"Roque N. Albuquerque has written a detailed, data-rich, clear, and meticulously nuanced work on a very specific grammatical phenomenon: the anarthrous aorist participle in the nominative case followed by a verb. The participle is 'upgraded' pragmatically to the mood of the main verb. The author makes a careful distinction between semantics and pragmatics, and follows the Hallidayan systemic linguistics school for his overall treatment. Interactions with others are respectful and irenic, with helpful critiques throughout. The ubiquitous constructions in which the upgraded participle occur in the New Testament have significant implications for the exegesis of the text. The author has shown repeatedly the value of syntax, semantics, and pragmatics for an accurate study of the sacred text. Albuquerque's monograph is a major advance over previous treatments of this construction; his study is itself an upgrade over previous works. It will be valuable for linguists, grammarians, exegetes, and even theologians."

—Daniel B. Wallace, Senior Research Professor,
New Testament Studies, Dallas Theological Seminary

"*Presupposition and [E]motion: The Upgraded Function and the Semantics of the Participle in the New Testament* by Roque N. Albuquerque invites us to a fascinating reflection about the participle. An old Greek professor once said that the participle is named as such for participation of grammatical classes, both the verb and the adjective, now with the proposal of Professor Albuquerque, we could complete that statement saying that the denomination of the participle is also to promote the participation of the reader/listener in the author's discourse."

—Ana Maria César Pompeu, Classical Studies and Greek Language Scholar,
Associate Professor, Federal University of Ceará, Brazil

"For those of us who teach Greek, we are blessed by God to live at a time when so many wonderful insights into the structure and function of Koiné Greek have been discovered. This 'embarrassment of riches' continues with this present study of the Greek participle by Roque N. Albuquerque. The insights provided here, especially in relation to the upgraded participle ('attendant circumstance' as it has traditionally been labeled), are so helpful in correcting previous assumptions and mistakes made in interpreting the numerous places in the New Testament where this function of the participle occurs. There is no doubt in my mind that our theological students will benefit immensely from this study, which will in turn ultimately improve the preaching and teaching of God's Word in our churches. And this blessing will be the greatest of them all. So I thank the Lord for Roque Albuquerque and the work he has labored to produce for the glory of our great God."

—Jon Pratt, VP of Academics and Professor of New Testament,
Central Baptist Theological Seminary of Minneapolis

"Roque N. Albuquerque skillfully analyzes what the authors of the Greek New Testament intend to communicate when they begin a sentence with an adverbial participle before the main clause."

"This research is of great relevance for both teaching and discourse practice in every area that involves humanities and language studies, especially considering that within textual analysis related to semantic features, presupposition is the decisive element to the utterance of the desired meaning by the speaker. Using Systemic Functional Linguistics (SFL) Roque N. Albuquerque draws us into a fascinating ideational world of the Greek participles."

Presupposition and [E]motion

This book is part of the Peter Lang Humanities list.
Every volume is peer reviewed and meets
the highest quality standards for content and production.

PETER LANG
New York • Bern • Berlin
Brussels • Vienna • Oxford • Warsaw

Roque N. Albuquerque

Presupposition and [E]motion

The Upgraded Function and the Semantics of the Participle in the New Testament

PETER LANG
New York • Bern • Berlin
Brussels • Vienna • Oxford • Warsaw

Library of Congress Cataloging-in-Publication Data

Names: Albuquerque, Roque N., author.
Title: Presupposition and [e]motion: the upgraded function and the
semantics of the participle in the New Testament / Roque N. Albuquerque.
Description: New York: Peter Lang, 2020.
Includes bibliographical references and index.
Identifiers: LCCN 2019021535 | ISBN 978-1-4331-6394-4 (hardback: alk. paper)
ISBN 978-1-4331-6395-1 (ebook pdf)
ISBN 978-1-4331-6396-8 (epub) | ISBN 978-1-4331-6397-5 (mobi)
Subjects: LCSH: Bible. New Testament—Language, style. | Greek language,
Biblical—Semantics. | Greek language, Biblical—Participle. |
Presupposition (Logic)
Classification: LCC PA857 .A43 | DDC 487/.4—dc23
LC record available at https://lccn.loc.gov/2019021535
DOI 10.3726/b14918

Bibliographic information published by **Die Deutsche Nationalbibliothek.**
Die Deutsche Nationalbibliothek lists this publication in the "Deutsche
Nationalbibliografie"; detailed bibliographic data are available
on the Internet at http://dnb.d-nb.de/.

The paper in this book meets the guidelines for permanence and durability
of the Committee on Production Guidelines for Book Longevity
of the Council of Library Resources.

© 2020 Peter Lang Publishing, Inc., New York
29 Broadway, 18th floor, New York, NY 10006
www.peterlang.com

To my dear mother Maria Rosa
who is with the LORD
and
to my beloved wife
Adriana
for twenty-six years by my side

Table of Contents

Figures

Abbreviations

In addition to the standard *SBL* abbreviations, the following have been used.

ACF   The Brazilian Portuguese Almeida Corrigida Fiel
ARA   The Brazilian Portuguese Almeida Revista e Atualizada, 2nd ed.
ATR   Robertson, *A Grammar of the Greek NT*
BDAG   Bauer, *A Greek-English Lexicon of the NT*, 3rd ed.
BDF   Blass, Debrunner, Funk, *Greek Grammar of the NT*
BMT   Burton, *Syntax of the Moods and Tenses in NT Greek*
DMG   Dana-Mantey, *A Manual Grammar of the Greek New Testament*
ESV   English Standard Version
FN   *Filologia Neotestamentaria*
HQ   *Hartford Quarterly*
GCG   Greenlee, *A Concise Exegetical Grammar of the NT Greek*
GGBB   Wallace, *Greek Grammar Beyond the Basics*
LDF   Levinsohn, *Discourse Features of New Testament Greek*
NA^{28} Novum Testamentum, 28th ed.
NASB   New American Standard Bible (1977)
NIV   The New International Version (2011)
NRSV   New Revised Standard Version
PVA   Porter, *Verbal Aspect in the Greek of the NT*

RSV   Revised Standard Version

SRG   Runge, *Discourse Grammar of the Greek New Testament*

TBF   Martín-Asensio, *Transitivity-Based Foregrounding in the Acts*

TDNT   *Theological Dictionary of the NT* (ed. Kittel and Friedrich)

UBS[5]   The Greek New Testament, 5th ed.

Preface

My first contact with the "Porter Fanning debate" was presented by the late Dr. Rodney Decker in our Advanced Greek class in the Summer of 2010 at Central Seminary in Minneapolis. Dr. Decker had assigned me to write a paper on the so-called "attendant circumstance participle" according to the new researches on verbal aspect and systemic linguistics. I decided on that time to develop that paper to be my Ph.D. dissertation. Dr. Decker never saw my final work, but he was the first one to direct me to the subject. After participating in his class, I came away convinced that verbal aspect was important for the advance of the New Testament exegesis, but also that modal semantics could contribute to the semantic studies of the Greek Language.

This book, then, is an update of my Ph.D. dissertation submitted to Central Baptist Seminary in Minneapolis in 2013. I changed my main presupposition about the typical context for the use of the Greek participle. By analyzing the concept of register in systemic functional linguistics I came to conclude prematurely that when the context of the situation presents any kind of emotion, the participle is the preferable form adopted by the author/writer to utter a specific meaning, that is, emotion. Dr. Buist Fanning, my dissertation external examiner, tried to point that out to me, but I was not able to tackle that issue at that time. Later on, I reformulated my main thesis about the upgraded participle specifically and all the Greek participles in general. My conclusion is that the author/writer has so many options available to him for uttering a meaning if the context of the situation involves emotion. He can use factive adjectives, factive verbs, emotional lexis, and the like, however, when the author chooses to use a participle in a context of the situation in which he wants to describe some sort of emotion, the participle is one of the most fascinating options since by its nature, they invite the reader to get involved ideationally within the context of the situation. By the choice of the participle, the writer is demanding the participation of the readers in the discourse at hand. If a given context involves emotion, the participles draw the reader into that environment.

Finally, I need to express how much I am thankful for guidance, interaction, and a shared love for the Greek language from Dr. Jon Pratt, vice president of academics and professor of New Testament at Central Seminary. Dr. Buist M. Fanning (Dallas Theological Seminary), also deserves thanks for his contribution. I could see so many times where he would disagree with me, but his kindness and Christian humility taught me a lot. There are other who contributed to the completion of this book and I would be remiss if I did not express my heartfelt gratitude to my dear friends Jeff Scott, and Craig Muri. I am so thankful for the review of my first draft by Alli Balts as well.

Roque N. Albuquerque

December 2019

UNILAB – Fortaleza, Ceará, Brazil

CHAPTER ONE

Introduction

The semantics of the participle, that is, presupposition, has such as a suitability that begs for the readers experiential participation to construe meaning in context. The range of the participial function is too big to be dealt with here, therefore, we decided to select the upgraded participles as a case proof for the semantics and the several functions of the participles.

One of the more confusing, and therefore, misunderstood functions of participles in New Testament Greek is the upgraded function.[1] The upgraded function is related to the anarthrous (adverbial or predicate) aorist participle in the nominative that precedes the main clause.[2] The participle in this function refers to an action that is so connected with the action of the main verb that the two are seen as one process/action. The main characteristic of this function of the participle is that the aorist participle becomes so associated with the main verb that the "mood"[3] of the participle is upgraded into the same mood of the main verb, whether an imperative, indicative, subjunctive or infinitive.[4] Although the following examples will be discussed later with full semantic range, here they are presented as an illustration.[5]

Matthew 2:13 Ἀναχωρησάντων δὲ αὐτῶν ἰδοὺ ἄγγελος κυρίου φαίνεται κατ' ὄναρ τῷ Ἰωσὴφ λέγων· ἐγερθεὶς **παράλαβε** τὸ παιδίον καὶ τὴν μητέρα αὐτοῦ καὶ φεῦγε εἰς Αἴγυπτον καὶ ἴσθι ἐκεῖ ἕως ἂν εἴπω σοι· μέλλει γὰρ Ἡρῴδης ζητεῖν τὸ παιδίον τοῦ ἀπολέσαι αὐτό (And having departed, behold, an angel of the Lord appeared to Joseph in a dream, saying, "*Get up* [and] **take** the Child and His mother, and flee to Egypt, and remain there until I tell you; for Herod is going to search for the Child to destroy Him").

The author could have chosen to coordinate the two clauses (embedded and nuclear) with a καί, but the meaning and its effect could be slightly different, if he or she would have chosen to use a participle with καί, or even use a participle following the main verb without any other term in between as the example above. So, the choice of a nominative participle in a given structure can concede to the embedded participial clause a very suitable function because the participle is a semantic presupposition. What that means is that the participle is reader-oriented, in such a way that it's use always occurs as an invitation to readers to participate in an imaginative way, whether getting involved emotionally with the context or filling some relationship between all the parts of the discourse.

The nominative participle in the upgraded structural function is so remarkable as a semantic presupposition that its use makes the reader in his or her mind to take the nominative participle as being in the same mood of the main/nuclear verb. This is a mental effect as a result of the semantics of the participles in a given structure. The semantics of the participles is presupposition, and it will always be a presupposition in contrast with mood or Greek modality.

The context of the situation and the specific structure in the relationship between the embedded clause and the main clause, in this specific function and structure of the participle is very self-evident that the participle is a grammatical presupposition. The participle is always a semantic presupposition independent of any context or co-text. The structure of the participles and their relationship with the main verb can vary establishing so many intriguing meanings that makes the participles the most fascinating subject matter in the study of Greek language.

In the example above, we note that as the angel is speaking to Joseph, the participle ἐγερθείς relates to the imperative παράλαβε, creating a clause chain. The participle (ἐγερθείς) here is grammatically subordinated to the main clause in the imperative (παράλαβε). The participle is an anarthrous aorist participle that precedes the main clause in the imperative. Due to several reasons, as we will show later, this aorist nominative participle adopts, from a translational perspective, the same mood of the main clause, that is, an imperative.

The context of the situation shows a sort of urgency that the character who is listening to the command of the angel, understood the emergency and took the nominative participle in a specific structural relationship as having the modal domain of the imperative. Therefore, the semantic explanation for such possibility is that the Greek participle is a grammatical presupposition that helps an author/speaker to involve the readers/hearers in the cultural environment of the discourse.

The nominative participle could logically be taken as some kind of temporal relationship with the main, but the occurrence of νυκτός (genitive—time during the night) in verse 14, and the urgency of the context of the situation, not only eliminates the possibility of translating ἐγερθείς as a temporal adverb like "*after you have risen,*" or "*when you rise,*" but also shows the emergency of this command.[6]

The word order or structure of the clauses can change the logical mental relation between the nominative participle and the main verb. The relation between both can be temporal. For example, Eph. 1:20 "Ἣν ἐνήργησεν ἐν τῷ Χριστῷ *ἐγείρας* αὐτὸν ἐκ νεκρῶν καὶ καθίσας ἐν δεξιᾷ αὐτοῦ ἐν τοῖς ἐπουρανίοις (... "which he exercised in Christ [when] *he raised/by raising* him from the dead"). It can be causal, for example, Matt. 1:19 "Ἰωσὴφ ... δίκαιος *ὢν* ..." ("Joseph ... [because] *he was* a righteous man ..."). These are just some examples, and so many other could be pointed out such as conditional participles, concessive participles, telic participles, and so on.

The verbal stems, the position of the participle in relation to the main verb and so many other features help the readers/hearers to interact with the discourse. This is only possible because the participles are semantic presuppositions that allow the readers to move on to get involved to fill some of the nuances of the discourse by relating the participles with the other parts of the clause obtaining different functions of them.

Back to the context of the situation of Matthew chapter 2, in verse 14. In verse 13, the same anarthrous nominative aorist participle preceding the main verb occurs, but now the main verb is an indicative, that is, "ὁ δὲ *ἐγερθεὶς* **παρέλαβεν** τὸ παιδίον καὶ τὴν μητέρα αὐτοῦ νυκτὸς καὶ ἀνεχώρησεν εἰς Αἴγυπτον." ("And he *got up* [and] **took** the child and his mother by night and departed to Egypt."). Rather than translate it as "Get up" (2:13), here the participle is upgraded to the same notion described by the indicative mood (... he *got up* [and] **took**).

The main reason why the nominative participle can be taken as an imperative in verse 13 and in the same type of structure can be taken as an indicative in verse 14 is because its semantics. As a presupposition the author/speaker is bringing the participants of the discourse, both immediate (listeners) and distant (readers) to take a part in this drama by giving priority to what is stated without losing track of the color that embellishes what is to be presupposed.

Another example that has some exegetical implication is Matthew 28:19 "*πορευθέντες* οὖν **μαθητεύσατε** πάντα τὰ ἔθνη, βαπτίζοντες αὐτοὺς εἰς τὸ ὄνομα τοῦ πατρὸς καὶ τοῦ υἱοῦ καὶ τοῦ ἁγίου πνεύματος" ("*Go,* then, [and] **disciple** all the nations, baptizing them in the name of the Father and the Son and the Holy Spirit").[7]

The main verb is an aorist imperative μαθητεύσατε (disciple) which is then complemented by three anarthrous participles—one that precedes (aorist πορευθέντες [going]) and two that follow (present βαπτίζοντες[8] [baptizing] and present διδάσκοντες [teaching]). What all these participles have in common is their semantics. They are hearers/readers oriented. The author/speaker could have chosen two coordinates clauses, but taking language as reflection, he chooses a nominative participle, and all the other choices that involve the participles in this construction contribute to how and which role the participants is to take in the reading process.

The upgraded function is more helpful in this passage to illustrate the semantic feature of the participle because its particular phenomenon that makes the reader/listener to move the participle in a very close semantic relationship with the main verb that causes the reader to take it as in the same mood or modality of the nuclear verb.

The focus for the sake of clarity is on *πορευθέντες* because its semantic function makes the reader to upgrade the participial clause as mentally coordinated with the main clause and having the same mood or modality of the nuclear clause. Why is that possible? It is not that the nominative participle leaves its participial nuance, rather, it where the participial semantics can be clearly seen.

For instance, there are two extreme views regarding this participle: 1) there is a tendency to render πορευθέντες as an imperative so that the great commission is not seen as a great suggestion.[9] 2) there are others that de-emphasized πορευθέντες so strongly to the point of omission in translation. Paul Gaechter purposes this omission when he says that "'Geht' hat also keinen eigenen Akzent und ist darum nicht wörtlich zu übersetzen."[10]

As will be seen, the anarthrous aorist nominative participle that precedes the main clause and has the upgraded effect is not to be weakened to a secondary, unimportant option.[11] On the other hand, it should not be seen as equally important, since not all actions are equal, and that is one of the most significant functions of the aorist participle. Therefore, a right understanding of the upgraded function has important exegetical implications for the interpreter, but it is of paramount importance to master its semantics in order to grasp it in its full meaning.

The thesis of our book is that factive presupposition is the semantics of all Greek participles, and the upgraded participial effect is a good study case to prove it, since its pragmatic effect illustrates the suitability of this semantic category.

Linguists typically take the idea of factive verbs to be a matter of presupposition and we will analyze it in chapter two. Here however, considering the adverbial participial clause, two main questions are asked: first, how does the participle relate to factivity? Second, what does factive presupposition means in this study?

The relation of the aorist nominative participle as factive presupposition involves the relation of the adverbial participial clause to the main clause. The majority of secondary embedded clauses in Greek are participial and infinitival clauses. Our goal is to deal with the semantics of the participles as a whole, and the upgraded effect as a case study.

Semantic classifications of the participle are connected to the semantic classifications of the adverbial clauses. Adverbial clauses have traditionally been based on the relation between the secondary clause and the primary clause. Recently, Hengeveld established a new semantic classification by applying four parameters.[12] In his first approach, he proposes only two parameters for the adverbial clauses, Entity Type and Factivity.[13] Thus, this study will use the factivity parameter as it deals with the adverbial participle in Greek. Again, all Greek participles (adjectival or adverbial = adjuncts) are a grammatical factive presupposition, which is an important category to understand the participles after verbal aspect.

One of the main distinctives of factivity is its semantic characteristic of introducing a presupposition of which the embedded clause expresses a true proposition. According to Kiparsky and Kiparsky, "the speaker presupposes that the embedded clause expresses a true proposition and makes some assertion about that proposition."[14] In other words, factive predicator has the property of implicating the presupposition from which the completive proposition is factual (it expresses the fact that the completive clause is true).[15] Language does *not* necessarily indicate what an author believes or what is true. In the case of the participle, it invites the readers to take the presupposition as such for the sake of his point at hand.

Lightfoot seems to be the first one to attempt to distinguish the participle and the infinitive on this base. He explains the supposed difference with the participle as a complement, the so-called complementary use of the participle.[16] The way he distinguishes the participle from the infinitive is because the participle "is used only where the truth or actuality of the complement clause is presupposed to be true by the speaker or author."[17] He holds that in a choice between a participle and an infinitive, the choice of the participle should be made if the presupposed truth claim of the proposition is in view. He presents several passages involving infinitives and participles and concludes that the participle has a clearer "factual" presupposition than does the infinitive.[18]

The argument is not about facts or truth in itself, but language as a tool to establish the linguistic "reality" or the imaginative world that language can create as the reader is drawn into the discourse knowing what his/her part in that specific context is.

For example, Luke 8:46 "ὁ δὲ Ἰησοῦς εἶπεν· ἥψατό μού τις, ἐγὼ γὰρ **ἔγνων** δύναμιν *ἐξεληλυθυῖαν* ἀπ᾽ ἐμοῦ" ("But Jesus said, 'Someone touched me; for I *know* that power *has gone out* from me'"). The semantic uniqueness of the complements of verbs of perception is that the nominative participial clause is used when the author is trying to communicate a direct perception. It is language creating reality to set an interaction between the readers and the text or speech.

In this complex clause "power *has gone out* from me" is the complement of the secondary clause with a verb of perception (for I know …). From Lightfoot's perspective, the speaker in this case presupposes the proposition "power *has gone out* from me" to be true. Truthfulness of this proposition does not seem to be the main point, the use of a participle as a complement of the verb of perception is more reader-oriented in order to draw him or her to connect the main clause with the secondary clause. The author could have used two finite forms, but by using a verb of perception and the participle as a complement of this type of verb, the semantic rule of the participle followed by the syntax of verbs of perception indicates that the author wants the reader/hearer to take the participial clause as uttering a direct perception of the event described.

"Power *has gone out*" and the context of situation shows the healing domain and every reader is able to put the two clauses together in a sort of hierarchy— the assertion (I know) and the presupposition attested by the reader/hearer that "power *has gone out*." The semantic of the participle helps reader to participate in the interpretative role of the discourse.

Another example by Lightfoot is 2 Cor 8:22 "συνεπέμψαμεν δὲ αὐτοῖς τὸν ἀδελφὸν ἡμῶν ὃν **ἐδοκιμάσαμεν** ἐν πολλοῖς πολλάκις σπουδαῖον ὄντα …" ("And with them we will send our brother whom we *tested* many times **to be** diligent …"). In this case "**to be** diligent" completes the thought of the other secondary clause "whom we tested many times." Paul, then, presupposes the proposition "**to be** diligent" to be true.[19]

Lightfoot is correct in seeing the complementary participle as a semantic presupposition. He also is correct in pointing out some slight difference between the participle and the infinitive. However, to affirm that the participle in the complement is distinguished to the infinitive because "the author of the sentence presupposes and wishes the hearer to think that he presupposes that the complement reflects a real, actual, existing state of affair,"[20] needs clarification.

Lightfoot seems to base his argument on the contrast between what is "actual" or "non-actual."[21] In addition, although no explicit affirmation was made, it seems that his concern with "real" or "actual" propositions implies that he believes that the indicative mood grammaticalizes "facts."[22] In fact, the non-indicative mood may be used to describe factual process and indicative mood may be used describe non-factual process. What an author/speaker is asserting is different than what he is saying with no assertion. While the former grammaticalizes attitude in the verbal system, the latter does not assert but presupposes something, bringing the readers to be part of the world created in the context of the situation.

The semantic difference between the indicative mood and the other non-indicative mood is the key to understand the semantic of presupposition. Further, the conception of the relation of the process expressed by the verbs starts with the author's choice of the finite system in the verbal network. +Finite is followed by the attitude system, while -Finite unlocks the factivity system and locks the attitude verbal choices.

To say that a proposition is "factive" it is not to say that it is "factual." Factuality moves through the two major categories of the attitude system (+assertion and -assertion), while factivity is outside of factuality. Factive is language that is a reflection working in the ideational metafunction as we will see.

Palmer indicates two features highlighted here. First, factivity refers to a "presupposition" indicated by a variety of verbs such as regret, resent, among many others, that are used in "factive predicates." Second, Palmer sees that the term can be misleading when referring to the verb "know" as the classic example of a factive predicator. He says, "the complements of KNOW are not Factive in the presuppositional sense."[23] The reason, he explains, is that "although know clearly suggests that the speaker accepts the information as factual, presupposition is not involved – it does not suggest that the addressee equally accepts the factuality."[24]

The lexical statement and the grammar of Greek language have a continuum or cline in between them that has to do with lexical-grammar, not lexical and grammar. The factive presupposition we are using here is set against the choice of the finite or non-finite options in the verbal system. The description of a factual or a non-factual is related not to the main point with the participle, but the presupposition of a process as being factive for the understanding or the author's intention to describe a process or state.

Porter elaborates Palmer's assumption and sees the difference between the infinitive and participle with his ±factive presupposition. He states, "it is better to characterize the difference between the Participle and the Infinitive as the Participle grammaticalizing a factive presupposition."[25] Presupposition is the imaginative or mental exercise done by the reader or hearer to reflect, complement, or react to what is being said. It is as though the author/speaker wants to make the readers participants of some assigned task by him within the discourse.

Porter illustrates his point with 2 Cor 7:12 "ἄρα εἰ καὶ ἔγραψα ὑμῖν, οὐχ ἕνεκεν τοῦ ἀδικήσαντος οὐδὲ ἕνεκεν τοῦ ἀδικηθέντος ἀλλ᾽ ἕνεκεν τοῦ φανερωθῆναι τὴν σπουδὴν ὑμῶν τὴν ὑπὲρ ἡμῶν πρὸς ὑμᾶς ἐνώπιον τοῦ θεοῦ" ("consequently if I write to you not on account of the *one wrongdoing* nor on account of the *one being wronged*, but in order that your desire be manifested in our behalf before

God"). He concludes from this verse, "Paul appears to presuppose at least for the argument one who acts/acted unjustly and one wronged, in this instance probably referring to actual individuals who figure in the Corinthian correspondence, while he merely refers to their manifested desire, not presupposing anything about it."[26]

Porter's analysis is too short, and the examples presented limit any further evaluation of his tenets, although his assertion seems to be greater than the amount of proof to make his case. However, it must be said that his objective is basically to present verbal aspect semantics of the infinitive and the participle. His analysis presents passages where verbs of perception occur with both the infinitive and the participle,[27] but he only discusses 2 Cor 7:12 in order to highlight the difference between these two modulations. This passage shows the complementary (supplementary) participial clause, which usually goes with the object of the main verb in the accusative case, and sometimes the genitive when it speaks of physical perception.[28]

The complementary participial clause has the tendency to occur with verbs of perception, which is divided into two categories, verbs of physical perception (seeing, hearing), and verbs of mental perception or cognition (knowing, recognizing, finding, confessing, and so on).[29] A third category could be presented, that is, audio perception (listen, hear, and notice, and so on).

So far, the discussion by Lightfoot, Schmidt, and Porter is aligned to the fact that the participle is a presupposition, although Porter disagrees with both Lightfoot and Schmidt when he states that the participle does not presuppose any "actual" or "factual proposition." He is right to take the participle as a semantic presupposition, that is, it is readers taking language as reflection.

Porter's main assertion is that "the semantic distinction [±factive presupposition] appears to hold for the Participle and Infinitive throughout their range of usage, and is thus a necessary semantic feature in analysis."[30] All three authors use the complementary verbs of perception to make their case.[31] Further, all of them see an essential difference between the semantics of the participle and that of the infinitive. The process contemplated by the participle can be easily related by the readers with a logical relation to find subjects involved in the description of the process, while the infinitive focuses more the action itself without relating to any subject of the process. The representation of reality is the concern in a linguistic text with all the abstraction involved. It is not a search for fixed points in the actual world.

An analysis of the distinction between these two modulations shows that the complement participial clause of a verb of perception denotes something imaginary, whose existence is only ideational, but it has a "direct perception," while the infinitive seems to refer to something of "indirect perception" (not presupposed).[32]

The best explanation for this phenomenon is that the semantics of the participle invites the readers to an imaginative world.

The semantics of the infinitive is beyond the scope of this study, but because the common use of these verbs with both participle and infinitive, a few examples will be presented.[33] Both the participle and the infinitive are presupposition. The difference is that the participle presupposes a factive process while the infinitive does not presuppose factivity. This difference is observable by take other syntactical elements and categories into account.

For instance, the semantic difference between the complements of the verbs of perception with a grammatical presupposition indicates a difference in terms of the perception. If the complement of the verb of perception is a non-factive presupposition (infinitive), the author wants the reader to notice an indirect perception of the process described at hand. It does not matter whether the verb of perception is audio, mental, or visual perception. The complement with the infinitive will render the perception as an indirect perception.

Audio Perception (ἀκούω) with an infinitive complement: 1 Cor 11:18 "πρῶτον μὲν γὰρ συνερχομένων ὑμῶν ἐν ἐκκλησίᾳ **ἀκούω** σχίσματα ἐν ὑμῖν <u>ὑπάρχειν</u> καὶ μέρος τι πιστεύω" ("For, in the first place, when you get together at church, I **hear** that <u>there are</u> divisions among you. And I believe it in part"). The verb of perception has as its complement a secondary clause with an infinitive. When the complement of the verb of perception comes with a non-factive presupposition, the perception is rendered as an indirect one.

Audio Perception (ἀκούω) with a participial complement: Acts 14:9 οὗτος **ἤκουσεν** τοῦ Παύλου *λαλοῦντος* ὃς ἀτενίσας αὐτῷ καὶ ἰδὼν ὅτι ἔχει πίστιν τοῦ σωθῆναι (He **was hearing/is hearing** Paul *speaking*. [Paul] looking directly to him and seeing that he had faith to be saved). The context of the situation with verbs of seeing in these clauses reinforce the analysis of this type of syntactical relation with its semantical core. When a verb of perception (**ἤκουσεν**) has as its complement a participial clause (*λαλοῦντος*), the readers are invited to take the perception as a factive presupposition, that is, a direct perception. A similar passage is Acts 6:11 τότε ὑπέβαλον ἄνδρας λέγοντας ὅτι **ἀκηκόαμεν** αὐτοῦ *λαλοῦντος* ῥήματα βλάσφημα εἰς Μωϋσῆν καὶ τὸν θεόν (Then they instigated men who said, "We **have heard** him *speaking* blasphemous words against Moses and God").

The semantic difference between the complements of the verbs of perception according in the New Testament is that the participle as a complement of the verb ἀκούω indicates a direct perception of the event in the examples above and the infinitive seems to indicate a general or indirect perception.[34] Thus, the difference between a participle and infinitive complement is semantic ± factive presupposition. The factivity result of the verb ἀκούω with the participle in the complement indicates some sort of direct perception, while with the infinitive indicates an indirect perception.

Mental perception (γινώσκω) with an infinitive complement: Matthew 16:3: "τὸ μὲν πρόσωπον τοῦ οὐρανοῦ **γινώσκετε** <u>διακρίνειν</u>, τὰ δὲ σημεῖα τῶν καιρῶν οὐ δύνασθε" ("you know to judge the face of heaven, but you cannot the signs of the times?"). Luke 24:18 "... οὐκ ἔγνως *τὰ γενόμενα ἐν αὐτῇ ἐν ταῖς ἡμέραις ταύταις;*" ("...do not you **know** the things that *have happened* in it?") The strength of the presupposition is present in both complements the non-factive and factive presupposition. Again, the semantic feature that distinguishes them is that of direct (participle) or indirect (infinitive) perception.

Different conclusions by different theories—Lightfoot's and Naturalness theory—have noticed the suitability of the Greek presupposition. While Kavčič would state that the verb γινώσκω indicates mental perception and it governs both participle (direct perception) and infinitive (indirect perception) complements,[35] Lightfoot sees the use of the participle as the speaker's desire for the readers to presuppose the truth of the proposition. Both conclusions are possible only because the factive and non-factive presupposition are available in the verbal system of the Greek language, which is confirmed by the theory of language adopted here, that is, systemic functional linguistics.

Factive and non-factive presuppositions are realized in Greek by the choice of the participle and infinitive consecutively. Presupposition is a deductive process of collecting some information not quite explicit from some explicit facts. Factive presupposition is a deductive process of presupposing a proposition as factual for the sake of the main verbal process. It is not about what is actual or factual in itself, but how an author wants the readers to assume a particular description for linguistic purpose.

That the participle is reader-oriented seems to be unanimous. Although Kavčič does not call it presupposition, she thinks that the author/speaker chooses the structure of the predicate by means of a verbal group with a complementary participle with verbs of perception to describe a direct perception of the process of the main clause. Lightfoot takes the participle as a presupposition of a true proposition since it presupposes wishes the hearer/reader to take the complement as reflecting an actual state of affair.[36]

Systemic Functional Linguistics (SFL), broadly applied to the study of Greek, uses systemic display of the Greek verbal network conjugated with contrast analysis to explain the semantic function of the participle. Contrast analysis relates the components within a given network where one term is always chosen in relation to the other to find meaning.

At the rank of clause, one author/speaker chooses how he or she wants to communicate the process based on the available options from the verbal network. Each form has its own semantic feature and its own thread in the verbal network. The choice to communicate a process includes two simultaneous broad choices: Aspectuality and Finiteness. The focus of this book is on the finiteness choice.

The semantic distinction within the finiteness system is defined by the choice on the expression of the verb through person. If the verbal form grammaticalizes the person of the verb, for example, γινώσκ-ω, φημ-ί, the -ω ending and ι- ending are what indicate the person of the verb (first person singular, I). The verbal form is +finite when its forms point out the person of the verb. The limitation of person in the verbal form expresses the -finite. If there is no person identified in the verbal form, then, the verbal form blocks the person of the verb. For example, λαβών, λαβεῖν do not have the person ending in their form.

The components find their meaning within a given network defined by the relation between the members of the system categories. The choice of the -finite blocks the choice +finite available. It is the -finite choice that grammaticalizes presupposition. By blocking the person of the verb in its form, invites the reader/hearers to fill the parts in whether as elements in the structure of the predicate or as elements in subjects, complements and adjuncts—adverbial or adjectival.

Two further choices are available following the choice of -finite, +factive and -factive. Veracity of a proposition can be checked by implication based on a lexis, by epistemic modal if the embedded clause is under a modal scope, and by factivity, which is presupposition.

The lack of limitation of person in the verbal form makes the reader move from the embedded clause and beyond of the person limitation for perceptual knowledge. The use of a participle makes the reader to evaluate the factivity of an event or state of affair in a text based on his/her decoding of the author's presentation of the relation of the participial clause with the process of the event or state of affair uttered by the main clause, and on his/her understanding about the context of the situation and about the author's reliability that the presupposition invites the readers to embrace.

The difference between the infinitive and the participle is that the participle is +factive, while the infinitive is -factive. Schwyzer states, "… das Ptz. Bezeichnet Tatsächliches, Anschauliches, der Inf. Steht als Beziehung der abstrakten Verbalbedeutung auch für Vermutetes, Gedachtes, Mögliches."[37]

Both the participle and the infinitive are presuppositions. The participle, however, is a what allows the reader to conclude that an event has happened, must have happened or will happen or that a state of affairs pertains, must pertain, or will pertain in the form of presupposition. Again, it is not the actuality of the event or state of affair, but the presupposition of it as true proposition for the sake of the description of the process of the main clause.

With the complementary participle, the lexical and the syntactical play an important role. We observed that a direct perception is to be presupposed when the participle is used, and an indirect perception when the complement comes with an infinitive.

Physical perception (εὑρίσκω) with infinitive complements: Luke 6:7 "... ἵνα **εὕρωσιν** <u>κατηγορεῖν</u> αὐτοῦ" (that they might find to accuse him). Rev. 5:4 "καὶ ἔκλαιον πολύ, ὅτι οὐδεὶς ἄξιος **εὑρέθη** <u>ἀνοῖξαι</u> τὸ βιβλίον οὔτε <u>βλέπειν</u> αὐτό." (I was weeping much, because no one worthy **was found** <u>to open</u> the book or <u>to see</u> it).

Physical perception (εὑρίσκω) with participle complements: Rev. 3:2 "... οὐ γὰρ **εὕρηκά** σου τὰ ἔργα *πεπληρωμένα* ἐνώπιον τοῦ θεοῦ μου." (for I **have** not **found** your works *complete* in the sight of my God). Acts 5:23 "... τὸ δεσμωτήριον **εὕρομεν** *κεκλεισμένον* ἐν πάσῃ ἀσφαλείᾳ ..." (... we **found** the prison *locked* with all security ...).[38]

The use of the participle in the complement seems to indicate a factive presupposition, which means that the complement is a shared information between the speaker and the readers and must be presupposed as a true proposition. In the examples above the verb εὑρίσκω with the infinitive indicates an indirect perception, while with the participle indicates a direct perception.[39]

Neither the participle nor the infinitive is used to grammaticalize the speakers' attitude. Semantically the participial dependent clause denotes something imaginary, whose existence is only ideational with a "direct perception," while the infinitive seems to refer to something of "indirect perception." In itself, Palmer's statement can be adopted here, "it is not factuality, certainty or truth that is at issue here. What is at issue is that nothing is being asserted, that there is no information value, because both the speaker and hearer accept the proposition."[40]

The relation of the participle with the context in itself manifests the reader-oriented usage of it. Wallace says, "the *context* has more influence on participles than on any other area of Greek grammar."[41] However, much more than the context, from a systemic display the choice of a participle enters into a number of lexical, and syntactical relations which have semantic consequences.

Adopting the Kiparsky's definition of factivity that the writer presupposes that the embedded clause to which the participle belongs in the adverbial use expresses a true proposition, from which the readers recognize its presuppositional properties of constructions. Several examples of the logical relation of the participial clause are pointed out below.

Mat 7:11 εἰ οὖν ὑμεῖς πονηροὶ *ὄντες* **οἴδατε** δόματα ἀγαθὰ διδόναι τοῖς τέκνοις ὑμῶν, πόσῳ μᾶλλον ὁ πατὴρ ὑμῶν ὁ ἐν τοῖς οὐρανοῖς δώσει ἀγαθὰ τοῖς αἰτοῦσιν αὐτόν. (If you, although [you] **are evil**, *know* to give good things). Jesus and his listeners must assume that the proposition of the embedded clause is a true proposition for the main clause to be an accepted assertion. The contrast here is between what is presupposed with what is asserted. Furthermore, Jesus is not asserting that they are evil, but sharing with them a proposition that they would agree with for the sake of the argument.

A similar example is Luke 9:25 "τί γὰρ **ὠφελεῖται** ἄνθρωπος *κερδήσας* τὸν κόσμον ὅλον ἑαυτὸν δὲ *ἀπολέσας* ἢ *ζημιωθείς*;" ("For how **does it benefit** a man [*if he*] *should gain* the whole world but [*if he*] *perishes* or *loses himself*?"). The same conditional idea is presented here, but without the explicit conditional εἰ. "Should gain" and "loses" are not being asserted, but the speaker chooses to communicate the idea in the form of presupposition for the sake of the argument.

2 Cor 10:3 Ἐν σαρκὶ γὰρ *περιπατοῦντες* οὐ κατὰ σάρκα **στρατευόμεθα**, (for [*although*] *we are walking* in the flesh, **we are not fighting** according to the flesh). The participial clause must be held by the readers as a true proposition if the assertion is to make sense. Paul is not asserting that they are walking in the flesh, although this is true; his intention, rather, is to invite the readers to embrace the truthfulness of the proposition expressed by the participle in order to set the main statement (οὐ κατὰ σάρκα στρατευόμεθα) in the spotlight.

Phil 2:6 ὃς ἐν μορφῇ θεοῦ *ὑπάρχων* οὐχ ἁρπαγμὸν **ἡγήσατο** τὸ <u>εἶναι</u> ἴσα θεῷ, (who, **although he existed** in the form of God, **he did not count** equality with God a thing <u>to be</u> grasped). There is a discussion if the participle in this passage is causal or concessive. Wallace presents an interesting discussion on the issue and because of its importance will be quoted at length.

> There are two interpretive problems in Phil 2:6–7 relevant to the treatment of this participle. First, of course, is the grammatical problem of whether this is concessive or causal. Second is the lexical problem of whether ἁρπαγμόν in v 6 means *robbery* or *a thing to be grasped*. The grammatical and the lexical inform one another and cannot be treated separately. Thus, if ὑπάρχων is causal, ἁρπαγμόν means *robbery* ("who, *because* he existed in God's form, did not consider equality with God as robbery"); if ὑπάρχων is concessive, then ἁρπαγμόν means *a thing to be grasped* ("who, *although* he existed in God's form, did not consider equality with God as a thing to be grasped"). As attractive as the first alternative might be theologically, it is not satisfactory. Ultimately, this verse cannot be interpreted in isolation, but must be seen in light of the positive statement in v 7– "but he emptied himself" (the participle ὑπάρχων equally depends on both ἡγήσατο and ἐκένωσεν). Only the concessive idea for the participle and *a thing to be grasped* translation for ἁρπαγμόν fit well with v 7.[42]

Wallace's conclusion is correct on a logical and exegetical base. The participle ὑπάρχων depends on both ἡγήσατο and ἐκένωσεν. The assertion "he did not count equality with God a thing to be grasped" is the main clause, the participial embedded clause is a factive presupposition, thus, the readers must share this information with Paul so that the main clause could be asserted. The participle is still a participle and Paul is not asserting that Jesus existed in the form of God, although this is true, but the truthfulness of this proposition must be accepted as such by the readers so Paul could make sense of the primary clause.

Mat 1:19 Ἰωσὴφ δὲ ὁ ἀνὴρ αὐτῆς, δίκαιος ὢν, καὶ μὴ θέλων αὐτὴν παραδειγματίσαι, ἐβουλήθη λάθρα ἀπολῦσαι αὐτήν (But Joseph, her husband, because *he was* a just man and *did not wish* to expose her, determined to divorce her secretly). The participle ὢν has the causal logical relationship with the primary clause. Matthew does not assert that Joseph is just, he presupposes it and the participle indicates that. The reason why he determined to divorce her secretly is assumed as a true proposition, Joseph is a just man.

δίκαιος is an adjective and ὢν is a verbal adjective. Factivity is a very broad subject matter in grammar. There is factivity in the word group, for example a choice of lexis. Factive adjective is a way to express or try to express the veracity of a world outside the direct perceptual knowledge of the reader. There is also, pragmatic factivity, which helps the reader to infer some properties of a construction base in the broad context or even outside the text but present in the world. Our main concern in this book is semantic presupposition realized by the choice of a Greek participle.

Linguists typically take the idea of factive verbs to be a matter of presupposition. From a lexical perspective, factive verbs are divided into two types: those that concern knowledge of facts (cognitive factive verbs), and those that concern emotional attitude toward facts (emotive factive).[43] At the level of lexis, factive is related to adjective and verbs, for example *regret, believe, think, guess*; the Greek language seems to be connected not only with lexis specifically, but also with a grammatical form, that is, the Greek verbal participle.[44]

We do not take the place of lexis in the Greek language system as having priority over grammatical forms, rather, grammar takes priority over the linguistics choices in relation to lexis. For instance, in Matt. 1:19 the reader's curiosity is increased by the choice of the three presuppositions in this narrative: ὢν, θέλων (participles), and παραδειγματίσαι (infinitive). "Put her [Mary] to public shame" is a clear inference of what could happen if he divorces her. The embellishment of these complex clauses is reinforced by the embedded clause with the participles.

The assertion (indicative) that Joseph wants to divorce (ἐβουλήθη λάθρα ἀπολῦσαι) Mary secretly is a statement of fact, at least in the author's description of the event. In order to make sense of the author's broader purpose (acquits Joseph), the reader/hearers are supposed to render the two participles as true propositions (factive presupposition) that Joseph is a just man and that he does not want to put her to public shame.

Factuality is in the real world and outside the text here. Factivity is related to presupposition grammaticalized by the participles. The author invites us to bear with him and to presuppose that Joseph "is just" and "did not want" are a true proposition for the sake of the drama of the narrative.

In sum, the examples above are just a sample of the normal semantics of the verbal use of the participle in the New Testament. The assertion here is that the verbal participle is a factive presupposition, which an author uses to invite the reader to share with him the truthfulness of a proposition in order to make sense of the main clause.

It is a matter of choice on the verbal network where the contrast occurs between the members of the particular entrance. In contrastive ways, the author has a choice to grammaticalize finiteness (+finite or -finite). Runge seems to assume this contrast, even without adopting the systemic display of the verbal network, as he states, "If a writer chose to use a participle to describe an action, he has at the same time chosen not to use an indicative or other finite form."[45]

The choice involved is between the embedded participial clause and its relation to the main clause. A finite clause could be an option, but the speaker has a choice of an factive presupposition (readers' orienting) in order to share with them the truthfulness of the proposition expressed by the participle as a linguistic interaction to draw the reader into the context of the situation at hand for a communicative propose.

For instance, Phil 3:17 "Συμμιμηταί μου *γίνεσθε*, ἀδελφοί, καὶ σκοπεῖτε *τοὺς* οὕτω *περιπατοῦντας* καθὼς **ἔχετε** τύπον ἡμᾶς" ("Become my imitators, brothers, and watch out *for those who walk* according to the example you **have** in us"). The participle fills the place of a noun here, but even here one can observe the semantic of the participle. The Philippians must agree that the proposition in the participle is a true statement; otherwise the command would not make sense at all. The proposition indicates there might be some among the Philippians who walk according to Paul's conduct. Further, the readers must hold as true proposition that Paul's conduct is correct as well.

Mark 6:36 ἀπόλυσον αὐτούς, ἵνα *ἀπελθόντες* εἰς τοὺς κύκλῳ ἀγροὺς καὶ κώμας ἀγοράσωσιν ἑαυτοῖς τί φάγωσιν. ("Dismiss them *to go* into the surrounding countryside and villages [and] *buy* themselves something to eat"). There is a secondary clause introduce by ἵνα (ἵνα … ἀγοράσωσιν ἑαυτοῖς τί φάγωσιν) and an embedded clause ἀπελθόντες εἰς τοὺς κύκλῳ ἀγροὺς καὶ κώμας. What the disciples are asking Jesus is to dismiss the multitude in order to buy something to eat, but they also presuppose that they would go to the countryside and villages to find it. The crowd could decide to stay anyway, but the disciples presuppose that they would rather go somewhere else.

The purpose is announced, to buy food, but they presupposed that they would go to do so. The secondary clause asserts then the purpose and the participial clause expresses a factive presupposition. The analysis of any presupposition should occur in the relation between the two clauses since there is an essential semantic difference between them in a syntagmatic analysis. At the paradigmatic axis the choice from the verbal system is available if the author wants to assert or to presuppose a process. The basic reason is that the proposition in the participle is presupposed, in contrast to mood (attitude system), where it is asserted.[46]

In this study, modulation is what grammaticalizes factive presupposition in the -finite choice of the process on the verbal network. Since the "fact" resides at the semantic level, the truth lies in the meaning shared by the reader. Therefore, by using a factive presupposition (Greek participle), a discourse extends beyond the relationship between the writer and his writings. The essential feature of the -finite system is the participation of the readers in the construction of meaning while it blocks the person of the verb in its form for this very purpose. Thus, the lack of limitation of person in the verbal form opens up the slot for the readers to interact with the discourse.

Now we are back to the most visible instances and most exegetical relevant features of the study of Greek participle, that is, the upgraded function. The interaction of lexis, grammar and pragmatics plays a very important role to the analysis of this particular feature of the participle. The reason why a participle can be suitable to be upgraded into the same mood of the main verb is because its semantic feature.

The participles are out of the attitude system with +finite choices. The choice -finite blocks the attitude system by opening up a space for the readers. If the presupposition is a factive presupposition, then the participle is the option available to indicate or point the readers toward the author's linguistic purpose.

One other intriguing feature of the participles that occurs by the interaction of lexis of factive adjective, or factive verbs and the semantics of the participle as a verbal adjective is the strong presence of some sort of emotion embedded in the use of the participle in the New Testament, and even in the ancient Greek as well. Of course, the author has different options to communicate the idea of emotion, but it seems that when emotion is desired, and the author wants to draw the readers into the emotive environment of the context of the situation, the participle seems to be a good option.

With verbs of movement, within the verbal complex, the author can choose the participle not only to express the speaker's feelings so as to affect the readers of the passage at hand,[47] but also to prepare the readers for future events in the context providing a logical association with, and motivation for, the action that follows. Therefore, any discussion of any specific function should not ignore how the semantics of the participle interacts with pragmatics and lexis in order to describe meaning.

Statement of the Problem

The frequent occurrences of this particular effect of the participle in the New Testament eliminate any excuse of rarity and provide an opportunity to consider the relationship of the aorist participle's semantics and its pragmatics. Scholars dealing with this function of the participle have confused the similarities of this participial usage and its several different effects produced by different contexts of the same structure of the aorist participle. For this reason, the function of the upgraded participle has been a challenge to those who propose to present it since some of them do not properly handle the semantics of the participle in general, and its resulting function.[48]

The upgraded function of the participle is a natural feature of Greek language as a result of being a factive presupposition. The various kinds of meaning are carried out at the rank of clause. Clauses combine to form clause complexes with all sorts of abstraction involved. The upgraded feature occurs in the participial embedded clause where a logical function creating clause complexes in relation to each other.

The logical and experiential function constitute the potential meanings in a broad metafunction, ideational. The close relationship between the process of the aorist participle and the main verb, connected to the structure in the syntagmatic axis makes the participle to be upgraded, in the reader's perspective, into the mood of the main verb.

The upgraded participle is always dependent on the main verb, although the association of the clause complexes by the choice of a factive presupposition giving the readers a need to assume the embedded participial clause as a true proposition to the point of being treated ideationally as in the same mood of the main verb.

The process described by the participle is used in such a way that the reader seems to be drawn into the narrative/discourse that the participle's action appears to be coordinated with the main verb. This apparent coordination is a result of a complex combination of several features.

Definition of Terms

Since the English participle fails to extend its use sufficiently to take care of the entire force of the upgraded participle,[49] it is imperative that its form and function be defined in such a way as to clarify this. Concerning form, the upgraded participle is just a function of the participle, which is always a participle by form no matter what function it may have. However, in identifying the upgraded effect of the participle there are three primary features that must be included: structure, context, and semantics. Thus, the "upgraded participle" is a complex effect of the participle, which can be presented as follows:

(a) It expresses an action or circumstance that accompanies the action of the main verb.[50] This participle is grammatically dependent[51] on the main verb. The reader, by seeing a formal designation, that is, the aorist nominative participle, accepts the embedded clause as uttering a true proposition in order to make sense of the main clause.

(b) It appears in the context as a prerequisite to the main verb though the action of the participle is in some sense upgraded to that of the main verb. From a translational perspective, the participle is upgraded to the same mood of the main action.

(c) The presupposition announced by the participle is so closely identified with the main verb that the reader ideationally, i.e., in thought,[52] relates the participle with that of the mood or modality of the main verb—either indicative, imperative, infinitive, or subjunctive[53]—but this is only a pragmatic effect of the functional roles of the semantics of the participle. Generally speaking, the addition of a coordinate conjunction "and" needs to be supplied in English since "translation must also be guided by the characteristics of the intended audience of the translation."[54]

The History of the Upgraded Participle

Here we present a brief summary with special attention to two points: neglect of the upgraded function, and absence of definitive guidelines.

Neglect of the Upgraded Function of the Participle

As Porter states, "the traditional terminology for defining the functional uses of the Participle often fails to make explicit the intricacies of Participle use."[55] This is the case not only of the adverbial participle as a whole but also of the specific functions of it. The terminology varies between two major terms: adverbial and circumstantial.

There is no essential difference between these two categories. By calling it a circumstantial participle, some authors emphasize the description of the relationship of the participle to the event ("circumstantial"), while others, in calling it "adverbial," point out the nature of the participle from a syntactical perspective.[56] To avoid any ambiguity, the terminology adopted for this complex effect of the aorist participle is *upgraded participle*.

On one hand, the dispute about terminology is unnecessary once it is recognized that "circumstantial" and "adverbial" are just two angles for looking at the same thing. On the other hand, the upgraded effect of the participle not only has been neglected, but also confused. While the semantic characteristics of a +factive presupposition (participle) remain unchanged throughout, its pragmatic functions and contextual effects vary.

The first grammarian to mention the upgraded participle effect was Ernest DeWitt Burton.[57] Burton dedicates only three paragraphs with a few instances in the New Testament.[58] Despite being short, his analysis anticipates what is going to be argued here because he notices that the sense of coordination between the participle and the main verb is logical and not syntactic.[59] Further, his analysis takes into account the fact that what occurs between the aorist participle and the main verb includes the reader's perspective: "the participle in such cases becomes *in thought* assertive, hortatory, optative, imperative, etc., according to the function of the principal verb."[60]

Burton affirms that the participle is not independent of the main clause. However, though he takes note of these features, his analysis of the upgraded participle misses some parameters, for example, "the action of a Participle of Attendant Circumstance [upgraded] may precede the action of the principal verb, accompany it, or even follow it."[61] In other words, there is no way of determining this relation of the participle by previous rule. He adds, "as respects logical relation, it is presented merely as an accompaniment of the action of the verb."[62] However, the examples presented show that both aorist and present participles are used, and no logical relation is determinative.

Blass-Debrunner-Funk include the upgraded participial function under the rubric of idiomatic or pleonastic[63] or even under the conjunctive participles.[64] They recognize the lack of prominence of the participles when they say, "the participles are asyndetic if they do not have equal value in the sentence."[65] Part of the semantics of every adverbial Greek participle is not being prominent. For the pleonastic example, they quote from the LXX Gen 32:23 ἀναστὰς δὲ τὴν νύκτα ἐκείνην ἔλαβεν τὰς δύο γυναῖκας καὶ τὰς δύο παιδίσκας καὶ τὰ ἕνδεκα παιδία αὐτοῦ καὶ διέβη τὴν διάβασιν τοῦ Ιαβοκ (*Rising* [he rose] that night [and] **took** his two wives and his two female servants, and his eleven children, and crossed the ford of the Jabbok).

BDF see this function as a sort of Hebraism. The conjunctive participle in BDF is their umbrella term for all adverbial participles that show agreement with a noun or pronoun from the main clause as opposed to absolute participle.[66] The upgraded participial effect is just one aspect of the conjunctive participle in BDF. They cite Acts18:23 Καὶ ποιήσας χρόνον τινὰ **ἐξῆλθεν** *διερχόμενος* καθεξῆς τὴν Γαλατικὴν χώραν καὶ Φρυγίαν, ἐπιστηρίζων πάντας τοὺς μαθητάς (Spending some time there, he **departed** [and] *went* successively *through* the region of Galatia and Phrygia, strengthening all the disciples).[67] They believe that the main verb and the participle (**ἐξῆλθεν** *διερχόμενος*) are similar to ἐξῆλθεν καί διήρχετο thus being equal to two finite verbs. However, they see the use of the participle by Luke as a matter of style.[68] No clear rules are presented as to why this participle both precedes and follows the main verb.

Moulton adopts Blass' description of the conjunctive participle, but he puts the upgraded participial effect under the umbrella of the pleonastic participle. He rightly notes the tendency of the authors to use verbs such as λάβων and ἀναστάς. However, he ends his analysis saying, "the large use of participles in narrative in grammatical connection … is more a matter of style than grammar and calls for no especial examination here."[69]

Like Moulton, Robertson includes the upgraded participle under the pleonastic participles. He combines the pure pleonastic participles (with verbs of saying) with that of the upgraded function of the participle. Using Moulton, he says, "there are other pleonastic participles like the common ἀποκριθεὶς εἶπεν (Mt. 3:15) which is somewhat like the vernacular: 'He ups and says' (Moulton *Prol.*, p. 15 f.)."[70] Robertson states, "it is not always *easy* to discriminate between the temporal participle and that of attendant circumstance [adverbial participle in general] or manner."[71]

The upgraded participial function for him is used to distinguish among other temporal ideas. But it is still viewed as an adverbial participle. Robertson, in discussing the above, does include the example of Acts 21:32 and even says, "παραλαβών (cf. λαβών in ancient Greek) may be regarded as merely the attendant circumstance."[72] It must be said that for him the attendant circumstance has a broad meaning and it is not used to describe the upgraded effect. However, he rightly notes "it is usually a mistake to try to reproduce such participles by the English 'when,' 'after,' etc., with the indicative … it is generally sufficient to preserve the English participle or to co-ordinate the clauses with 'and.'"[73]

Robertson's terminology does not fit the recent discussion in use of the term attendant circumstance (upgraded participle). However, he rightly notes, "Burton makes a separate division for the participle 'of attendant circumstance,' but this is not necessary and leads to over refinement."[74] He goes on to say that "Blass' term 'conjunctive' (*Gr. of N. T. Gk.*, p. 249) throws no particular light on the point."[75]

He comments, "it is easy to split hairs over the various circumstantial [adverbial] participles and to read into them much more than is there."[76] This demonstrates that determining an appropriate translation does not define the meaning associated with a particular verbal choice. Sim agrees with Robertson about the idea that the terminology such as causal, temporal, concessive conflates syntax and pragmatics. As a result, this common terminology hides a necessary logical and cognitive process. Sim's conclusion is that "we then wrongly place the result within the grammatical form of the participle, rather than in its relationship to the context."[77]

Dana-Mantey see the circumstantial participle (adverbial participle) not as a wide category, but as a specific category named attendant circumstance [upgraded effect]. There are only ten lines in their book dealing with the topic. They recognize the legitimacy of the upgraded effect of the participle, commenting that the best rendering in English for the upgraded function is adding the conjunction "and" with a finite construction.[78] They go on to say, "Here the English participle fails to extend its use sufficiently to take care of the entire force of the Greek participle, and at the same time, it is doubtful if a separate clause is an exact translation."[79]

They present only few instances which demonstrate what they establish as a possible rendering in English. Mark 16:20 ἐκεῖνοι δὲ *ἐξελθόντες* **ἐκήρυξαν** πανταχοῦ, τοῦ κυρίου συνεργοῦντος καὶ τὸν λόγον βεβαιοῦντος διὰ τῶν ἐπακολουθούντων σημείων (but they *went out* [and] **preached** everywhere, the Lord working with them and confirming the word through accompanying signs). Luke 4:15 καὶ αὐτὸς ἐδίδασκεν ἐν ταῖς συναγωγαῖς αὐτῶν *δοξαζόμενος* ὑπὸ πάντων (He taught in their synagogues, *being glorified* by all).

Both Burton and Wallace cite Luke 4:15 in their discussion of the adverbial participles. It is possible that Dana-Mantey might have been influenced by Burton who also classifies the participle in Luke 4:15 as upgraded.[80] Wallace, however, identifies this participle as the result participle.[81] It may be that many issues in language and interpretation are actually judgment calls on how to assess the evidence. In fact, good interpreters may differ even in the face of quite clear "rules." Whatever aspect one sees, their differing classifications show the development and advance of rules that help to identify the upgraded function of the participle.

Brooks and Winbery call the upgraded participle an imperatival participle. The so-called "imperatival participle" is rare, but the example presented is not imperatival at all.[82] The example is from Mark 5:23 - καὶ παρακαλεῖ αὐτὸν πολλὰ λέγων ὅτι τὸ θυγάτριόν μου ἐσχάτως ἔχει, ἵνα ἐλθὼν **ἐπιθῇς** τὰς χεῖρας αὐτῇ ἵνα σωθῇ καὶ ζήσῃ (and implored him insistently saying, "My little daughter is at the point of death. *Come* [and] **lay your hands** *on* her, so that she may be made well and live.").[83] This is a rare use of ἵνα with a subjunctive, and it has the force of a command.[84] The relation of the participle to the main verb shows that the participle is upgraded by the mood of the main verb coordinated by "and" in the English translation.[85]

Greenlee has two different categories, the attendant circumstance and coordinate circumstance. The attendant circumstance is used to refer to the general adverbial participle. According to him attendant function "describes a circumstance as merely accompanying the leading verb, with the sense of 'and in addition, this,' and semantically in the same mood as the leading verb." He goes on to say, "the participle of attendant circumstance is merely an *accompanying action* which does not qualify the action of the leading verb."[86] He presents the following examples for the attendant circumstance.

John 19:5 ἐξῆλθεν οὖν ὁ Ἰησοῦς ἔξω, *φορῶν* τὸν ἀκάνθινον στέφανον καὶ τὸ πορφυροῦν ἱμάτιον. καὶ λέγει αὐτοῖς· ἰδοὺ ὁ ἄνθρωπος (So Jesus *came out, wearing* the crown of thorns and the purple robe. And Pilate said to them, "Behold the man!"). John 19:17 καὶ *βαστάζων* ἑαυτῷ τὸν σταυρὸν **ἐξῆλθεν** εἰς τὸν λεγόμενον Κρανίου Τόπον (and *carrying* his own cross **he went out** to the place called "The Place of the Skull".). Greenlee's first example follows the main verb while the second precedes it. He does not follow his own translational clue (and in addition, this). In the first example the present participle develops the idea of the main verb with the sense of "and in addition, this," but this would not easily fit in his second example.

Greenlee presents another class that he calls coordinate circumstance that seems to fit the upgraded participle. Notwithstanding, Levinsohn says that "the term 'coordinate circumstances' … is unfortunate, since the circumstances are always of secondary importance with respect to the action of the nuclear [main] clause."[87] Levinsohn adds that this participle "describes an action coordinate with, prior to, and of the same mood semantically as the leading verb, although often not equal in importance with the leading verb."[88]

He goes on to say that "it may be translated by the same tense and mood as the leading verb and connected with it by an 'and'."[89] In a later 2005 article, Greenlee discusses the upgraded participle, but he does not add the distinction between the attendant circumstance and the coordinate participle, though the very same examples are quoted.[90]

In the 1990s, three Greek grammars were published. Young's *Intermediate NT Greek* was the first to approach the participle by considering linguistic features. His treatment of the upgraded participial effect has only three NT instances.[91] Young says, "the [upgraded] participle … expresses an action or circumstance that accompanies the action of the leading verb."[92] Among several grammarians, he advances the analysis of the participle in general. About the upgraded function he recognizes that "the participial phrase represents a deep structure proposition that is semantically less prominent than that represented by the main clause."[93]

In this binary relation, the focal point is on the main verb, so he sees a semantic implication of a factive presupposition. Although Young advances the analysis of the adverbial functions of the participle, his examples in general do not fit the upgraded structure, syntax, and contextually. Matthew 3:1 Ἐν δὲ ταῖς ἡμέραις ἐκείναις **παραγίνεται** Ἰωάννης ὁ βαπτιστὴς *κηρύσσων* ἐν τῇ ἐρήμῳ τῆς Ἰουδαίας (John the Baptist **came** *preaching* in the desert).

First, the upgraded effect always appears in the aorist participle. Second, the upgraded function always precedes the main verb, but in the above example it does not precede the main clause. Third, although the participle is adverbial, its logical relation does not show the aorist participle being upgraded to the mood of main verb. Fourth, he establishes a criterion for the upgraded effect, but his example does not fit his criterion.[94]

The history of the upgraded function shows that the majority of scholars consider it as a dependent adverbial participle, with the exception of few grammarians that decided to take the upgrade function as an independent class. In terms of guidelines and other features, Daniel Wallace has the clearest presentation on the upgraded participle. He delineates the basic structure to identify this participle; he includes some of its semantic implications; and he presents and discusses examples both indisputable and debatable.[95] Wallace's approach is very useful and if it needs some refinement this would be only in regard to semantics but well recommended for its works on the structure (word order) and pragmatics of the upgraded.

The analysis so far of many grammars and grammarians and the varying terminology for the "apparent" similar function of the upgraded participle show two needs: an explicit theory concerning modal semantics in the Greek language and detailed examination in order to avoid any misunderstanding of the matter.

First, we choose to present an explicit theory laying out a procedure for dealing with modal semantics. This will be presented later in chapter three. Porter provides a recent analysis of modal semantics, although his emphasis is upon verbal aspect, it is useful for the understanding of grammatical presupposition. He points out,

> The indicative is used for assertive or declarative statements […] while the non-indicative forms grammaticalize a variety of related attitudes, having in common that they

make no assertion about reality but grammaticalize simply the 'will' of the speaker, and are therefore deontic. Thus, the Imperative grammaticalizes [+direction], the Subjunctive grammaticalizes [+projection], and the Optative, marked in relation to the Subjunctive grammaticalizes [+ projection: +contingency].[96]

As will be seen, in contrast to the indicative (mood) and the non-indicative (modals), there is modulation (participle and infinitive) that does not grammaticalize attitude.[97] He clarifies the point stating, "the confusion arises when analysis is reduced to asking whether the Participle is an Imperative or an Indicative. Then extrapolations about the Participle are implied on the basis of the nature of the, for example, Imperative, failing to realize that the Participle remains a Participle."[98] The main tenet used here is that the participle is a factive presupposition.

Not only is there a need for an explicit theory of modal semantics applied to the participles, but it must also be admitted that the pressure on the traditional categories (e.g., causal, temporal, concessive, manner, etc.) normally conflates semantics and pragmatics and consequently puts too much attention on secondary points. Therefore, it is necessary to include a treatment of what is a semantic presupposition and what are some of its functions.[99]

The obsession for classifying the participles according to translational aspects has relegated the semantics of the participle to a secondary place while distracting students from the importance of the Greek participle in discourse studies of the New Testament. Translation is very important, but it is better to treat the Greek participle on its own and then move to fit any translation.

The analysis of the upgraded effect includes a complex study of language at different levels of meanings with enormous degree of abstraction. All kinds of feature combinations, such as discourse analysis, semantics, syntax, lexis, pragmatics must be included in its own place and in its relations to meaning. On the discourse and structural side, two linguists in particular have given a great contribution: Stephen Levinsohn and Steve Runge.[100]

Absence of Definitive Guidelines

The lack of a theory of modal semantics and the conflation of semantics and pragmatics in dealing with the participle explain the absence of definitive guidelines for the participle in general and upgraded effect in particular. The absence of it for this participial effect has occurred because this effect, though related to the main verb, does not fit in any of the categories for the so-called adverbial usage of the participle. Perhaps the obstacle is the collective interest to classify the participles for the sake of translation into English and other languages at the same time some ignore the transitivity functions that are so important to distinguish "logical" from "grammatical" categories.

Among the classical Greek scholars, Goodwin presents some guidelines, but only one paragraph about the circumstantial participle (adverbial participle). His discussion of the upgraded participle is too short to allow any adoption of guidelines. There are two examples cited, and one of them fits the upgraded effect; the other example probably indicates the logical function of the adverbial participle known as "manner."[101] Smyth follows the same path as Goodwin on the idea of the preposition "with" to translate this participial function into English. Again, he does not seem to be interested in developing any guidelines for the study of aorist adverbial participle.[102]

Adolf von Schlatter gives the first direction to future guidelines on the study of the upgraded effect of the participle. He observes that the upgraded function of the participle is common in the Gospel of Matthew. He perceives Matthew's structure and explains it as Matthew's style. What he does to Matthew, BDF does to Luke.[103] He comments that if two actions appear to be connected with only one process, then the aorist participle acts as a prerequisite for the action and should be placed before the main verb in translation.[104]

Schlatter seems to perceive the importance of the word order. In fact, the aorist nominative participle in the embedded clause placed at the beginning of a clause or sentence does in fact indicate a close relation between the embedded clause and the primary clause. As a point of departure, Schlatter's observation will be proven to make sense with circumstantial roles of the participles that fit in the upgraded effect. Again, the issue is of deep-order and includes many different features.

The tendency to conflate semantics and pragmatics have led to a diversity in terminology and have indicated the need for a modal semantic theory. Despite these characteristics some advances were made. Burton recognizes that the relation between the participle and the main verb in this type of construction is logical. It is logical in the sense that not only the author and his writing are related to the discourse, but also the reader's perspective is stimulated by the participle. Systemic functional linguistics combined two functions in one metafunction: experiential and logical into the ideational metafunction. Logically, the nominative participle within the upgraded effect depends on the main clause, and the association with the participle causes the purpose intended so that the readers can track the sematic feature and its function.

The relation between the participle and the main verb is that of dependence, and no matter what kind of translation would result, the semantics of the participle is different from that of the verb. To see this difference and the contrast between the function of the participle and that of the main verb will enrich one's understanding or appreciation of the text. Again, the semantics of the participle's factive presupposition will be compared and distinguished from the semantics of the indicative and non-indicative moods, that is, ±finiteness.[105]

Burton says that the upgraded effect of the participle is equivalent to a coordinate verb with καί. He affirms that the position of this participle is not determined by any fixed rules.[106] His assertion is much more from an English translation than from the Greek language itself, but we will see that the writer did have a choice of having two coordinated verbs with καί or even have a participle καί with a verb in any mood. However, to say that this choice is the equivalent of the upgraded participial effect is to conflate semantics and pragmatics as well as to miss the functional roles of the aorist nominative participle's semantics.

In sum, among those who have written about the upgraded participle, Wallace should be recommended for working in this subject matter. From the actionality perspective and pragmatics, he is still an asset for intermediate grammar studies. Our research tries to advance some of the semantic aspects pointed out in his grammar while recognizing that most of the Greek grammarians have not emphasized the semantic of this participle in contrast to the semantics of the mood and modals.

The Purpose of the Study

We desire in this book to advance some of the best semantic insights from Porter's doctoral thesis on the system of finiteness on Greek verbal network according to systemic display, published in his Verbal Aspect (1989). There is an application of the theory of modal semantics of the participle. Therefore, our research has its significance within the context of a larger problem—the devalued semantics of the Greek participle, and a narrow problem—the upgraded effect of the participles. This latter one is taken as a study case to present the semantics of the participle.

The upgraded participial effect is meaning in its complexity where a lexical item, a sentence structure, syntactical arrangement, pragmatic analysis are at the service of semantics. Our approach is top-down. We start with semantics to move from there to the lower levels of meaning. A semantic item has its own function derived of its semantic role. For example, once we accepted that factive presupposition is the semantics of the participle that cannot be cancelled, then we proceed to analyze the effect of the participle in some contexts which can be seen and better explained if the functional result (hierarchization) is taken together with the semantics of the participle (+factive presupposition).

There are couple of questions we try to answer in this book. The following questions serve a road map for our approach. The main concern in this book is to answer this question: What are the semantics grammaticalized by the participles? Other questions are: 1) What is the upgraded effect of the aorist participle? 2) What is the context of situations that most attract the use of the nominative participle in general, and the upgraded effect of the aorist participle in particular? 3) What is the contribution of this function of the participle to New Testament exegesis?

We will discuss modulation in chapter three as a suitable explanation for the understanding of the participle -finiteness system in contrast to mood and modality +finiteness system. In this book we use a modal semantics theory, and take modulation as what communicates semantic presupposition, which is a morphologically based feature of the verbal system within Greek grammar.

Because presupposition functions at levels higher than that of simple morphology, chapter two will discuss the participle as a semantic presupposition. The problem appears to be like this, "saying that presuppositions are not part of what is asserted but of what is assumed does not in itself provide any practical method to identifying presuppositional constructions in language."[107]

The problem above needs to be taken seriously, so there is an attempt to include a fair analysis of the aorist nominative participle in the broad sense, that is, its relation to the narrative and discourse, but much more attention is given to the rank of clause. Clause-level analysis demonstrates the potential semantic pattern that helps to determine a semantic value of a particular form, which in turn provides evidence to confirm the initial semantic assumption of this book.[108]

Factive presupposition in our analysis functions up to the level of the clause complex, and it is used by the author to indicate relative prominence of events that are being narrated.[109] Therefore, the analysis of the semantics of the participle in general, and of its functional roles is a supplement to the former analysis and a starting point for further research of modal semantics.

Prominence is indicated by motivated markedness within a given discourse. Callow helps to understand what prominence as she states,

> A story in which every character was equally important and every event equally significant can hardly be imagined. Even the simplest story has at least a central character and a plot, and this means one character is more important than the others, and certain events likewise. Human beings cannot observe events simply as happenings; they observe them as related and significant happenings, and they report them as such.[110]

Callow's definition is adopted throughout this study. She defines prominence as "any device whatsoever which gives certain events, participants, or objects more significance than others in the same context."[111] What are these features that signal peaks in the clause or narrative? Greek like other languages has different devices to signal that, however, we will be arguing that the participle is one of these devices that signals prominence.

Fanning and Porter have noted that verbal aspect has the function of highlighting peaks of information, such as background and foreground.[112] This study will argue that modal semantics of presupposition is another motivated marked element that New Testament authors used to signal prominence.

Therefore, a careful attempt to analyze the Greek semantics of the participle will indicate if the NT writer's discourse wants not only to be "accurate" but also convincing. We will show that by using a factive presupposition (participles), a discourse extends beyond the relationship between the writer and his writings so that the reader could be impacted by the situation presented.

An author uses a participle in the embedded clause to invite the reader into the environment of the narrative requiring him to assume the truthfulness of the proposition expressed by the participle in order to set the main clause on the spotlight.

The Method of the Study

This research relies heavily on linguistic methods in establishing its understanding of +factive presupposition (the reader's mental action) achieved by Greek modulation (participle). It accepts a modified version of Halliday's systemic linguistics as the general framework within which research is conducted.[113] The reason to include Halliday's language theory is related to the fact that he is among few linguists that have included a discussion of modal semantics.

Palmer's typological approach is very helpful in the distinction between mood and modality, although his discussion of the non-indicative mood emphasizes more the subjunctive and imperative (Irrealis).[114] Givón in his functional perspective sees the participle as adding background information into the narrative.[115] His view, that points of departure are as much from a backward perspective as a forward one (which we will discuss in chapter four), is foundational to the analysis of the structure of the upgraded participle in the embedded clause that initiates the sentence.[116] However, it must said that his perspective is oriented by generative transformational grammar, and Van Valin states, "the most serious difficulty with Givón's assumption is that much of the use of language in every society and culture appears to have a primary *social* rather than informative function."[117]

Rijksbaron sees the distinction between the infinitive and the participle as that of semantics. He sees the participle in the complement of verbs of perception as indicating a direct perception in contrast to the infinitive, which shows some sort of indirect perception (something already presented above).[118]

What can be seen from the scholars above is that no extensive discussion of the participle has included a study of register and modulation with special attention to the analysis of the adverbial participle. Even Halliday's systemic linguistic theory tends not to include any cognitive analysis.

Teuen van Dijk points out several critiques of systemic functional linguistics, in fact, of several functional approaches: 1) systemic functional linguistics has a limited field of work, that is, too much linguistic (lexico-syntactic) sentence; 2) he sees the systemic linguistics as anti-mentalism with a lack of interest in cognition; 3) van Dijk accuses systemic linguistics of being a limited social theory of language, since it works only with grammar, which limited to verbal context and co-text.[119]

Some functional linguists perceived some of these failures and they have tried to implement Halliday's theory by adding a methodology that includes the analysis of the social and cultural "contexts" of language and language use, with a specific emphasis on register.[120] One of these scholars, as will be seen, is widely used in this study in order to balance Halliday's theory.[121]

Considering the strength of some of these critiques, the present study does interact with the discourse analysis approach of Stephen H. Levinsohn and Steve E. Runge.[122] This latter especially, has presented recently one of the strongest critiques of systemic functional linguistics. Although critiquing SFL, both are useful for the present research since both Levinsohn and Runge see the participle as a presupposition in contrast to mood. Levinsohn in his treatment of the participial background function states, "the primary significance of using the participial clause is … the counterpoint from the assertion of the nuclear clause."[123] If we adopt the systemic display of the verbal network, the system of finiteness has two available options: +finite (mood) and -finite (presupposition). Runge affirms that the choice of using a participle represents a choice not to use other moods.[124]

Runge's critiques focus on the methodological and theoretical flaws of systemic linguistics. He sees systemic linguistics as limited in some aspects. One element of this limitation has to do with the realization statement, which is used to describe the set of options available in the verbal network typically faced as markedness, that is, each element is heavily marked, and we identify it using systemic display with the signs + plus or − minus. He states, "SFL is well-suited to describing simple systems of language, ones that do not have multiple variables simultaneously in operation."[125] Further, he states, "There is a tendency to claim that a device can only do one thing or another, that it cannot accomplish more than one discourse task at a time."[126] He sees language more as multi-tasking than specializing.

Acknowledging that this subject is broad in scope and that the debate so far has not received any response from the systemic functional linguists, just some clarifications are sketched here. First, the contrastive display relation adopted in this study, that sees the choice of the aorist participle over other possibilities does not seem to disagree with Runge. Our presupposition is that choice implies meaning, and in this specific topic Runge says, "if a writer chose to use a participle to describe an action, he has at the same time chosen not to use an indicative or other finite verb form."[127]

If systemic functional linguistics is well-suited to describing simple systems of language, it is assumed that the modal semantics adopted here is part of this well-suited system, which seems to be in agreement with Runge's discursive perspective. The terminology used for us to describe markedness is prominence. Markedness theory presupposes that in a pair of relations one member in the opposition is the most basic while the other is what stands out.

In the relation between the participle and the indicative, for instance, the indicative in this pair of opposition is what stands out.[128] Thus, as Runge states, "the choice to use a participle to grammaticalize an action represents the choice to use a verb that is less-specific than a finite verb, whether paratactic [coordinate] or hypotactic [subordinate]."[129]

Second, the contrastive relation between the participle and infinitive in this study is marked within modal semantics as +factive presupposition and −factive presupposition. All of the verbal forms in Greek seem to be marked and each form has its specific features. The ± does not mean that sometimes one of the members does not contribute to the total meaning. Rather, both the participle and the infinitive contribute with their semantic features to the verbal component of the clause.

From a verb oppositional perspective, both the participle and the infinitive are established in terms of marked pairs. A marked pair asserts the presence of an established feature specified by a linguistic sign. The participle and infinitive are marked terms that assert ±factive presupposition respectively.

All the choice available in the system network are heavily marked formally.[130] In the process description the finiteness system comes with two further options +finite and -finite. The choice of -finite blocks the person of the verb form while it opens up the slot to the reader's participation in the construal of meaning.

The choice of aspectuality and finiteness are simultaneous. Aspect is primary to the verbal choice and continues through the process. By choosing -finite, two new options are available ±factive presupposition. There is a slight contrast that occurs as the -finite system is picked up, the attitude option is blocked. Thus, all the mood options on the up level continue by all the choices of ±assertion.

±Assertion has no limitation in the description of the verbal person since it belongs to the +finite system, while -finite is marked by the limitation of the person of the verb. The conclusion is that the relation between these two clauses indicates to the readers that the choice to use a participle represents the choice *not* to use another verb form."[131]

Since choosing to describe a process with -finite blocks the person of the verb but opens up the slot for the readers to participate in the construal of meaning, the reader/listener must accept the truthfulness of the embedded participial clause so the main clause can be on the spotlight without losing track of the parts communicated. For instance, Matthew 28:19 πορευθέντες οὖν μαθητεύσατε … (Go, therefore, make disciples).

The participle gives prominence to the main verb, but the readers must accept "go" as a true proposition in order to make sense of the main clause. In the case of the upgraded function, the interpreter must recognize that the translation makes the participle appear to have the same "mood" as that of the of the main verb, but ultimately, the aorist adverbial participle is a factive presupposition and not a command.

The method applied is similar to what other scholars have applied to their research. Systemic functional linguistics is a system-structure theory, which views language as a network of interrelated sets of options. This study will not focus too much on this theory because often systemic seems to limit its discussion to system-level meaning, something very abstract and general and could fail to see the possible sense that occurs in actual usage when the system interacts with various contextual features to produce specific meanings in actual usage.

Our readers should expect to deal with verbal aspect since this subject matter has already been the focus of so many books. Our research, rather, relies upon the modal semantics realized by modulation in contrast to mood and modal/modality.[132]

The functional paradigm indicates that there is a difference in meaning when an author chooses to utter something with a participle.[133] The choice that the language user makes not only highlights the meaning of that choice but also eliminates the meanings of the other options.[134] Our functional paradigm is a *framework* for investigation rather than fixed points that the data must fit in with.[135]

Another important point included here is the distinction between semantics and pragmatics. This division is much more for didactical purpose, but it is deeper that we are willing to accept. It is not just the relation between what is cancelable and what is not (context or pragmatics), rather, it is philosophical, on which the interaction of the verbal classes with lexical, syntactical, and semantic feature have to take for a careful analysis. Recognizing that there is much debate about grammar as a "closed system" this research holds that any supposed meaning of a grammatical feature that can be canceled in a specific use of this feature demonstrates that this meaning is not part of the semantics of the form but rather of its context.[136] It does not mean that a specific form that normally occurs in a determined context would not occur where it is not expected. The point here is that the variety of contexts changes the contextual semantic, but not the semantics of the form.[137]

In addition, any study of a dead language that includes semantics and pragmatics must add the study of register, which, according to a version of systemic linguistics, will indicate the most common context where a speaker/writer uses the participle. By investing the text with diverse viewpoints on the action and highlighting key elements or episodes through lexico-grammatical means, the skilled narrator is able to impose an 'evaluative superstructure' upon the text, aimed at effecting the desired response(s) in the reader.

For the set of data, we use Gramcord, Logos 4, and Bible Works 10 to present multiple samples where the participle and the upgraded function occur in the NT. Grammar, articles, reviews, and commentaries are all used in order to track the various ways authors have dealt with this subject.

Ramifications of the Study

The nature of the participle as part of -finite system is what turns the participle to be readers-oriented. What are the roles that the readers play as they follow the author's choice of a Greek participle? The answer to this question is not simplistic, but complex. For instance, the complementary participles use a participle as a complement to communicate different meaningful features according to the author's intention.

A signal that confirms that the Greek participle is a factive presupposition, in this case, is that with verbs of perception, the choice of the participle indicates a direct perception of the event, while the infinitive, non-factive presupposition communicates an indirect perception.

Another confirmation of the participle as a factive presupposition is that every example of the participle in the New Testament show that if we consider only the process of the embedded clause, the use of the nominative participle occurs when an author wants to draw the reader to play a role in the discourse, that is, the reader is invited to embrace the process participial clause as a true proposition in order to make sense of the action of the main clause.

If we take the upgraded effect as a case study, two other ramifications can be discussed. First, the structure of the upgraded participle, that is, an anarthrous aorist nominative participle that precedes the main verb sets the main verb in the spotlight and gives the readers a road map to a meaningful strategy. This is a reader-oriented tool to make sense or highlight the points the author wants to emphasize. Second, the participle serves as a background information connected with the action of the main verb.

Finally, we suspect based in the study of register or the context of the situation, where some emotion is involved, the author has different options to describe whether by a factivite adjective of emotion, or any lexis available. However, some authors give preference to communicate emotion and in so many contexts the participle is their favorite since it is reader-oriented. Thus, the author uses it in order to draw the reader into some emotional environment. The participle is one option, but by choosing it, the author opens up the slot to get the reader into it.

The discourse feature of the participle, including the upgraded effect, shows that by using a participle, a writer is able to express details without giving the participle a prominence that would distort the perspective. This feature is a right observation of the semantics of the participle. Thus, the main verb outlines the action while the participle gives color to the process. This is where an analysis that draws on wider discourse units involving a semantic presupposition loses strength.

Summary of the Study

Campbell states the following assumption: "a model will be deemed more successful than another on the basis that it more successfully demonstrates the non-cancelability of its semantic content; in other words the model with the least 'exceptions' will win the day."[138] Thus, the present analysis seeks to demonstrate that in a description of process the finiteness system follows to choices in the verbal network. The communication of the person of the verb (+finite) moves toward the attitude system, followed by another choice ±Assertion.

When an author intends limitation, he or she has the -finite option, which blocks the +finite system and opens up the slot to the reader with the choice ±factive presupposition. The +factive presupposition on the verbal network is the choice encoded by the participle and the upgraded participial effect is an interesting example of this linguistic phenomenon since multiple tasks occur.

Chapter two is entitled *the participle as semantic presupposition*. Discussion here has a wider purpose, that is, it analyzes the semantics of the participle in general so that the specific results of it may be applied to the upgraded participial effect in chapter five. A necessary balance of any analysis of an ancient text is the inclusion of register, which is added here to interact with the assumption that the verbal participle, specifically, the aorist nominative participle is one possible choice among others to communicate emotion, but when it occurs in emotional context it opens up a slot in order to draw the reader into such an environment. After discussing that, this chapter presents the discussion of presupposition as both a semantic and a pragmatic feature and their relation to systemic functional linguistics.

Chapter three includes a model semantic discussion arguing that the relationship between the anarthrous aorist (adverbial) participle that precedes the main clause has a semantic value contrasting what is ±asserted (mood/modality) to what is presupposed (modulation). Furthermore, it will argue that the two major categories of mood, epistemic (+ assertion [Realis]) and deontic (-assertion [Irrealis]),[139] must be seen in opposition to each other, and both together must be seen in opposition to the participle as well as to the infinitive. Communicating an action by means of a participle states something different from the way a mood would do it. In addition, the importance of differentiating semantics from pragmatics, at the same time combining them within a specific context, is the key to understand the pragmatic effect of the upgraded participle.

Chapter four sketches the functional roles of the aorist adverbial participial. There is an attempt to relate pragmatic and semantic. Since the semantics of the aorist adverbial participle is that of presupposition, the main functional role of it is hierarchization. Therefore, hierarchization has two further functional roles: background and prioritizing. These two functional roles occur in a pair with the action of the main clause setting the main verb in the spotlight. This chapter will include also a brief analysis of the typical context preferred by the aorist participle, that is, emotional contexts.

Chapter five narrows down all the research to analyze the specific semantics related to the upgraded function. It is a place to see how the specific semantics of the participle in general are applied to the specific function of upgraded participles. The relation between semantics and pragmatics plays an important role to understanding the upgrade function of the participle.

Chapter six deals with the New Testament examples. A brief introduction will be presented as a way of reviewing the relation of the moods with modulation. The valid examples will be presented with the indicative, subjunctive, imperative, and infinitive consecutively.

The conclusion of this study shows that the core semantic values of the participle are capable of issuing a range of pragmatic implicatures, of which the upgraded participial effect is one; but the failure to see how these elements work together within a semantic environment is the cause of several unbalanced conclusions.

Notes

1. The upgraded function of the participle is also known as participle of attendant circumstance in many grammars. However, to avoid any ambiguity in terminology between adverbial participle or circumstantial participle, the term "upgraded participle" will be used throughout this study.

2. Here it refers to the anarthrous (participle without an article preceding it) aorist participle that functions as a verb in a dependent clause.

3. We will argue below strictly; a participle is not a mood.

4. This upgraded function is not a formal designation. There are several adverbial implicatures of the Greek participle. Wallace notes at least 12 under the dependent adverbial participle. *GGBB*, 622–649. Young rightly points out, "the adverbial force [of the participle] is not indicated by the grammar." See Richard A. Young, *Intermediate New Testament Greek: A Linguistic and Exegetical Approach* (Nashville, TN: Broadman & Holman, 1994), 152.

5. The main verb throughout the dissertation is quoted in bold, the participle in italics.

6. The majority of the versions in English, Portuguese, Spanish, and German translate it as a coordinate clause. Some versions use a comma to separate the participle from the finite verb.

7. οὖν is missing from א A 0148^vid f^13 etc. bo^pt. νυν ('now') in D. The first part of Matt 28:19 has a firm textual tradition. Codex Bezae D05 illustrated the upgraded participle with its hindrance. D05 reads πορεύεσθαι (verb infinitive present middle from πορεύομαι) which could be only a misspelling of the imperative form πορεύεσθε. Tischendorf understood it as an imperative transcripted wrongly. See Constantinus von Tischendorf; Gregory, Caspar René (Hrsg.); Abbot, Ezra (Hrsg.): *Novum Testamentum Graece*. Lipsiae: Giesecke & Devrient, 1869–94, Mt 28:19. Origen wrote two finite verbs without any coordinate conjunction, he reads πορεύεσθε μαθητεύσατε.

8. B and D read an aorist participle βαπτίσαντες, but evidence confirms the present tense-form for this text. Cf. Karl Barth, "An Exegetical Study of Matthew 28:16–20," in *The Theology of the Christian Mission*, edited by Gerald H. Anderson (New York, 1961), 67.

9. Cleon Rogers, Jr. "The Great Commission," *BSac* 130 (1973):258. Wallace is the grammarian that has one of the most complete presentations of the upgraded function. He says, "to turn πορευθέντες into an adverbial participle is to turn the Great Commission into the Great Suggestion!" See *GGBB*, 645. Although Wallace states this, it must be said that the upgraded participle is an adverbial participle since it is dependent on the main clause. It is only from a translational perspective that πορευθέντες sounds independent from the main clause. Thus, a more precise way to say this would be, "to translate πορευθέντες into an adverbial clause in English is to turn the Great Commission into the Great Suggestion!" He recognizes this caveat as he says, "certainly no participle should be explained as an independent participle if there is any other way to explain it" (quoting Brooks and Winbery). See *GGBB*, 653.

10. Paul Gaechter, *Das Matthäus-Evangelium* (München: Wien, 1963), 965.

11. Roger, "The Great Commission," 262.

12. The four semantic types and expression formats of adverbial clauses are: Entity Type, Time Dependency, Factuality, and Presupposition. Kees Hengeveld, "Adverbial Clauses in the Languages of Europe," in *Adverbial Constructions in the Languages of Europe*, edited by Johan van der Auwera (Berlin: Mouton de Gruyter, 1998), 345.

13. Kees Hengeveld, *Non-Verbal Predication Theory, Typology, Diachrony* (Berlin: Mouton de Gruyter, 1992), 11–13. Note that "factivity" was replaced by presupposition in his recent work.

14. P. Kiparsky, and C. Kiparsky, "Fact," in *Semantics: An interdisciplinary Reader in Philosophy, Linguistics, and Psychology*, edited by D. Steinberg and L. Jakobovits (Cambridge, MA: Cambridge University Press, 1971), 348.

15. Maria Helena de Moura Neves, *Gramática dos Usos do Português* (São Paulo: UNESP, Ed. Universidade Estadual Paulista, 2000), 32.

16. *ATR*, 1119. See *GGBB*, 646.

17. David Lightfoot, *Natural Logic and the Greek Moods: The Nature of the Subjunctive and Optative in Classical Greek*. Janua Linguarum: Series Practica, 230 (The Hague: Mouton, 1975), 41.

18. See Luke 8:46, Matthew 16:3, John 7:32, John 12:18, 2 Cor 8:22, and 1 Thess 2:4. Schmidt sketches a brief summary of the history of Greek grammar and adds a contemporary linguistic discussion of the Hellenistic Greek follows Lightfoot. See Daryl Schmidt, "The Study of Hellenistic Greek Grammar in the Light of Contemporary Linguistics," *Perspective in Religious Studies* 11 (1984), 36.

19. See Schmidt, "The Study of Hellenistic Greek Grammar," 37.

20. Lightfoot, *Natural Logic*, 41–42.

21. See Palmer for a critique of such ideas. Frank Robert Palmer, *Mood and Modality*, 2nd ed. Cambridge Textbooks in Linguistics (Cambridge, MA: Cambridge University Press, 2006), 3.

22. See *PVA*, 391.

23. Palmer, *Mood and Modality*, 11.

24. Ibid.

25. *PVA*, 391.

26. Ibid., 391.

27. Ibid., 390.

28. James L. Boyer, "The Classification of Participles: A Statistical Study," *GTJ* 5 no. 2 (1984):175.

29. This explanation [of the complementary participle] is dependent upon Boyer, "Classification of the Participle," 174–175.

30. *PVA*, 391.

31. Jerneja Kavčič in her recent monograph follows the same semantic definition of the participle. However, she sees factuality much with the infinitive. She states, "the difference between the participle and an infinitive dependent clause is that the latter refers to something actual, whereas the former denotes something imaginary, whose existence only assumed." Jerneja Kavčič, *The Syntax of the Infinitive and the Participle in the Early Byzantine Greek: An Interpretation in Terms of Naturalness Theory* (Ljubljana: Znanstvenoraziskovalni inštitut Filozofske fakultete, 2005), 87.

32. This is an opposite perspective to Lightfoot and Schmidt who think that the participle refers to something "actual." The above assumption depends partially on Kavčič, *Syntax*, 103.

33. The main verb will be in **bold**; the <u>infinitive</u> is in underline and the participle in *italics*.

34. The participle occurs in indirect discourse, but is rare in the NT. The infinitive and the ὅτι clause are the favorite forms. The participle is used in indirect discourse 6 times with ἀκούω. See Boyer, "Classification of the Participle," 175.

35. Kavčič, *The Syntax*, 87.

36. Lightfoot, *Logic*, 42.

37. Eduard Schwyzer, and Albert Debrunner, *Griechische Grammatik: Auf der Grundlage von Karl Brugmanns*, Griechischer Grammatik, Syntax und syntaktische Stilistik 2 (Münich: C. H. Beck 1959), 395. Schwyzer sees that the verb γινώσκω in the Hellenistic Greek shares the idea of 'erkennen' when the participle is the complement, and 'urteile' with an infinitive clause. See Ibid., 396.

38. See *PVA*, 390 for several passages with the verb εὑρίσκω with the participle as a complement.

39. See Matt 12:44; 21:2; 24:46; Mark 7:30; 11:2, 4; 13:36; 14:37, 40; Luke 2:12; 7:10; 8:35; 11:25 with the participle as the complement of the verb εὑρίσκω showing that the presupposition shared by the author and reader must be a "true proposition." In contrast to the infinitive the presupposition described by the participle indicates a direct perception, while the examples with the infinitive indicate a indirect perception of the complement.

40. Palmer, *Mood*, 4.
41. *GGBB*, 613. Porter states, "these relations ... are for the most part not grammaticalized but are inferred from context and tend to be subject to much discussion and debate." Stanley E. Porter, *Idioms of the Greek New Testament*, 2ⁿᵈ ed. Biblical Language 2 (Sheffield: Sheffield Academic Press, 1999), 190.
42. *GGBB*, 634–635.
43. Lauri Karttunen, "Some Observations on Factivity," *Papers in Linguistics* 5 (1971):55–69.
44. The linguists' debate if these two types of factivities are actually two separated behaviors. See Stalnaker, R. "Pragmatic Presuppositions," in *Context and Content* (Oxford University Press, 1999), 45–62. See also Ewan Klein, "Two Sorts of Factive Predicate," (*Pragmatics Microfiche* 1975), microfiche 1.1, Frames B5-C14; Gerald Gazdar, *Pragmatics: Implicature, Presupposition and Logical Form* (New York, NY: Academic Press, 1979), and Gerald Gazdar, "Pragmatics and Logical Form," *Journal of Pragmatics* 4 (1980):11–12; Paul M. Postal, "A Frew Factive Facts," *Linguistic Inquiry* 3 no. 3 (1972): 396–400.
45. *SRG*, 3.
46. See chapter three on Modulation: Participle a *Quasi*-Modality for definition of modulation.
47. This assertion only includes the dependent verbal participles having any of the adverbial function. See chapter three.
48. This confusion can be illustrated by the interpretation of Luke 4:15 καὶ αὐτὸς ἐδίδασκεν ἐν ταῖς συναγωγαῖς αὐτῶν δοξαζόμενος ὑπὸ πάντων (He taught in their synagogues, **being glorified** by all). Dana-Mantey and Burton classify δοξαζόμενος as that of attendant circumstance, while Wallace rightly sees it as a participle of result. See *DMG*, 228, *BMT*, 173–174, and *GGBB*, 638.
49. *DMG*, 228.
50. Young, *Intermediate New Testament Greek*, 158. This participle must be treated as a dependent verbal participle because it cannot stand by itself in a sentence.
51. *BMT*, 174.
52. We will show, especially in chapters two and three. "Ideationally" refers to the ideational meta-function in systemic linguistics, which "corresponds to what people usually think of as 'meaning' in the ordinary sense; that is, 'content', especially 'referential content'." See M. A. K. Halliday, *The Essential Halliday*, edited by Jonathan J. Webster (London: Continuum, 2009), 272.
53. Wesley J. Perschbacher, *New Testament Greek Syntax: An Illustrated Manual* (Chicago, IL: Moody Press, 1995).403.
54. Greg Clark, "General Hermeneutics," in *The Face of New Testament Studies: A Survey of Recent Research*, edited by Scot McKnight and Grant R. Osborne (Grand Rapids, MI: Baker Academia/ Apollos, 2004), 106.
55. *PVA*, 367.
56. Ibid.
57. *BMT*, §§ 450–451, pp. 173–174.
58. Ibid.
59. Ibid., 173.
60. *BMT*, 174, Italics added.
61. Ibid., 173–174
62. Ibid., 174
63. *BDF* points out that "λαβών and other descriptive participles are common in pleonastic usage following the Hebrew pattern." See *BDF*, § 419.
64. Ibid., 217.

65. Ibid.
66. *BDF*, §§ 411, 418.
67. When the adverbial participle is a present tense form there is no upgraded participle effect.
68. Ibid.
69. Ibid., 231.
70. Robertson quotes Moulton's *Prolegomena*, p. 15 as the reference for his quotation. See *ATR*, 1110, 1125., 1135. Cf. also τοῦτο εἰπὼν λέγει (Jo. 21:19), ἀπελθὼν πέπρακεν (Mt. 13:46), 'he has gone and sold.' So also, ἀναστὰς ἦλθεν (Lu. 15:20), 'he *arose* and came.' Once again note λαβοῦσα ἐνέκρυψεν (Mt. 13:33), 'she took and hid.' Pleonasm belongs to all tongues.
71. *ATR*, 1126–1127. Attendant circumstance for Robertson is a general term for the adverbial participle, and not the upgraded effect itself.
72. Ibid., 1127
73. *ATR*, 1126
74. Ibid.
75. *ATR*, 1127
76. Ibid., 1128.
77. Margaret Sim. "Undeterminacy in Greek Participles," *BT* 55 (2004): 359. The title is a little confusing since throughout the article she is talking about "*underdeterminacy*". Perhaps it is only a typographical error in the title.
78. *DMG*, 228.
79. Ibid., 228–29. This agrees with what Moulton states, "our own language comes much nearer, but even with the help of auxiliaries we cannot match the wealth of Greek …."
80. *BMT*, 173.
81. *GGBB*, 638.
82. The imperatival participle is not dependent on any finite verb explicitly. Zerwick says "in general it may be said that no participle should be explained in this way that can properly be connected with a finite verb." See Max Zerwick, and Joseph Smith, *Biblical Greek* (Rome: Scripta Pontificii Instituti Biblici, 1963), 99.
83. James A. Brooks, and Carlton L. Winbery, *Syntax of New Testament Greek* (Washington, D.C.: University Press of America, 1988), 152.
84. *GGBB*, 476–77.
85. Greg Clark, "General Hermeneutics," 106.
86. J. Harold Greenlee, *A Concise Exegetical Grammar of New Testament Greek*. 5th edition Revised (Grand Rapids, MI: Eerdmans Publishing Co, 1986), 57–58. Italics his.
87. *LDF*, 183 note 5. The adverbial participle is dependent upon the verb it qualifies, since the upgraded effect occurs with an adverbial participle, there is no real coordination syntactically, but only logically. See Campbell, *Verbal Aspect and Non-Indicative*, 5.
88. *LDF*, 58.
89. Ibid. He presents one example with the other moods and modalities. Cf. John 12:36 (indicative); John 12:24 (subjunctive); Act 16:9 (imperative); Luke 11:7 (Infinitive).
90. J. Harold Greenlee, "New Testament Circumstantial Participles," *JT* 1 no. 1 (2005): 57–59.
91. Richard A. Young, *Intermediate New Testament Greek*, 158–159.
92. Ibid., 158.
93. Ibid.
94. Ibid., 154. He even recognizes that some scholars classify this very same example as a participle of manner.

95. *GGBB*, 640–645.
96. *PVA*, 165–166.
97. See *PVA*, 390.
98. Ibid., 375.
99. See Sim, "Underterminacy," 359.
100. See *LDF*, 183, and *SRG*, 145.
101. Different scholars have approached the classification of the adverbial participle with different terminology, as already mentioned, but in general scholars have used "circumstantial" to refer to all the verbal participles. William Watson Goodwin, *Syntax of the Moods and Tenses of the Greek Verb* (Boston: Ginn and Co, 1897), 336.
102. Herbert Weir Smyth, *Greek Grammar*, Revised by Gordon M. Messing (Cambridge: Harvard University press, 1956), 459. Originally this grammar was published in 1920.
103. See *BDF*, § 419.
104. Adolf von Schlatter, *Der Evangelist Matthäus: seine Sprache, seine Ziel, seine Selbstständigkeit: ein Kommentar zum ersten Evangelium* (Stuttgart: Calwer Verlag, 1929), 23.
105. As will be shown, ±assertion indicates markedness within the verbal system network. If an author wants to grammaticalize attitude two options will be available: +assertion (indicative) and −assertion (subjunctive, imperative, and optative). Again, the + sign is a attempt to show prominence in the discourse.
106. *BMT*, 174.
107. David I. Beaver, 13.
108. Campbell, *Verbal Aspect and Non-Indicative Verbs*, 5.
109. This is a *segue* into Porter's contention of the role of verbal aspect. Verbal aspect is just one of the multiple semantic features of the verbal system. See, Stanley E. Porter, "Verbal Aspect and Discourse Function in Mark 16:1–8: Three Significant Instances," in Studies in the Greek Bible: Essays in Honor of Francis T. Gignac, S.J., edited by Jeremy Corley and Vicent Skemp, *The Catholic Biblical Quarterly Monograph Series*, 44 (Washington, DC: The Catholic Biblical Association of America, 2008), 126.
110. Kathleen Callow, *Discourse Considerations in Translating the Word of God* (Grand Rapids, MI: Zondervan, 1974), 49.
111. Ibid., 50.
112. See Fanning, *Verbal Aspect*, and *PVA* for more information. Porter adds a third peak of prominence, frontground. Porter, *Verbal Aspect and Discourse Function*, 127. Porter's frontground has been criticized. See Steve Runge, "Verbal Aspect and Discourse Prominence: A Reassessment of Porter's Linguistic Model." Paper presented in 2010 in the "Greek Grammar and Exegesis" Section of the ETS Annual Meeting, Atlanta, GA, Nov. 17–19.
113. Systemic Functional Linguistics has several variant versions. Gotteri defines systemic linguistics as a "theory in which language is interpreted as essentially a vast network of interrelated sets of options. The structure of a language (wording or other syntagmatic realizations) is regarded as manifesting choices made from interdependent paradigmatic options, which added together constitute the language's potential for conveying meaning. See. Nigel. J. C. Gotteri, "Toward a Comparison of Systemic Linguistics and Tagmemics: An Interim Report and Bibliography," *JMALS* 7 (1982):31. For a recent improvement of systemic functional linguistics see Helen Leckie-Tarry, *Language and Context: A Functional Linguistic Theory of Register* (London: Pinter, 1995), 31–50. See also Gustavo Martín-Asensio, *Transitivity-Based Foregrounding in the Acts*

of the Apostles: A Functional-Grammatical Approach to the Lukan Perspective, JSNTSup, 202 (Sheffield: Sheffield Academic Press, 2000), 21–49.

114. Palmer, *Mood*, 1–18.

115. Talmy Givón, "The Binding Hierarchy and the Typology of Complements," *Studies in Language* 4 no. 3 (1980): 333–377.

116. Talmy Givón, *On Understanding Grammar* (New York, NY: Academic Press, 1987), 182.

117. Robert D. Van Valin, Jr. "Toward Understanding Grammar: Forma, Function, Evolution," review of "On Understanding Grammar," by Talmy Givón, Lingua 54 (1981):59.

118. Albert Rijksbaron, *The Syntax and Semantics of the Verb in Classical Greek: An Introduction*, 3rd ed (Chicago, IL: The University of Chicago Press, 2002), 17.

119. Teun A. van Dijk, *Discourse and Context: A Sociocognitive Approach* (Cambridge, MA: Cambridge University Press, 2008), 29–55.

120. See chapter two of this study for the analysis of register as a tool for the analysis of the aorist participle.

121. See Helen Leckie-Tarry, *Language and Context: A Functional Linguistic Theory of Register*, edited by David Birch (London: Pinter, 1995).

122. *LDF*, 181–187, and *SRG*, 194–204.

123. Stephen H. Levinsohn, *Discourse Features of the New Testament Greek: A Coursebook on the Information Structure of New Testament Greek* (Dallas, TX: International, 2000), 184.

124. *SRG*, 19

125. Steve Runge, Why I am not a Systemic Functional Linguist – SFL. *NT Discourse: Removing the mystery from discourse grammar.* Jul 7, 2013. http://www.ntdiscourse.org/2009/07/why-i-am-not-a-systemic-functional-linguist/ (accessed April, 24, 2013).

126. *SRG*, 102.

127. Ibid., 3.

128. Runge warns, "Caution is called for when appealing to statistics …. The more complex a set of items becomes (i.e., beyond a binary opposition), the more misleading and unrepresentative the insights from statistics become." See *SRG*, 6.

129. *SRG*, 197.

130. See Buist M. Fanning, *Verbal Aspect*, 56–57, *PVA*, 88. Battistella confirms this idea stating that "Jakobson took the term *opposition* to mean the privative opposition between the presence of a property and its absence." See Edwin L. Battistella, *Markedness: The Evaluative Superstructure of Language* (Albany, NY: State University of New York Press, 1990), 16.

131. *SRG*, 195.

132. Mood here is particularly related to the indicative mood, while modal/modality applies to the imperative, subjunctive, and optative. Modulation is only applied to the participle and infinitive.

133. M. A. K. Halliday, *Language as Social Semiotic: The Social Interpretation of Language and Meaning* (London: Edward Arnold, 1978), 137.

134. See *PVA*, 7.

135. *PVA*, 375. Paradigmatic environment exploits the opposition or contrast existing between words and thus may be referred to as contrasting relations, while syntagmatic sense relations are seen in their combinatory relations. See Moisés Silva. Biblical Words and Their Meaning: An Introduction to Lexical Semantics. Revised and Expanded Edition (Grand Rapids, MI: Zondervan Publishing House, 1994), 100. Jean-Pierre Delville presents a fair definition of both paradigmatic and syntagmatic environments. He says, "syntagmatique correspond

à l'ensemble du discours qui est formulé et qui fournit un cadre d'interprétation des mots et des phrases qui y sont employés. [while] paradigmatique vise à établir le sens indirect sans chercher ancrage dans le discours énoncé, mais dans tous les 'lieux communs', c'est-à-dire les références les plus courantes, sur fond desquelles il se déroule." Jean-Pierre Delville. L'Europe de L'exégèse au XVIe Siècle: Interprétations de La Parabole des Ouvriers à La Vigne, Matthieu 20:1–16 (Leuven: University Press, 2004), xxix.

136. Campbell, *Verbal Aspect and Non-Indicative Verbs*, 26.

137. The historical present has been the center of the debate about the above assertion. Although recognizing that there are divergent positions on this matter, this study holds to a definition of grammar as a closed system. Therefore, the semantics of form is non-cancelable while the contextual meaning may vary. However, it does agree with Runge when he says, "if a device is not needed for semantic reasons, it still plays a semantic role, but it also is doing something more." *SRG*, 104.

138. Campbell, *Verbal Aspect and Non-Indicative Verbs*, 26.

139. Frank Robert Palmer, *Mood and Modality*, Cambridge Textbooks in Linguistics, 2nd ed. (Cambridge, MA: Cambridge University Press, 2006), 2. cf. PVA, 165.

CHAPTER TWO

Participle as Semantic Presupposition

A Theory of Grammar

The study of any particular feature of a language brings with itself a theory, which in turn presents the framework within which the analysis of the parts is put together by a theory of grammar. In this book we see grammar as based on the notion of choices. On the system of every language one finds a set of options, a set of things to be chosen following the entry condition under which the choice can be picked up.

The entry condition clause opens three simultaneous choices for the analysis of a dead language such as ancient Greek. The choice of information is not necessary since everybody who spoke the ancient Greek is dead. Those three choices are mood, transitivity and theme. We believe that "system network specifies what are the possible combinations of choices that could be made; each permitted path through the network is thus the description of a class of linguistic items."[1]

Our task is a hermeneutic one, that is, to construct meaning based in the choice already made in order to indicate how those particular choices are realized in structural terms. In language there are two worlds to be dealt with to create reality in social settings: the perception of reality and the expression of reality. How an author perceived some real-world event is not an easy task to investigate, but how he wants us to relate with what he is describing through the realization of systemic choices, can be achieved by interpretation.

When an author decides to communicate certain events, he has the statement of choices opened, which we call class, but when we consider it to interpret the choices already made, we are dealing with function. Let's take a couple of near related events by the same ancient writer and look at how he is imposing his framework upon what he is describing and how he wants his readers to interpret what is communicated.[2]

Xen. Anab 4.3.2	τοτέ μὲν οὖν ηὐλίσθησαν μάλα ἡδέως καὶ τἀπιτήδεια ἔχοντες καὶ πολλὰ τῶν παρεληλυθότων πόνων μνημονεύοντες. [...] μαχόμενοι διετέλεσαν, καὶ ἔπαθον κακὰ ὅσα οὐδὲ τὰ σύμπαντα ὑπὸ βασιλέως καὶ Τισσαφέρνους. ὡς οὖν ἀπηλλαγμένοι τούτων ἡδέως **ἐκοιμήθησαν**.	Therefore, in that occasion, they went into their quarters very happily, *having* provisions and *remembering* many hardships that *were now gone*. [...] *fighting* ceaselessly, and they suffered more evils than all which they had suffered taken together at the hands of the King and Tissaphernes. Therefore, *being out of trouble*s such as those, they **went to sleep** happily.

There are a couple of questions to be addressed in this section: what are the main factors underlying the author's choice? The study of register will be a *sine qua non* as the interpreter adopts his or her hermeneutic tool. But if one adopts the SFL language theory, he or she will know, "register," which is a set of features that occur and co-occur in a regular fashion. Another question: what would be the difference between the choice of communicating a process with +finite or -finite?

Xenophon in the example above could have communicated this episode in different manners, but the context of the situation is surrounded by some emotional context, and that attracts the author for setting up the readers in. He starts and ends this particular event with ἡδέως (happily, with good feeling). If we take only the last main clause of the last line, we see a state of affair in a background position (ἀπηλλαγμένοι – perfect participle) in order to set the main verb (ἐκοιμήθησαν), "they went to sleep" on the spotlight.

Xenophon described the process making simultaneous choices on the finiteness system. One +finite choice, realized by the choice of +assertion (ηὐλίσθησαν) followed by the two embedded clauses (ἔχοντες καὶ μνημονεύοντες), realized by -finite. In the same passage, the author communicates a process with the embedded clause (ἀπηλλαγμένοι) preceding the main clause (ἐκοιμήθησαν).

Xen. Ages. 2.15	τότε μὲν οὖν (καὶ γὰρ ἦν ἤδη ὀψέ) συνελκύσαντες τοὺς τῶν πολεμίωνvεκροὺς εἴσω φάλαγγος **ἐδειπνοποιήσαντο καὶ ἐκοιμήθησαν.**	Then—it was already late—having dragged the enemy's dead within the battle line, they **had dinner** and **went to sleep.**

There are several parallel passages with ἐκοιμήθησαν that provide some data for the examination of our theory of grammar. The difference is that the author decided to coordinate the two process with +assertion (ἐδειπνοποιήσαντο καὶ ἐκ οιμήθησαν). The author chose to communicate this process with two indicative verbs. Note that there is a participle in the embedded clause that precedes these two main verbs and serves as a background information.

Xen. Hell. 4.3.20	τότε μὲν οὖν, καὶ γὰρ ἦν ἤδη ὀψέ, δειπνοποιησάμενοι ἐκοιμήθησαν.	Then—it was already late—*having taken dinner* they **went sleep.**

Buijs analyzes a very extensive parallel passages with ἐκοιμήθησαν in narrative in the works of Xenophon in his book Clause Combining in Ancient Greek Narrative Discourse.[3] His hermeneutic method sees the activity of the ancient Greek historian in three level: the reality-level, which is what happened in the real world, but not yet codified in the text; the level of the real World construction by a mimetic mode. He seems to follow Bakker's mimetic mode here. Finally, his level of text articulation, which involves the organization of the text.

Buijs believes that "when … the narrator does not want to indicate a Real-World relation between the events expressed in the subordinate clause and the matrix clause, he uses a participial clause."[4] His main assertion is that "the participle refers to a state of mind rather than an event and resumes previously expressed information (propositional overlap)."[5] Although from a different theory of grammar, it seems that there is an agreement with our thesis that the choice of participle communicates something different of the choice of the indicative, for example. In this particular discussion, we can say that he sees the participles as a sort of presupposition.

Another aspect in his analysis is that the choice of a participle indicates a clause chain and it is not set as a pair with the finite verb of their sentence.[6] The use of the aorist participle followed by a finite verb serves to communicate two independent events with a hierarchical indication with the other parts of the discourse. Further, another function of the participles is that of an unspecific movement, which helps the reader/hearer to keep track of the narrative situation.[7] Again, this is exactly what we will see occurring with the upgraded effect.

The near similarity of the different events having the same finite verb (ἐκοιμήθησαν) in the aorist demonstrates that the author had different options to communicate a process on which the following choices were used: PARTICIPLE + FINITE VERB, FINITE VERB καί FINITE VERB, PARTICIPLE + FINITE VERB. The choice of +finite verb demonstrates a limitation toward the person of the verbal stem while the choice of -finite lacks limitation of the person of the verb in its stem. Blocking the person of the verbal stem provides an opening. for the readers to play a role in the process described. The invitation for the readers to provide some information to construct meaning is what we call here presupposition.

Considering the two natures of the participle—adjectival and verbal, there are at least, twelve logical variations with the understanding of it. The dependent verbal participles, according to some grammars, have about six different nuances of meaning. The traditional adverbial usage has about eight specific nuances. The study of the participles has a large spectrum since it is done from a logical perspective, syntactical analysis, pragmatic studies, and most recently, semantic approach. All these nuances are possible because of the semantics of the participle.

The study of the participle has to do with the understanding of transitivity, which is understood to be a grammatical category related to the ideational metafunction in systemic functional linguistics. In other words, transitivity is taken in this book as the clause grammar, as a structural unity that serves to express particular ideational or cognitive meanings.

The transitivity system enables the readers/speakers to identify actions and human activities expressed in the discourse and what reality is being communicated. There are six types of process (verbs) with the transitivity system: material, mental, relational, verbal, behavioral, and existential. Three out of the six process types are considered as more important: material, mental, and relational. Associated with these processes we have the three components in the transitivity system: participants, process, and circumstance.

Transitivity reflects the way a finite clause relates itself with participants, the process, and circumstance. Greek participles are connected with all these three categories, whether as a nominal adjunct or adverbial adjunct. Of particular interest is the circumstances, since they present the additional information attributed to the processes, which in turn are realized by the means of the participles and other adverbs.

When the participle is dependent, it comes in the embedded clause referring to the conditions and cohesion related to the verbal process. For instance, 1 Pet 1:8 "ὃν οὐκ ἰδόντες ἀγαπᾶτε" ("[although] *you have* not *seen* him, you **love** him"). The relation between the primary clause with the assertion "you love him" and the embedded clause "not seeing" indicates that the assertion of the primary clause is true *in spite of* the action of the participle.

The implication of the circumstantial functions seems to be less essential to the process described by the main clause. Observe that this analysis occurs in the syntagmatic axis at the rank of clause. In the paradigmatic axis the emphasis is upon the choices made in the verbal system network. -Finite was chosen instead of +finite. The choice of the participles blocks any person of the verbal form, thus -finite.

There is no person encoded in the participial form - ἰδόντες. No explicit person comes with the participial form because it is blocked. On one hand, the use of a participle blocks the person of the verbal form, on the other hand, it opens up a slot so that the reader can fill it. This is language as reflection and the choice of -finite opens up two other choices: +factive presupposition (participle) or -factive presupposition (infinitive).

The contrast is not about assertion and non-assertion. Rather, it is about what is asserted and what is presupposed. Ideationally, the author invites the readers to assume "ἰδόντες" (seeing) as a true proposition. The point is not a real-world type of deal, but a mental exercise about a proposition in order to strengthen the process of the main clause. He is not saying that they have not seen Christ, he is assuming that this is a true proposition to enforce how much they love Jesus, even though they have never seen him.

The participle as a factive presupposition can even occur by itself without describing any circumstance of any given verbal process. For instance, Rom 12:9 "ἀποστυγοῦντες τὸ πονηρόν, κολλώμενοι τῷ ἀγαθῷ" ("*Hate* the evil one, *cling* to what is good"). Despite of the dispute involved with the independent use, the participle in this relation is an acceptable use. There is no primary clause explicit, and it may be unnecessary to have one.

The imperative belongs to the Attitude -assertion grammaticalized by its proper form. The participles do not pertain to the attitude system, rather, its use blocks the attitude system. Participle remains a participle even though it can appear in contexts where an indicative or imperative were expected. This example of usage is where the participle is seen in its own place, that is, reader's oriented as a factive presupposition.

Based on all that Paul has said, he does not command them to behave in such or such way using an imperative, although that was the most common form. If he would have done it in this way, it is possible that the readers could easily fill the commands by pointing someone's name that needs to obey, except themselves. Therefore, by using a participle in a context of situation that encompasses exhortation, the choice of the independent participles with its pragmatic effect of "imperative" brings the readers to take every participle to themselves rather to apply in someone else's life.[8]

The upgraded complex effect is not an independent use of the participle, but at the rank of clause the participle in the embedded clause adds a background action or state to the main clause, sets the main event on the spotlight, and indicates an unspecified movement toward the action of the main.

On the semantic side of the participle as a factive presupposition, the readers are invited to share the information uttered by the participle as a true proposition. The use of presupposional meaning describes the circumstance of the main event with a participle that functions as a clause chain, enabling the readers to make the right connection to keep the focus on the main verb by assuming a prerequisite to it. This chain of the participle with the main clause in the upgraded function seems to designate one single, though complex, event.

It is this complexity that surrounds the participles that demands from the interpreter an interaction with presupposition both on philosophical and linguistic terms. Furthermore, this complexity occurs in an exchange between grammar, lexis, semantics, and pragmatics. We believe a linguistic theory is a *sine qua non* to assess a linguistic work, that the interpreter needs a framework that will provide a general understanding of language.[9]

Following Firth, Halliday has defined key terms that show the differences between language and the importance of a system that deals with language at its different levels.[10] There are four fundamental categories within the theory of grammar: unit, structure, class, and system. Grammar is related to a "closed system"[11] which stands as the dividing line between grammar and lexis.[12]

Grammar expresses the *formal meaning*, which is a meaning morphologically based, while *contextual meaning* is that network of semantic factors comprised by grammatical and contextual factors within a particular set.[13] Even though they are distinct, the contextual meaning has a logical dependence on the formal meaning.[14]

The main tenet of this book is that the only semantic value grammaticalized by the Greek participle is factive presupposition. An author uses a factive presupposition when he or she wants the readers to participate in the construction of meaning. He or she invites the readers to render the embedded clause with the factive presupposition as a true proposition that is essential for his/her communicative purpose.

Semantics deals with meaning while pragmatics deals with use, and the relation between these elements shows that the participle has several other functions: first, *prioritizing the action of the main verb*, and *serving* whether *as a background to the main clause* when the participle precedes the main verb or developing the verbal main idea when it is placed following the main verb.[15]

The study of the Greek participle, and the upgraded effect as a showcase, must carefully distinguish pragmatics and semantics. While the pragmatic effects are many according to several other features and change in different contexts, semantics is what determines pragmatics and it is fixed at most, that is, semantics is a closed system.

Based on form, Halliday sets three criteria that define a "closed system". First, there are a limited number of terms; second, the choice of a term is at the cost of others; third, if a new term is added to the system this will change the contextual meaning of the other terms.

The first criterion means that in any given system all choices will not always be available.[16] For example, the semantics of the Greek verb in its system network contains so far fourteen systems from a probabilistic point of view. The verbal forms are what give realization to the verbal network.[17] The difference between semantics and pragmatics can be described in the following way: semantics can be defined in terms of the number of closed systems, which in Greek goes from one to fourteen.

The systems 1–14 are part of the verbal system (semantics) and all other numbers, 15 and up, are outside the system (pragmatics).[18] In other words, semantics, or grammar, has to do with the network of fourteen main choices related to the verb in the Greek system and everything outside of this "closed system" belongs to pragmatics. By choosing a participle, an author blocks the attitudes that are expressed by the Greek moods.[19]Attitude is semantic while mood is the form that grammaticalizes attitude.

Halliday establishes a second criterion. In a "closed system," the choice of a term is done at the cost of others, that is, they are mutually exclusive. A given term, A, cannot be identical with B, C, or D.[20]

The third criterion set by Halliday to define a "closed system," states that if a new term is added to the system this will change the contextual meaning of the other terms.[21] This implies that terms that are mutually exclusive will likely have a contextual distinction.[22] This shows that "an element is only meaningful if it is defined wholly in terms of other elements."[23] This is the principle of contrastive substitution, which proposes that if a specific grammatical feature can function in opposing contexts, then it is evident that the difference in the contexts is not due to this grammatical feature.[24] In other words, any semantic analysis must include a theory of pragmatics.

The section below will present Halliday's linguistic approach that includes some of what has already been asserted here. There will be an attempt to relate systemic function linguistics to the analysis of the adverbial aorist participle. Next, the systemic concept of register will be analyzed, since register is the study of the context as a way of speaking.

Systemic Functional Linguistics

An adequate theory of language is required for explaining the various lexico-grammatical structures in a text as purposeful choices. Systemic functional linguistics[25] has been implemented since Halliday to include several other features that were seen as necessary to improve any analysis of a text.

The aim of this study requires demonstrating the suitability of the proposed theory of language and its perspective. The following part is a brief summary of the general perspective of language embraced by systemic functional grammar according to Halliday.

Language serves the speaker or writer to express his or her experience of his or her external world and inner world, that is, the world of his or her own consciousness. Halliday's theory is socio-linguistic, rather than psycho-linguistic.[26] SFL sees language as a means of social behavior, rather than as "'competence' stored in people's brains."[27] Thus, language serves to establish and preserve social relation.[28] In order to fulfill its role, language must provide the links and connections that enable both the speaker/writer and the listener/reader to distinguish a speech act from a random set of sentences.[29]

Two important features are so useful for our approach in this book: language function and register. SFL does not confuse function and register. The former is a product of interrelating situational variables, but the latter is the product of functional variation, that is, language appropriate to the context.[30] SFL, as well as several other functional systems, understands that "whereas a variety of language refers to *language according to user*, register refers to *language according to use.*"[31] Therefore, among different linguistic theories, systemic theory can be set within a defined class of functional grammars that are identified by certain orientations. It is oriented as follows:

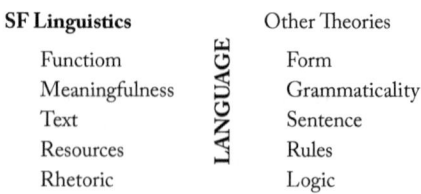

Figure 2.1. SFL theory. (Adapted from Decker, *Temporal Deixis*, pp. 11–14; *PVA* 7–16.)

Halliday argues that the failure of many text-descriptive theories is rooted in an inability to properly account for the paradigmatic relations.[32] This means that the main concern is with the meaning of verbal forms in relation to each other rather than with the meaning of a specific verbal form in relation to the rest of the clause. It is necessary in order to move beyond a simple description of syntax to account for the contextually determined networks of options (paradigmatic axis) from which particular textual choices occur.[33]

Halliday argues that two possible levels must be considered in the analysis of texts. The first level has to do with the comprehension of the text achieved by the study of lexis and grammar as shown above. The second level concentrates on the situation it is designed to address. The more Halliday's functional grammar is applied, the more the links between text and its context of situation will be seen, which promises to approach a "dead" language from a "formal" model.[34] He says, "we shall ... expect to find the situation embodied or enshrined in the text, not piecemeal, but in a way which reflects the systematic relation between the semantic structure and the social environment."[35]

So far, it has been seen that a suitable functional grammar focuses on the lexico-grammatical system, that is, the network of options having a functional input, and a structural output (realization). The functional input is the set of social functions that language must serve, and the structural output is the set of linguistics items that are joined to form a text.[36] The network that can be used to model options between features at various levels of language, and any system network is incomplete without a set of realization (output) rules.[37]

What Halliday is arguing so far is not only applied to verbal aspect but also to the finite system network. The set of options is available in the pairs of opposition with the choice of ±finite simultaneous to the choice of aspect. This −finite subsystem is split into two other subsystems, + factive presupposition and −factive presupposition.

The choice of a participle blocks the attitude system (±assertion), but opens the opportunity for an external person, not expressed with the verbal form, that is, the participation of the readers/hearers. This will be developed later, however, a brief summary can be presented here. Applying this to Greek participles, it may be said that if an author wants to express a factive presupposition, he or she uses a participle.

If he or she wants to make an assertion, the indicative is available and so on. Assuming this basic principle, it may be said that if an author wants to coordinate two assertions, he or she would use two indicative forms coordinated by καί, and if he or she wants to utter two commands, he or she would choose two imperatives.

How one can explain the upgraded participial effect—the aorist adverbial participle in the nominative that precedes the main clause, which is upgraded to the same mood of the main clause? For instance, Matthew 28:19 πορευθέντες οὖν **μαθητεύσατε** πάντα τὰ ἔθνη, βαπτίζοντες αὐτοὺς εἰς τὸ ὄνομα τοῦ πατρὸς καὶ τοῦ υἱοῦ καὶ τοῦ ἁγίου πνεύματος (*Go*, then, [and] **make disciple** all the nations, *baptizing* them in the name of the Father and the Son and the Holy Spirit). The answer to this phenomenon resides in the very nature of the semantics of the participle: factive presupposition.

A sound exegesis will seek to avoid two extremes regarding this aorist adverbial participle with the upgraded effect: the tendency on the one hand to render πορευθέντες as an imperative so that the great commission is not seen as a great suggestion, and on the other hand deemphasizing πορευθέντες to the point of omitting it altogether in translation.

Having an anarthrous aorist participle dependent on and preceding a main verb in the imperative would not change the fact that imperative and participle are formal designations and not functional ones.[38] Thus, in order to explain why a participle is upgraded to the mood of the main verb, one must find a better analysis so that semantics and pragmatics are not conflated, yet at the same time not left unrelated.

The relation of the verbal participle and the Greek mood shows that language is a complex and highly-developed system of communication.[39] This relation must be included in any discussion of a finite system network. Thus, part of the general linguistic theory is that which explains how language works. The attempt to explain this phenomenon has contributed to the methods of descriptive linguistics.[40] Even though description is not theory, general linguistics and descriptive linguistics are by no means unrelated.[41] All description is specifically related to that part of the theory that is concerned with how language works.[42]

A theory sketches the scheme of the interrelationship of the categories that are set up to deal with the data (the "text" is the data, which describes observed events or prescribes conduct. What relates the categories to the data and to each other is a set of scales of abstraction.[43] How the text should be related to the categories of the theory is the rule of description.[44]

There are three types of grammatical categories to be established in the description: units, elements, and classes. Elements and classes are categories set up to describe the units.[45] A unit is that "category to which corresponds a segment of the linguistic material about which statements are to be made."[46]

There are three units: sentence, clause, and word.[47] The fundamental unit of organization in functional grammar is the clause within which all the elements of language are expressed.[48] The Halliday SFL, especially the version popularized by

Porter, has been criticized for limiting itself almost entirely to the clause, ignoring the broad spectrum of language, such as the sentence and broad discourse.[49] Although clause analysis is important, the relation of the aorist adverbial participle with the main verb demands that one include the analysis of the sentence since it is its departure point for our analysis.

Halliday concisely points out,

> Our most powerful conception of reality is that it consists of 'going-on': of doing, happening, feeling, being. These goings-on are sorted out in the semantic system of the language and expressed through the grammar of the clause. Parallel with its evolution in the function of mood, expressing the active, interpersonal aspect of meaning, the clause evolved simultaneously in another grammatical function expressing the reflective, experiential aspect of meaning.[50]

The function of expressing the reflective and experiential aspect of meaning is part of the function of the participle in its relationship with the goings-on of the main clause. The above description shows how language enables humans to construct a mental portrait of a speech event. It gives them the discernment to relate language to what goes on around them (the register [context of situation] and the metafunctions [context of culture]) and to what they have individually experienced during their lives.[51] The grammar of the clause achieves these functions by means of processes, participants in the process, and circumstances related to the process.[52]

The fundamental unit of organization in functional grammar is the clause, and it is from there that the integrated expression of all the functionally distinct elements of language goes forth. The options in the mood system of Greek are expressions of the participants in the process (interpersonal),[53] and choices of participle, agent, medium, and process are the expression of the *ideational* function of language.[54] This is what we call reader's oriented, since it presents meaning by way of reflection.

The speaker either gives his assessment (the attitude system) or demands the addressee's assessment. An author indicates to the readers when he demands any assessment from them by blocking the finite system. The speaker's own assessment is interpersonal, and that which demands the addressee's assessment is ideational. For instance, in a Greek clause such as ὃς ταύτην τὴν ὁδὸν ἐδίωξα ἄχρι θανάτου (Acts 22:4) there are grammatical elements that are the structural expression of the ideational, interpersonal and textual functions.[55] Analyzing this clause syntactically there is a subject (ὃς) and a finite (ταύτην τὴν ὁδὸν ἐδίωξα). The elements of subject and finite, options in the mood system of Greek, are expressions of the *interpersonal* function of language. Paul is acting as a narrator and this is expressed by means of a simple declarative statement in the indicative mood.

The very same clause can be analyzed as the expression of a process. There is a material process encoded, which contains the elements of agent (ὅς the relative and a non-explicit first person singular in ἐδίωξα), medium (ταύτην τὴν ὁδὸν) and process (ἐδίωξα), ἄχρι θανάτου being an adjunct.

Moving from here to the adverbial participle, it must be said that semantic classifications of the adverbial participle have been based on the kind of semantic relation, which exists between the embedded clause and the primary clause (actually the secondary clause).

Act 22:3 introduces the primary clause and verse 4 presents the relative clause (secondary) to which the embedded clause is attached, δεσμεύων καὶ παραδιδοὺς εἰς φυλακὰς ἄνδρας τε καὶ γυναῖκας (*binding* and *delivering* to prison both men and women). It has been shown that agent (ὅς the relative and a non-explicit first person singular in ἐδίωξα), medium (ταύτην τὴν ὁδὸν), and process (ἐδίωξα) are the expression of the *ideational* function of language. In this relative clause, there are logical components that need to be connected to each other and at the same time that signal the relation to the primary clause. The embedded clause connected to the dependent clause results in the creation of a clause complex. "The complexing of clauses foregrounds the type of logico-semantic relationship that exists between the two connected clauses."[56]

The ideational logico-semantic between the embedded and secondary clauses can occur in several ways.[57] First, the embedded clause expands the secondary clause ἐδίωξα. Thus, ἐδίωξα *δεσμεύων* καὶ *παραδιδοὺς* ... ([I] persecuted binding and delivering ...). This is common with a present participle that follows the main clause. Levinsohn notes, "Participial clauses that *follow* the nuclear clause may be concerned with some aspect of the nuclear [main] event. Alternatively, they may describe 'a circumstance as merely accompanying the leading verb.'"[58] This expansion offers a characterization, clarification, evaluation or exemplification to the main clause.

Second, the embedded clause sometimes extends the main clause. In this sense, the embedded clause adds something to the main clause by offering a reference to time, condition, place, reason, etc. For instance, Eph 1:8–9 τὸ ὑπερβάλλον μέγεθος τῆς δυνάμεως αὐτοῦ εἰς ἡμᾶς τοὺς πιστεύοντας κατὰ τὴν ἐνέργειαν τοῦ κράτους τῆς ἰσχύος αὐτοῦ, ἣν *ἐνήργησεν* ἐν τῷ Χριστῷ *ἐγείρας* αὐτὸν ἐκ νεκρῶν ("the surpassing greatness of his power toward us who believe, according to the working of the strength of his might, which *he exercised* in Christ [when] *he raised* him from the dead").

Ἐγείρας qualifies the main clause by offering a time frame to the main verb ἐνήργησεν.[59] An adverbial participle has dependent or determined time reference if its time reference is a necessary consequence of the meaning of the predicate. It is not always that the interpreter needs to find a time reference or even a logical reference for the participle. Matthew 21:22 πάντα ὅσα ἂν *αἰτήσητε* ἐν τῇ προσευχῇ πιστεύοντες **λήμψεσθε** (Whatever you *ask for* in prayer, *if you believe*, you will receive it). The participial embedded clause qualifies the main clause by offering a logical condition. The point is that they will receive what they ask if the condition in the embedded clause is a true proposition.

The *ideational* functional component is what enables a writer to track participants (interpersonal realized by the moods) with participles (*ideational*).[60] Christie observes that the ideational metafunction is not involved

> directly in the building of the meanings within the clause, but rather in the matter of building connectedness between the meanings of clauses. Such a logical connectedness is realized in those resources in the grammar which are involved in two different sets of relationships: those to do with interdependency or 'taxis' between clauses; and those to do with the logico-semantic relations between clauses brought about by either projection or expansion … [while] the interpersonal metafunction refers to those grammatical resources in which the relationship of interlocutors is realized, including those of mood, modality and person.[61]

The anarthrous participle that begins a sentence indicates that there is continuity between sentences.[62] Thus, the ideational functional component is realized by the Greek participles, among others. Lang saw this very same feature in Herodotus as she states that the participle makes the transition from one state or action to another.[63] This ideational continuity can be better seen with the upgraded function.

For instance, Act 19:19 ἱκανοὶ δὲ τῶν τὰ περίεργα πραξάντων *συνενέγκαντες* τὰς βίβλους **κατέκαιον** ἐνώπιον πάντων καὶ συνεψήφισαν τὰς τιμὰς αὐτῶν καὶ εὗρον ἀργυρίου μυριάδας πέντε (and a number of those who had practiced magic arts *brought* the books [and] **burned** before all and they counted the value of them and found it came to fifty thousand pieces of silver). The logico-semantic connectedness in this passage is made by the hearer/listener and not by the text itself. Levinsohn states, "I present specific instances in Acts in which a continuity of situation and other factors is implied that might not be immediately evident were it not for the participle."[64]

When the participial embedded clause is placed right before the primary clause with which it is related, the participial embedded clause indicates a point of departure with renewal. It should be said that the emphasis is much more on the renewal aspect than on the point of departure. Act 21:15 μετὰ δὲ τὰς ἡμέρας ταύτας *ἐπισκευασάμενοι* **ἀνεβαίνομεν** εἰς Ἱεροσόλυμα (After these days *we made preparations* [and] **went up** to Jerusalem). The ideational logico-semantic operates at two levels in the readers mind; first, it makes the readers to see some sort of coordination, and second, it gives the readers the impression that both the participle and the indicative have the same mood.

Acts 23:16 *ἀκούσας* δὲ ὁ υἱὸς τῆς ἀδελφῆς Παύλου τὴν ἐνέδραν *παραγενόμενος* καὶ *εἰσελθὼν* εἰς τὴν παρεμβολὴν **ἀπήγγειλεν** τῷ Παύλῳ (and the son of Paul's sister, *hearing* of their ambush, *went* and *entered* the barracks [and] **told** Paul). The participles in this passage make a clause chain that connects one sentence to another as they make the transition from one action to the next. There is a logico-semantic connection between them, but the upgraded function of the last participle creates in the readers mind an ideational coordination connected by an imaginative καί. Lang includes Luke as following a normal rule for a storyteller by which he occasionally provides a topic sentence (participial clause), which gives direction to the narrative. This topic sentence is the means by which "both speaker and hearer know where they are going."[65]

There is no other form in the Greek language that is more reader/listener oriented than the participle. What that means is that every time an author chooses a participle, two subcategories of the ideational component come into play: 1) the *experiential* subcategory by means of which humans represent processes, participants in the process, and circumstances accomplished with the process;[66] and 2) the *logical* subcategory, where humans represent experience in terms of certain fundamental logical relations in natural language.[67]

Halliday points out that although these logical components are not those of formal logic, they are "the ones from which the operations of formal logic are ultimately derived."[68] Formal logic and the ideational functional component, along with the interpersonal component, is where the speaker takes the role of choosing and assigning meaning to the hearer.[69] The choice of a participle is a choice not to use an assertion, choosing to presuppose something rather asserting it.

Verbal Aspect, Modal Semantic and SFL: Caveat and Implementation

As a way of reviewing, SFL places the function of language as central (what language does, and how it does it), and systemic semantics includes what is usually called 'pragmatics'. Thus, semantics is divided into three components, Ideational Semantics (the reflective content), Interpersonal Semantics (the expression of attitude grammaticalized by the moods), and Textual Semantics (how the text is structured as a message, e.g., theme-structure, given/new, rhetorical structure, and so on).

Systemic Functional Linguistics seems to be based on contrastive options available in the verbal network. Two of these options are being analyzed, aspectuality and finiteness. The primary focus is on the finiteness system since it is related to modal semantics. The relation of these two sets of options can be seen in Halliday when he states, "all acts of meaning embody both—i.e., both reflection and action—not just on components, but as sets of options, each constituting a distinct dimension of choice."[70]

There is a crucial question to be answered by the proponents of verbal aspect, especially from the concept of markedness. If we adopt the contrastive analysis of verbal aspect, then, all the verbal tense is heavily marked. However, this complexity of options needs to present a clearer response to the question of how closely it models the actual decision making of the speaker. Runge rightly recognizes, "if the modeling is off base, the tree becomes a theoretical exercise rather than a functional description."[71]

According to verbal aspect theory, the primary semantics of the Greek verb is verbal aspect. The choices of verbal aspect occur simultaneous to the finiteness system. For example, based on the concept of markedness the stative aspect is formally the most heavily marked (perfect tense-form) and forms an opposition with the perfective aspect (aorist) which is the least marked.[72] If we take Porter's assertion that within the Present/Aorist opposition, the imperfective aspect (present) is the more heavily marked,[73] how can we explain Acts 27:15–16 where the most heavily marked choice does not seem to be the most heavily marked one?

In these passages, there are five aorist forms[74] and three present forms:[75] συναρπασθέντος δὲ τοῦ πλοίου καὶ μὴ δυναμένου ἀντοφθαλμεῖν τῷ ἀνέμῳ ἐπιδόντες ἐφερόμεθα. νησίον δέ τι ὑποδραμόντες καλούμενον Καῦδα ἰσχύσαμεν μόλις περικρατεῖς γενέσθαι τῆς σκάφης (And [when] the ship *got caught* and not *being able* to face the wind, *giving way* to it we were driven along. *Running under the shelter of* a small island called Cauda, we **were** barely able **to secure** the ship's boat.

Based on Halliday's implication, applied in the New Testament by some scholars and popularized by Porter, δυναμένου ἀντοφθαλμεῖν and καλούμενον (Present Tense) are more prominent than συναρπασθέντος, ἐπιδόντες, ὑποδραμόντες, ἰσχύσαμεν, γενέσθαι. The question (regardless the tense forms) is: How is it possible that 'being seized' (συναρπασθέντος) is less marked, while 'not being able to face the wind' (δυναμένου ἀντοφθαλμεῖν) is most heavily marked?

There is a need for more information and more details in the narrative. Thus, the assumption here is that on the basis of the Greek verbal aspect alone it is difficult to judge Halliday's theory, which was applied primarily to the English language. A good way to answer the problematic question would be: Is the author making any assessment of his own or is he demanding the reader's assessment? What the author assesses must be contrasted on its own categories and what he invites the readers' assessment must be contrast within the readers' own spectrum.

Another difficult situation showing the complexity of the present analysis is Acts 16:9 Καὶ ὅραμα διὰ [τῆς] νυκτὸς τῷ Παύλῳ ὤφθη, ἀνὴρ Μακεδών τις <u>ἦν</u> <u>ἑστὼς</u> καὶ παρακαλῶν αὐτὸν καὶ λέγων· *διαβὰς* εἰς Μακεδονίαν **βοήθησον** ἡμῖν (And a vision appeared to Paul during [the] night: a man of Macedonia <u>was standing</u>, urging him and saying, "*Come* over to Macedonia [and] **help** us"). Again, on the basis of verbal aspect the stative aspect (perfect tense-form) is more heavily marked than both present and aorist and the present tense-form is more heavily marked than the aorist.

Using a prominence description, to say that "was standing" is the most prominent point of the narrative because is a perfect tense is unimaginable, unless a necessary distinction must be made between the markedness on the finite system and markedness on -finite choice. Further, to say that "urging him" and "saying" (both present tense-form) is more prominent than the two aorist tense "come" and "help" is equally senseless.

The most prominent point in this passage is βοήθησον ἡμῖν (Help us). Following the implication with planes of discourse related to verbal aspect, one can ask on what basis can it be argued that a clause is backgrounded or foregrounded (highlighted).[76] How does an instance of foregrounded morphology relate to the complex surrounding the text?

These questions are valid since they imply that the task which the verbal forms have in language use, is not exhausted by the basic grammatical functions.[77] The point here has already been asserted by Fleischmann who warns that "the work that verbal forms perform in language use is by no means exhausted by their 'basic grammatical functions.'"[78] Thus, the assumption here is that among others, modal semantics must be added to the analysis of the Greek verbs to avoid misinterpretation.

What must be said about Act 16:1–5, 9 is that interpreters seem to be unfamiliar with the fact that there is an essential difference in nature between the participle and the mood (including indicative and the non-indicative moods).[79] It must be noted that the first three verbs (ἑστώς, παρακαλῶν, λέγων) are participles.[80] By using these adverbial participles, Luke describes some actions that are less specific than that of the finite verb (βοήθησον).

We will show in chapter four that the adverbial participles have their value in their ideational metafunction, and the relative semantic in this construction seems to be preparing the circumstance described in order to place a greater emphasis on the action of the main verb.[81] Furthermore, it seems that one of the functions of the aorist nominative participles that precede the main verb is to convey information that is of secondary importance.[82]

Another passage can be considered in order to see modal semantics at work. Matthew 9:18 Ταῦτα αὐτοῦ λαλοῦντος αὐτοῖς ἰδοὺ ἄρχων εἷς ἐλθὼν **προσεκύνει** αὐτῷ (While he was saying these things to them, behold, a ruler *came in* [and] **knelt** before him). Taking ἐλθών and προσεκύνει as a sample with regard to the verbal system, ἐλθών has its own opposite in the branch of aspect, being in contrast to other choices in its set of options (perfective, imperfective, stative). It is assumed here that the analysis of verbal aspect should include modal semantics in its particular clause.

The adverbial participle establishes a chain between its own clause and the clause to which it is related. Thus, there is a necessary relation created with the finiteness system, that is, "the adverbial participles modify a verb, typically by specifying some kind of dependent action."[83]

The participle ἐλθών in this passage functions as an adverbial adjunct that provides an indication of the circumstances associated with the process described by the primary clause. Matthew announces a true proposition "coming," which is a prerequisite for the action of the main clause.

Matthew could have chosen two finite verbs to utter this sentence, such as ἦλθεν and προσεκύνει both being an assertion, but he chooses one presupposition (the participle) and one assertion (indicative). The connection between the embedded clause and the primary is such that the presupposition grammaticalized by the embedded clause is so closely related to the primary clause that they together describe a complex event. Palmer makes the same point when he says, "propositions that are presupposed are not asserted."[84]

The readers must interact with these two sentences at the same time. Palmer states, "what is at issue is that nothing is being asserted, that there is no information value, because both speaker and hearer accept the proposition." Thus, as Bekalu affirms, "presuppositions are the ones the reader must find uncontroversial in order to find the assertions relevant"[85]

A partial conclusion here is that the indicative utters an assertion and as such is prominent, while the participle draws the reader/listener's attention to what is prominent—the main clause. In the Jairus and Jesus episode where a participle occurs, neither the aspect of the aorist participle nor the aspect of the main verb is canceled.[86] The same opposition is preserved on the side of the attitude system because the adverbial participle, which is outside of that system, makes the readers relate it to the main verb's attitude in order to make sense of the process.

The analysis of the participle moves on to combine two systems from the Greek network. The aspectuality system occurs simultaneously with the finiteness system and those two systems are considered the broadest choice within the verbal system.[87] The finiteness system is distinguished in verbal expression through person (προσεκύνει – 3rd person singular imperfect indicative) or lack of person (ἐλθών – participle nominative singular).

The grammaticalization of the person of the verb in the form sets the verb in the attitude system (+finite). If the form of the verb does not encode the person, then it is outside of the attitude system (-finite). Being outside of the attitude system it provides an opening for the readers to participate in the construal of meaning.

Matt 4:2 καὶ *νηστεύσας* ἡμέρας τεσσεράκοντα καὶ νύκτας τεσσεράκοντα, ὕστερον **ἐπείνασεν** (And *fasting* forty days and forty nights afterward **he was hungry**). English versions add "after" before the adverbial participle forgetting that "after" is before the main verb in this example. Sim observes, the "relations between participles and the main clause must be identified but this identification is possible only by inference from the context, there being no temporal or logical markings in the participle itself."[88] In other words, by choosing ±factive presupposition, aspectuality must be chosen simultaneously. However, by choosing –finite (±factive presupposition), + finite (attitude) is blocked because its dual entry condition is not met.[89] However, the opposition in this case occurs between these two systems, and this perspective must be at the forefront of exegetical work.

The participle is that choice of the writer through which he informs the reader about things the reader already knows so that he can add new information, whether asserting, commanding or projecting. The adverbial participle has a relative relational ambiguity with the main verbal action, and because of this ambiguity, the participle depends on the context in order to express itself.[90] Thus, the participle indicates continuity between the embedded clause and the primary clause.

As stated above, the participle is a formal designation and its semantics can be demonstrated by analysis of the essential meanings of individual verbal form, which in turn occurs in a variety of contexts. Then, the main entry of the participle is that of factive presupposition, which can appear in a variety of contexts without altering its semantics while features such as "temporal," "causal," "concessive," "conditional," or "final" are the result of several items within the context, therefore pragmatics.

Semantics and Pragmatics: Closed and Open Systems in Linguistics

Caution is necessary so the interpreter will not confuse semantics with pragmatics. Since the participle grammaticalizes a semantic presupposition, the upgraded effect because of the context is a pragmatic result. In summary, the only semantics grammaticalized by a participial form is that of presupposition. The chart below shows how meanings are related.

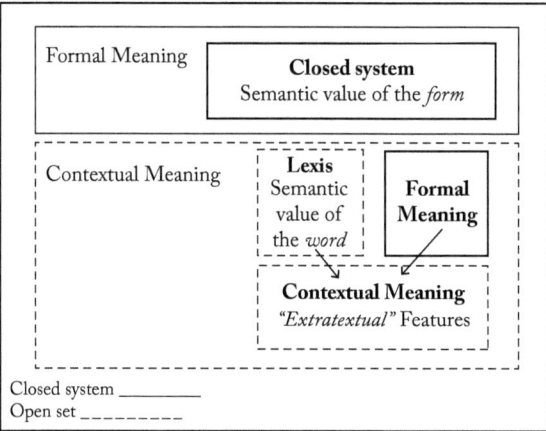

Figure 2.2. Closed system patterns and open set patterns. (Adapted from Decker, *Temporal Deixis*, p. 28.)

The chart above by Decker more or less represents Halliday who describes context as "the relation of the form to non-linguistic features of the situations in which language operates, and to linguistic features other than those of the item [form] under attention."[91] Therefore, our research distinguishes formal meaning and contextual meaning, but also sees form in two related levels, that is, grammar and lexis.[92] Systemic linguistics sees these two levels as a cline (or continuum) of coordinated systems having grammar at one end and lexis at the other.[93]

The need for balancing semantic and pragmatic analysis is stated by Van Dijk who recognizes that "Las relaciones entre proposiciones o frases en un discurso no pueden describirse exhaustivamente sólo en términos semánticos."[94] Therefore, the study of any function of the participle must include the distinction between semantics and pragmatics, since speakers choose from this system on a functional basis.[95] By definition, pragmatics is "the study of the way signs or symbols are used in context, whereas semantics concerns the meaning of a symbol in abstraction from its use."[96]

The basic difference between pragmatic phenomena and semantics is that the former is cancelable while the latter cannot be canceled. This agrees with what Comrie states, "the distinction between the meaning of a linguistic item, in terms of its conventionalised semantic representation, and the implicatures can be drawn from the use of a linguistic item in a particular context."[97] Therefore, this distinction explains why the same participial structure can mean different things in different contexts. It reveals also what kind of contexts are preferred with the Greek participle, and the study of register has been useful for such an analysis.

The Study of Register

Register is the term used to talk about the study of the context. The basic function of register is to observe the language appropriate to a given context. Only a couple minutes of listening to the radio are necessary in order to determine if one is listening to a talk show, a football game, or a news broadcast. The same individual uses different varieties of language depending on the situation. A change in the context of situation involves a change that affects the idea of the text. Thus, the text and "the context of situation" should not be considered as separate entities.[98] Further, the search for meaning must include three types of contexts: the social, cultural, and that of the situation.

This book is limited to analyzing the context of situation assuming that, as Reed states, "speakers conform their discourse to the context of situation, and consequently draw upon accepted forms of language which others recognize as appropriate for that situation."[99] What is going on restricts who is taking part and how meaning is exchanged. These aspects are what the study of register aims to know.

By applying register in this book, two characteristics will become evident. 1) When aorist nominative participle is used in contexts expressing some sort of feeling or emotion, the readers are drawn into the emotional environment. Further, the use of the participles in general seems to be a proper semantic function for emotional environment since it invites the readers to take a part in it. In other words, assuming that the context of situation constrains those taking part and how meaning is exchanged, it may be that the participle is preferred for contexts in which emotion is involved. 2) The pragmatic effect of upgrading indicates some sort of movement within the narrative from one point to another. An unspecified movement toward the main process.

This movement seems to be a result of two features.

First, the use of the anarthrous adverbial participle of the embedded clause when it is placed at the beginning of the sentence, indicates that no discontinuity is being assigned within the context. For instance, Acts 10:20, ἀλλὰ ἀναστὰς **κατάβηθι** καὶ **πορεύου** σὺν αὐτοῖς μηδὲν διακρινόμενος ὅτι ἐγὼ ἀπέσταλκα αὐτούς (*Get up* [and] **go down** and **go** with them nothing doubting, for I have sent them). There is a movement from the embedded clause initiated by ἀναστάς to the main clause with κατάβηθι καὶ πορεύου. The embedded clause establishes a chain so that the main clause can be in the spotlight.

Second, based on the large context, it can be said that the adverbial use of the participle is preferred for a context where some emotion occurs. We are not saying that the participles are reserved for emotional context as the only option, but that as a result of being readers' oriented, the participles are usually used in emotional context to get readers' involved ideationally in the event.

Acts 10:17–23a shows the culmination of Peter's vision, and while he was recovering from the shock of the vision on the roof of the tanner's house, the Spirit told him the messengers from Cornelius had arrived in Joppa.

The point here is that by investing the text with diverse viewpoints (directional movement and feeling) on the action, a writer is able to impose an attractive environment aimed at effecting the desired response(s) in the reader. This rhetorical function occurs in the interaction between several features, mainly, the relation of the participle with the main verb.

Examples and basic discussion in the New Testament will be in chapter four. The Greek language seems to connect factive ideas not with lexis specifically, although there will be times where this happens, but with a grammatical form—the participle. It is not being argued that all factive verbs from an English perspective occur in the New Testament with the aorist participle. Rather, it seems that the factivity that concerns perception, i.e., cognitive factive verbs, and that which concerns emotional attitude toward facts, i.e, emotive factive, are part of the verbal complex in the New Testament in environments where any sort of perception and emotions are involved.

The study of complementation in Greek provides a foundation for the analysis of the verb, which may take an infinitive or a participle. Hebrews 6:1 Διὸ ἀφέντες τὸν τῆς ἀρχῆς τοῦ Χριστοῦ λόγον ἐπὶ τὴν τελειότητα **φερώμεθα**, μὴ πάλιν θεμέλιον καταβαλλόμενοι μετανοίας ἀπὸ νεκρῶν ἔργων καὶ πίστεως ἐπὶ θεόν (therefore *let us leave* the elementary doctrine of Christ [and] **go on** to maturity, not laying again a foundation of repentance from dead works and of faith toward God). The moving on of the author of Hebrews presupposes truth of "the leaving" in the embedded clause. The author expects them to move on in the perfection (New Covenant), but he is committed, and his readers should be as well, to the truth of the proposition Διὸ ἀφέντες τὸν τῆς ἀρχῆς τοῦ Χριστοῦ λόγον, which functions as a complement of **φερώμεθα**.

Matthew 9:13 πορευθέντες δὲ **μάθετε** τί ἐστιν· ἔλεος θέλω καὶ οὐ θυσίαν· οὐ γὰρ ἦλθον καλέσαι δικαίους ἀλλὰ ἁμαρτωλούς ("But *Go* and **learn** what is, 'I desire mercy, and not sacrifice.' For I did not come to call the righteous, but sinners."). As we will see, the use of the participle as a factive presupposition with its functional role serves as the background and prioritizes the action of "learning." He invites the readers to feel the environment of [e]motion assigned by ἔλεος θέλω καὶ οὐ θυσίαν (I desire mercy, and not sacrifice). It is as though Jesus is saying to the reader as well "**Go** and *learn*" what I expect from you.

Systemic functional linguistics is helpful for the understanding of register, although Halliday limited his treatment to the context of situation. This limitation was perceived by other functional scholars, so they added the analysis of the social

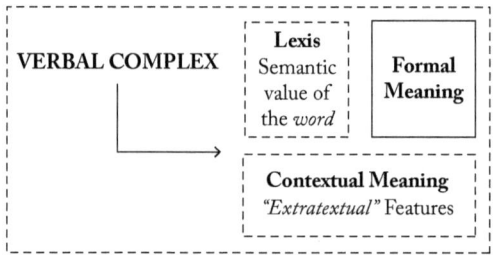

Figure 2.3. Verbal complex.

This verbal complex chart shows a simple closed system with the solid line having the formal meaning inside while the others are open. The inclusion of other features will not change the formal meaning. See Decker's verbal complex chart for more details. Rodney J. Decker, *Temporal Deixis of the Greek Verb in the Gospel of Mark with Reference to Verbal Aspect*, SBG 10 (New York, NY: Peter Lang, 2001), 26.

and cultural context.[100] It is necessary to understand the logical association with, and motivation for, the action that of the participle, and a tool available to guide the interpreters in this quest is the study of register.

In the treatment of the context of situation, Halliday adopts explicitly Malinowski and Firth's orientation.[101] Malinowski saw language as a "mode of action,"[102] that is, a mode of cultural behavior carried to its logical conclusion. He believes that the usage of language is not mere thought or "contemplation" rather it is action and experience,[103] and this use of language leaves behind a path that shows the structure of language itself.[104] Although Malinowski had little to say about linguistic theory, he laid the background that contributed to Firth's theory, which shaped Malinowski's ideas about language into a consistent linguistic theory.[105]

For Firth, linguistics should start through "the active participation of men in the world,"[106] and this participation in the event of language forms part of this "context of situation."[107] Firth's definition of context of situation is succinct: first, relevant features of the participants, including persons and personalities that encompass their verbal and non-verbal actions; second, relevant objects; and third, the effect of the verbal action.[108]

Firth also adopts a notion of "typical context of situation" that "considers the limited variety of social situations and within each context finds a context-specific language variety."[109] The same speaker can produce a different variety of language in close temporal succession having a variety of goals for which language is being used.[110] This is what is known as register.[111]

As pointed out above, Malinowski saw language as a "mode of action" and coined the term "context of situation" to account for the various environments within which speakers behave through language.[112] Firth developed it into the necessary abstraction to become a linguistic theory, but Firth's student, Michael Halliday set out the research of the functional basis of language following Malinowski and Firth.

Halliday states, "'Text is meaning and meaning is choice, an ongoing current of selections each in its paradigmatic environment of what might have been meant (but was not).'"[113] Halliday sees language as fundamentally functional and the primary attribute of social man.[114] In the same behaviorist mindset as Malinowski and Firth, Halliday sees that what it "can do" (the behavioral potential of a society) is realized by the social-semantic ("can mean") that can only be achieved by the lexicogrammar ("can say").[115]

In summary, the function of the language as a semiotic system through the above-mentioned realities, "can do," "can mean," and "can say," form the register. It is this part of linguistics which determines and constrains the meta-function or macro-function (ideational, interpersonal, and textual), and it is important in setting the structure of the language.[116] "Can do" is the *field*, "can mean" is the *tenor*, and "can say" is the *mode*. Matthiessen states that "the context can be characterized with the help of systemic theory, using field (*the social action* and *subject matter, what's going on* [can do]) tenor (*the social relationship, who's taking part* [can mean]), and mode (*how are the meanings exchanged* [can say]."[117]

As Halliday argues, to relate a text to "higher orders of meaning, whether social, literary or of some other semiotic universe," it is necessary to move beyond the mere description of syntax to an account of the contextually determined networks of options from which particular textual choices emanate.[118]

Features of situation	establishes...	Meta-function	Functional Roles	Realization in text
Field ('what is going on')	**REGISTER** A context-specific, function-based language variety	Ideational>	Transitivity Modulation	Participles/ Infinitive
Tenor ('who's taking part')		Interpersonal>	Mood, Modality	Indicative/ Non-indicative
Mode ('how are the meanings exchanged')		Textual>	Theme/rheme/ Given/new Information	
'Can mean' (semantics)				'Can say' (Lexico-grammar)

Figure 2.4. Register: context of situation.

This chart is adapted from *TBF*, 36.

Figure 2.4 above points out that beyond syntax, there is much more. There are, among others, the context of situation, which means that in any social context, certain semantic resources are characteristically employed; certain sets of options are as it were 'at risk' in the given semiotic environment. Considered in terms of the notion of meaning potential, the register is the range of meaning potential that is activated by the semiotic properties of the situation, as already mentioned: What is going on? Who is participating in it? How is meaning exchanged?[119]

The context of the situation determines what changes are necessary to be made to the material as the context changes. Reed states, "speakers conform their discourse to the context of situation, and consequently draw upon accepted forms of language which others recognize as appropriate for that situation."[120] Consequently, a given linguistic structure is determined by the intention of meaning that invokes the common interpretive ground for readers. Thus, it provides predictability.

Register requires some sort of predictability that encompasses five major aspects of discourse: first, subject-matter (this is the semantic content of the discourse); second, context of situation; third, participants (who is who, and what is what in the communicative process); fourth, mode (e.g., imperative, interrogative, persuasive, and explanatory discourse); and fifth medium (spoken or written).[121]

The above five major aspects are described by three specific functions. First, transitivity which analyzes text in terms of the process expressed in the clause (what is going on), participants in this process (who is taking part), and the various attributes and circumstances of the process and the participants.[122] As will be seen, the participle is part of the ideational metafunction, and as such it does not grammaticalize the speaker's attitude.

The second function is mood, which deals with the options such as indicative (declarative, interrogative [yes/no and wh- types]), and imperative.[123] Mood and modality are concerned with the interaction between speakers and addressees.[124] The third function, theme-rheme, is what enables the speaker or writer to build or connect parts of the speech act that are situationally relevant, and enables the listener or reader to discern what is a text and what is a sentence.[125]

Lang is one of few scholars to indicate Herodotus' and Thucydides' preference to express motivation ([e]motion) using a participle.[126] Rijksbaron presents a series of verbs whose complement can be either infinitive or participle.[127] He sees the difference between the participle and the infinitive semantically. "The participle may also be used in such a way that the state of affairs expressed by the participle is indispensable for a correct interpretation of the sentence as a whole."[128] When the participle and infinitive are related to verbs of perception, he argues that the participle is used as the complement when there is a direct perception, while the infinitive when there is an indirect perception.[129]

Note that the treatment of the several functions of the participle is related to the classification of the different types of entity that are applied to the analysis of the internal structure of the adverbial clause. Rijksbaron deals with the function of the satellite (an optional modifier of the main verb) realized by the embedded clause with the main clause, which is taken into account, analyzing the layer of the hierarchical structure of the clause it modifies (predicate, predication, proposition or illocution). In the end, what Rijksbaron is doing is an analysis of the adverbial participle but seen from an external perspective.[130]

Figure 2.5 not only includes the functional components themselves, but also goes on to relate their functional roles. Modulation, mood and modality are concerned with the interaction between speakers and addressees.[131] The interaction of these features is what indicates focus or prominence. These prominent features are called here theme-rheme/given-new.[132]

The present study is interested in *language according to use*.[133] As Halliday bluntly asserts: "we are interested in what a particular writer has written, against the background of what he might have written … in what it is about the language of a particular work of literature that has its effect on us as readers …."[134] Therefore, the aim of functional grammar is the study of texts,[135] "which may be regarded as the basic unit of semantic structure."[136] Of particular interest here is the interaction of the meta-functions to their related functional roles. Using a participle expresses something different than using any other mood and/or modals.

In summary, the choice of a participle is a choice to not use an assertion, thus, the choice of participle is a choice of presupposing something rather asserting something. This is what is going to be discussed below.

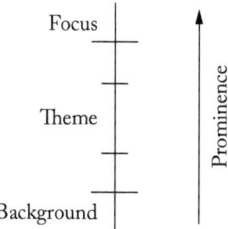

Figure 2.5. Cline of prominence

This chart is from Jeffrey T Reed, *A Discourse Analysis of Philippians*, 108.

Presupposition

Semantic and Pragmatic Presupposition

What this study is arguing is that the key to explaining the upgraded effect of the participle in the New Testament is to include the semantics of the participle with its functional results. As stated above, the participle's only semantic value is that of presupposition, which characterizes every Greek participle; the upgrading is only a pragmatic effect as a result of the suitability of the factive semantics of the participle. Therefore, the main point here is that the use of a presupposition represents a process of hierarchization that draw the readers into part of the construction of meaning.

The fact that the participle in certain contexts appears to be upgraded to the same mood/modal of the main clause is best explained by including the fact that this happens only because the participle is a semantic presupposition. Presupposition is a necessary common ground between the reader/listener and an author as he or she moves the narrative (or *parenesis*) forward. In the specific case of the upgraded effect of the participle this common ground is so connected that the reader tends to read it in close association as though the participle were grammaticalizing attitude along with the mood/modal. The connection is so tight that the same event is described by different evangelists with different choices.

Let's take Mark 2:9–12; Matthew 9:5–7; Luke 5:23–25 as an illustration for our future discussion.

The analysis of these clauses must include the largest discourse spectrum to grasp a fair understanding of the use of the participles in these passages. All three evangelists present the authority of the exalted Son of God as the main point in this discourse involving a healing story. The paralytic healing is used as a means to show the authority of the Son of Man to forgive sins. The verb of perception (εἰδῆτε) places the focus of all these parallel passages ("in order to know") on the fact that Jesus Christ has the authority to forgive, something that only the true God has.

The complement of the primary clause comes with a complex clause having one subordinate clause followed by one embedded clause with the infinitive. The perception of "forgiving sins" cannot be directly perceived by the readers. They need to reflect about it, and decide if they would take as a "true proposition" or not. The use of the infinitive indicates that they did not accept the utterance of forgiveness as a true proposition, so something else would be necessary to make such an assumption into a real accepted proposition.

The movement from an abstract reflective world with the infinitive changes into the author's assessment in the direct discourse uttered by Jesus. From a presuppositional world (infinitive), a material process is described by a combination of imperatives ἔγειρε καὶ ἆρον ... καὶ περιπάτει (three imperatives in Mark 2:9, and two imperatives ἔγειρε ... καὶ περιπάτει in both Matthew 9:5, and Luke 5:23. The direct discourse unfolds by showing that what Jesus compares is an indirect perception with a direct grasp of his powerful ministry.

After asking what is the easiest, Jesus moves on to address the paralytic with another three imperatives in the book of Mark (2:11) ἔγειρε ἆρον ... καὶ ὕπαγε. Matthew 9:6 does not have three imperatives as Mark. He actually takes a different construction having one aorist nominative participle preceding a finite verb (imperative) in the following order: _ἐγερθεὶς_ **ἆρόν** ... καὶ ὕπαγε. This particular phenomenon happens with Luke 5:24, but his structure is different from both Mark and Matthew. He uses an imperative ἔγειρε with καί and switches Mark's imperative (ἆρον) into an aorist nominative participle preceding an imperative according to the following structure: ἔγειρε καὶ _ἄρας_ ... πορεύου.

Mark 2:11	ἔγειρε ἆρον ... καὶ ὕπαγε	Imperative + imperative + καί + imperative
Matthew 9:6	_ἐγερθεὶς_ **ἆρόν** ... καὶ ὕπαγε	Participle + imperative + καί + imperative
Luke 5:24	ἔγειρε καὶ _ἄρας_ ... **πορεύου**	Imperative + καί + participle + imperative

The same event described with special subtlety serves for the understanding of the upgraded effect we are going to study. In narrative, this was common in the classical Greek as we already saw with Herodotus above and it happens in the Koiné Greek. The direct discourse is what initiates the movement in the narrative that goes on with a clause complex combination allowing several different choices to describe the same process. The choices available are many, but each different choice implies a different nuance in the meaning.

The description of the process moves on with the +finite system toward the attitude system, which occurs with two other options ±assertion. The choice of the imperative is that of -assertion with the focus in +direction. The reason why a participle may function in a place where there was originally an imperative verb is because of the semantics of the participle. The participle as a factive presupposition makes such a possibility available, but the semantic meaning of participles is different from that of the imperative.

The use of καί sets the two clauses in some sort of equal status, while the relation of the aorist nominative participle is a kind of clause chain. Rather than take all the clause as having equal status, the participial embedded clause works altogether to present the circumstances of the process of the main clause. This structural chain serves as the background circumstance of the main process, it is used as the reader's invitation to participate in the construction of the meanings. It sets the main clause on the spotlight, and if the context of the situation has any emotional tone, it invites the readers to get involved with what is going on by means of reflection.

The readers know, by an indirect perception, that the Son of Man forgives sins at first by the use of the infinite, then, they know who the Son of Man is by the material description of healing of a paralytic man, but they are drawn into the narrative as they take the factuality of the healing by assuming the participle as a true proposition (ἐγερθείς, ἄρας) to make sense of the process at hand. While Mark extends the invitation to the readers by means of reflection only in the final outcome of the healing (2:12), Matthew and Luke draw the readers right into the healing event happening by the direct discourse of Jesus.

The Study of Presupposition

Logicians used to distinguish meaning and reference as they set up a theory of semantics. While the theory of meaning has to do with intention or sense, the theory of reference is related to denotation or extension.[137] The study of presupposition is closely connected to the theory of reference and thus it has an important role for the production and understanding of the speech act.[138]

Presupposition was originally part of the field of philosophy and was proposed by a German philosopher, Friedrich Ludwig Gottlob Frege in 1892 in his *Über Sinn und Bedeutung*. In the 1950s and 1960s, Peter Frederick Strawson brought the discussion into a linguistic field as a pragmatic issue.[139] The debate concerning presupposition increased because of Bertrand Russell's objections to Frege's theory of sense and reference.[140] Russell made two claims: that *the present King of France is bald* is part of two assertions: first, *there is one and only one King of France*, and second, *whoever is the King of France is bald*. Russell claimed that the relation between the two statements is one of entailment.

The logical definition of entailment is that "one sentence entails the second if the truth of the second necessarily follows from the truth of the first."[141] The concept of presupposition contrasts with entailment, although both are defined in terms of the relation between two statements.[142]

This philosophical theory of presupposition and the divergent subjectivist view of the study of presupposition, forced Levinson to state the difficulty of having a semantic theory of presupposition.[143] From Levinson a semantic presupposition is untenable, thus, there is only pragmatic presupposition.[144]

Levinson is right in seeing presupposition as implications that are often felt to be in the background—assumed by the speaker to be already known to the addressee. What he seems to ignore is what Reed states, "each element of grammar is treated in terms of a linguistic system, emphasizing that speakers choose from this system on a functional basis."[145] From the verbal network, the finiteness system enables the writer to choose how he wants the reader to apprehend the action.

The system enables the writer to present the information in a manageable and concise form so that the reader can comprehend the meaning with a minimum effort. By finding a Greek participle, the reader tracks the elements that precede the main event with that which follows the narrative. This is more than logic, it is experiential as well, and these two together form the ideational metafunction of language. It is a feature available in the Greek verbal network realized by the *ideational* functional component, grammaticalized by the Greek participle.

Strawson and Kempson claim that presuppositions stand in direct contrast to both assertion and entailment. She states, "one [is] associated with statements and the other associated with the speaker of an utterance, of which the latter stood in contrast to assertion in the sense of what the speaker is actually asserting."[146] While the contrast between assertion and presupposition is important, the difference between presupposition and entailment is of no particular interest for a dead language such as Koiné Greek, unless one sees the importance of both and the fact that one depends on the other. Since the validity of this distinction could only be applied from an oral perspective, presupposition and entailment are seen as the same in this study.[147]

Presupposition and Given-New/Theme-Rheme

The above relation contrasts these features and it represents an increase in the abstraction of meanings. A non-finite morphologized structure occupies the middle ground between verbal and nominal structures, and by being related to a verbal clause, serves to highlight prominent parts of a discourse.[148] Prominence refers to the means by which speakers/authors draw the listener/reader's attention to important topics. What is asserted must be more prominent than what is presupposed.[149] This dynamic act of speech rests firmly on the linguistic concept of theme-rheme and given-new.[150]

The different theories of information structure today distinguish what originated in the Prague school *theme* and *rheme/given* and *new*. Halliday assigned different categories to these information structures. Given–New became associated only to "tone group," not related to clause or sentence, but intonation or prosody. Theme-Rheme are understood as related to syntax.[151]

Theme-rheme and given-new represent different types of informational choices. Theme-rheme,[152] and Given-new[153] are part of the functional roles. Reed applies Halliday's definition to the study of New Testament Greek. He says, "it is important to emphasize that theme and given, rheme and new, do not always correspond … [and] to conflate the two ways of information structuring is to err in the same way the Prague School of linguists did."[154]

Errors that Reed sees in the Prague School have been turned against SFL because of Halliday's insistence on confining given-new to intonation and theme-rheme to the clause. SFL has been criticized from both outsiders and insiders regarding the limitation of Given-New to prosody.[155] Because Halliday's definition of "focus" was exclusively related to intonation, Runge rightly states, "in its present form, SFL is ill suited to tackle flexibly ordered languages such as Greek and Hebrew."[156]

The concepts of Given and New are described by functional sentence linguists in terms of communicative dynamism. Given elements, functioning as presupposition, contribute less to the development of communication, while new elements uttered by the main verb contribute more.[157] The relation between two sentences, the embedded clause and the main clause form a hierarchical clause chain that signals prominence for the readers. However, it does not mean that new information is limited only to what the main verb expresses.

Language is too broad to deal exhaustively with all nuances. It is too complex, so the present study limits itself to only one theory of grammar in every aspect. The main point of Given is not that it introduces the chronological information presented in the previous context, although that happens often. The use of Given-New deals with prominence, which means that the presupposed information is the least marked serving as a background, prioritizing, then new information, which is the focal part of the clause or sentence.

It is assumed here that almost every adverbial participle in the New Testament functions as Given so that the main clause may function as New.[158] The participle in the New Testament seems to fit with the concepts of Given. Theme is equated with the subject matter (transitivity), which deals with some sort of definite description of the topic that carries a presupposition of existence and uniqueness, but the focus (Rheme) is on the main verb and its closely related elements (objects, κ. τ. λ) in the Greek.

Generally speaking, "presupposition … concerns knowledge which a speaker/writer does not assert but presumes as part of the background of a sentence, knowledge presumed to be already known to the hearer/reader."[159] What indicates to readers the information already known are the participles, which help the readers to keep track of the clause chain giving prominence where it should.

Seeing it this way, presupposition on the one hand deals with the relation between statements or sentences, and on the other it has to do with what a writer/speaker assumes in uttering a given statement.[160] Thus, how this relation can be established will be seen in the relation of the ideational metafunction with the other metafunctions and their respective functional roles.

It is necessary for a clause to have thematic organization in order to deliver a message. Halliday argues that there are two kinds of thematic system: first, "those which assign structure to the whole clause"; and second, those that "assign sub-structures at certain points in the clause."[161] These organizational systems act in a sub-network within the network of systems that are organized in three sets: the information system (Given-New), thematization system (Theme-Rheme),[162] and identification system (Known-Unknown).[163]

The information unit represents the speakers' organization of the speech act into message units, and it shows the information focus.[164] Halliday states, "the system of information focus is thus dependent on the information structure; it involves the selection, within each information unit, of a certain element or elements as points of prominence within the message."[165] Thus, the speaker has a choice in the network of what he or she wants to present as focal.

If the speaker's choice is lightly marked, "the non-focal components are unspecified with regard to presupposition, so that the focal is merely culminative in the message."[166] Reed asserts, "focal elements often express feelings or arouse emotions ... [and] the reader cannot help but be drawn to focal elements. It is as if the speaker/author is slapping the listener/reader across the face and saying, 'Pay attention'."[167]

HEBREWS 6:1			
Planes of Discourse	Background	Foreground	Foreground Development
Greek	ἀφέντες ...	φερώμεθα	καταβαλλόμενοι
English	let's us leave	go on	Laying down

This is a cluster of clauses with a very complex relationship between them. The semantic projection of the subjunctive is the center point around which the other two form a chain unit in two embedded clauses. The focus is upon the foreground information with φερώμεθα (let's go on) and two other circumstances help to develop the author's argument in this passage. These two clauses have a negative tune, one with an explicit negative μὴ πάλιν (not again) καταβαλλόμενοι (laying down) and the other with a proper lexis ἀφέντες (leaving).

The information with the two participles keeps the main clause on the spotlight. The exhortation to go on presupposes two circumstances that the readers must take as a "true proposition" in order to move on to perfection: leaving and not laying down. The readers play their roles because the author assigns them such a task by using the participles. The first one serves as background information so closely related to the main clause that ideationally the readers cannot avoid reading it as a subjunctive, and the other develops the action of the main process.

Those three clauses within a complex relationship give us the idea on how to interpret factive presuppositions in Greek. The concept of a clause in Greek does not fit the conventional and traditional grammar in English. It is not necessary to have a subject and a predicate to form a clause in Greek. The debate on how to classify a participle as being adverbial or not is debatable. It is not unanimous, but we adopt here Culy's thesis.

First, Martin Culy has written an article questioning the function-focused way of teaching the classification of participles. In his article "The Clue is in the Case: Distinguishing Adjectival and Adverbial Participles," he says that "scholars have overlooked an important, simple rule for distinguishing adverbial participles from adjectival participles."[168] His rule states, "Adverbial participles will always be nominative, except in genitive absolute constructions or when they modify an infinitive."[169]

The two exceptions occur because there are sometimes cases when it is necessary to indicate a circumstantial idea with a participle whose subject is not coreferential with the main verb. In this case, the author uses a switch-reference device, namely the genitive absolute participle construction. The other exception is when the verb that the participle is modifying is an infinitive. Since infinitives normally take accusative subjects, then adverbial participles modifying them will also be accusative. The crux of his argument is that in many cases when an adjectivally functioning participle is confused to be adverbial, this is often because translation is being confused with syntax.[170]

The other observation about the adverbial participle is related to the nominative as well. In Matthew 28:18–19, the four participles are all nominative adverbial participles. The semantic of the nominative with the adverbial participle indicates that this nominative case "creates the expectation that the subject of the participle will also be the subject of the main clause."[171] The clause chain established by the adverbial participle acts on the readers, who then expect to see both the (logical) subject of the participle and that of the main verb as one.

Starting a sentence in a vacuum with προσελθών (approaching) would not make sense. The readers must connect it with what happened before (Matthew 28:16–17) in the broad discourse, that is, οἱ δὲ ἔνδεκα μαθηταὶ ἐπορεύθησαν εἰς τὴν Γαλιλαίαν εἰς τὸ ὄρος οὗ ἐτάξατο αὐτοῖς ὁ Ἰησοῦς, καὶ *ἰδόντες* αὐτὸν **προσεκύνησαν**, οἱ δὲ ἐδίστασαν (And the eleven disciples went to Galilee, to the mountain to which Jesus had pointed to them and *seeing* they **worshiped** him, but they hesitated.) The movement in this set established by the logical clause chain has this pattern.[172]

Matthew 21:29 ὁ δὲ ἀποκριθεὶς εἶπεν οὐ θέλω ὕστερον δὲ *μεταμεληθεὶς* **ἀπῆλθεν** (And answering, he said, 'I do not want to' but afterward he *repented* [and] **went**). *μεταμεληθείς* is an aorist adverbial participle in the embedded clause. The new information is called the focus of the clause because it is what the speaker wants the hearers to know in the whole utterance. These sentences contain a mix of presupposed (ἀποκριθείς, μεταμεληθείς) and newly asserted information (εἶπεν, ἀπῆλθεν).

Typically, studies in Greek language attribute the issue of prominence to several features, one of them being information structure, which focuses on the ordering of clause components. Runge discusses information structure in his Discourse Grammar starting from the perspective that "no single linguistic theory is robust enough on its own to adequately account for every aspect of language."[173] He introduces two main features: information structure is related to a mental representation of the discourse, and it is connected to the natural information flow of the language. He states, "speakers tend to start with what is already established or knowable in the context and then add new or "non-established" information to it."[174]

There is intent in writing that guides the readers so that they can build a mental representation of the discourse. Through this mental representation, the readers reflect on how the content comes together and then store it in their mind. Dooley and Levinsohn state, "the forms of language that the speaker uses certainly play a part in this, but psychological research shows that the way hearers understand, store, and remember a discourse corresponds only partially with what was actually said."[175]

The writer can organize his message in terms of markedness by combining established information and non-established information. Runge argues, "The established information may derive from the preceding discourse content, or from generally accessible knowledge about the world around us."[176]

The focus of the clause may be more specifically defined as the difference between what is presupposed in a context and what is asserted in a given proposition."[177] It can be concluded that the writer would treat the non-focal components as presupposed.[178] Thus, presupposition is broadly accepted as one of the writer's devices to attract the readers into the environment communicated.[179] Runge's treatment in chapter nine of his book is much more from an English perspective.

Chapters ten and eleven of his book apply the discussion of frame devices to the Greek language. Although Runge mentions the inclusion of information structure with the embedded clause, such as subordinate or relative, he does not include the occurrence of the participle in the embedded clause within any of categories presented in these chapters.

Runge reserves chapter twelve to analyze circumstantial frames, but he does not seem to follow the same pattern as the preceding chapters. In chapter 10, he includes several of the adverbial logical functions and he does admit, "Koiné Greek is a verb-prominent language, where the least-marked and most basic order of clause components is for the verb to be placed in the initial position. When other elements are placed in the initial position, such placement is motivated by some pragmatic reason."[180] For example, there is a common tendency of the upgraded pragmatic function to occur when the aorist participle in the embedded clause not only precedes the main clause, but is placed in the beginning of the whole sentence.

Runge is correct in seeing the adverbial participles with two main functions: prioritizing the main clause and providing background for its action.[181] Thus, he is right to see the distinction between the participle and the other moods or modality in terms focal and non-focal points in the discourse.

There is a mental representation that shows that the speaker is not only doing something himself, but also demanding something of the listener since he or she can give meaning by "inviting [the reader through assertion] to receive," and demands meaning by "inviting [the reader through presupposition] to give."[182]

In summary, presupposed information is the complement of focus, and it represents the information that the speaker assumes (Given) is already part of the common ground, i.e., meaning shared by both the speaker/writer and the hearer/reader.[183] Focus, on the other hand, is that part of the discussion that is assumed by the writer not to be shared by the hearer. The New items of information are presented by the main clause and its complements.[184]

Levinsohn says, "the primary significance of using the participial clause is that [it] provides the counterpoint for the assertion of the nuclear [main] clause."[185] Focal prominence is presented by New, while Given (participle) sets the main verb in the spotlight. Of course, this does not mean that prominence is a result of one grammatical structure such as information structure, but the participle being an adverbial seems to work in the same capacity. Therefore, the assumption is that information structure motivates the pragmatic effect of focus, which commonly occurs with the adverbs.

What is common to the adverbs shows itself to be very common with the aorist adverbial clause of the embedded clause that initiates the sentence with the upgraded effect. In others, as Reed warns, "the analyst should not depend on the presence of one grammatical category to determine prominence, but an analysis of all signaling devices,"[186] the aorist adverbial participle being one of these features.

Presupposition as Shared Information

The Greek participle is a semantic presupposition that does not exhaust the information, but it is open, that is, it lacks certain information that is added by the relation to the main verb, which can be caught by the hears in a logical/experiential way. Sematic finiteness points to readers what is presupposed and what is communicated with the attitude system with ±assertion. The connection between established information and non-established information forms a clause chain between the participle of the embedded clause and the main clause.

There is an essential distinction that will be followed throughout this analysis between what is presupposed and what is asserted. This basic relation has to do with the finiteness system realized by the moods and modulation. The upgraded function occurs because of the close relation between the aorist adverbial participles of the embedded clause and the main verb, which provokes a mental representation of the embedded clause's circumstance, making the participle seem to have the same mood as the main clause. Runge states, "adverbial subordinate clauses that are placed before the main clause serve the pragmatic purpose of establishing an explicit frame of reference for the clause that follows."

Verbs of perception such as ἀκούω, γινώσκω, δοκιμάζω, ἐπιτρέπω, εὑρίσκω, οἶδα, ὁμολογέω, αἰσχύνομαι, δεικνύω, χαίρω, μεταμέλομαι can have as their complement either a finite clause, an infinitive, or a participle, the last two being (more/very) common. They occur where no assertion is made with the embedded clause where they belong. One can observe that with verbs of perception, the difference between the participle and infinitive is that this latter describes an indirect perception while the former indicates a direct perception.

Rijksbaron states, "The participle may also be used in such a way that the state of affairs expressed by the participle is indispensable for a correct interpretation of the sentence as a whole."[187] The speakers and the hearers accept the proposition of the presupposition as a true proposition in order to make sense of the focal clause.

Lightfoot seems to see the participle as concerning to factuality. He states, "the use of a participle construction indicates that the author of the sentence presupposes and wishes the hearer to think that he presupposes that the complement reflects a real, actual, existing state of affairs."[188] It is not factuality, actuality or truth in themselves that is the point here. The truth of the proposition refers to a common ground where the speaker and hearer should stand and accept the shared information so that the main point can be the focus.

Presupposition drawns the readers' attention as it calls them to agree with the proposition at hand. For instance, John 9:25 ἀπεκρίθη οὖν ἐκεῖνος· εἰ ἁμαρτωλός ἐστιν οὐκ οἶδα· ἓν οἶδα ὅτι τυφλὸς ὢν ἄρτι **βλέπω** (therefore he answered, "if he is a sinner I do not know, one thing I know that **being** blind now I see"). The participle of the embedded clause in this passage serves as a complement to the verb of mental perception οἶδα. Being asked by the Pharisees, the formerly blind man obliges by reiterating the truth that he knew and had experienced. If Jesus is a sinner, he answered "I do not know," but one thing he knows, and the Pharisees must share this information—being blind now I see.

The blind man was not lying, and the Pharisees can share this information. Not only the Pharisees, but the writer assumes that the readers also were following the flow of the narrative: direct perception (τυφλὸς ὢν "*being* blind") as a true proposition in order to make sense of the assertion (ἄρτι βλέπω now I see).

Mark 6:12 καὶ *ἐξελθόντες* **ἐκήρυξαν** ἵνα μετανοῶσιν (So *they went out* [and] **proclaimed** that they should repent). Established information tends to be asserted in Greek like "they preached," (ἐκήρυξαν) followed by a subjunctive in the secondary clause. The embedded clause is right before the main clause. Runge recognizes, "placing presupposed information in a place of prominence has the effect of establishing an explicit frame of reference, providing the reader with the primary basis for connecting what follows with what precedes."[189] There is no information value with ἐξελθόντες because both speaker and hearer accept the proposition. The focal point is that they proclaimed repentance. The unspecified movement is a typical participial chain.

Luke 11:8 λέγω ὑμῖν εἰ καὶ οὐ δώσει αὐτῷ ἀναστὰς διὰ τὸ εἶναι φίλον αὐτοῦ διά γε τὴν ἀναίδειαν αὐτοῦ *ἐγερθεὶς* **δώσει** αὐτῷ ὅσων χρῄζει (I say to you, though he will not give anything when he gets up because he is his friend, yet because of his impudence he *will rise* [and] **give** him whatever he needs). ἐγερθείς of the embedded clause sets the main verb clause in the spotlight. The information uttered by the participle must be a true proposition that both speaker and reader accept, so that the main verb δώσει can be the focus.

To understand factivity it is necessary to look at the three types of transitivity role—process, participant, and circumstance.[190] Verbal groups express processes, while nominal groups express participants. The participle is a declinable verbal adjective.[191] From its verbal nature derives tense and voice; from its adjectival nature, case, number, and gender. All participles are either verbal or adjectival in their emphasis.[192] However, no matter if it is in a verbal group or nominal group, its semantics is that of factive presupposition.

	HEBREWS 6:4		
Semantic	**Aorist Participle**	**Present Infinitive**	**Present Participle**
	factive presupposition	Non-factive presupposition	factive presupposition
Planes of Discourse	Background	Foreground	Foreground
Greek	φωτισθέντας γευσαμένους 2x γενηθέντας παραπεσόντας	ἀνακαινίζειν	ἀνασταθροῦντας παραδειγματίζοντας
English	enlightened tasted become fallen	to restore	crucifying putting to shame

This chart is adapted from Rômulo Monteiro, p. 164.

All these adjectival participles are united by one article only. They are referring to one group altogether that encompasses all these verbal qualities. The basic difference between an adverbial and adjectival is that of emphasis. The adjectival participle emphasizes the person or thing described or thought. What kind of person are the qualities in form of actions describing? The author presents a general description of these qualities in the aorist.

Nothing about reality or factuality is asserted. Language as reflection is the main focus in these passages. The exercise of language shows that the author is giving his readers a mental/ideational part to play in the communication of the event by taking all aorist participles φωτισθέντας, γευσαμένους [2x], γενηθέντας, παραπεσόντας as a true proposition. Not only does the author want the readers to think but also to make them identify themselves with this idealized group. It is not a hypothesis, it is a factive presupposition. Observe that the aorist participles occur as a background of ἀνακαινίζειν (to restore) while ἀνασταθροῦντας (crucifying) and παραδειγματίζοντας (putting to shame) develop the reason why it is impossible to restore for repentance.

The author of Hebrews wants the readers to put themselves in the skin of this qualified group by way of language. The author expects identification and reflection using language by putting the readers as part of this ideational group. The focus among the factive presupposition lies on the present participles (ἀνασταθροῦντας and παραδειγματίζοντας) in contrast to the aorist participles, and these two together set the non-factive presupposition on the spotlight. The "impossibility of restauration" is so clear that nothing better than an infinitive to describe, it is a non-factive presupposition, it is out of consideration.

While the author of Hebrews assigns to the readers the reflection of the participles as a true proposition, for instance, they are part of the group with these qualities in form of action including the "fallen" ones, and they are supposed to take the two other participles as a true proposition, "crucifying" and "putting to shame", the infinite does not need to be taken as a true proposition. Thus, it is impossible to restore those with all the characteristics pointed out, since by doing it they would supposedly crucify Christ again. In sum, those who belong to the New Covenant (the perfection) logically cannot crucify Christ again, therefore, stop playing with the Old Covenant and move on in the New.[193]

Factivity and Presupposition:

Why is the participle called factive and why is it called a presupposition?

The answers to these two questions go together. The speaker has a choice in the information status he wants to present as focal. Presupposition is a social exchange since the writer is not only doing something herself/himself, but also demanding something of the listener.[194] The readers/listeners act upon the speech/text to fill some slots of information necessary to qualify or to complete a process in a communicative event. It is a sort of mental process clause without necessarily using words that specifically describe it.

We use factive to mean a presupposition of true proposition. We avoid the ideal of factuality. Factive here is an assumption of something as a true proposition, not some external reality. This true proposition can be a description of any reality, but that is not the point of factive presupposition. By being a presupposition, there are further implications. Assuming that the Greek participle is a semantic presupposition, therefore, listener/reader oriented, it evokes a broad range of responses on the scale of abstraction.

First, *perception*—how the writer wants the reader to see the event speech. For example, Matt 2:13 ἰδοὺ ἄγγελος κυρίου φαίνεται κατ' ὄναρ τῷ Ἰωσὴφ *λέγων·* *ἐγερθεὶς* **παράλαβε** τὸ παιδίον καὶ τὴν μητέρα αὐτοῦ καὶ φεῦγε εἰς Αἴγυπτον. The first participle λέγων is a shift[195] in the narrative that captures the reader's attention for what is about to come. It signals a transition from a narrative proper to a sort of dialogue-speech within the narrative.[196]

Observe that there is no grammatical subject for λέγων, but only a logical subject ἄγγελος κυρίου. While the participle λέγων has the effect of attracting the attention of the reader to the speech or even the segment of speech that follows, the other participle ἐγερθεὶς draws him or her into the event so that he perceives himself/herself as being part of the dynamic of the narrative, most preferred in direct discourse, wanting to shake Joseph and help him to get moving. Verse 14 provides the reader some type of relief with the same participle following an indicative pointing out that Joseph obeyed the command and fled.

Second, not only does presupposition evoke *perception*, but also *reaction*. For instance, Matt 9:13 πορευθέντες δὲ **μάθετε** τί ἐστιν· ἔλεος θέλω καὶ οὐ θυσίαν· When the writer uses a participle to describe an action, he has at the same time a choice of an imperative or indicative, or even other kinds of constructions from the network at his disposal. However, by choosing a participle he communicates something that could not be conveyed had he chosen another mood.[197] Learning is the direction, but the hearers/readers must take the unspecified movement as a true proposition closely related to the main process.

In the case above, for instance, if Matthew had chosen to use two imperatives rather than a participle and an imperative, he would have been giving equal weight to both of them.[198] In this case, the focus of the text is not on πορευθέντες but on μάθετε. That is, a necessary reaction must happen—πορευθέντες, being a sort of background action[199] for the main verb μάθετε.

Third, the "mental process" related to the participle is *cognition*. For instance, Acts 9:26 καὶ πάντες **ἐφοβοῦντο** αὐτὸν μὴ *πιστεύοντες* ὅτι ἐστὶν μαθητής. The participle here is an extended chain elaborating on what is meant by the main action of the clause ἐφοβοῦντο.[200] *They were afraid of Paul* is an assertion uttered by Luke, while the adverbial participle invites the reader to presuppose the reason for it by appealing to a cognition seen in πιστεύοντες that follows the main verb and has a secondary function of showing continuity of the situation.[201]

Fourth, the mental process clause uses a participle of verbalization such as *say* or *speak*. For instance, Matthew 3:2 λέγων· **μετανοεῖτε·** ἤγγικεν γὰρ ἡ βασιλεία τῶν οὐρανῶν. The participle λέγων has the effect of attracting more attention from the reader to the segment of speech that follows. The objective, as Runge states, is "to create something of a dramatic pause just before a (or the) significant point of the speech."[202]

Further, the anarthrous nominative aorist adverbial participle that begins a sentence assigns a point of departure involving renewal of what precedes to that which follows. The first structural indication of the upgraded participle is that the aorist participle is placed at the beginning of the sentence, pointing in two different directions: backward and forward. The forward direction seems to be the most common direction, since the aorist adverbial participle assigns continuity. It has this double function. The intention is to enable the reader to connect the circumstances, or the process of the previous narrative with the focal point of the following clause or sentence.

The adverbial participle of the embedded clause placed at the beginning of the sentence serves a backward-forward point of departure with renewal. When that happens, the focal point is on the main clause. Because it is a semantic presupposition the participle is listener/reader oriented and when it is used in this way, it invokes some sort of *reaction* from the readers. Finally, all the participles involve a "mental process," a sort of *cognition, however, a clause with an aorist adverbial participle forms* a chain elaborating on what is meant by the main action. The Greek participles as a factive presupposition are so suitable of different nuances that we need to set them on their own place to be able to enrich our understanding of their several functions in the interpretation of the New Testament.

Notes

1. Halliday, On Language, p. 182.
2. It does not look like the classical Greek has changed from the Koiné Greek in this matter.
3. BUIJS, *Clause Combining*, 24–35.
4. Ibid., 14.
5. Ibid., *Clause Combining*, 32.
6. Ibid.,
7. Ibid., 36.
8. Most of the NT instances of the independent participle occur in Romans 12 and 1 Peter. Cf. Rom 12:10, 11, 12, 13, 14, 16, 17, 18, 19; 1 Peter 2:18, 3:7.
9. H. A. Gleason, Jr. "Some Contributions of Linguistics to Biblical Studies," *HQ* 4 (1963): 48.
10. M. A. K. Halliday, *On Grammar*, Collected Works of M. A. K. Halliday, edited by Jonathan J. Webster, 1 (London/New York, NY: 2002), 41. Systemic linguistics is not a monolithic theory and as such it has different versions.
11. Halliday, *On Grammar*, 40.
12. Ibid., 40. This distinction is presented by Decker in his Temporal Deixis. See Rodney J. Decker, *Temporal Deixis of the Greek Verb in the Gospel of Mark with Reference to Verbal Aspect*, SBG, 10 (New York, NY: Peter Lang, 2001), 26.
13. Decker seems to call the "*contextual meaning*" as being that of "verbal complex," by which he means "… the total semantic value of the verb and its adjuncts in a particular context, including aspect, lexis, *Aktionsart*, and contextual factors." Decker, *Temporal Deixis*, 27. Systemic linguistics distinguishes between form and function of a given linguistic item. See *PVA*, 11.
14. Halliday, *On Grammar*, 40.
15. Runge sees these two as the most of important functions of the aorist participle that precedes the main verb. See *SRG*, 195.
16. *PVA*, 9.
17. Stanley E. Porter, and Matthew B. O'Donnell, "The Greek Verbal Network Viewed from a Probabilistic Standpoint: An exercise in Hallidayan Linguistics," *FN* 14 (2001): 17. Porter's dissertation presents only 11 major systems, and he later added 3 other systems that were lacking in his Verbal Aspect, that is, Causality, Number, and Participation. Porter states, "Any meaningful component is part of a system of similar available choices, and these systems of choices are arranged into a network, this system network is the grammar." See *PVA*, 8.
18. Halliday, *On Grammar*, 41.

19. Robertson corroborates that idea by saying that "the addition of these verbal functions [tense, voice and case-government] does not make the participle a real verb, since, like the infinitive, it does not have subject." See *ATR*, 1101.

20. Ibid.

21. Ibid., 41.

22. Ibid., 75.

23. *PVA*, 8.

24. *PVA*, 77.

25. Hereafter, SFL.

26. Teun A. Van Dijk accuses Halliday's theory of language as being [somewhat] anti-mentalist. See van Dijk, *Discourse and Context: A Socio-cognitive Approach* (Cambridge: Cambridge University Press, 2010). See the whole chapter entitled context and language. Van Dijk seems to follow Michel Foucault in his thematic approach of "the abuse of power and reproduction of inequality through ideologies. For a response to Van Dijk's view see Stanley E. Porter, "Is Critical Discourse Analysis Critical?: An Evaluation Using Philemon as a Test Case," in *Discourse Analysis and the New Testament: Approaches and Results*, edited by Stanley E. Porter and Jeffrey T. Reed, JSNTSup 70 (Sheffield: Sheffield Academic Press, 1999), 50.

27. *TBF*, 37

28. Halliday, *On Grammar*, 175.

29. Ibid.

30. Helen Leckie-Tarry, *Language and Context: A Functional Linguistic Theory of Register* (London/New York, NY: Pinter, 1995), 7.

31. Reed, "Language of Change and the Changing of Language," 131.

32. See Figure 2.1.

33. Halliday, *Language*, 137.

34. *PVA*, 7.

35. Halliday, *Language*, 141.

36. Halliday, *On Grammar*, 200.

37. Robin P. Fawcett, "What Makes a 'Good' System Network Good?: Four Pairs of Concepts for Such Evaluations," in *Systemic Functional Approach to Discourse: Selected Papers from the 12th International Systemic Workshop*, edited by James D. Benson and William S. Greaves Advances in Discourse Processes 26 (Norwood, NJ: Ablex Publishing Corporation, 1988), 9.

38. *PVA*, 375.

39. John Lyons, *Language and Linguistics: An Introduction* (Cambridge, MA: Cambridge University Press, 2002), 27.

40. Descriptive Linguistic deals with how language is used rather than how language should be used. See Henry A. Gleason, *An Introduction to Descriptive Linguistics* (London: Holt, Rinehart & Winston, 1978).

41. Lyons, Language *and Linguistics*, 34.

42. Halliday, *On Grammar*, 37.

43. Ibid., 38.

44. Ibid.

45. M. A. K. Halliday, *Halliday: System and function in language, Selected papers*. Ed. Gunther Kress (London: Oxford University Press, 1978), 36.

46. Halliday, "Grammatical Categories in Modern Chinese," 212. See Butler. *Systemic*, 14.

47. Halliday, *On Grammar*, 27.

48. M. A. K. Halliday, *Explorations in the Functions of Language* (London: Edward Arnold, 1976), 42.

49. See *SRG*, 200–204.

50. M. A. K. Halliday, *Introduction to Functional Grammar* (London: Edward Arnold, 1994), 101.

51. Ibid.

52. Ibid.

53. While a verb in English does not necessarily grammaticalize subjects, the Greek verb does. For example, in English the verb "want" does not say anything about the participants, that is, who is who, unless the personal and oblique pronouns are used. This is not the case with Greek finite verbs. For example, θελώ, (I want). The verb ending grammaticalizes the person. Those concepts will be studied in chapter 3.

54. *TBF*, 41.

55. The discussion here depends on *TBF*, 40.

56. Suzanne Marie Swiderski, *Assessing Reasoning Through Writing: Developing and Examining Approaches Based on Psychological and Linguistic Theories* (Ann Arbor, MI: UMI, 2006), 53.

57. See Gregory P. Fewster, *Creation Language in Romans 8: A Study in Monosemy*, Linguistic Biblical Studies 8 (Leiden: Brill, 2013), 42.

58. *LDF*, 184. Italics his.

59. See *GGBB*, 625 for a discussion of this passage.

60. An interesting study on the participle with special attention to the genitive absolute was written by the Healeys. Of course, they did not relate it to SFL. See Phyllis M Healey, and Alan Healey, "Greek circumstantial Participles: Tracking Participants with Participles in the Greek New Testament," *Occasional Papers in Translation and Text-Linguistics* 4 no. 3 (1990):173–259. The Healeys' discussion focuses in the genitive adverbial participial clause (Genitive Absolute) but seeing the need to compare the genitive adverbial participial with the nominative circumstantial participial clause, they present a fair discussion of the adverbial participle in the New Testament. Among seven characteristics presented, they state, "Circumstantial participial clauses have a semantic relationship to another whole clause or larger unit." See Ibid., 180.

61. Frances Christie, *Classroom Discourse Analysis: A Functional Perspective* (London: Continuum, 2005), 12.

62. *LDF*, 181.

63. Mabel L. Lang, *Herodotean Narrative and Discourse* (Cambridge, MA: Harvard University Press, 1984), 2.

64. *LDF*, 181.

65. Lang, *Herodotean*, 2.

66. Halliday, *Introduction to Functional Grammar*, 101.

67. Halliday, *On Grammar*, 198.

68. Ibid., 198–99.

69. Ibid., 199.

70. Halliday, *On Grammar*, 356.

71. Runge, Why I am not a Systemic Functional Linguist, § 12.

72. *PVA*, 90.

73. Ibid. See Decker, *Temporal Deixis*, 22.

74. Italics.

75. Bold letters.

76. The impression drawn for this part is that more than a clause analysis is necessary in the discussion of the verbal aspect and discourse prominence. Thus, this research departs from Porter's

arguments about aspect solely in terms of clause and either-or option, and discourse prominence. A wider analysis seems to be necessary in a number of places, especially in those with greater clause complexity.

77. Fleischmann, *Discourse-Pragmatics*, 2.

78. Suzanne Fleischmann, and Linda R.Waugh, "Introduction," in *Discourse-Pragmatics and the Verb: The Evidence from Romance*, edited by Suzanne Fleischmann and Linda R (London: Routledge, 1991), 2.

79. The present research is arguing for a threefold distinction, that of, mood (indicative), modal (subjunctive, optative, and imperative), and modulation (participle).

80. There are at least 2.600 verbs that Porter thinks are aspectually vague (εἰμί, φημί, κεῖμαι [even ἵστημι]. Thus, ἦν ἐστώς (periphrastic participle) could be added in this class. See *PVA*, 181.

81. *GGBB*, 642–43.

82. See *LDF*, 183.

83. *SRG*, 195.

84. Palmer, *Mood*, 4.

85. Mesfin Awoke Bekalu, "Presupposition in News Discourse," *Discourse & Society SAGE Publication* 17 no. 2 (2006):152.

86. *Contra* Daniel Wallace who thinks that in the "historical present" the aspect collapses. See *GGBB*, 643. See *SRG*, 200–204.

87. See *PVA*, 94.

88. Margaret G. Sim, "Particles and Participles: A Helpful Partnership," in *Discourse Studies & Biblical Interpretation: A Festschrift in Honor of Stephen H. Levinsohn*, edited by Steven E. Runge (Bellingham, WA: Logos Bible Software, 2011), 225.

89. Ibid., 94.

90. BDF confirms this saying that "the logical relation of the circumstantial participle to the rest of the sentence is not expressed by the participle itself (apart from the future participle), but is to be deduced from the context." Robertson also agrees as he states, "in itself … the participle does not express time, manner, cause, purpose, condition or concession. These ideas are not in the participle, but are merely suggested by the context." *ATR*, 1124

91. Halliday, *On Grammar*, 39. With regarding to verbs in Greek there is *Aktiosart* which is a combination of the pragmatic value of lexis + context. See Decker, *Temporal Deixis*, 28 from whom the chart above was borrowed and adapted.

92. Ibid, 39. Lexis is the denotative value of the word itself. See Decker, *Temporal Deixis*, 27 for further explanation. Halliday points out that "there is no one /one correspondence in exponence between the item which enters into lexical relations and any one of the grammatical units." There is even a distinction between lexis and word. "Word" is related to a grammatical unit. Halliday, *On Grammar*, 59. See M.A.K. Halliday, "Lexis as a linguistic level," in *Memory of J.R. Firth*, edited by C. E. Bazell et al. (London: Longman, 1996), 150–61. See also M.A.K. Halliday, "Language as System and Language as Instance: the Corpus as a Theoretical Construct," in *Directions in Corpus Linguistics: Proceedings of Nobel Symposium* 82 no. 4–8, edited by Jan Svartvik (Berlin: Mouton de Gruyter, 1991), 61–77.

93. Stanley E. Porter and Matthew Brook O'Donnell, "The Greek Verbal Network," 14 (2001):12. Cline is here used as a system of terms related along a single dimension made up of a continuum carrying potentially infinite gradation. See M. A. K. Halliday, *Halliday: System and function in language*, Selected papers, edited by Gunther Kress (London: Oxford University Press, 1978), 55–56.

94. Teun A. Van Dijk, *Texto Y Contexto: Semántica y Pragmática del Discurso* (Madrid: Cátedra, 1980), 290. Translation: the relationships between proposition or phrases in a given discourse cannot be described exhaustively only in terms of semantics.

95. Jeffrey T. Reed, *A Discourse Analysis of Philippians: Method and Rhetoric in the Debate Over Literary Integrity. JSNTSup* 136 (Sheffield: Sheffield Academic Press, 1997), 59.

96. Nathan Salmon. "Two Conceptions of Semantics," in *Semantics vs. Pragmatics*, edited by Szabó, Zoltán Gendler (Oxford, UK: Clarendon Press [u.a.], 2005), 317.

97. Bernard Comrie, *Tense*, Cambridge Textbooks in Linguistics (Cambridge, MA: Cambridge University Press, 1985), 23. He recognizes that "the major test for distinguishing between what is part of the meaning of a sentence and that sentence's implicatures is that the latter, but not the former, can be cancelled."

98. Juliane House, *Translation Quality Assessment: A Model Revisited*, Tübingen Beiträgen zur Linguistik 410 (Tübingen: Narr, 1997). 37.

99. Jeffrey T Reed, "Language of Change and the Changing of Language: A Sociolinguistic Approach to Pauline Discourse," in *Diglossia and Other Topics in New Testament Linguistics*, edited by Stanley Porter, *JSNTSup* 193 (Sheffield: Sheffield Academic Press, 2000), 131.

100. See van Dijk, *Context and Language*, 40–41.

101. M. A. K. Halliday, *Language as Social Semiotic: The Social Interpretation of Language and Meaning* (London: Edward Arnold, 1978), 28 ff, and 109 ff.

102. B. Malinowski, "The Problem of Meaning in Primitive Languages," in *The Meaning of Meaning*, edited by C. K. Ogden and I. A. Richards (New York, NY: Harcourt, Brace and Company, 1956) 312.

103. Ibid., 327.

104. Ibid.

105. Gustavo Martín-Asensio, *Transitivity-Based Foregrounding in the Acts of the Apostles: A Functional-Grammatical Approach to the Lukan Perspective*, *JSNTSup* 202 (Sheffield: Sheffield Academic Press, 2000), 32.

106. J. R. Firth, "Selected papers of J. R. Firth, 1952–1959," edited by F. R. Palmer (London: Longmans, 1968), 169.

107. Ibid., 13.

108. J. R. Firth, *Speech* (London: Benn's Sixpenny Library, 1930), 155.

109. J. R. Firth, "Selected papers," 29.

110. Matthew B. O'Donnell, "Designing and Compiling a Register-Balanced Corpus of Hellenistic Greek for the Purpose of Linguistic Description and Investigation," in *Diglossia and Other Topics in New Testament Linguistics*, edited by Stanley E. Porter, *JSNTSup* 193 (Sheffield: Sheffield Academic Press, 2000), 255.

111. Halliday, *Language*, 31–35, 60–63; Christopher S. Butler, *Systemic Linguistics: Theory and Applications* (London: Batsford, 1985), 67; Stanley E. Porter, "Greek Grammar and Syntax," in *The Face of New Testament Studies: A Survey of Recent Research*, edited by Scot McKnight and Grant R. Osborne (Grand Rapids, MI: Baker Academia/Apollos, 2004), 92–96; Matthew B. O'Donnell, "a Register-Balanced Corpus of Hellenistic Greek", 255–287.

112. *TBF*, 34.

113. Halliday, *Language*, 137. See chapter 1, footnote 143.

114. M. A. K. Halliday, *Learning How to Mean—Explorations in the Development of Language* (London: Edward Arnold, 1975), 51.

115. Ibid., 51–53.

116. M. A. K. Halliday, *Language*, 68.

117. Christian Matthiessen, "Representational Issues in Systemic Functional Grammar," in *Systemic Functional Approach to Discourse: Selected Papers from the 12th International Systemic Workshop*, edited by James D. Benson and William S. Greaves, Advances in Discourse Processes 26 (Norwood, NJ: Ablex Publishing Corporation, 1988), 138. Italics added.

118. Halliday, *Language*, 137.

119. Halliday, *Learning How to Mean*, 126.

120. Jeffrey T Reed, "Language of Change and the Changing of Language: A Sociolinguistic Approach to Pauline Discourse," in *Diglossia and Other Topics in New Testament Linguistics*, edited by Stanley Porter, *JSNTSup* 193 (Sheffield: Sheffield Academic Press, 2000), 131.

121. Ibid.

122. M. A. K. Halliday, "Notes on Transitivity and Theme in English. Part 1," *Journal of Linguistics* 3 no. 1 (1967): 38. Transitivity has to do with the "'deeper' aspects of the relations between verbs and the phrases associated with them." See Butler, *Systemic*, 164.

123. Halliday, *On Grammar*, 189–190.

124. Butler, *Systemic*, 172.

125. Halliday, *On Grammar*, 175.

126. Lang, *Herodotean Narrative*, 2. See also Mabel L. Lang, "Participial Motivation in Thucydides," *Mnemosyne* 48 (1995):49. Linguistic motivation has as a point of departure cognition, which is the "information-processing system that we consider central to the human condition ...." They include, amongst others, bodily experience, emotion, perception, action, social and communicative interaction, culture—and language. See Klaus-Uwe Panther and Günter Radden, "Introduction: Reflections on motivation revisited," in *Motivation in Grammar and the Lexicon*, edited by Klaus-Uwe Panther (Amsterdam: John Benjamins, 2011), 1.

127. He states, "several verbs discussed in this section may also be construed with a dynamic or declarative *infinitive*." Rijksbaron, *The Syntax and Semantics*, 121.

128. Ibid., 121, he calls this participle "dominant."

129. Ibid., 118. Hayase states, "Perception is in general closely related to Cognition, the prototype of the dangling participle situations, and serve as one of its metaphorical source domains." Naoko Hayase, "The Cognitive Motivation for the use of Dangling Participles in English," in *Motivation in Grammar and the Lexicon*, edited by Klaus-Uwe Panther and Günter Radder (Amsterdam: John Benjamins, 2011), 96.

130. Bernd Kortmann, *Adverbial Subordination: A Typology and History of Adverbial Subordinators Based on European Language* (Berlin: Mouton de Gruyter, 1997), 31–32.

131. Butler, *Systemic*, 172.

132. Halliday, *On Grammar*, 175. The definition of *text* here follows Halliday who says, "a text is an intersubjective event, in which speaker and listener exchange meaning in a context of situation." See Halliday, *Essentials*, 362. A *sentence* is a grammatical unit which consists of two or more words that bear minimal syntactic relation to the words that precede or follow it. See Halliday, *On Grammar*, 26.

133. Reed, "Language of Change and the Changing of Language," 131. Italics his.

134. Halliday, *Language*, 56–57.

135. Butler, *Systemic*, 25.

136. Halliday, *Language*, 60. Halliday defines unit as "that category to which corresponds a segment of the linguistic material about which statements are to be made." M. A. K. Halliday, "Grammatical Categories in Modern Chinese," in *Studies in Chinese Language*. The Collected

Works 8, edited by M. A. K. Halliday and Jonathan Webster (London: Continuum, 2006). 212. See Butler, *Systemic*, 14.

137. John Lyons, *Structural Semantics: An Analysis of Part of the Vocabulary of Plato* (Oxford, UK: Basil Blackwell, 1963), 51.

138. Ruth M. Kempson, *Presupposition and the Delimitation of Semantics*, Cambridge Studies in Linguistics 15 (Cambridge, MA: Cambridge University Press, 1975), 31–32.

139. P. F. Strawson, "*On Referring*," Mind LIX (1950), 320–344, reprinted in *Strawson, Logico-Linguistic Papers* (London: Harvard University Press, 1962). Strawson, *Introduction to Logical Theory* (Abingdon, Oxon: Routledge, 2011).

140. Bertrand Rusell, "On Denoting," *Mind* 14 no 56 (1905): 479–93.

141. Kempson, *Presupposition*, 33–4. Linguists, such as Strawson, condemn the idea of a presupposition of sentences arguing that true or false belong to statements not to sentences. See P. F. Strawson, "*On Referring*," Mind LIX (1950), 320–344, and Strawson. *Introduction to Logical Theory* (Abingdon, Oxon: Routledge, 2011). However, Kempson and Lemmon think that both sentences and statements have true or false condition, thus it does not matter which terminology one chooses. See Kempson, *Presupposition*, 52, and E. J. Lemmon. "Sentences, statements, and propositions," in Bernard Arthur Owen Williams, and Alan Montefiore, *British Analytical Philosophy* (New York: Humanities Press, 1966), 91 respectively.

142. Ibid., 47. Linguists who see presupposition as entailment include C. J. Fillmore. "Types of lexical information," in *Studies in Syntax and Semantics*, edited by Ferenc Kiefer (Dordrecht: D. Reidel, 1969), 109–37; and E. L. Keenan, "Two Kinds of Presupposition in Natural Language," in *Studies in Linguistic Semantics*, eds. C. J. Fillmore, and D. T. Langendoen (Holt: Rinehart & Winston, 1971), 45–54.

143. Stephen C Levinson, *Pragmatics* (Cambridge, MA: Cambridge University Press, 2000), 199.

144. Levinson's arguments have found a strong response by some scholars. See Gennaro Chierchia, and Sally McConnell-Ginet, *Meaning and Grammar: An Introduction to Semantics* (Cambridge, MA: MIT Press, 2000), 355.

145. Reed, *A Discourse Analysis of Philippians*, 59.

146. Ibid., 188–189.

147. This agrees with C. J. Fillmore, "Types of lexical information," 109–137.

148. Leckie-Tarry, *Language and Context*, 159.

149. Reed, *A Discourse Analysis of Philippians*, 105–106.

150. Jeffrey Reed states, "as of yet no convincing research has been proposed which applies to large selections of Koiné Greek discourse" concerning given-new applied to the study of Greek in the New Testament. Jeffrey T. Reed, "Identifying Theme in the New Testament: Insights from Discourse Analysis," in *Discourse Analysis and Other Topics in Biblical Greek*, edited by Stanley E. Porter and D. A. Carson. *JSNTSup* 113 (Sheffield: Sheffield Academic Press, 1995), 79.

151. M. A. K. Halliday, "Notes on Transitivity and Theme in English, Part 2," *JL* 3 (1967):199–244. While Halliday's distinction of the information categories had broad acceptance in New Testament studies, seen, especially in the writings of Reed and Porter, Halliday's perspective provokes significant differences between SFL and Functional Grammar, on the one hand, and Role and Reference Grammar on the other. Christopher S. Butler, "Focusing on Focus: A Comparison of Functional Grammar, Role and Reference Grammar and Systemic Functional Grammar, *LS* 27 (2005): 585–618.

152. Theme is information central to the author's message, and in narrative it consists of major participants. See *TBF*, 202.

153. Given information is that which is presented as recoverable from the previous discourse and is indicated by the participles. See Reed, "Identifying Theme in the New Testament", 79.

154. Reed, "Identifying Theme in the New Testament", 80.

155. See Robin Fawcett, *A Theory of Syntax for Systemic Functional Linguistics* (Amsterdam: John Benjamins, 2000), 33–43.

156. *SRG*, 203.

157. M. P. Williams, "Functional Sentence Perspective in the Context of Systemic Functional Grammar," in *Pragmatics, Discourse and Text: Some Systemically-Inspired Approaches*, edited by Steiner and Veltman (London: Pinter Publishers, 1988), 77–78.

158. Further studies should prove this assumption.

159. G. Hudson, Essential Introductory Linguistics (Grand Rapids, MI: Blackwell Publishers Inc. 2000), 322. See Kempson. *Presupposition*, 50. See also R. Garner, "Presupposition in Philosophy and Linguistics," in *Studies in Linguistic Semantics*, edited by Charles J. Fillmore and D. Terence Langendoen (New York, NY: Holt, Rinehart and Winston, 1971), 23–42.

160. Ibid., 53.

161. Halliday, *System and function in language*, 174.

162. There are three types of prominence. The first is "thematic" (what a person is talking about). This type of prominence is typically what theme-rheme describe. Another type is "focus" (the most important information in a given setting). The third type of prominence is called "emphasis" proper (expression of feeling or indication of an unexpected event). These last two are related to the functional role of Given-New. See Callow, *Discourse Considerations*, 50–52, and Simon C. Dik, *Functional Grammar* (Amsterdam: N-Holland, 1978), 19.

163. Ibid.

164. Ibid., 179.

165. M. A. K. Halliday, *English Language*. The Collected Works of M. A. K. Halliday, edited by Jonathan J. Webster 7 (London/New York, NY: Continuum, 2005), 60.

166. Either the speaker is giving something to the listener (a piece of information, for example) or he is demanding something from him … giving means 'inviting to receive', and demanding means 'inviting to give'. The speaker is not only doing something himself; he is also requiring something of the listener. Halliday, *Introduction to Functional Grammar*, 68.

167. Reed, "Identifying Theme in the New Testament," 80.

168. Martin Culy, "The Clue is in the Case: Distinguishing Adjectival and Adverbial Participles," *PRS* 30.4 (2003): 441. Culy has not been without opposition. One of them is Grant Edwards in his thesis entitled *The Validity of Oblique Adverbial Participles in the Greek of the New Testament*. Grant Edwards, *The Validity of Oblique Adverbial Participles in the Greek of the New Testament* (ThM thesis, Dallas Theological Seminary, 2007). The core of Edwards' critique of Culy's proposal is an examination of every oblique participle in the New Testament, evaluating each to see if it is functioning adverbially or adjectivally. He begins with a group of 1303 accusative and dative participles and narrows this down to 75 oblique participles which he believes may possibly be functioning adverbially. He concludes that there are 28 unambiguous examples of oblique adverbial participles, 14 compelling examples, and 33 inconclusive examples. Culy is right in his conclusion that adverbial participles will always be nominative. Oblique participles are marked as modifying words functioning in other capacities. Edwards seems to overlook much of these pieces of information. In his analysis, he focuses more on determining function first, apart from a word's case. Take, for example, Acts 9:39 ἀναστὰς δὲ Πέτρος συνῆλθεν αὐτοῖς· ὃν παραγενόμενον ἀνήγαγον εἰς τὸ ὑπερῷον (So rising, Peter went with them, who, having arrived,

they led to the upper. Edwards classifies παραγενόμενον as an adverbial participle of time, since "it is hard to imagine a participle attributively modifying a relative pronoun" (p. 32). But this is the case only in English; in the Greek it is exactly what is going on. Here, παραγενόμενον, being in the accusative case is modifying ὅν, which is in the accusative case since it is the direct object of ἀνήγαγον. The case agreement and the fact that it immediately follows ὅν both point toward the fact that this participle is functioning as an adjectival modifier of a pronoun. Edwards takes both πορευομένῳ and ἐγγίζοντι as adverbs of time in Acts 22:6 (pp. 27–28). Yet again the syntax is clear, they are dative because they are modifying μοι adjectivally. Edwards classifies ἀναγομένοις in Acts 28:10 as a temporal adverbial participle (p. 48), which is how most Bible versions also translate it. However, a close examination of the context shows that ἀναγομένοις is dative because it is functioning as the substantive dative indirect object of the main verb of the clause. It tells to whom something was being bestowed. While it is probably accurate to say that they bestowed on them when they were leaving, the syntax of the verse makes it clear that in this case the participle is serving as the indirect object of the verb, thus indicating who was the recipient of the bestowing. Many other examples such as these could be found to demonstrate the differences in classification between this study and Edwards', but they all follow generally the same pattern. Edwards tends to examine the participle's function first before he has fully dealt with the syntax of the verse, which leads him to look to translational or English based arguments to defend an adverbial classification of an oblique participle.

169. Ibid.
170. Ibid., 453.
171. *SRG*, 199.
172. The relation between Given-New regards the understanding of the distinction between the presupposed information that provide the framework for processing and handling of the focal information. Runge states, "each clause contains a mix of presupposed and newly asserted information, the focus of the clause may be more specifically defined as the difference between what is presupposed in a context and what is asserted." See *SRG*, 189.
173. *SRG*, 204.
174. Ibid., 187.
175. Robert A. Dooley and Stephen H. Levinsohn, *Analyzing Discourse: A Manual of Basic Concepts* (Dallas, TX: SIL International, 2001), 10.
176. *SRG*, 188.
177. Ibid.,189. Italic his.
178. Danny D. Steinberg, and Leon A. Jakobovits, *Semantics: An Interdisciplinary Reader in Philosophy Linguistics and Psychology* (Cambridge: Cambridge University Press, 1978), 261.
179. See Simon Dik, *The Theory of Functional Grammar: Part 1: The Structure of the Clause* (Dordrecht: Foris, 1989), 363.
180. *SRG*, 207.
181. Ibid., 244–245.
182. Ibid.
183. Deborah Schiffrin, Deborah Tannen, and Heidi Ehernberger Hamilton, *The Handbook of Discourse Analysis* (Malden, MA: Blackwell Pub, 2007), 120.
184. Knud Lambrecht, *Information Structure and Sentence Form: Topic, Focus, and the Mental Representations of Discourse Referents* (Cambridge, MA: Cambridge University Press, 1994), 207. Phrased negatively focus refers to those constituents which cannot be omitted without "depriving the utterance of some information value." See Ibid., 215. However, Lambrecht does not

allow for the existence of multiple focus within a clause which is contrary to Halliday's systemic functional linguistic that asserts that focus may be separated into more focal and less focal elements in a clause. Halliday, "Notes on Transitivity", 200–2008.

185. *LDF*, 184.
186. Reed, "Identifying Theme in the New Testament," 83.
187. Rijksbaron, *Syntax*, 121.
188. Lightfoot, *Logic*, 41–42.
189. *SRG*, 194.
190. Halliday, *On Grammar*, 180.
191. *GGBB*, 613.
192. Ibid., 616.
193. Romulo Monteiro in his book *Caminhando na Perfeição: a perseverança dos santos em Hebreus.* Niteroi, RJ: 2018, applies the idea of the participles as a factive presupposition for the interpretation of the warning passages.
194. Halliday, *Functional Grammar*, 68.
195. *GGBB*, 642.
196. *SRG*, 145.
197. Ibid., 6.
198. *GGBB*, 643.
199. Donald E. Hardy, *Narrating Knowledge*, 48–51.
200. *SRG*, 243.
201. *LDF*, 187. See another example in Act 28:23 "... πείθων τε αὐτοὺς τὰ περὶ τοῦ Ἰησοῦ ...."
202. *SRG*, 151.

CHAPTER THREE

Greek Participles: Modulation Versus Modality and Mood

One of the basic tenets of this study is that the distinction between semantics and pragmatics, and a careful analysis of the nature of a semantic presupposition, present the guidelines to avoid any misunderstanding in the study of the participles. The most common understanding of the upgraded participial effect must include a clear analysis of the differences between a factive presupposition (modulation) and the meaning conveyed by the moods.

The specific distinction between modulation and mood will help us to consider the explanation for the phenomenon of having an anarthrous aorist adverbial participle that precedes the main verb and that is so closely connected to the main clause that the readers get the impression in their mind that the aorist participle is upgraded to the mood of the main clause. This is the reason we call it an upgraded participle.

The way the word mood occurs here varies. In the system network—grammar, all the Greek moods are related to assertion. However, in SFL, all the options in the verbal system network occur in opposition to each other. Thus, assertion (moods) is divided into two subsystems, + assertion (mood - indicative), and – assertion (modal/modality - imperative, subjunctive, and optative). In this study, if the contrast described is between the participle modal semantics and assertion, the use of the word mood encompasses both mood and modal/modality, whether +assertion or –assertion.

If the contrast is with the indicative alone, the word mood will be used in the more restricted sense, excluding the modal/modality forms, since the assumption of this study is that, strictly speaking, only the indicative grammaticalizes +assertion. If, on the other hand, the contrast is between the participle and –finite, the word modal or modality will be used. In other words, the participles are out of the attitude system.

Having made this qualification, it is important to proceed to a semantic discussion that considers the difference between the verbal form used to grammaticalize attitude (mood and modal) and the verbal form that blocks attitude and grammaticalizes presupposition (modulation). Specifically, it will stress the relation of the participle that suffers the upgraded effect. Although closely connected and even being upgraded into the mood/modal of the main clause, the participle always will be a participle by form, and it is out of the attitude system ±assertion (mood/modal).

Jeffrey Reed is among a handful of writers who have done a modest analysis of the role of modalities and their focal task in New Testament Greek. Unfortunately, the relation of the participles with mood and modality has not been included, except by Levinsohn and Runge in their Discourse Grammar. Reed mentions the importance of this matter and is quoted here at length:

> Modality plays a role in distinguishing between background and thematic prominence. Under normal circumstances one would expect an audience to be more interested in what is asserted as real or factual (indicative mood). What someone asserts as actually happening is likely to be the centre of attention in discourse as opposed to what is merely projected or purported to happen (i.e., what might, may, could occur). Accordingly, the indicative mood tends to grammaticalize thematic material. The subjunctive and the optative, because their function is essentially that of 'non-assertion' or 'projection', are used with background material. This partly explains their frequent use in subordinate clauses (e.g., purpose clauses) which typically play a rhetorically supportive role. The imperative mood, however, regularly plays a thematic role, probably because of its forceful pragmatic function.[1]

To understand how modulation, mood and modality relate to each other, it is necessary to know the relationship between the semiotic components of the situation and the functional components of semantics involved. Since the participle belongs to the ideational metafunction, which is one of the functional components, more attention is given to it.

To determine the semantic meaning of the modulation-form (participle) both the principle of contrastive comparison and the principle of cancelability are accepted. Since a participial form is used in context with varying meaning, then the conclusion is that this difference of meaning in the context is not a result of the formal designation but some other feature in the context. Therefore, if any meaning that has been related to a formal designation can be changed in certain contexts, we must conclude that this meaning is not part of the modulation-form semantic meaning.

Function and Form: Semiotic Component and Functional Component

Function is seen here as a result of contextual factors and linguistic forms.[2] Halliday has already established relationships between these features.[3] There are three functional components in a grammar of a natural language according to systemic linguistics: ideational, interpersonal, and textual.

The first functional component in a grammar is the ideational metafunction by which human experiences are construed. Through this function, humans make sense of reality as it is perceived, both the world outside of them and the world of their own inner consciousness.[4] This ideational function "corresponds to what people usually think of as 'meaning' in the ordinary sense; that is, 'content', especially 'referential content'."[5]

Halliday explains this function as "language taking over the material processes and conditions of human existence and transforming them into meanings."[6] By choices from the transitivity network, the writer seeks to guide the readers through the text, and he or she highlights episodes or themes at various levels of meaning according to his writing strategy.[7] As already mentioned, transitivity within which choices have to do with the representation of experience describes the functional elements of process, participants, and circumstances.[8] The discussion of the participles (modulation) belongs to this metafunction, while the Greek moods/modals are related to the interpersonal metafunction.

The second component in a grammar is the interpersonal metafunction by which social and personal relationships are enacted.[9] There is an exchange between the ideational and interpersonal functions. Human experiences are understood "in the course of, and by means of, being acted out interpersonally."[10] At the same time that human experiences are construed interpersonally, the interpersonal relations are "enacted in the course of, and by means of, being construed ideationally."[11] Through the interpersonal function, identity and self-awareness are established.[12]

Halliday's model aims to relate linguistics to the effects they have on the readers, and mood which describes the speaker's attitude is related to this function.[13] The concept will play an important role between the upgraded effect of the aorist participle and its relation to the other moods. The ideational metafunction (participle) and the interpersonal metafunction (mood and modal/modality) are so closely related to each other contextually that the formal designation (participial form) fluctuates in the readers' perspective. For instance, Hebrews 6:1 "ἀφέντες … φερώμεθα" (Let us leave … let us go on). The urgency of the exhortation makes the participle (in the readers' mind) to be upgraded into the same subjunctive mood of the main process.

A specific formal designation (aorist participle) that is outside of the attitude system, acts as though it is inside of the attitude system realized by the moods that belong to the interpersonal metafunction. This relation that occurs within a given context gives the impression that the participial modulation is "upgraded" (cognitively) to the same mood of the main clause.[14] The explanation for this pragmatic phenomenon has to do with the ideational function of the participle.

The third functional component in a grammar is the textual metafunction. This metafunction is what materializes the semiotic and the functional components since it is what creates discourse by combining human experience and their personal relations into a spoken or written text.

Assertive and Non-assertive Attitudes

Since meaning exists as an interaction of these components within a particular context, the relationship between the participle (seen in this study as a modulation) and the moods (±assertion) will be discussed.

The interpersonal metafunction provides for interaction between people by allowing social and individual attitudes, assessment, and the like. Mood is that grammatical feature that defines roles which people may take as they communicate with each other whereby the writer/speaker can choose his or her own communication role by making assertion, commanding something, expressing doubts, and the like.[15]

If communication is to take place between a speaker/writer and the listener/reader, he or she "must impose a particular perspective on the text, a 'patterning of patterns' that unifies the composition, investing it with at least a minimal amount of structure and direction."[16] The speaker is an intruder into reality[17] and the choices made by him or her at one point tend to determine and be determined by the choices he makes at another.[18]

Within the network of the Greek verb, two simultaneous systems are involved: Aspectuality (not included in the chart below) and Finiteness. Considering finiteness of verbs as in the chart above, there is a semantic distinction between limitation and lack of limitation, and the person of the verb is a mark of

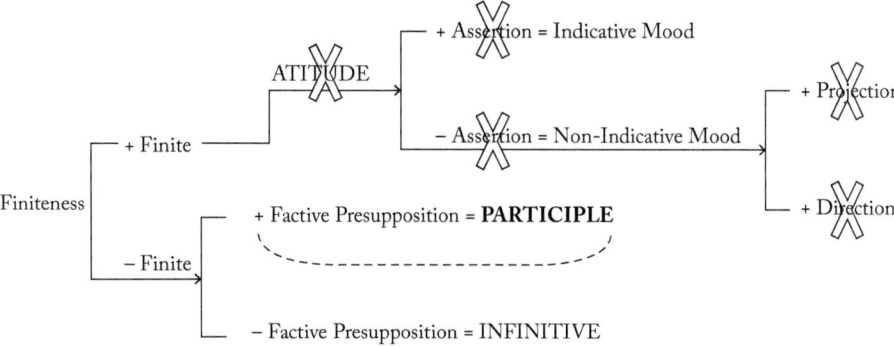

Figure 3.1. Semantic network with a choice of the participle.

this limit. For instance, Matthew 2:14 ὁ δὲ *ἐγερθεὶς* **παρέλαβεν** τὸ παιδίον καὶ τὴν μητέρα αὐτοῦ νυκτὸς … (Then he *got up* [and] **took** the child and his mother by night …). The main verb in this clause is παρέλαβεν, and this verbal form grammaticalizes among other things, the pronoun *he* (the subject of this verb), thus the writer is making one assertion, that is, *he took*.

On one side, by the indicative mood, the author makes an assertion about what is put forward as the condition of reality; in other words, the writer sees this event as a reality whether or not there is a factual basis for such an assertion.[19] On the other side, the participle ἐγερθείς is not even a part of the attitude system, therefore it does not grammaticalize the "user's perspective on the relation of the verbal action to reality."[20] There is no person in the participle. There are number (singular), and gender (masculine), that help the readers to make the logical relation on the entire discourse or the order of the constituent, among other features. Blocking the person of the verb takes it out of the attitude system where ±assertion is available. This choice sets the participles on the -finite choice, leaving out two other options: ±factive presupposition.

Halliday points out that the interpersonal metafunction depends on the systems of mood, and a text is an intersubjective event in which speaker and listener exchange meaning in a context of situation.[21] Modulation demands from the reader/listener much more than mood or modal. As a modulation, the participle blocks its attitude so that the attention should be directed to the main verb.

By choosing a participle, an author blocks his assessment about any given action having the attendant circumstances opened so that the reader can be drawn into the discourse in order to connect the parts, infer some points, or assume something. Thus, being part of the ideational metafunction, the adverbial participle as a *presupposition sounds like an impetus to action and it is used to effect a transition from one state or action to another.*[22] For instance, Matthew 2:13–14 has four adverbial participles ἀναχωρησάντων, λέγων, ἐγερθείς [2x] that form a logical clause chain that connects the embedded clauses to the main clause indicating this transition as it keeps the reader involved in mental exercise.

"Departing" (ἀναχωρησάντων) draws them to the event that follows, while "saying" (λέγων) introduces a dramatic pause, creating a sort of expectation. "Get up" (ἐγερθείς) in close association to the main imperative verb "take" (παράλαβε) hurries up the pace that finally finds some relief with another upgraded effect, this time with the indicative "then he rose and took the child and his mother by night and departed." The tension is raised by the first upgraded effect, but it occurs as a relief with the second upgraded effect. In this passage, the presupposed information items indicated by the participles in each embedded clause change with each new clause, based upon what kind of mental exercise the writer wants to share.

The chart above also demonstrates that +finite describes verbs whose form makes the person clearly explicit, while –finite describes verbs in which person is not part of its form. This lack of limitation makes it possible for these -finite verbs to function both as elements in the structure of the predicate and as elements in subjects, complements, and adjuncts. As a speaker/writer selects to use a -finite verb, two further semantic features are available: +factive presupposition, and – factive presupposition.[23] The +factive presupposition is the only one discussed here.

Porter uses the language of slot and filler for both mood and the participles in Greek. He says that whenever a finite verb[24] is picked up to fill a slot, the content that fills that slot brings an indication of the attitude as grammaticalized by choosing the mood.[25] In accordance with this feature, Rijksbaron expresses what is involved with the Greek moods when he asserts, "the moods enable the speaker to 'clothe' his utterances in such a way as to express his attitude towards their contents, according to the situation in which he produces the utterance and the nature of the information which he wants to convey."[26]

In his grammar, Daniel Wallace appears to disagree with two types of definition with regard to mood: first, he disagrees with a definition that treats mood as having an objective correspondence to reality.[27] Second, he states that "to say that mood 'indicates how the speaker *regards* what he or she is saying with respect to its factuality'[28] seems to suggest that the speaker is attempting to draw an accurate portrayal of the verbal action."[29] Thus, Wallace defines mood as "*the morphological feature of a verb that a speaker uses to **portray** his or her affirmation as to the certainty of the verbal action or state (whether an actuality or potentiality).*"[30] Regardless of the different definitions, one common element of the semantics of the mood is the speaker's (subjective) attitude, and even Wallace's definition will accommodate it.[31]

Porter accuses the traditional analysis of considering the subjective nature of the mood only on the non-indicative moods.[32] However, a close analysis of the several grammarians will show that this not the case. They see both the indicative and the non-indicative moods as having subjective features.[33] Thus, some of these recent critiques must be discounted.[34] Following his typological approach, Palmer suggests Realis and Irrealis for grammaticalization of the status of a proposition.[35]

Regardless of the bulk of discussion on definitions in Greek, mood grammaticalizes the speaker's attitude by the indicative and the non-indicative forms, and since Greek does not have the equivalent of modal verbs in English,[36] how can the participles be classified in this modal semantic?[37] The answer is related to the ideational metafunction.

While the interpersonal meaning relates to language as a social action, the ideational meaning relates to language as reflection.[38] Through the ideational meaning, "language … gives structure to experience, and helps to determine our way of looking at things, so that it requires some intellectual effort to see them in any other way than that which our language suggests to us."[39]

Even without dealing with the ideational function, grammarians like Wallace point out that the participles and the infinitives should not be put under the rubric of mood.[40] So how can they be classified? Most grammars label according to class that which will indicate such things as noun phrase, verb phrase, noun, verb, adjective, or adverb.[41] In this case the participle is a verbal adjective.[42]

The procedure here is to emphasize the meaning in relation to each other (paradigmatic choice) rather than the meaning in relation to the rest of the clause (syntagmatic). Thus, the two major categories of mood, such as epistemic (+ assertion [Realis]) and deontic (-assertion [Irrealis],[43] must be seen in opposition to each other, and the participle is out of the attitude system. Porter introduces the subject of modal semantics saying that,

> the Indicative is used for assertive or declarative statements …, while the non-Indicative forms grammaticalize a variety of related attitudes, having in common that they make no assertion about reality but grammaticalize simply the 'will of the speaker, and are therefore deontic.[44]

Strictly speaking, there is only one mood, which grammaticalizes assertion (indicative). The other supposed moods are actually modals or modalities that grammaticalize the "will of the speaker" (imperative, subjunctive, optative).[45] The choice of the participle implies something completely out of these two options. Modulation is on the side of the readers/listeners so that they can fill the open slot of the communication at hand, while mood is used for assertion, which is the author/speaker's own assessment of the action.

Mood is used to describe the will of the speaker, modulation presupposes shared knowledge where the readers/listener are committed to the truth of the proposition and is not concerned with statements of fact. Therefore, modulation is the third party in this set of options that will occur outside of the finiteness system that includes both mood and modal.

The modal semantics for the indicative is that of assertion. J. Gonda rightly states,

> If we may describe the verbal category of mood (such as it appears in Greek or Sanskrit) as a means of intimating the speaker's view or conception of the relation of the process expressed by the verb to reality, it will be clear that the main distinction made is between what the speaker puts forward as fact (whether it be true or not) and what he does not regard as such.[46]

The non-indicative moods in Greek (imperative, subjunctive, optative) are not used for assertion, but they describe some deontic attitude hypothesized or projected to a non-existent state, and they have in common the fact that they grammaticalize the volition of the speaker.[47] Another common element is their finiteness. Considering the finiteness of verbs, there is a semantic distinction between limitation and lack of limitation, and the person of the verb is a mark of this limit.[48]

For example, in the clause ἐλάλησεν ἡμῖν ἐν υἱῷ (*he has spoken* to us by Son), ἐλάλησεν grammaticalizes tense-form *aorist*, voice, *active;* mood, *indicative;* the person, *third person;* and number, *singular*. Easily the person of the verb is identified by the personal ending -ν. The same is true of both subjunctive κατέχωμεν τὴν ὁμολογίαν (present, active, subjunctive, first person plural), and optative χάρις ὑμῖν καὶ εἰρήνη πληθυνθείη (aorist, passive, optative, third person singular), and imperative πληροῦσθε ἐν πνεύματι (present, passive, imperative, second person plural).

The grammatical subject[49] is a meaningful function in the clause. The grammatical subject chosen by the speaker is used to accomplish the communication role he or she wants. In functional grammar, there are three "kinds of subject:" grammatical subject, logical subject,[50] and psychological subject.[51] Ephesians 5:18–21 poses an interesting illustration for this discussion. Paul says καὶ μὴ μεθύσκεσθε οἴνῳ, ἐν ᾧ ἐστιν ἀσωτία, ἀλλὰ πληροῦσθε ἐν πνεύματι, λαλοῦντες ... ᾄδοντες ... καὶ ψάλλοντες ... εὐχαριστοῦντες ... ὑποτασσόμενοι. There are couple of questions to be asked in this passage.[52]

If there is no dative for content, for the genitive renders this function,[53] then the Spirit is not the content with which believers are filled. With what are they filled then? ἐν πνεύματι [ἐν + dative] cannot be the subject of this verb, thus who is the subject of πληροῦσθε? Finally, what is the function of Spirit here? The speaker's communication role is found in clauses of all moods, but in this passage, Paul requires some action (even with passive) on the part of the Ephesians, but only they (not the Spirit) have the capacity to obey or disobey Paul's command.[54]

The subject grammaticalized by the imperative (-assertion) πληροῦσθε is deontic (or modal, Irrealis), that is, the listener who accedes fulfilling the function defined by the speaker's role. Thus, the grammatical subject here is the listener. ἐν πνεύματι is the logical subject, since it is the personal instrument for the filling. The logical subject is known as the actor that is part of the ideational function, the grammatical subject belongs to the interpersonal function realized by the mood.

The passive voice here begs for a psychological subject. It is not explicit in this passage, but it seems that Paul is assuming his readers followed his argument in the whole letter. Ephesians 1:23 points to Christ as the one who fills his church ἥτις ἐστὶν τὸ σῶμα αὐτοῦ, τὸ πλήρωμα *τοῦ* τὰ πάντα ἐν πᾶσιν *πληρουμένου*. The content that the believers are filled with is described in 3:10 ἵνα πληρωθῆτε εἰς πᾶν τὸ πλήρωμα τοῦ θεοῦ.[55]

Who is the subject of the participles λαλοῦντες … ἄδοντες … καὶ ψάλλοντες … εὐχαριστοῦντες … ὑποτασσόμενοι? While the indicative mood and the non-indicative moods grammaticalize subject, the participle and the infinitive do not. Having said that, the participle is not a mood at all, it is not a modal either. So, what is it?

The Greek participle is considered as a modulation, which is part of the modal semantics that in turn has as its semantic core the +factive presupposition.[56] In sum, with the exception of the Bible software that list the participle and infinitive with the moods, every grammar identifies the participle and infinitive as a verbal adjective outside the attitude system.[57] The upgraded effect in its combination of several features involves informational structure, pair of opposition between a modulation and a mood. The modulation is the non-focal part that points to the focal point realized by the moods.[58] This is what a participle is, a subject-blocked to open a slot that can be filled by the readers/listeners. In other word, it is quasi-modality as we will see below.

Modulation: Participle a *Quasi*-Modality

The closest function of the participle regarding its definition can be seen in the imperative. In the imperative, the speaker requires some action from the listener who accedes to it.[59] With the imperative, the listener/reader can either obey or disobey, and with the participle, the speaker/writer expects the listener/reader to meet certain conditions in order for the sentence to make sense.[60] Through a participle, a speaker/writer addresses the listener/reader who must accept the proposition in order for the utterance to be relevant for her/him.[61]

Following the analogy above, in one sense modulation is a *quasi*-modality (-assertion [deontic]). The verb itself is formed on the verb-stem, while the participle is formed on the tense-stem.[62] With the exception of the future participle, whose use diminished in the New Testament, the participle is widespread in the major tense forms (aorist, present and perfect).[63]

As a Greek modulation, the participles are subject to the main tense systems. So far ± assertions are being distinguished among themselves. Palmer rightly says, "Modals (-assertion=modality) have an important part to play in discourse, as the participants express their opinions and attitudes and, in general, interact with one another."[64] In Greek both indicative and non-indicative moods describe the speaker's attitude, therefore they are all moods.

Rijksbaron describes mood as enabling "the speaker to 'clothe' his utterances in such a way as to express his attitude towards their contents, according to the situation in which he produces the utterance and the nature of the information which he wants to convey."[65] Because the indicative is +assertion, it is called here mood, while −assertion, even though it is a mood, is called modal or modality since it is, to some extent, an invitation to the hearer/reader to play some limited part in the discourse.[66]

In ±assertions, either the speaker or the hearer/reader is grammaticalized by the verbal form. For instance, ἐλάλησεν (he has spoken); here the writer grammaticalizes the subject (-ν) and it is clearly an +assertion. If the verb is an −assertion, for instance, πληροῦσθε (*be filled* - imperative) the speaker chooses to address the listener/reader in some way as to require something from him or her. Observe that by the verbal form explicitly only the *modal subject* is grammaticalized, that is,

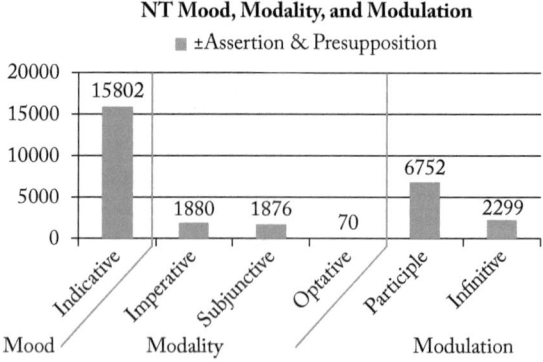

Figure 3.2. NT mood, modality, and modulation.

According to Logos Bible there are 3,741 present participles, 2,299 aorist participles, 699 perfect participles, and 13 future participles in the New Testament.

πληροῦσθε (-σθε). The subjunctive grammaticalized the speaker's projected mind, for instance, διέλθωμεν (-μεν [subject] – *let us go*).[67] In other words, only the indicative is an assertion; the other moods (subjunctive, optative, and imperative) are not assertion; and the participle is none of the above.

Both modulation and transitivity are part of the ideational metafunction in contrast to the interpersonal. Within a language system, three main areas of syntactic choices in the clause are available: transitivity, mood, and theme. Greek seems to work in the same way. We already defined transitivity as related to language with its cognitive content."[68] These characteristics work together to engage the reader in the dynamic of language, which, in the case of the participles, are used to relate the processes and things of the real world, a typical function of modulation.[69]

In summary, the participle is an inflected verbal adjective[70] and as such it shares two natures: verbal and adjectival. In its verbal nature there are tense and voice, and its adjectival nature grammaticalizes gender, number, and case.[71] The complex nature of the relationship between mood (mood and modality – indicative and non-indicative) and modulation (participle) is considered below.

λαλοῦντες does not grammaticalize person, but only number (plural), gender (masculine), and case (nominative). The participle does not have a grammatical subject but only a logical subject found in its relationship with the main verb, which is indicated by the nominative case.[72] It does not grammaticalize attitude, since it is not a mood, not even a modality.

The participle is on the side of the ideational metafunction, while mood (± assertion) is on the side of the interpersonal metafunction. However, as Halliday argues "nearly every utterance has both an ideational meaning, relating to the processes and things of the real world, and the interpersonal meaning relating to the roles and attitudes adopted and assigned by the speaker."[73] The independent participle, although rare in the NT, is a good illustration of an ideational meaning related to things of the real world without a need to be in the embedded clause of the main process.

Establishing these features in terms of marked pairs +assertion is uttered by the indicative mood, -assertion is accomplished by the non-indicative (subjunctive, optative, and imperative). Using verbal opposition, -assertion can be further divided in ±modal. +Modal, which is not an assertion but the speaker's attitude, is still grammaticalized even though the semantic role is much more on the side of the listener/reader (realized by imperative, subjunctive, and optative).

–Modal blocks the attitude, leaving the participle (even the infinitive) open as though it is fluctuating so that the listener/reader can play the most important part, that is, he or she is invited to presuppose something with the speaker that could not be uttered any other way.[74] Of course, the double entrance in systemic linguistics is ±finite. -Finite blocks the attitude system of which the mood and modality belong to.

The basic distinction between ±modal, is that if the qualification of the process resides in the speaker's own mind, then it is interpersonal, thus attitude is grammaticalized; *if the qualification of the process resides in the circumstances*, then it is ideational in function—it relates to a specific part of the content of the clause.[75] This does not mean that this analysis does not rely upon the discourse structure of Greek narratives, but only to the observance of the clausal structure. The clause is of paramount importance since it is within it that the relation of the participle to the main verb may be seen.

The observance of a given context in which the different nuances of the aorist participle occurred demonstrates that specific forms favor a specific context, which in turn reveals the various functions of the participle as a result of its semantics. Although the semantic core of the participle is factive presupposition, its functional role is so suitable that it able to have many pragmatic effects, one of which is the upgraded effect. Thus, we will use a study of this specific effect with its versatility of the participles as a result of being a factive presupposition. One participle connects with several features that make the participle to upgrade into the same mood of the main verb, and still being a participle as such, deserves our attention to which we start below.

Notes

1. Reed, "Identifying Theme in the New Testament," 86.
2. Leckie-Tarry, *Language and Context*, 31.
3. Halliday, *Language*, 123.
4. Halliday, *The Essential Halliday* (London: Continuum, 2009), 272.
5. M. A. K. Halliday, *The Collected Works 6: Computational and Quantitative Studies*, edited by Jonathan J. Webster (London: Continuum, 2005), 201.
6. Ibid.
7. *TBF*, 52.
8. Halliday, *Functional Grammar*, 101–44.
9. Halliday, *The Essential Halliday*, 272.
10. Halliday, *Computational and Quantitative Studies*, 201.
11. Ibid.
12. Halliday, *The Essential Halliday*, 272.
13. Halliday, *On Grammar*, 189.
14. A. C. Moorhouse, *The Syntax of Sophocles*, Mnemosyne, Bibliotheca Classica Batava, Supplementum 75 (Leiden: E. J. Brill, 1982), 250.
15. Halliday, *On Grammar*, 189.
16. *TBF*, 51–52.

17. Halliday, *On Grammar*, 199.
18. Ibid., 200.
19. *ATR*, 915; K. L. McKay, *Greek Grammar for Students: A Concise Grammar of Classical Attic with Special Reference to Aspect in the Verb* (Canberra: Dept. of Classics, Australian National University, 1974), 148; Porter, *Idioms*, 51.
20. Porter, *Idioms*, 50.
21. Halliday, *The Essential Halliday*, 362.
22. Lang, *Herodotean*, 13. Italics added.
23. *PVA*, 365–400.
24. Finite verbs, that include both indicative and non-indicative moods, are those that grammaticalize person, whether first, second or third.
25. Porter, *Idioms*, 50.
26. Rijksbaron, *Syntax*, 6.
27. *GGBB*, 444. Wallace acknowledges that this criticism is related to the indicative and not with the general definition of mood. Wallace is regarded as a grammar of reference for its treatment of the moods. See Decker. *Temporal Deixis*, 239 footnote 163.
28. Wallace cites Dana-Mantey's grammar as defining it in that way. See *DMG*, 168 (§ 162). Dana-Mantey actually see mood as having both that which is real and that which is possible. See *DMG*, 166 ((§ 161).
29. *GGBB*, 444. Italics his. Wallace sees the verbs as the portrayal of reality, not perception of it.
30. Ibid., 445. Emphasis his. McKay seems to be aligned with Wallace even though he phrases it in a different way. He says that function of the finite forms of the verb indicates the manner of presentation by distinguing between simple statement of fact or intention, expression of will, wish, generality, potentiality, etc. See K. L. McKay, *A New Syntax of the Verb in New Testament Greek: An Aspectual Approach. Studies in Biblical Greek 5* (New York: Peter Lang, 1994), 53.
31. *GGBB*, 444, footnote 3.
32. *PVA*, 165.
33. See *ATR*, 915–924; *BMT*, 73–74; Moulton, *A Grammar*, 164 (especially his indicative *modus irrealis*, 199–201); *GGBB*, 448–460.
34. Porter is too hard as he says, "[the tradition analysis] has clearly erred in positing an objective nature for the indicative mood." *PVA*, 164.
35. Palmer, *Mood and Modality*, 2.
36. Modal verbs or modality are used in this dissertation to refer to either the imperative, subjunctive, or optative. In English, modal verbs are *can, could, may, might, must, shall, should, will* and *would*. There are no modal verbs in Greek.
37. *PVA*, 165. By modal verbs Porter means verbs such as *can, might, should, must* and the like.
38. Halliday, *Functional Grammar*, 26–27.
39. Halliday, *On Grammar*, 175.
40. *GGBB*, 444 footnote 3.
41. Halliday, *On Language and Linguistics*, 182.
42. See H. P. V. Nunn, *The Elements of New Testament Greek* (Cambridge: Cambridge University Press, 1923). 179. See Nunn, *A Short Syntax of New Testament Greek* (Cambridge: Cambridge University Press, 1920), 12; *BMT*, 163; *ATR*, 1095; Michael S., *Glossary of Morpho-Syntactic Database Terminology* (Logos Bible Software, 2005); Herbert Weir Smyth, *Greek Grammar* (Oxford, UK: Benediction Classics, 2010), 311 (§ 1263); Rijksbaron, *Syntax*, 95; Campbell, *Verbal Aspect and Non-Indicatives*, 19–22; McKay, *A New Syntax*, 53; *GGBB*, 613; Young. *Intermediate*

New Testament Greek, 147; Anders Cavallin, "Zum Verhältnis zwischen regierendem Verb und Participium coniunctum," *Eranos: Acta Philological Suecana* 44 (1946): 280–85.

43. Palmer, *Mood and Modality*, 2; cf. PVA, 165.

44. *PVA*, 165–66.

45. The generalization above would not change the fact that the readers will see the close association of the aorist adverbial participle with the subjunctive and he or she will get the impression that the participle was "upgraded" to the subjunctive.

46. J. Gonda, *The Character of the Indo-European Moods with Special Regard to Greek and Sanskrit* (Wiesbaden: O. Harrassowitz, 1956), 6.

47. *PVA*, 168, 322. Wallace seems to pose the subjunctive and optative on the side of the indicative in the sense that they address cognition, that is, an appeal to the mind, and the imperative apart once it addresses to the volition. However, this dichotomy (volition and mind) is hard to maintain. See *GGBB*, 446.

48. N. Clayton Croy, *A Primer of Biblical Greek* (Grand Rapids, MI: Eerdmans, 2007), 8.

49. Halliday argues that the idea of "grammatical subject" is an oddity since it implies a structural function with only one purpose, i.e., to define a structural function. See Halliday, *On Grammar*, 189–90.

50. Henry Sweet, *A New English Grammar: Logical and Historical* (Oxford, UK: Claredon Press, 1898), 125. Here the subject of the participle in English if it is not an absolute participle, having a Logical subject (cf. § 2353).

51. Halliday, *On Grammar*, 189.

52. Arnold sees some sort of cognitive approach of Paul in this passage. See C. E. Arnold, *Ephesians: Power and Magic: The Concept of Power in Ephesians in Light of Its Historical Setting* (Cambridge, MA: Cambridge University Press, 1989), 70, and R. Schnackenburg, *Ephesians: A Commentary* (Edinburgh: T & T Clark, 1991), 47–49, 67–69. An analysis of the participle based in the context of situation will show that the most preferred grammatical feature to prove, highlight or even engage the readers sometimes in emotional context of situation is the adverbial participle. In the letter to Ephesians Paul uses the participle 107 times in 76 verses, and chapter one has 21 participles. In chapter 2 where Paul contrasts Jews and Gentiles in order to consider the reconciliation of both, there are 24 participles (17 verses). Chapter three, which continues to deal with reconciliation and God's plan to create the new humanity, has 10 (7 verses). In the *paraenesis* (exhortation) part, the occurrence of the participles is basically related to various emotions and there are 23 participles in 15 verses. Chapter 5 there are 15 participles and finally in chapter 6 there are 14 participles.

53. *GGBB*, 94.

54. Halliday, *On Grammar*, 190.

55. Theme (Psychological Subject), Actor (Logical Subject), and the Modal Subject (Grammatical Subject) are identical unless there is good reason for them not to be. Cf. Halliday, *On Grammar*, 191.

56. Any attempt to define a grammatical term stumbles on the range and the degree of abstraction, therefore, grammatical nomenclature is never so clumsy as in the effort to express the delicacy in the *nuances* of Greek reflected in the synthetic and manifold forms of its verb. See F. W. Farrar, *A Brief Greek Syntax and Hints on Greek Accidence: With Some Reference to Comparative Philology, and with Illustrations from Various Modern Languages* (London: Longmans, Green, and Co, 1905), 136. Porter admits that the terminology of the participle varies from grammar to grammar. Cf. Porter, *Idioms*, 181.

57. *GGBB*, 444, note 3. Bible software usually includes the participle and infinitive under the mood label search.
58. Palmer, *Mood and Modality*, 1–4; *PVA*, 165–81.
59. Halliday, *On Grammar*, 190.
60. Bekalu, "Presupposition," 152.
61. Ibid., 5.
62. *ATR*, 1098.
63. Porter, *Idioms*, 180.
64. Palmer, *Mood and Modality*, 58.
65. Rijksbaron, *Syntax*, 6.
66. Assertion is not an assertion formally, but some type of presupposition. Lunn rightly suggests that only the indicative is an assertion, and the choice of the subjunctive at least is non-assertion. See Patricia Lunn, "The evaluative function of the Spanish Subjunctive," in *Modality and Grammar in Discourse*, edited by Joan Bybee and Suzanne Fleischman, Typological Studies in Language 32 (Amsterdam: John Benjamins, 1995), 430.
67. This Projected mind does not mean a future event, it is just a projected realm. See. Porter, *Idiom*, 57.
68. M. A. K. Halliday, *Studies in English Language*, Collected Works of M. A. K. Halliday, edited by Jonathan J. Webster 7 (London: Continuum, 2005), 55.
69. Halliday, *Essentials*, 3. See Halliday, *On Language and Linguistics*, 84.
70. *GGBB*, 613. From a didactic perspective, Daniel Wallace has one of the most complete treatments of the participle for an intermediate level student.
71. Ibid. Nunn confuses his reader by saying that the participle is a verbal adjective and resembling verbs can have subjects. cf. H. P. V Nunn, *A Short Syntax*, 61. The participle does not grammaticalize subject.
72. *GGBB*, 623. He says that "since the subject of the participle is usually the subject of a finite verb, the participle will usually be in the nominative case (almost 70 % of the time)." Strictly there is no grammatical subject, but a logical subject for the participle.
73. Halliday, *On Language and Linguistics*, 84.
74. *SRG*, 6.
75. Although Halliday is dealing with modality and modulation in English, his theory can effectively be applied to the Greek verbal system, but the differences should not be ignored. Thus, the dependence of systemic functional linguistics can be seen in this approach. See Halliday, *System and function*, 209. Italics added.

CHAPTER FOUR

Functions of the Participle

The following approach is aligned with Halliday who affirms that "a language is almost certainly the most complicated semiotic system we have; it is also a very fuzzy one, both in the sense that its own limits are unclear and in the sense that its internal organization is full of indeterminacy."[1] Any utterance would become cumbersome and exhausting for the reader/listener to grasp any meaningful thought if a speaker/writer chose to say in detail everything he or she means by supplying all the referents and the like.[2] The Greek participles are described as heavily underdetermined. This means that the participle forces the reader/hearer to presuppose what the speaker/writer means.[3]

The analysis of the participle so far has included the study of the semiotic component of the situation—*field*; the analysis of the functional component of the semantics—*ideational*; and the analysis of syntactic choices in the clause—*transitivity*.[4]

We are arguing that the study of register and its components applied to the participles shows the purposeful nature of linguistic choices made by the writer or speaker within a text in order to evoke the attention and involvement of the reader. This notion of linguistic prominence can be shown to be consistent and motivated in the participle's relationship to the main verb.

A high degree of abstraction is seen with the participle since the verbal and adjectival forms converge in it, and this combination determines its semantics, that is, a factive presupposition with its functional roles within different pragmatic effects by which the participle is upgraded. The nominative aorist adverbial participle seems to derive its main functional role from its semantic core (factive presupposition), which represents an ultimate stage of hierarchization, an abstraction of meaning.

Finite and non-finite clauses are stages in the process of hierarchization of clausal relationships. The syntactical complexity and lexical density join together forming a common ground where the participle occurs, since within it verbal and adjectival meanings are converged. In other words, the participial formal structures represent the interface between verbal and nominal structures, being able to realize complex meanings at various points on the presuppositional scale.

The presence of a formal designation such as the participle by itself indicates a clausal relationship where an embedded participial complex clause involves the need to process dependency relationship at the same time that it indicates a high degree of compression of meaning, this is what is meant by an abstraction of meaning.

The semantic core of the participle is presupposition, whose core functional role is hierarchization from which two further functions come: background and prioritizing functions. Whatever the circumstances the participles describe, they must be taken as a true proposition so that the meaning communicated by the main clause hits its purpose.

Background Function

The most important clue to understand the participle is to connect it to the ideational metafunction. The grammar of the clause achieves this function by means of processes, participants in the process, and circumstances related to the process.[5] Choices in the mood system of Greek are expressions of the participants in the process (interpersonal), and choices of the participle, agent, medium, and process are the expression of the *ideational* function of language.[6]

The relation between these two functional components establishes the *background* and the *prioritization* functions. Within the sentence these two functions are set in the relation between modulation and mood, and transitivity helps to clarify this matter. Transitivity has to do with the "'deeper' aspects of the relations between verbs and the phrases associated with them."[7]

In the discourse, everything is important, but not important for the same reason. The role of the participle is to mark exactly that degree of importance, as though the adverbial participle were the spotlight illuminating the main verb.

Steve Runge makes this point by saying that "the Greek [adverbial] participle allows the writer to make one finite verb (e.g., indicative or imperative) central to the entire sentence by rendering the rest of the actions as participles."[8] Such a feature shows the preference for the participle in Greek, as Anders Cavallin confirms when he says, "es mag dies uns vielleicht als ein drastischer Ausfluss der Vorliebe des Griechen für Partizipilkonstruktionen erscheinen."[9]

Cavallin thinks that, in classic Greek at least, the main verb is used to set the participles in the spotlight. Unfortunately, his idea is the opposite of that which is presented here. Cavallin does not defend his point or even present a minimal set of data to be evaluated here. Of course, his purpose is to show the dependence of the participle on the main verb. Contrary to Cavallin, the center of the action in Koine Greek, at least, is found in the main verb, not in the participle. Although not limited to it, the participle has the double role of providing the background for and prioritizing the action of the main verb.[10]

The modal semantic seems to be the best way to explain the participial phenomenon but only a few scholars have included any discussion of it in their books. Burton says of the participle, "as a verb it has both tense functions and functions which may be designated as modal functions, being analogous to those, which in the case of verbs in the Indicative, Subjunctive, or Optative, belong to the mood."[11]

All the subtleties of the participles as a semantic presupposition open a range of logical relations that function in many logical capacities as means, cause, result, and the like.[12] Wallace's intermediate grammar is still very useful and helpful for a student interested to master Greek with numerous exegetical examples. He does deal with a modal semantic that includes the fair discussion of participles from a pragmatic perspective. He notes, "*a greater emphasis is placed on the action of the main verb than on the participle.*"[13] His intermediate grammar should not be despised since it brings a considerable number of examples from an exegetical-contextual perspective.

Generally speaking, Wallace's statement above about the upgraded participle (participle of attendant circumstance for him) can be applied to all the adverbial participle. In other words, it is a valid aspect for all adverbial participles both preceding and following the main verb. In terms of prominence, the presupposed information is given by the participle so that the ±assertion can be made prominent.[14]

To perceive the background and prioritization functions, it is necessary to give more attention to the relationship between mood and modulation. Indicative and imperative are formal designations that grammaticalize the attitudinal features (mood); and the participle is a formal designation that is outside of the attitude system.[15] Therefore, both systems should be analyzed within this spectrum first and then their relationship to verbal aspect can be considered. This section is built upon all the other resources on verbal aspect.

The sophistication of the clause chain between an embedded clause and the main clause likely indicates the literary taste for the Koiné more seen with Luke. The anarthrous participle that precedes the main verb, whose modal semantic of presupposition produces hierarchization, that is background and prioritization. These features work together in different contexts having different pragmatic effects, one of which is the upgraded participial effect.

Levinsohn, for instance, recognizes that,

> Anarthrous participial clauses that *precede* their nuclear clause [main clause] present information that is backgrounded. This means that the information they convey is of secondary importance vis-à-vis that of the nuclear clause. This claim does not hold for anarthrous participial clauses that follow their nuclear clauses.[16]

Some questions are in order here. First, is the background function of the aorist participle a result of being a participle (modulation) or a function of the perfective aspect? Similarly, Levinsohn states that the adverbial participle which precedes the main verb describes an event that is of secondary importance,[17] so is this secondary importance of the dependent clause a result of being an adverbial participle or because it has a perfective aspect (aorist)?

There is an essential distinction between the meaning of a proposition in the context and the individual semantic value of its component.[18] Porter, in discussing patterns of constituent order and clause structure in the New Testament Greek says, "the flexibility of Greek syntax because of its inflected endings and its various ways of forming clauses does not mean that the order of various elements makes no difference."[19] Therefore, the answer to these questions cannot ignore the issue of Greek word order.

Background: Theory of Verbal Aspect and the Aorist Adverbial Participles

This part will answer what was asked above, that is, is the background function of the participle a result of being a participle (modulation) or a function of the perfective aspect (verbal aspect of the aorist)? As a matter of fact, the theory of verbal aspect relates this background function to the semantics of the aorist tense-form. This part will not be exhaustive, because of the vast amount of literature on this subject. Five key authors—McKay, Porter, Fanning, Decker, and Campbell—have expounded on aspect in the New Testament.[20] The main thread of the discussion below is related to Porter's contention that the perfective aspect realized by the aorist indicates background. The assumption in this section is that although Porter seems to be correct for most part, there are cases where the aorist does not fit his assumption.

We present here only a brief summary as an attempt to contribute to the understanding of aspect in the adverbial participle. Following Decker's advice, it is essential to identify and define key terms when describing languages, since the difference between languages must be evaluated based on a standard set of definitions.[21]

Porter defines verbal aspect as "A semantic category (meaning) by which a speaker or writer grammaticalizes a [subjective] perspective on an action by selecting a particular tense-form in the verbal system."[22] The verbal aspects are therefore morphologically based (i.e., form and function are matched).[23] This means that verbal tense-forms are selected by language speakers not on the basis of the action itself but on the basis of how a language speaker wishes to conceive of and conceptualize the action.[24]

The theory of verbal aspect advances the Greek knowledge by differentiating the semantics of *Aktionsart*, which is a description of the kind of action that a verb can have because of its inclusion into a verbal complex.[25] Further, Decker clarifies that the difference between lexis and *Aktionsart*: "Lexis refers to the semantic, denotative value of the word itself, while *Aktionsart* is a descriptive category for the kind of a situation described."[26] Since language is an exchange of meaning, an ancient writer must impose his or her specific point of view on the text in order to highlight various levels of meaning[27] as though he knew the modern features such as *boldface, italics, underline* and the like. This is a rhetorical strategy. How does a particular author draw the readers' attention to his/her points of prominence? Markedness is such a tool.[28] The terminology to describe this markedness varies among the scholars.

Based on the concept of markedness, the stative aspect is formally the most heavily marked (perfect tense-form) and forms an opposition with the perfective aspect which is the least marked.[29] Decker has a figure to represent this aspectual opposition.

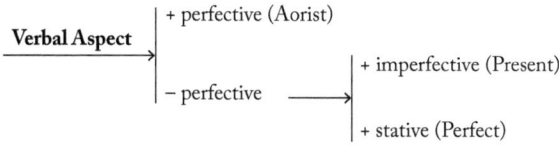

Figure 4.1. Verbal opposition. Decker, *Temporal Deixis*, 21, figure 5.

The aorist would be the expected form if a particular author wants to describe an event that precedes another action or is already complete. Since this is the role of the aorist (perfective aspect), one can see why it is often found in historical narratives, especially when a writer wants the reader to understand the action as a complete whole. However, when a writer/speaker wants a reader to see an event as taking place (especially as overlapping with a current action or even still to come), the writer/speaker uses the imperfective aspect, which is grammaticalized by the present tense-form.[30] Decker translated the opposition into planes of discourse when he concludes that

> The aorist is the tense normally used to carry the storyline of the narrative—it moves the account along by specifying the basic events. Narrative writers normally employ the imperfective aspect for descriptive purposes: the present form for emphasis and/ or detailed description, the imperfect for describing the events that are more remote from the main story. The remoteness may serve to supply supporting details, to record events simultaneous with other events (that may be either aorist or present), or it may record or introduce conversation.[31]

According to verbal aspect theory, the semantics of a tense-form indicates only the writer/speaker's subjective portrayal of an action. However, Fanning's warning must be followed, "aspect properly defined is central in the Greek verb, but it interacts in predictable ways with closely related features to produce important secondary effects."[32] The aorist tense-form describes an action as complete, and the imperfect and present tense-forms describe an action as a process.

We can see a lack of uniformity in discourse analysis on what function each aspect performs. There are significant areas of agreement in terminology to indicate that the aorist is perfective (the author's external viewpoint).[33] There are conflicting views regarding the function of the perfective aspect. This disagreement seems to start with the conceptuality of the system. It is necessary to differentiate foundational principles of the system from notions, which are applications of these principles. It may be that there is disagreement because those who see the aorist as having a *foreground* function use the term to refer to the position of it in the mainline, while the term *background* has to do with a position off the mainline.[34]

Porter's *foreground* signals non-mainline events or descriptions according to Fanning, while background refers to mainline events, that which carries the main movement of the narrative proper.[35] For Porter, the perfective aspect realized by the aorist carries the mainline or storyline of the narrative. This statement is the exact opposite of Hopper's usage of the term:

> It is evidently a universal of narrative discourse that in any extended text an overt distinction is made between the language of the actual story line and the language

of supportive material, which does not itself narrate the main events belonging to the skeletal structure of the discourse—as FOREGROUND and the latter as BACKGROUND[36]

Porter's foundational principles seem to be the same for Hopper, but their application of the principles is different. Porter sees the aorist setting the background, while the imperfect, and the present tense-forms being used to highlight points in the narrative. The reason for this difference might be that Porter's starting point in distinguishing between these features is prominence, while other scholars start with the movement of the narrative.

Campbell seems to perceive this in his analysis of background and foreground when he makes the following qualification, "it is important to remember that the term background has to do with the position off the mainline, rather than prominence."[37] We use the roles of background or foreground as having less or more prominence, respectively; therefore, it sees the aorist (external viewpoint) as less significant since it is used for an undefined sequence of events. However, this does not mean that the verbal aspect should be the only feature to be considered in the analysis of the verbal system. On the contrary, we argue here that modal semantics is one of the essential features of the verb in the study of discourse analysis.[38]

Aspect of the Participle

Having sketched a summary of the theory of verbal aspect, now we turn to establish the relation of the theory of verbal aspect to the modal semantics of the participle. Analysis of verbal aspect should struggle to stay in the verbal entrance of the system network. If the system of +finiteness is the choice than the aspect contrastive analysis moves in the very same process toward the attitude system. If it is -finiteness, the attitude system is blocked, then the choice made in the contrastive analysis stays in the ±factive presupposition.

Markedness involves both tense-form and mood, therefore it is necessary to include the discussion of aspect with the participle here. Wallace argues that since participles share two natures, these two natures work together, and affect the verbal nature of the participle by diluting the strength of the aspect.[39] However, is aspect theory valid when considering the participle? Wallace carefully qualifies his assertion by saying that "in particular when a participle is *substantival*, its aspectual force is more susceptible to reduction in force."[40] On the verbal side, the nature of the participle participates in all ranges of the aspect of a normal verb.[41]

Another issue linked to the discussion of the participle is the relation between time and aspect. Scholars are not unanimous. There are some that insist that both aspect and time are grammaticalized in the verbal tense-form. The issue is very complex and so many features are involved. The starting point will determine the direction to land. Is the approach top-down (from pragmatics to semantics) or down-top (semantics to pragmatics)? Most of the issue revolves around this departure line and the conclusion in either way must carefully include lexicogrammar and several other linguistic subtleties.

The differences can be seen in Mark 5:40 "καὶ κατεγέλων αὐτοῦ. αὐτὸς δὲ *ἐκβαλὼν* πάντας **παραλαμβάνει** τὸν πατέρα τοῦ παιδίου καὶ τὴν μητέρα καὶ τοὺς μετ' αὐτοῦ καὶ εἰσπορεύεται ὅπου ἦν τὸ παιδίον" ("And they were laughing at him. But *putting* them all *outside*, he **took** the child's father and mother and those who were with him and went in where the child was").

There is an aorist participle (ἐκβαλὼν) preceding a main clause whose main verb is a present indicative (παραλαμβάνει).[42] Wallace includes this participle as an example of the attendant circumstance [upgraded effect] related to the so-called historical present. He argues that the relation between the aorist participle and the present tense in the attendant circumstance construction tends to support the view that the aspect collapses in historical present.[43] Wallace argues that the historical present has zero aspectual value.[44] However, Decker hits precisely the point when he asserts that

> The objection that a progressive aspect is not evident in the context, and thus that 'the historical present has suppressed its aspect,' confuses aspect with lexis or *Aktionsart*. There may not be any contextual indication of the actual progress of the action intended—but that is not the meaning of imperfective aspect (which describes the author's view of the situation).[45]

In summary, the historical present is used by Wallace to defend zero aspect for it,[46] Porter, uses it to argue that this verb provides important proof for the non-temporal nature of the tense-forms in Greek, and points to verbal aspect as the distinguishing semantic feature.[47]

Two observations need to be made at this point. First, what does it mean when scholars disagree or even have different assessments of the same data? It may be because they had different methods that oriented their conclusion. A conception of grammar as a "closed system" and the presupposition of the non-cancelability of a semantic of the verb will lead one to a different conclusion from that of one who does not hold to this conception. Thus, Wallace' assertion seems to be pre-defined by his assumption that tense-form is time-embedded. Porter and Decker see grammar as a "closed system," so they will not admit exception.

The second observation is that the researcher, when finding such disagreement, decides which side he or she should take based on his or her own presuppositions. In this particular case, it must be stated that simultaneity, by definition, excludes distinctions of temporal distance—if two time-points coincide, then it is possible to say only that they are coincident.[48] Of course, the debate over time in the Greek verb and over how the historical present works are being oversimplified here, but since they are not central to the topic of this study, they will be left out.[49]

A New Approach in the Analysis of the Participle

A ramification of the study of the participle argues that the background function of the participle is a result of being a semantic presupposition, its functional role is that of hierarchization, and one of its functions is that of background coupled with the prioritizing function of the action of the main verb. Transitivity studies indicate that participial and infinitival clauses serve as supporting background for foreground information.[50]

Steve Runge following Levinsohn holds that in the case of participles which precede the main verb, the action of the participle suffers the effect of backgrounding, setting it as something secondary in importance to the main verb.[51] He goes on to say, "since the participle is dependent upon the main verb to supply the information that it does not encode on its own (e.g., mood), the participle does not obtain the same status as a finite verb."[52]

Both Runge and Levinsohn seem to assume some theoretical definitions of this particular participial form and then read these assumptions into the contexts in which the anarthrous aorist participle occurs. Although their conclusions do not seem incorrect, they do not declare how they arrived at their definitions and pragmatic conclusions. A better explanation of this phenomenon must include perfective verbal aspect, and modulation, which grammaticalizes factive presupposition. Because of the interrelation between these two, verbal aspect will be dealt with first, and then modulation.[53]

Those who attribute the background function of the participle only to the aorist verbal aspect by and large use the systemic functional approach to support their position. They note that a systemic functional approach to the Greek verb has revealed that patterns of usage show some sort of textual conditions that in the case of Greek verbs become associated with particular tense-forms.[54] In the New Testament narratives, when desiring to select a chronological thread or background event, the Greek speakers used the most compatible aspect, the perfective (aorist).[55]

Therefore, as Porter puts it, "in many instances the Aorist Participles are antecedent and the Present coincidental. However, rather than looking at the Participle by itself, verbal aspect and syntax must be taken into consideration."[56] As Campbell has pointed out, Porter seems to assume promptly a theoretical definition of the tense-form and then reads this definition into the contexts in which the forms occur, using these as evidence for his own definition.[57]

If Porter is being rightly understood, he relates the background function not to the participle but to the combination of contextual features and the semantic function of verbal aspect. However, he has not been very specific as to how he arrived at his conclusion on this specific matter. Levinsohn and Runge seem to put this background function on the combination of contextual features and the participle word order.[58] Levinsohn and Runge's claim is correct when they state that a participle conveys something of secondary importance compared to the main clause.[59] However, the statement that the "anarthrous participial clause that *precedes* their nuclear clause [main clause] presents information that is backgrounded,"[60] needs further examination.

In terms of word order in the NT, there are four different types of order involving the Greek participle.[61] However, only two of them will be used to interact with Runge's and Porter's point of view on the participial function.

There are instances where the aorist participle precedes the main verb and the present follows the main verb.[62]

Mark 9:25	ἰδὼν δὲ ὁ Ἰησοῦς ὅτι ἐπισυντρέχει ὄχλος, **ἐπετίμησεν** τῷ πνεύματι τῷ ἀκαθάρτῳ <u>λέγων</u> αὐτῷ·
	Jesus, *seeing* that a crowd was following together, he **rebuked** the unclean spirit, <u>saying</u> to it.
Matt 14:30	καὶ *ἀρξάμενος* καταποντίζεσθαι **ἔκραξεν** <u>λέγων</u>·...
	and *beginning* to sink he **cried out** saying ...
Luke 10:34	καὶ *προσελθὼν* **κατέδησεν** τὰ τραύματα αὐτοῦ <u>ἐπιχέων</u> ἔλαιον καὶ οἶνον ...
	And *approaching* he **bound up** his wounds, <u>pouring on</u> oil and wine ...
Acts 13:12	τότε *ἰδὼν* ὁ ἀνθύπατος τὸ γεγονὸς **ἐπίστευσεν** <u>ἐκπλησσόμενος</u> ἐπὶ τῇ διδαχῇ τοῦ κυρίου.
	Then *seeing* the existing situation, the proconsul **believed**, <u>being astounded</u> at the teaching of the Lord.

Keaton's lexham propositional outlines glossary brings definition for a considerable number of terms. About background information he says, "the speaker is describing someone or something undergoing or being affected by an action or event relative to a main statement; all background statements precede a foregrounded main statement in a discourse."[63] Porter's comment, "this common pattern, in which two processes are described in their completeness and then a statement is made that in some way grows out of this series of events,"[64] is not that different from Runge who says, "those [participles] that precede the main verb have the effect of backgrounding the action of the participle indicating that it is less important than the main verbal action."[65]

Runge goes on to say that "the participles that follow elaborate the main action."[66] Although the data shows the tendency of the aorist to precede the main verb,[67] in those cases where it comes after the main verb, it also seems to spotlight the main verb.[68]

Second, there are also instances where both the aorist and the present participles precede the main verb.[69]

Matt 16:1	Καὶ *προσελθόντες* οἱ Φαρισαῖοι καὶ Σαδδουκαῖοι <u>πειράζοντες</u> **ἐπηρώτησαν** αὐτὸν σημεῖον ἐκ τοῦ οὐρανοῦ ἐπιδεῖξαι αὐτοῖς.
	And *coming*, the Pharisees and Sadducees <u>testing</u> him **asked** him to show them a sign from heaven.
Luke 7:37–38	καὶ ἰδοὺ γυνὴ ... *κομίσασα* ἀλάβαστρον μύρου καὶ *στᾶσα* ὀπίσω παρὰ τοὺς πόδας αὐτοῦ <u>κλαίουσα</u> τοῖς δάκρυσιν **ἤρξατο** βρέχειν τοὺς πόδας αὐτοῦ ...
	And behold a woman ... *bringing* an alabaster flask of perfume and *standing* behind, <u>crying</u> at his feet, **began** to wash with tears his feet ...

When both participles (aorist/present) precede the main verb, both indicate a background idea. Luke 7:37–38 shows that the woman could not begin to use her tears before she cried them. It may not be the aorist tense-form that indicates the background action since in this example the present participle has the very same function. To attribute the backgrounding function in the participle to verbal aspect, looking at it only from the plane of discourse, seems to assume too much since the data shows the close relationship between both aorist and present participles in this matter.[70]

Background provides the context within which the main events (foreground) take place. Thus, from the observed data, a balanced position that couples Porter's statement with that of Levinsohn and Runge must be preferred. So then, the anarthrous aorist participial clause that precedes its main clause presents information that is backgrounded in the New Testament.[71] This does not mean that the verbal aspect theory has no value, but rather that the semantic function of Greek modulation and that of verbal aspect should both be included right from the start with any analysis of the Greek verb.

Prioritizing Function

The analysis of the New Testament data has shown so far that the only semantic core of the participle is presupposition, whose functional role is hierarchization. The first result of such hierarchization is background. The second result, namely, prioritizing function, will now be analyzed.

Markedness and Modulational Prioritizing Function

There are several different ways to formulate the semantic qualities of a Greek verb. One that should be included is verbal opposition, to specify not only the aspectual function but also the subjective choice from the Greek verbal system realized by the attitudes (moods).[72] The several options of describing attitude occur in terms of opposition, that is, by choosing a participle over the attitude system (+finite), the original writer made a decision of emphasis and meaning.[73] Thus, when a term is combined with others, there is a logical opposition[74] between the central meaning of one term and the central meaning of the other term.[75]

The opposition is between a presupposition, which is often contrasted with the assertion. It is not as though the action described by the participle has no importance - it does. However, at the same time that human experiences are construed interpersonally (realized by the moods), the interpersonal relations are "enacted in the course of, and by means of, being construed ideationally" (realized by modulation).[76] Thus, Halliday's model aims to relate linguistics to the effects they have on the readers.[77] What that means is that for each sentence in the discourse, the writer/speaker wants to assign something to the reader/listener both on the semantic level and in the structure used in order to specify how new sentences relate to the preceding sentences, and how presupposed information appeals to the reader/speaker about the meaning uttered.[78]

Interpreters need to understand that the use of a participle grammaticalizes an action in different ways than if a writer/speaker were to use a finite verb. The participle is less specific than other grammatical options in rendering cause, manner, time, result, and the like. Funk noticed that as he states, "Greek circumstantial [adverbial] participle is therefore a less precise form of expression than corresponding subordinate clauses of time, condition, concession, etc."[79]

Adverbial participles are used as clause chains. The relation established between the participial clause and the main clause operates in the high level of abstraction. That is, "the specific semantic relationships between a prenuclear [preceding the main clause] anarthrous participial clause and the following nuclear clause [main clause] may be deduced from the context."[80] This open spot is filled by the readers association within the discourse or co-text.

The reader virtually will deduce this relation at a pragmatic level. In this relation, the adverbial participle depends upon the main verb, which the readers assess to supply the information that the adverbial participle does grammaticalize. Therefore, if the participle of the embedded clause depends on the main verb to supply information necessary to be understood, it is logical to conclude that the adverbial participle is not in the same status as the main clause.

Having said that, now it may be said that the anarthrous aorist adverbial participle in the nominative has a double function. That is, this participle functions as a coin with two sides, one is background, the other is prioritization. Thus, by choosing an adverbial participle to describe some action a writer/speaker is condensing one action at the same time that he/she is prioritizing another action. "The clause chain participles are not on a par with the finite verb of their sentence."[81] It is as a "'second fiddle' to the main action rather than being on an even par with it."[82] The participles have a very important function, that is, *prioritization of the action.*"[83] The action prioritized is that of the main verb.

No matter if the participle comes before or after the main verb, the prioritizing function still works whether presenting background information for the main clause or developing information of the main clause. By being an adverbial participle, the nominative establishes the relation of the participle with the main verb. It indicates that the grammatical subject of the main verb can be presupposed as the logical subject of the participle.

The following examples of the participles both before and after the main verb show the second main function of the participle, namely, prioritizing the main verb.

Mark 2:14   Καὶ *παράγων* **εἶδεν** Λευὶν τὸν τοῦ Ἀλφαίου καθήμενον ἐπὶ τὸ τελώνιον, καὶ λέγει αὐτῷ· ἀκολούθει μοι. καὶ *ἀναστὰς* **ἠκολούθησεν** αὐτῷ.

         Passing by he **saw** Levi the son of Alphaeus sitting at the tax booth and he **says** to him, "Follow me." And *getting up* he **followed** him.

Having decided to communicate a particular process, Mark then chose to grammaticalize the description of this event by means of a verbal group, which consists of verb forms, each of them having a specific semantic feature. The primary clause has two embedded clauses. The first participle (παράγων) is an example of a present participle preceding the main verb in that clause. There are different logical functions of this participle, but the main one, even without considering the word order, is that of putting the main verb in the spotlight (ἀκολούθει – "follow").

With some internal adverbial participial clauses, even if one removes the participle the sentence would still make sense (cf. Καὶ εἶδεν Λευὶν τὸν τοῦ Ἀλφαίου καθήμενον ἐπὶ τὸ τελώνιον, καὶ λέγει αὐτῷ· ἀκολούθει μοι. καὶ ἠκολούθησεν αὐτῷ. He saw Levi the son of Alphaeus sitting at the tax booth and he says to him, "Follow me." And he followed him). The participle is what gives color to the narrative at the same time that it points to the main verb. Participles work like a mental exercise to draw the readers into the core of the event as we will see below.

Since modulation does not grammaticalize a subject, it draws the reader into the narrative. The main verb here is εἶδεν, an assertion, while the participle παράγων (passing by) is a semantic presupposition. By placing the embedded clause at the beginning of this complex relation, the adverbial participle expresses continuity between the prior context and that which follows. The readers, seeing this clause chain, do not lose focus since they are able to see the new information in contrast to the additional circumstance to color the narrative.

There is a possible pragmatic corollary that belongs to the nature of the adverbial participle that helps to clarify this aspect: if a potential point of departure is the primary basis for relating the sentence to its context, the adverbial participle will be placed in the beginning of the sentence.[84] If the adverbial participle that is placed in the beginning is followed by another adverbial participle, the principle applies to both of them.

In this verse παράγων is the point of departure that alerts the readers to relate the sentence to its context. The readers are able to do that and perceive that there are two statements showing what happened, each of them highlighting its importance, that is, Jesus saw (aorist) Levi, and he says (present).

To summarize what we already stated, it can be said that by choosing a participle one chooses to set the action of the participle as a backdrop so that the action of the main verb can be prioritized in the story line. Factive presupposition transcends information of the "real world" to help the readers in their creative imagination. Thus, the participle related to the aorist indicative seems to create some sort of suspense to some main future event. The culmination of the narrative connected by a couple of verbs and the answer of the suspense action described by the participle is found in the present imperative: ἀκολούθει μοι (follow me). Again, the participle puts the focus on the main verb: Levi getting up (ἀναστάς) followed him (ἠκολούθησεν).

Acts 13:16	Ἀναστὰς δὲ Παῦλος καὶ κατασείσας τῇ χειρὶ εἶπεν· ἄνδρες Ἰσραηλῖται καὶ οἱ φοβούμενοι τὸν θεόν, ἀκούσατε.
	And *rising* Paul and *making a signal* with his hand **said**: Men of Israel and those who fear God, listen.

In sum, the attitude grammaticalized by the Greek mood is blocked in the participle so that the reader can be drawn into the narrative.[85] As a modulation, the two participles both preceding the main verb and connected by καί, have the function of drawing attention to the main verb.

The pragmatic upgraded effect of the aorist adverbial participle is but one possibility among many other options. The point here is that the semantics of the participle sets limits on interpretation by indicating the two main functional roles of the verbal participle: it not only creates a background to the main clause but also prioritizes the action of the main verb. Both the participle and the main verb with which it relates are set in a clause chain without being a pair, having this hierarchization function to highlight the prominent parts of the discourse.

Aorist Participle: Background/Prioritization and Clause Chain

A presupposition has as its functional role the establishment of a hierarchization of the speech as a writer indicates to the readers what is secondary, although important, and what is primary and more important. For instance, by starting a sentence with an anarthrous aorist participle, no discontinuity has been assigned.[86] In other words, the author has given new information in the previous context and by using an aorist participle, he wants to prepare the readers for more new information. It is necessary to create in the readers' mind a type of suspense that signals for them a continuity, moving from what is in the previous description to what is coming. This feature is called here a clause chain.[87]

This clause chain is more logical than grammatical. For example, Luke 15:23 "καὶ φέρετε τὸν μόσχον τὸν σιτευτόν, θύσατε, καὶ *φαγόντες* **εὐφρανθῶμεν**," ("And bring the fattened calf and kill it, and *let us eat* [and] **celebrate**"). The understood "and" between the participle (φαγόντες) and the subjunctive verb (εὐφρανθῶμεν) is a result of the contextual meaning that shows an *association étroite* between the modulation and the mood.[88] In this example, eating is clearly part of the way the subjunctive verb (εὐφρανθῶμεν) is to take place.[89]

The role of the aorist participle within the upgraded context shows that there is a chain between the participle and the main verb, but this chain that assigns continuity occurs only on the side of the readers, namely, ideationally.[90] This phenomenon is old enough and common in the ancient Greek.

Sicking and Stork observing the use of the aorist participle in Classical Greek, point out that participial clauses are instances of the "mode of coding 'discourse structure' commonly described by discourse linguists as 'clause chaining': 'information is presented in chains or thematic paragraphs.'"[91]

Having illustrated the point with Act 13:16, which brings two examples of modulation, it can be said that the function of the two participles in this passage, both the one proceeding and the one following the main verb, is to convey something of secondary importance compared to the main clause. To say that something is of secondary importance is not to say that there is no importance at all. For instance, ἀναστὰς … καὶ κατασείσας are aorist participles having a resumptive function.

By using these two aorist participles, Luke wants to bring the reader's attention (ideational component) into the drama of the narrative. The participles serve as transitions through which the author moves the narrative forward assuring that the readers are able to follow it by combining mood and modulation.[92] This clear transition is what keeps the main verb in the spotlight, that is, it is a prioritization of the main clause.

Other references set the participle as a point of departure giving the readers a signal to relate the participial sentence to its context with renewal forward focus.

Mark 5:33	ἡ δὲ γυνὴ *φοβηθεῖσα* καὶ *τρέμουσα*, *εἰδυῖα* ὃ γέγονεν αὐτῇ, **ἦλθεν** καὶ **προσέπεσεν** αὐτῷ καὶ **εἶπεν** αὐτῷ πᾶσαν τὴν ἀλήθειαν
	But the woman, *fearing* and *trembling, knowing* what her state of affairs was, **came** and **fell down** before him and **said** to him the whole truth.
Luke 8:47	*ἰδοῦσα* δὲ ἡ γυνὴ ὅτι οὐκ **ἔλαθεν**, **τρέμουσα ἦλθεν** καὶ **προσπεσοῦσα** αὐτῷ …
	And the woman *seeing* that she could not escape noticed, *trembling* she **came** e *falling down* before him …

Matthew omits this exchange, but Mark and Luke describe this healing event with richness of linguistic details. The structure of Mark is PARTICIPLE [aorist] + καί + PARTICIPLE [present] + PARTICIPLE [perfect]. Luke's structure is PARTICIPLE [aorist] + FINITE VERB [aorist]. Mark's setting is surrounded by emotional and the equal status of the two participles (*φοβηθεῖσα* καὶ *τρέμουσα*) connected by καί give color to the fearful atmosphere and the use of the participle take the readers to a dramatic environment.

Mark 5:25–34 is the fullest participial chain found in the New Testament.[93] The participle seems to establish a complex description of the event. It seems that the function of the participle is to recapitulate the previous information, so as to conclude a paragraph at the same time that it puts the main verb in the spotlight. In other words, the aorist participle here creates a starting point for further information in the narrative.[94] The preposed participles typically serve the purpose of preparing the audience for what will come next in order to keep the attention focused on the main action of 5:25–27 which is that of "touching".

Both Luke and Matthew summarize and omit many details, while Mark presents the information in "chain" so the reader will not get off track.[95] In the first part, her "touching" is the most important action in the sentence. In 5:33 her state of affairs (γέγονεν) is followed by a public confession, [she] εἶπεν αὐτῷ πᾶσαν τὴν ἀλήθειαν (Mar 5:33). Three adverbial participles (φοβηθεῖσα καὶ τρέμουσα, εἰδυῖα) cause an emotional suspense before getting to the main verb in this relation, and from there the reader goes to the open confession that culminates in the main statement: ἡ πίστις σου σέσωκέν σε.

What we see here is that "the choice to use so many participles has exegetical significance."[96] Further, the function of the participle of putting the main verb at the spotlight is confirmed in v. 30 where Jesus' question about who touched him and her telling the whole truth in v. 33 are all connected by the participle.

| Matthew 16:1 | Καὶ *προσελθόντες* οἱ Φαρισαῖοι καὶ Σαδδουκαῖοι <u>πειράζοντες</u> **ἐπηρώτησαν** αὐτὸν σημεῖον ἐκ τοῦ οὐρανοῦ ἐπιδεῖξαι αὐτοῖς. |
| | And *coming* the Pharisees and Sadducees, <u>testing</u> they **asked** him to show them a sign from heaven. |

Here both the participles precede the main verb.[97] Both the aorist participle (προσελθόντες) and the present participle (πειράζοντες)[98] seem to establish a frame of reference for what is to come next, that is, to focus attention on the main verb (ἐπηρώτησαν). The function of each of the preceding participles is to recapitulate a piece of information, thus creating a starting point for new information in the narrative. The new information is realized by the mood or modals while the participle backgrounds and prioritizes the action of the new information.

Greek participles are factive presuppositions and as such they are the ones the reader must find uncontroversial in order to find the assertions.[99] It is uncontroversial because it deals with a mental exercise in written form. The chain function can be perceived in the example above. The Pharisees and Sadducees were added into the narrative in two chains: coming and testing. The author could have chosen two indicatives, but he did not want to describe it in this way. The reason is twofold.

First, continuity would be compromised, unless other constructions had been added, such as prepositional phrases and the like.[100] However, he decided to set this sentence as a participial "clause chaining" so that the readers could be drawn to where he wants. Second, had he picked all indicatives to describe this event the reader could look at any verb as having the same importance.

He decided to utter these actions in a chain realized by the participle so that the main verb could have more importance. The indicative utters an assertion and as such it is prominent while the participle draws the reader's/listener's attention to what is prominent. For instance,

---

Eph 5:19–21   **πληροῦσθε** ἐν πνεύματι ... (19)*λαλοῦντες* ἑαυτοῖς [ἐν] ψαλμοῖς καὶ ὕμνοις καὶ ᾠδαῖς πνευματικαῖς, *ᾄδοντες* καὶ *ψάλλοντες* τῇ καρδίᾳ ὑμῶν τῷ κυρίῳ, (20) *εὐχαριστοῦντες* πάντοτε ὑπὲρ πάντων ἐν ὀνόματι τοῦ κυρίου ἡμῶν Ἰησοῦ Χριστοῦ τῷ θεῷ καὶ πατρί. (21)*ὑποτασσόμενοι* ἀλλήλοις ἐν φόβῳ Χριστοῦ

Be filled with the Spirit ... (19) *speaking* to one another in psalms and hymns and spiritual songs, *singing* and *praising* the Lord with your heart, (20) *giving thanks* always and for everything to God-Father in the name of our Lord Jesus Christ. (21) *Submitting* to one another in the fear of Christ.

From a pragmatic perspective, Ephesians 5:19–21 is controversial in regard to the function of its participles. While the first four participles are considered adverbial, many versions, including recent editions of the Greek NT, would render the last participle ('ὑποτασσόμενοι v. 21) as an imperative in English.[101] Of course, the dynamics of rendering long Greek sentences into understandable English could allow it. From a pragmatic perspective, Wallace treats these participles as that of result.[102] Further, from an internal or logical perspective, the participle presents the logical outcome of the verb. As an external or temporal result, the participles present the chronological outcome of the verb.[103] However, as has been stated, all of these ideas have a pragmatic meaning.

Sim notes that the way in which "many grammar books confidently identify 'temporal,' 'causal,' 'concessive,' 'conditional,' or 'final' participles" should be questioned."[104] The context is determinative to establish these logical relationships, but temporal or logical markings are not grammaticalized by a participial form. By using a participle, Paul is assuming the ability of the hearer to infer; that is why the functional component—ideational—is picked up.

The use of the participles works in a vague or ambiguous communication so that it describes a valuable and essential function of language. Therefore, the use of the participle allows the readers to minimize the communication itself (realized by the participles) and maximize what it actually communicates.[105]

The main verb πληροῦσθε is a present imperative. In one sense, the imperative is not a real mood, but a modality or modal. The basic distinction is that if the qualification of the process resides in the speaker's own mind, then it is interpersonal, thus attitude is grammaticalized; *if the qualification of the process resides in the circumstances*, then it is ideational in function, that is, it relates to a specific part of the content of the clause.[106] Here the imperative appeals to the hearer's/reader's volition[107] while the participles present the circumstance described by the process, appealing to the reader's capacity to presuppose something in order to make sense of the whole discourse.

There is a command first, and then the present participle in some way grows out of this command, thus developing it.[108] The present participles elaborate the main action (πληροῦσθε) at the same time that they have the effect of condensing and prioritizing the command.[109] Runge points out that "verse 19 begins a chain of participles that elaborate what it practically looks like to be filled with the Spirit: it looks like speaking to one another in song, like singing and making melody to the Lord, and like submitting to one another."[110]

The obedience resulting from the command (the participial clauses) provides the counterpoint for the command itself and in the whole discourse (Eph 5:19–6:9) husband-wife, parents-children, father-children, and master-slave are all filled by the Spirit. By choosing a participle, an author signals that the participle is of secondary importance compared to the assertion, whether + or -assertion.[111] The imaginative world created by the participial chain is fascinating since it makes the readers to take the direction by the imperative and creatively develop into a mental exercise in written form (participles): λαλοῦντες … ᾄδοντες καὶ ψάλλοντες … εὐχαριστοῦντες … ὑποτασσόμενοι.

In sum, what is true for the aorist participle in Greek, is true for the upgraded contextual effect, noting that the clause chain happens more logically than the explicit usage of the connective conjunction. Thus, the participle, a clause chain, has the functional role of hierarchization which in turn has the pragmatic effect of background and prioritization of the main verb.

Greek Participles and [E]motion

We already stated the goal of our study: to deal with the semantics of the participles as a whole, and the upgraded effect as a case illustration for the study of factive presupposition in the New Testament. Our intention in this part is not to present the results of the analysis of the semantics of the participle connected to emotions as something to be verified with absolute certainty. We are not saying that participles like emotional contexts. The author has several different options to communicate feelings in the New Testament. There are the factive adjectives that describe emotions, factive verbs of emotion among other features. The author depending on the context of the situation chooses how he wants to utter a communicative meaning dealing with emotions.

We have noted that when the context of the situation indicates emotion and the participle is used, the author is drawing the readers into the emotional environment. In cases such as these the use of participles become one of the most fascinating features in the New Testament. We understand that the semantic meaning of the participle for this matter cannot be checked with absolute certainty, but there will be seen clear evidences for such possible analysis.

We already observed that presupposition is the imaginative or mental exercise done by the reader or hearer to reflect, complement, or react among others to what is being said. It is as though the author/speaker wants to make the readers a participant of some assigned task by him within the discourse.[112] The Greek participle with verbs of perception, verbs of emotion, and verbs of movement creates an environment that involves feeling or emotion that the author can use to invite the readers to participate in the emotional overtone at hand.[113]

There are several occurrences of exchange among modality and modulation in the New Testament. Some events occur with the same verbal lexeme stem with different semantic choices, that is, in the parallel passage one or other evangelist chooses to communicate the circumstances of a process using a factive presupposition. There may be more going here than mood choices, therefore, caution is always needed. For instance, Matthew and Luke use a participle where Mark uses an imperative or indicative (Mark 2:9–11; Matthew 9:5–6; Luke 5:23–24).

There are several finite choices in Mark linked by καί, but Matthew and Luke take exactly the one that is asyndetic (ἔγειρε ἆρον) in Mark and put a different emphasis. Both Matthew and Luke set the participle in a clause chain with the main process by setting the main verb in the spotlight. Matthew replaces ἔγειρε for an aorist participle of the same lexeme (ἐγερθείς)[114] preceding ἆρον. Luke preserves Mark's original lexeme (ἔγειρε), but he changes Mark's imperative form (ἆρον) into a participle (ἄρας)[115] and coordinates ἔγειρε with καί and the participle ἄρας preceding the following imperative verb πορεύου.

Matthew is interested to make a clause chain between rise (ἐγερθείς) [and] take (ἆρον) on which the participle set the main clause (ἆρον - take) as one of the focal points to Jesus' sonship vindication. First, the participle serves as a hierarchization device that prioritizes the action of the main verb in this structure; second, the participle presents the background circumstance to the main process in this relation; third, it indicates an unspecified movement toward the main action; fourth, laid out that the paralytic could not take his own bed unless some further action occurs before. Thus, Matthew takes both the embedded clause and the main and set them as one connected event. Fifth, it is exactly the participle that draws the reader to the drama of the direct discourse, since the participle signals to the readers that ἐγερθείς is a true proposition so that the following action could be possible. Finally, the sequence of the narrative after a direct discourse makes possible that this aorist nominative participle preceding the main verb upgrades itself to the same "mood" of the main verb.

Luke follows the same options of Matthew, with one difference: he chooses the participle instead of the imperative ἆρον. He connects ἄρας with the verb of movement, πορεύου leaving the culmination of Jesus' vindication to the end of the direct discourse. These different choices are available to the author, since he is the one who decided how he wants his readers to handle this event. If we assume Mark as the first Gospel written and Matthew and Luke used his Gospel and other unknown sources, Matthew and Luke made a deliberate choice.

Admitting that choice implies meaning, they decided to include the readers participation right in the communication of the process, where Jesus' intent to make himself known is vindicated by a healing activity, which can be taken as true by the circumstance that cooperates to the visible manifestation of the cure. *Rising* or *taking* is so readers-oriented that they now are immersed into the drama of the narrative and Jesus' vindication extends itself beyond the primary audience. It is for everybody to confirm it altogether.

There are examples in the New Testament with the participle following a subjunctive verb in one Gospel and an imperative main clause in the same event description.

Mark 14:12	"… Ποῦ θέλεις *ἀπελθόντες* **ἐτοιμάσωμεν** ἵνα φάγῃς τὸ πάσχα;"
	"Where do you want us *to go* [and] **prepare** for you to eat the Passover?"
Luke 22:8b	"… *Πορευθέντες* **ἐτοιμάσατε** ἡμῖν τὸ πάσχα ἵνα φάγωμεν."
	"… *Go* [and] **prepare** the Passover for us, that we may eat it."
Matthew 26:17b	"… Ποῦ **θέλεις ἐτοιμάσωμέν** σοι <u>φαγεῖν</u> τὸ πάσχα;"
	"Where do **want** us **to prepare** for you <u>to eat</u> the Passover?"

Only Mark and Luke (*ἀπελθόντες* and *Πορευθέντες* respectively) use the participle in the embedded clause forming a clause chain of the main verbs. Matthew opts to present the process of preparation without using any participle. Each author decided how they want to communicate the Passover preparation. Mark uses a subjunctive preceded by an aorist participle while Luke use an imperative in a direct discourse. Both participles indicate an unspecified movement as although there is only one action being described. The clause chain is too close to the main verb that Matthew leaves out the participle but uses the same modality of Mark.

The connection of the two participles with the main process is so visible that action of *going* serves as a background information as it sets the main verb on the spotlight. *Going* is just an unspecified movement to achieve the main process. Interesting enough is that when the main verb is subjunctive, the upgraded effect makes the readers to render the participle in the same "modality" of the main clause, and when in the direct discourse, the imperative occurs, the participle presents the same imperative "sense". Of course, taking the participle as a real imperative would set both action as coordinate. The upgraded participle makes the readers/listeners to render the embedded clause in chain with the main clause, never loosing track that there is only one direction (imperative) or projection (subjunctive) indicates by the participial movement.

Whenever the evangelist wishes to create a chain pertaining to the organization of the narrative, he marks the main structure but adds an on-going thematic presupposition that cause the readers/listeners to make in their mind the close connection of the two events having one as a true proposition to highlight the "heavy" linguistic attitude of the structure. As formal differences do not exist without purpose in any language, the use of the participle makes the two action to look one by drawing the readers to the movement of the narrative. Greek syntax offers different structures to grammaticalizes two events ideationally as one only colored event. For instance:

Mark 14:38	γρηγορεῖτε καὶ **προσεύχεσθε**, ἵνα μὴ ἔλθητε εἰς πειρασμόν·
	Watch and **pray** that you may not enter into temptation.
Luke 22:46	... *ἀναστάντες* **προσεύχεσθε**, ἵνα μὴ εἰσέλθητε εἰς πειρασμόν.
	... *rise* [and] **pray** that you may not enter into temptation.
Matthew 26:41	γρηγορεῖτε καὶ **προσεύχεσθε**, ἵνα μὴ εἰσέλθητε εἰς πειρασμόν·
	Watch and **pray** that you may not enter into temptation.

Luke is the only one to subordinate the participle to an imperative in Jesus' direction to his disciples to be praying with him in that hard moment. It is likely that Luke sees the action of praying as the most prominent, so he does not see the need for the verb γρηγορεῖτε since praying is to be alert. However, he changes the lexeme and puts in a participle probably to bring the readers to the environment by creating mental images of context of the situation in a clause chain. The prominent statement is the modality (imperative). The unspecified movement gives the necessary color to the main clause since the readers must take the participle as a true proposition in order to pray.

Without the syntactical hierarchization by the participle of the embedded clause, the verb to pray and to watch are of equal status. They are two different actions of equal importance, while Luke's choice sets the prominent action "to pray" in the spotlight by adding a participle before the main clause without any interruption. This thematic structure adds a strong aspect of continuity and is backward-forward pointing. It connects what comes before with what follows making the readers to keep track of the parts of the discourse while the participle opens the spot so that the readers can immerse themselves in the drama at hand.

Luke has an emotional note justifying the fact that the disciples were found sleeping (εὗρεν κοιμωμένους αὐτοὺς ἀπὸ τῆς λύπης). The context of [e]motion is well suitable to beg empathy and the participle is a very nice tool to draw the readers into the emotional event. Interesting enough is that Luke is the only one among the other evangelists that adds the emotive note (sleeping for sorrow). This does not prove that the participle is the preferred choice for the communication of feeling in the NT, but it indicates that when the context of the situation presents some sort of emotions, the participle is a very suitably form to draw the readers into to the [e]motional environment.

There are times when participles come following immediately the main clause and the impression is that only one action is being rendered followed by a state of mind (ideational metafunction) in written form. The co-texts sometimes inform us about the urgency of the circumstance toward the imperative that is difficult to ignore that the embedded clause works on the reader's imaginative way as the command is obeyed by those directly related to it. It is likely that the same direction is echoing to readers to obey the same command with the same urgency. For instance, Matthew 28:7 "καὶ ταχὺ *πορευθεῖσαι* **εἴπατε** τοῖς μαθηταῖς αὐτοῦ ὅτι ἠγέρθη ἀπὸ τῶν νεκρῶν ..." ("Now quickly **go** [and] tell his disciples that he has risen from the dead ...").

The participle *πορευθεῖσαι* seems to be more a mental exercise in written form (factive presupposition) than an event in itself. The urgency expressed by the adverb ταχὺ (quickly) reinforces the directional overtone of the participle because of the attraction that it suffered in the upgraded relation with the main action "**εἴπατε**" ("tell"). The position immediately preceding the main clause likely signals continuation as it resumes the previous circumstances. The emotional context of the situation is expressed by the Angel negative command ("Μὴ φοβεῖσθε ὑμεῖς") in Matthew's record of the announcement. Again, the parallel passage in Mark 16:7 "... ὑπάγετε εἴπατε ..." has two imperatives, of course, with a different lexeme. However, in Mark with two finite verbs there is no explicit statement of emotion in the context.

We are not saying that every time that there is some sort of emotional context a participle occurs, rather, we are stating that there are different options to communicate an event, but if a particular author wants to embellish the meaning of the action, a participle is available with one specific characteristic: its usage brings the reader into the emotional environment by way of reflection. The participle is not a pair with the main clause but acts like a mental exercise in written form setting the main verb in a clause chain. It is a self-contained set of information communicating one event in a colored way.

The episode of the healing of leper in Mark 1:42–44 brings some insight to our present discussion. The emotional overtone in the context is on Jesus himself. The parallel passages in both Matthew (8:4) and Luke (5:14) are relevant for our comparison. Mark and Matthew bring two asyndetic imperatives (ὕπαγε ... δεῖξον), while Luke replaces one of the imperative (ὕπαγε) for a different lexeme, but the passage is still a valid example (ἀπελθὼν δεῖξον) for the use of the aorist participle in the upgraded effect. Only Mark uses an emotive note (σπλαγχνισθείς),[116] but like Matthew, he uses two finite verbs. Among those three evangelists, Luke with his *literary Koiné* uses more often the participle for this relation.

Mark's use of emotional context indicates that it is still possible to use finite verbs normally if an author desires to, but if he uses an emotional factive adjective or similar and decides to add a participle (e.g., Luke), this mental exercise draws the readers into the emotional environment. The circumstance described by the participle is a written factive presupposition having the function of setting up the main clause in the spotlight giving the sensation that there is one real event (finite verb) and one ideational, cognitive, mental exercise to color the two events connected.[117]

Emotion and the Readers ≠ Participle and Emotion

We are not stating that the participle prefers context of emotion (feelings of some sort), since the author, as we will see, is the one who decides on how he wants to communicate a meaningful event. What we are saying is that the participle is a very fascinating tool for contexts of emotions because it draws the readers into the environment of feelings.

The several participial features we have been studying so far taken together demonstrate that the participle extends beyond the relationship between the writer and his writings. It may be supposed a third party can be included, the author, his writing, and his readers. Of course, the writer wrote for his readers. However, the point goes beyond this. By using the participle, the writer wants to involve the readers to the extent that they can be impacted by the situation that he presents to them.[118]

The indication of emotion is in the lexeme and in the co-text or in the lexeme of the participle as part of the clause chain. For instance, Act 2:13 "ἕτεροι δὲ διαχλευάζοντες ἔλεγον" ("but others *mocking* were saying …) or Act 5:41 "**ἐπορεύοντο** χαίροντες" ("they **went on** their way *rejoicing*"). Several examples fit in this category. When the participle precedes a lexeme that communicates emotion the participle anticipates a dramatic pause toward the main action. In either way the participle is readers oriented and the choice of it invites the readers to take the open spot to participate in the construction of meaning.

The emotional environment is not set necessarily by the participle. Factive verbs of emotion, factive adjectives of emotion, among other features are used to communicate feelings of any sort. The complex structure of the participial constructions is used by an author when he wants to get the readers to create a mental exercise and if that context of the situation involves some kind of feelings, the readers are invited to play a role within such an environment.

For instance, 1 John 2:9 "λέγων ἐν τῷ φωτὶ <u>εἶναι</u> καὶ τὸν ἀδελφὸν αὐτοῦ μισῶν ἐν τῇ σκοτίᾳ ἐστὶν ἕως ἄρτι" ("the one *saying* he is in the light and *hating* his brother is in the darkness even now"). John is creating a factive presupposition, a mental exercise. It is not a real world event but an imaginative exercise. The infinite projects an indirect perception, another mental exercise with a distant possibility. *Hating* (μισῶν) again brings a factive presupposition. He is not asserting anything but bringing an ideational feature to bring his readers into a logical conclusion.

The exercise is mental, the inferences are logical. It is difficult to deny the emotional atmosphere since some lexemes indicate it. The use of the factive presupposition is so readers oriented that John does not assert that a brother hates each other. Both *hating* and *saying* are just a mental exercise. Neither the one saying he is in the light nor the one hating hates his brother. If the participle would be taken as a true proposition the logical conclusion is that this brother is in darkness but not in the light. It is up to the readers to make the logical inferences through the attention to the participles and infinitives.

A group of lexemes can create the emotional environment while the participles are in charge of drawing the readers into the context by means of a mental exercise. For instance, 2 Corinthians 6:9–10 "ὡς ἀγνοούμενοι καὶ ἐπιγινωσκόμενοι, ὡς ἀποθνῄσκοντες καὶ ἰδοὺ ζῶμεν, ὡς παιδευόμενοι καὶ μὴ θανατούμενοι, ὡς λυπούμενοι ἀεὶ δὲ χαίροντες, ὡς πτωχοὶ πολλοὺς δὲ πλουτίζοντες, ὡς μηδὲν ἔχοντες καὶ πάντα κατέχοντες" ("as *unknown*, yet *well known*, as *facing death*, and yet, behold, we live on, as *punished* and yet not *killed*, as *sorrowful*, yet always *rejoicing*; as poor, yet *making* many *rich*; as *having* nothing, yet *possessing* everything").

The emotional environment involves the particular context of this passage. There are lexemes for emotions (λυπούμενοι, χαίροντες) in a chain with other lexemes that indicate tension, fear, desperation, and sorrow. In a sentence such as this the participles are indispensable for a correct interpretation of the sentence as a whole. The participle as presupposition indicates a common ground between the reader/listener and an author as he moves the narrative (or *parenesis*) forward. Paul appears to presuppose at least for argument's sake that these are mental exercises in written form to bring his readers to interact emotionally with what he is communicating.[119]

Upgraded Effect and [E]motion

Most of the data observed with the upgraded effect contribute to the analysis of passages with this structure. With verbs of movement within the upgraded effect, the lexeme in the participle indicates an unspecified movement toward the main action. The mental exercise is to make the readers to take two different events as one by prioritizing the main verb. When a different feature that compounds the context is surrounded by emotions indicated by several other nuances that present feeling of any sort, the presence of the upgraded effect is a linguistic sophistication to get the readers/listeners into the emotional environment.

Since the majority of the examples where the upgraded effect occurs within some context of emotion, especially in the Gospel of Matthew, we decided to include some discussion with data from Matthew.

The Gospel of Matthew have fifty-three anarthrous adverbial aorist nominative participles with the upgraded effect. Seven out of the fifty-three are ambiguous and it seems that the context indicates some emotion, but it is not easily seen. Only six do not occur in an emotional environment or do not indicate any related feeling or motivation.[120]

For example, the environment of worship usually has the upgraded effect, and it is introduced by a verb of movement, and the participle has the function of drawing the readers into the environment of feelings. For instance, Matthew 2:8 and 11 have the main verb—worship—preceded by the anarthrous aorist nominative participle with the upgraded effect. The two verses have in the embedded clause a verb of movement connected to worship, ἐλθὼν **προσκυνήσω**, πεσόντες **προσεκύνησαν**. *Coming* (ἐλθών) is an unspecified movement, a mental action to help the readers to set the main action in the spotlight.

The position of the participle communicates a linguistic feature as well. The use of these aorist nominative participles following the main verb without any interruption is to secure a clear transition from one section of the narrative to another.[121] The focal part is the New information (προσκυνήσω, προσεκύνησαν), while the participle placed before the main verb typically prepares the audience for what will come next whose relevance is reported in the main clause.[122] The assertion is that they worshiped, but both readers and speakers must share ground that is semantically presupposed, which is indicated by the preceding participle.

The atmosphere of worship is in contrast to an angry atmosphere when Herod perceived that he was deceived, Τότε Ἡρῴδης *ἰδὼν* ὅτι ἐνεπαίχθη ὑπὸ τῶν μάγων ἐθυμώθη λίαν, καὶ *ἀποστείλας* ἀνεῖλεν πάντας τοὺς παῖδας τοὺς ἐν Βηθλέεμ καὶ ἐν πᾶσι τοῖς ὁρίοις αὐτῆς ἀπὸ διετοῦς καὶ κατωτέρω, κατὰ τὸν χρόνον ὃν ἠκρίβωσεν παρὰ τῶν μάγων (Mat 2:16). Herod's anger is described by a direction perception pointed by the aorist participle ἰδών the emotional environment follows connected to ἐνεπαίχθη (he was mocked) plus ἐθυμώθη (he was angry).

There is a healing event in Matthew that shows the use of the participle in a context that involves feeling, suffering, and healing. Matt 8:6,7 "καὶ *λέγων·* κύριε, ὁ παῖς μου βέβληται ἐν τῇ οἰκίᾳ παραλυτικός, δεινῶς *βασανιζόμενος* καὶ λέγει αὐτῷ· ἐγὼ *ἐλθὼν* θεραπεύσω αὐτόν" ("and saying, Lord, my servant is lying para-lyzed at home, suffering terribly and he said to him, "*I will come* [and] **heal** him."). Three participles contribute to the creation of the environment. There is a clear indication of suffering described by βασανιζόμενος (tormented) follow by another embedded clause that sounds like a promise of comfort ἐλθὼν θεραπεύσω (I will come and heal).

One example with the participle with a verb of movement in the context of emotion. Matthew 8:25–26 "καὶ *προσελθόντες* **ἤγειραν** αὐτὸν *λέγοντες·* κύριε, σῶσον, ἀπολλύμεθα. καὶ *λέγει* αὐτοῖς· τί δειλοί ἐστε, ὀλιγόπιστοι; τότε **ἐγερθεὶς** ἐπετίμησεν τοῖς ἀνέμοις καὶ τῇ θαλάσσῃ, καὶ ἐγένετο γαλήνη μεγάλη" ("and *they went* [and] **woke** him, saying, "save us, Lord; we are perishing." And he said to them, "why are you afraid, O you of little faith?" Then he got up [and] rebuked the winds and the sea, and there was a great calm"). Matthew acts as a storyteller by which from time to time he provides a clause chain (participle), which gives direction to the narrative bringing this trial to a point of relief. Again, although subjectively, the environment of Matthew 8:25–26 is surrounded by emotion.

This emotional environment is a good moment to draw the readers into what is about to happen. Mark and Luke as well record this event surrounded by an emotional context. It is the analysis of the context that determines which form is the most adequate to utter meaning. Assuming that the participle must have its preferred context, the study of register is an important tool for understanding the upgraded participial implicature. The structure of register is semantic and the critical elements of it are primarily contextual and then linguistic.[123]

Register is included because its components indicate the purposeful nature of linguistic choices made by the writer or speaker within a text in order to evoke the attention and involvement of the reader.[124] The use of participles seems to place the reader right into the environment of the narrative by reproducing the feelings of the original readers, giving insight into their motivation for doing, perceiving, interacting, or knowing something.

The observation of the context of the situation that encapsulates the relationship between texts and social processes, suggests the participle's preference for contexts involving feelings or emotion if the author wants to draw the readers into such an environment.[125] Following this semantic circle, it may be said that the semantic domain of cognitive and emotive (i.e., factive presupposition) is aimed at the readers so as to draw them into the drama of the narrative or exhortation.

The perspective of these features that relates the preferred context for the use of the participle is not exclusive to this study, yet no systematic approach has yet been published. Different authors have stated the occurrence of the participle in context of [e]- motion. We have already seen that this emotional tone is sometimes a result of some specific lexis that expresses feelings. The contention here is that the study of register demonstrates that even a choice of any particular lexis is made by considering the context of situation. Thus, when the context of situation involves emotion, there is a considerable data that show the participles are very suitable for this type of atmosphere since to utter a process with a participle the writer is to present a clause chain that demands something from the readers/hearers.

This typical phenomenon is already attested to in the classical period as well. From a different linguistic theory and much more from lexical observation, Lang uses Herodotus to show that with verbs of perceiving and knowing (and it can be added, verbs of learning) the function of these verbs, especially, that of learning is like a narrative bridge, which has a double function according to her. On the one hand, it provides a temporal connection with the action to come, and on the other, it gives "motivation for the following action, and so gives the impression that the learning is everything."[126]

A possible clue for motivation is related to the use of factive verbs connected to its complement. Sometimes the complement is what indicates the presupposition and sometimes the factive verb comes as presupposition. The common environment seems to indicate the emotion of the atmosphere, although subjectively. In Hdt. 1.5.4 "τὴν ἀνθρωπηίην ὢν ἐπιστάμενος εὐδαιμονίην οὐδαμὰ ἐν τὠυτῷ μένουσαν, ἐπιμνήσομαι ἀμφοτέρων ὁμοίως" (Being Known [ὢν ἐπιστάμενος] that human happiness [εὐδαιμονίην] never **continues** so long in one state, I will discourse both equally).

In the classical Greek example above, the periphrastic participle precedes the main verb as a background and prioritizes the main verb by setting it on the spotlight, that is, "happiness never endures."

The participle as a logical clause chain connects with the main clause and leads the reader to assuming this presupposition (ὢν ἐπιστάμενος, "being known" is a shared information). The combination of these several features shows that Herodotus invokes the reader to agree with him that "happiness never endures … therefore …."

Another example from the classical period is E. Orestes 884–85 (480–406 B.C) ἐπεὶ δὲ πλήρης ἐγένετ' Ἀργείων ὄχλος, κῆρυξ *ἀναστὰς* **εἶπε**: Τίς χρήζει λέγειν, πότερον Ὀρέστην κατθανεῖν ἢ μὴ χρεών, μητροκτονοῦντα ("But when the crowd of the city of Argos got together, a herald *got up* [and] **said**: Who desires to say whether Orestes should be slain or not for the murder of his mother?") The connection of these participles marks some sort of motivation. Homer seems to use an adverbial participle in an emotive environment. Iliad 16.521 (7th Century B.C) "ἔγχος δ' οὐ δύναμαι σχεῖν ἔμπεδον, οὐδὲ **μάχεσθαι** *ἐλθὼν* δυσμενέεσσιν" ("and I choose not to have my lance firmly, neither *to go* [and] **fight** with the fool-ish-men."). In these examples, the use of the adverbial participle seems to indicate that there is a lack of feeling in the audience and calls on them to think about it.

We are saying that although the participle occurs in different types of contexts, commonly occur in contexts related to motivation or [e]motion when the writer wants to open a slot for the readers to participle in the construction of meaning as they put themselves in the emotional environment.

Furthermore, sometimes awareness of a situation (knowing or perceiving) may be enough; and sometimes there may be only calculation (thinking or expecting) or only emotion of some kind (fearing, hoping, suspecting, willing) or outside influence (trusting or being persuaded), but often a combination of two or even three participles with different thrusts provides a complex motivation for it.[127] Lang rightly concludes that

> The sameness of expression introducing action after action despite the great difference both among the individuals themselves and in Thucydides' knowledge of and feelings about them, suggests strongly that what we are dealing with here is neither a historian's s intimate knowledge of individuals' mind-sets and motives nor a closely reasoned interpretation of actions taken but rather a narrative technique which links actions and actors chainwise. It is obvious that on a factual plane actions do affect men when their awareness of them, with or without intellectual and emotional response, causes them to effect further action. But it is more obvious that a record of men's actions in narrative form forces this linking of actions for the sake of the connectedness that narrative expects.[128]

It seems that there is a parallel between the Classical Greek and Koiné in this matter. For instance, there are fifty-nine occurrences of the upgraded function in the book of Acts.[129] Thirty-four appear in the context of emotion. There are six examples where emotion is involved but it seems ambiguous. Only ten out of the fifty-nine do not occur in any emotional environment whether in the preceding context or in the following one.[130] Knowing that the participle is readers-oriented since it draws them into the emotional environment the New Testament writers used not only the upgraded function, but also other adverbial functions to invite the readers.

For instance, Acts 5:41 "… Οἱ μὲν οὖν **ἐπορεύοντο** *χαίροντες* ἀπὸ προσώπου τοῦ συνεδρίου, ὅτι κατηξιώθησαν ὑπὲρ τοῦ ὀνόματος ἀτιμασθῆναι" ("… they **went on** their way *rejoicing* …"). The adverbial participle of the embedded clause does not have the upgraded function, but it develops the idea of the main clause presenting the circumstance of the main clause. Wallace comments on this participle as being that of manner and he says, "this participle gives us quite a bit of the flavor of the narrative; since it adds flavor, it is a 'color commentator'." It does not matter the logical conclusion that the readers draw, the fact is that by being a factive presupposition the participles are suitable for so many nuances that the usage of them embellishes the description of any event.

In the example of Acts 5:41 the participle follows the main clause and still has the function of highlighting the main verb as it develops the action of it. Acts 2:13 Ἕτεροι δὲ *χλευάζοντες* **ἔλεγον** ὅτι Γλεύκους *μεμεστωμένοι* **εἰσίν** (but others *mocking* **were saying**, "Of wine they *are filled*"). In 2:13 the participle of the embedded clause precedes the main verb and describes one single, even if complex, event. The upgraded function seems to describe two independent events in *association étroite*. The participles in these two passages, the one preceding and the ones following, occur in the narrative indicating the feeling of the narrative at hand (rejoicing, and mocking respectively).

The [e]motional environment occurs outside Acts and the Gospel, for instance, Phillipians 3:18 πολλοὶ γὰρ περιπατοῦσιν οὓς πολλάκις ἔλεγον ὑμῖν, νῦν δὲ καὶ *κλαίων* λέγω, τοὺς ἐχθροὺς τοῦ σταυροῦ τοῦ Χριστοῦ (For many walk, of whom I have often told you and now tell you even *crying*, as enemies of the cross of Christ). The use of κλαίω 'to weep, cry' in this passage confirms a common used of this lexis that indicates a loud expression of pain or sorrow.[131]

There is another passage with κλαίω, a participial clause chain that creates an emotional atmosphere around the description of the event 1 Cor 7:30 "καὶ οἱ κλαίοντες ὡς μὴ κλαίοντες καὶ οἱ χαίροντες ὡς μὴ χαίροντες καὶ οἱ ἀγοράζοντες ὡς μὴ κατέχοντες" ("and the ones *mourning* as though not *mourning*, and the ones *rejoicing* as though not *rejoicing*, and the ones *buying* as though not *holding fast*" [i.e., as though it were not theirs to keep]). Sadness, rejoicing, and disappointment are all connected to transmit the emotional tone to the readers. By using a participle, Paul seems to indicate a mental exercise putting the readers to do the ideational task as they see themselves as insiders of the event at hand.

The progression of the passage flows from one participle to other to the cul-mination in verse 31 "… παράγει γὰρ τὸ σχῆμα τοῦ κόσμου τούτου" ("… For the present form of this world is passing away"). Paul draws the reader's attention with the participles within this emotional context, which will bring them to agree with him in the last assertion—the present form of the world is passing away, think and feel such an environment.

It would not be an overstatement to say that the Greek seems to have preserved this preference for context involving emotion. In the semantic domain where the context of situation involves [e]motion in Classical Greek, the participles play an important role. In the Classical Greek it was shown that Thucydides describes feel-ing by participles as he narrates, "… καὶ *μετεμέλοντο* τὰς σπονδὰς οὐ δεξάμενοι" (and *regretting* because they did not receive the treaty).[132] So does Sophocles who says "καὶ νῦν ποθῶ τοῦ σοῦ *θανοῦσα* μὴ **ἀπολείπεσθαι** τάφου" ("and now I wish *to die* [and] not **to be left out of** your tomb").[133] What is seen in the Classical can be seen in the Koiné with the upgraded function as well as with other functions of the participle.

Factive presupposition seems to demand from the readers a correct interpreta-tion of the sentence as a whole for the sake of the argument. Another scholar who noted these features is Bakker. He points out that by using a participle, the author is not exclusively concerned with "facts", but with types of stylistic features. For Bakker, an author, by using a participle, wants to draw the attention of the readers into the situation being narrated, so that they also participate in the drama of the event that follows.[134] Radermacher agrees with this idea, but sees it as motivated by style as he says "Bei den Verben des Wahrnemens …, Erkennens …, Wissens hat sich Partizip in Objektsbeziehung einingermassen gehalten."[135]

The richness of the Greek participle and its suitability explain the readers-ori-ented features of the participles in the Greek language. Thus, the frequency of the participle in Epic poetry, George M. Bolling asserts that it "constitutes one of the main causes of the vividness and swiftness."[136] This vividness and swiftness is highlighted by Lang when she says that the use of the participle is what gives "motivation for the following action."[137]

We are arguing that the participles as factive presupposition are a great tool because of its vividness and suitability. Their nature because of lack of limitation on the verbal form opens a slot for the readers to be drawn into the context ant that explains why some authors would use the participles to get them into the emotional environment. What is true for the Classical period can also be affirmed in Hellenistic Greek.

In the New Testament, for instance, we find good illustrations of the emo-tional domain and the use of the participle. Vividness is a remarkable characteristic relating the main clause and the participle.[138] As Robertson states, "when Paul's heart was all ablaze with passion, as in 2 Corinthians, he did pile up participles like boulders on the mountain-side, a sort of volcanic eruption."[139]

Mk 10:21	ὁ δὲ Ἰησοῦς *ἐμβλέψας* αὐτῷ **ἠγάπησεν** αὐτὸν καὶ **εἶπεν** αὐτῷ, Ἕν σε ὑστερεῖ· ὕπαγε, ὅσα ἔχεις πώλησον καὶ δὸς [τοῖς] πτωχοῖς …
	And Jesus, *looking* carefully at him, **loved him**, and **said** to him, "You lack one thing: go, sell all that you have and give to the poor …
Lk 18:22	*ἀκούσας* δὲ ὁ Ἰησοῦς **εἶπεν** αὐτῷ, Ἔτι ἕν σοι λείπει· πάντα ὅσα ἔχεις πώλησον καὶ διάδος πτωχοῖς
	And Jesus *hearing* this, he **said** to him, "One thing you still lack. Sell all that you have and distribute to the poor …"
Mt 19:21	ἔφη αὐτῷ ὁ Ἰησοῦς, Εἰ θέλεις τέλειος εἶναι, **ὕπαγε πώλησόν** σου τὰ ὑπάρχοντα καὶ **δὸς** [τοῖς] πτωχοῖς …
	Jesus said to him, "If you would be perfect, **go, sell** what you possess and **give** to the poor …"

Mark 10:22	ὁ δὲ *στυγνάσας* ἐπὶ τῷ λόγῳ **ἀπῆλθεν** <u>λυπούμενος</u>·· ἦν γὰρ ἔχων κτήματα πολλά.
	Shocked by the saying, he **departured** <u>saddened</u>, for he had great possessions.
Luke 18:23	ὁ δὲ *ἀκούσας* ταῦτα περίλυπος **ἐγενήθη**· ἦν γὰρ πλούσιος σφόδρα.
	And *hearing* these things, he **became** very sad, for he was extremely rich.
Matthew 19:22	*ἀκούσας* δὲ ὁ νεανίσκος τὸν λόγον **ἀπῆλθεν** <u>λυπούμενος</u>· ἦν γὰρ ἔχων κτήματα πολλά.
	And *hearing* the young man, he **departured** <u>saddened</u>, because he had many possessions.

All the three evangelists present the dialogue between Jesus and the rich young man surrounded by an emotional atmosphere. Even Mark, who usually does not use complex structure as often as the other evangelists, uses the participle in this episode. He introduces (Mark 10:21) the emotional environment pointing out that Jesus loved him ("ὁ δὲ Ἰησοῦς *ἐμβλέψας* αὐτῷ **ἠγάπησεν** αὐτὸν"). He is the only one to make a clause chain (*ἐμβλέψας* αὐτῷ **ἠγάπησεν**) in order to draw the readers more explicitly into the drama of the narrative. Mark's dramatic environment gets deeper as he opts for the lexeme στυγνάσας (*being shocked*), while the other Gospels have ἀκούσας (*hearing*).

Mark and Matthew follow the same structure PARTICIPLE [aorist] + FINITE VERB [aorist] + PARTICIPLE [present]. Luke poses his own structure PARTICIPLE [aorist] + FINITE VERB [aorist] + ADJECTIVE. Generally speaking, when a change is made from a finite construction into a participial, Luke is the one who does it, but here for an unknown reason he does not develop the action of the main verb with a present participle as Mark and Matthew do.

All three writers colored the event with a dramatic melancholic note whether with factive presupposition (participle) or factive adjective (Luke). The presence of the participles cannot prove that emotional atmosphere prefers the participles, but it indicates that when the emotional environment is involved, the presence of the participles draws the readers into the feeling atmosphere.

A similar example can be seen with another verb of sorrow-regret. Matthew 21:29 "ὁ δὲ ἀποκριθεὶς εἶπεν· οὐ θέλω, ὕστερον δὲ μεταμεληθεὶς ἀπῆλθεν" ("And he *answering* said, I do not want, but afterward *repenting* he went").

The reader was already caught by the redundant quotative frame ἀποκριθεὶς εἶπεν.[140] The participle in this tautological expression has the effect of slowing the discourse resulting in much more attention from the readers.[141] Runge declares the purpose for this feature in the narrative, that is, to draw "attention to a surprising or important speech that follows."[142] There are two different uses of the redundant participle.

The first function uses a verb of speaking in order to introduce a speech; the second function is to reintroduce the same speaker back into the same speech. In addition, Runge points out that "both of these uses have the pragmatic effect of highlighting a discontinuity in the text, specifically within the context of the speech (in this case, a different speaker). Both have the effect of attracting more attention to the speech or segment of speech that follows."[143]

While discontinuity is signaled by this redundant quotative frame, the anarthrous aorist participle μεταμεληθείς assigns continuity. The drama of the narrative is described by a logical clause chain (μεταμεληθείς) that points to the main verb (ἀπῆλθεν – he departed). The lack of limitation of the participle brings the reader into the narrative. The background or prioritizing function of the participle focuses his attention on the action of the main verb. How the son in Matthew 21 went away is described by the participle (repenting) - a clear combination of the [e]motion.

By using a participle, Matthew communicates something that the moods could not communicate. The participle seems to create a dramatic pause in the form of background before presenting the significant point. In this function, the aorist participle "creating the break in the flow also serves the same delay tactic seen with other forward-pointing devices, building suspense through the delay."[144] Having created this suspense, the context of situation is that of sorrow-regret sub-domain, and again the [e]motion participle (μεταμεληθείς) occurs, highlighting the drama. The main verb ἀπῆλθεν is a verb of movement so that the reader can keep track of the teaching in the narrative as he moves from the scenario to another place[145] bringing the readers into the event as an insider participant.

Mark 4:38–39	καὶ ἐγείρουσιν αὐτὸν καὶ λέγουσιν αὐτῷ, ... καὶ *διεγερθεὶς* ἐπετίμησεν τῷ ἀνέμῳ ...
	and **they woke** him and **said** to him, ... and he *woke* [and] **rebuked** the wind ...
Luke 8:24	*προσελθόντες* δὲ **διήγειραν** αὐτὸν <u>λέγοντες</u>, ... ὁ δὲ *διεγερθεὶς* ἐπετίμησεν τῷ ἀνέμῳ ...
	And they *came* [and] **woke** him *saying* ... and he *woke* [and] **rebuked** the wind ...
Matthew 8:26	καὶ *προσελθόντες* **ἤγειραν** αὐτὸν <u>λέγοντες</u> ... τότε *ἐγερθεὶς* ἐπετίμησεν τοῖς ἀνέμοις
	And they *came* [and] **woke** him <u>saying</u> ... so he *woke* [and] **rebuked** the winds ...

Generally, syntax offers different ways to express two or more events in one complex unity. All three Gospels bring this particular event of the windstorm and Jesus' resting moment in the midst of it. Mark uses καί to link the two clauses in equal status in verse 38 and sets the following complex clause into a clause chain with the aorist nominative participles establishing a continuity of equal status from the first two coordinate clause. The structure is καί + FINITE VERB + καί FINITE VERB. By setting the participle preceding immediately the main verb, it signals to the readers a backward-forward pointer and equal status of the compound finite clause signaled by καί.

Luke structures the same event in his typical style, that is, setting information in chain giving more cohesion to the communication. Different from Mark, he chooses two clause chains (participle and finite verb) both providing momentum in the narrative. The dramatic moment in Luke has the following sequence, PARTICIPLE + FINITE VERB (*προσελθόντες* **ἤγειραν**). Observe that while Mark uses the verb ἐγείρουσιν (they wake up) coordinated with λέγουσιν (they say), Luke adds the aorist nominative participles preceding immediately the aorist finite verb. This is the typical structure for the upgraded participle.

The upgrade occurs with Luke, and as Mark, he has the option to coordinate the two sentences by putting them as a pair. However, the upgraded function establishes an unspecified movement that because of the nature of the relationship between the aorist nominative participle and the main clause, it gives the impression that the embedded clause (participial clause) and the main clause are of equal status. The participial effect as part of the ideational metafunction triggers the readers mind to make a mental exercise, that is, the disciples were not right next to Jesus, and to wake him up they would need to approach him.

It is not the conjunction δέ between the participle and the main clause that indicates coordination. The use of δέ twice in Luke here is to mark a change of initiative through the action of different participants. So, the subject of the initiative with δέ were the disciples, then Luke signals that the participant changes from the disciples to Jesus and δέ signals it.[146] The effect of the participle causes the readers to take two sentences and to render them as one. The aorist participle is the mental exercise in written form that draws the readers into the event. The participle that follows the main clause (λέγοντες) presents a dramatic pause.

Jesus' action is described in a clause chain with the same logical sequence of the first clause complex: Jesus woke up [and] rebuked. The participle sets the main verb on the spotlight as it gives to the main clause the primary attention. Luke's structure is PARTICIPLE + δέ + FINITE VERB + PARTICIPLE for the first episode where δέ marks that the participants of the circumstances of the participles are the disciples. Following the unspecified movement to wake up Jesus, Luke sets the following structure, PARTICIPLE + δέ + FINITE VERB. Again, δέ does not coordinate the circumstance of the participle with the action of the main verb, it only signals to the readers that the participant of this aorist participle is Jesus, not his disciples as in the first clause complex.

Matthew does exactly what Luke did. They take Mark's cut-and-dried narrative and embellish it with the dramatic overtone colored by the participles. Both set the circumstances and the process in a clause chain two pairs of actions are taken as one pair. All three evangelists describe Jesus' action with the upgraded effect giving the readers a chance to participate in the event. Matthew and Luke describe both the action of the disciples and that of Jesus with the upgraded effect. It is not that they are coordinated, rather they are set in such a close association that they cause the two actions to look like one. The two-movement presented by the participles as factive presupposition, which by the lack of limitation of the verbal form draws the readers into in the drama of the narrative.

There is another aspect to observe in Matthew's usage of the upgrade in the passage above. ἐγερθείς contains no indication of time nor the structure of the upgraded effect.

τότε link low-level narrative units to indicate that the units share continuity of time and to introduce the next significant development in the storyline.[147] The logical relation with Mark indicates that the upgraded effect reflects an option available so that the author has the choice to communicate a process with a finite verb or with a clause chain with the participle. Whatever choice is made, the choice to communicate with a participle differs from that with a finite verb. With the participle, the close association with the main verb makes two sentences to seem like one only action where the participial clause becomes a mental exercise in written form so that the action of the main verb can be prioritized.

The power of synthesis of Greek participles can encompass in one lexeme meaning rendered with more than one lexis. Matthew (14:8–12) and Mark (6:25–29) with the record of the death of John the Baptist illustrate this point.

Mark 6:26	καὶ περίλυπος *γενόμενος* ὁ βασιλεὺς διὰ τοὺς ὅρκους …
	And the king *being* sad because the oaths …
Matthew 14:9	καὶ *λυπηθεὶς* ὁ βασιλεὺς διὰ τοὺς ὅρκους …
	And *grieving* the king because of his oaths …

There is a fundamental similarity between Mark and Matthew, both use participles. Mark's construction has a factive adjective to describe the emotional situation of the king because of the death of John the Baptist. Luke uses only one lexeme in the participial form to describe the same event. The hypothesis is that there are different ways to render emotional context, but the usage of the participle is more literary and demands a greater participation of the readers in the drama narrated.

The participle (λυπηθείς) functions as a 'coherence bridge' between two narrative paragraphs. On one hand, the participle makes clear to the reader in what way the next paragraph (New) is to be connected with what precedes (Given).[148] On the other hand, the participle creates some vividness that is perfect to invite the readers to take part of the description of the circumstance or process and the participle is a very suitable tool for it since it is a factive presupposition.

The sadness of the event (John's beheading) drags the reader into the feelings of the narrative at the time that Herod commanded his beheading. Herod's sorrow serves as a background so that the main verb ἐκέλευσεν could be in the spotlight. The central point is Herod's command but by adding the participle, an emotional environment, Matthew draws the readers in.

What is seen above in the Gospels can also be seen in Homer and Aeschylus. The participles come after the main verb, but all of these examples have the upgraded effect. This does not contradict the principle that the upgraded effect always precedes the main verb, since Homer is poetry, and it is not safe to define pattern of usage based on it.[149] The emotional tone is encountered first in the Classical, then in the Koine papyri, and finally in the apostolic fathers. The author has different options to communicate a sentence with other grammatical features, but if they use a participle, they want to draw the readers into the context of situation at hand.

Example in the Classical Period

Iliad 16.521 (7th Century B.C)	ἔγχος δ᾽ οὐ δύναμαι σχεῖν ἔμπεδον, οὐδὲ **μάχεσθαι** ἐλθὼν δυσμενέεσσιν
	and I choose not to have my lance firmly, neither *to go* [and] fight with the foolish-men
Iliad 16. 668 (7th Century B.C)	φίλε Φοῖβε, κελαινεφὲς αἷμα **κάθηρον** ἐλθὼν ἐκ βελέων Σαρπηδόνα
	Dear Phoebus, *go* [and] **cleanse** from Sarpedon the dark blood.
Aeschylus Supp. 928.	**λέγοιμ᾽** ἄν ἐλθὼν παισὶν Αἰγύπτου τάδε.[a]
	Herald *I will go* [and] **tell** Aegyptus' sons about this.
E. Orestes 884–85 (480–406 B.C)	ἐπεὶ δὲ πλήρης ἐγένετ᾽ Ἀργείων ὄχλος, κῆρυξ *ἀναστὰς* **εἶπε**: Τίς χρῄζει λέγειν, πότερον Ὀρέστην κατθανεῖν ἢ μὴ χρεών, μητροκτονοῦντα;
	But when the crowd of the city of Argos got together, a herald *got up* [and] **said**: "Who desires to say whether Orestes should be slain or not for the murder of his mother?"[b]

[a] Aeschylus, *Aeschylus with an English translation* (Cambridge, MA: Harvard University Press, 1926).
[b] The Greek edition of these two instances are from Homer. Homeri Opera in five volumes. Oxford, Oxford University Press. 1920.

The following examples are from the Greek prose.

Xen Ana 1. 6. 10	μετὰ ταῦτα, κύρου κελεύοντος ἅπαντες καὶ οἱ συγγενεῖς *ἀναστάντες* **ἔλαβον** τὸν Ὀρόντην τῆς ζώνης ἐπί θανάτῳ.
	After these things, Cyrus ordered [it], all even the siblings [of Orontes] *got up* [and] **took** Orontes with a strap until death.[a]
Xen Ana 1. 1. 7	ὁ δὲ κῦρος *ὑπολαβὼν* τοὺς φεύγοντας *συλλέξας* στράτευμα **ἐπολιόρκει** μίλητον καὶ κατὰ γῆν καὶ κατὰ θάλατταν καὶ ἐπειρᾶτο κατάγειν τοὺς ἐκπεπτωκότας.[b]
	But Cyrus *received* the banished ones, *collected* them an army [and] **laid siege** to Miletus by land and sea, and endeavored to restore the exiles.[c]

[a] Xenophon, *The Anabasis of Xenophon: with an interlinear translation, for the use of schools and private learners on the Hamiltonian system* (Philadelphia, PA: David McKay, 1887), 64. The Greek text is from Thomas Clark's edition, the translation is mine.
[b] The Greek text is from William W. Goodwin and John Williams White, *The First Four Books of Xenophon's Anabasis.* Revised Edition (Boston, MA: Published By Ginn and Co, 1896), the translation it is mine.

^c The analysis of the context of all these examples will show an emotional tune. See Sophocles, Antigone 1107 (496–406 B. V); Further instances in the Classical Period are Phe. Cor. 21; Thuc. 4.93, 112; Od. 6.7; Xen. An. 3.2.34; Xen. Cyr. 5.2.14; Ar. Nub 181.

Factive presupposition as readers-oriented occurs in context of emotion in the Koiné Period. The description of the circumstance with an emotional lexeme color even more the communication of such action bringing the readers to fill the open slot left by the lack of limitation of the participial form.

P. Teb. 42.5–8 (114 B.C)	*ἠδικημένος* καθ᾽ ὑπερβολὴν ὑπὸ ʿΑρμιύσιος συναλλαγματογράφου τῆς αὐτῆς, ὁ γὰρ ἐγκαλούμενος ἐν τὸ αὐτό, *συνείπαντος* θρακίδα Ἀπολλωνίου
	Being exceedingly *unfairly treated* H., the one who writes documents of the village mentioned. The accused *conspired* together with T. son of A.
P. Grenf. I 35.7–9 (99 B.C)	ἑαυτῶν δὲ *ἐπιμελόμενοι* ἵν᾽ ὑγιαίνητε ἐσμεν ἐν Πτολεμαιδι ἔρρωσθε
	taking care of yourselves so that you might go well. We are in P. keep well)
P. Teb. 12.12–13 (114 B.C)	τὰ ἀλλὰ σαυτοῦ *ἐπιμελόμενος*. ἵν᾽ ὑγιαίνης ἐρρῶσο
	for the rest *taking care* of your health. Be well.
P. Petrie II 19.1–9 (3rd cent. B.C)	ἀξιῶ σε μετὰ δεήσεως καὶ ἱκετείας οὕνεκα τοῦ θεοῦ καὶ τοῦ καλῶς ἐχόντες, *δοὺς* τὰ πιστὰ Μηζάκωι μηθέν με, εἰρηκέναι σοι καθ᾽ αὐτοῦ μηδέποτε ἄτοπον ὅπερ καὶ ἀληθινόν ἐστιν καὶ ὡς ἂν τοῦτο ποιήσηις *ἀξιώσας* αὐτὸν μταπέμψασταί
	I beg you with supplication and prayers on account of the god who good, *giving* faithful assurances to M. that I never said anything inappropriate to you against him in regard the truth and if you do this, *requesting* of him to send for me and to set me free out of prison.

Examples of the adverbial participle with emotional tone occurred in the Apostolic Father's writings, where one sees significant statements and intention to persuade with the possible intention of motivating the readers to some action, or attitude. The emotional tone can be seen by the father's desire of seeing them change or do something.

Barn. 6:11	Ἐπεὶ οὖν *ἀνακαινίσας* ἡμᾶς ἐν τῇ ἀφέσει τῶν ἁμαρτιῶν ἐποίησεν ἡμᾶς ἄλλον τύπον ὡς παιδίον ἔχειν τὴν ψυχήν ὡς ἂν δὴ *ἀναπλάσσοντος* αὐτοῦ ἡμᾶς

Therefore, *renewing* us by the forgiveness of sins, he made us to be another example, so that we should have the soul of children, as if he were recreating us.

Diogn. 2:1

Ἄγε δή *καθάρας* σεαυτὸν ἀπὸ πάντων τῶν προκατεχόντων σου τὴν διάνοιαν λογισμῶν καὶ τὴν ἀπατῶσάν σε συνήθειαν *ἀποσκευασάμενος* καὶ *γενόμενος* ὥσπερ ἐξ ἀρχῆς καινὸς ἄνθρωπος …

Come, then *clease* your mind from all of its prejudices and *lay aside* the custom that deceives you, and *become* a new man as it were from the beginning …

Diogn. 2:4

οὐ ταῦτα πάλιν τὰ νῦν ὑφ᾽ ὑμῶν *προσκυνούμενα* δύναιτ᾽ ἂν ὑπὸ ἀνθρώπων σκεύη ὅμοια γενέσθαι τοῖς λοιποῖς οὐ κωφὰ πάντα οὐ τυφλά οὐκ ἄψυχα οὐκ ἀναίσθητα οὐκ ἀκίνητα οὐ πάντα *σηπόμενα* οὐ πάντα *φθειρόμενα*

Are not these things that now *being worshipped* by you, made again by men vessels similar to rest? Are they not all deaf? Are they not blind? Are they not without life? Are they not destitute of feeling? Are they not incapable of motion? Are they not all liable *to rot*? Are they not all *corruptible*?

Ig. Ep 1:1

[Ἰγνάτιος ὁ καὶ Θεοφόρος *τῇ εὐλογημένῃ* ἐν μεγέθει θεοῦ πατρὸς πληρώματι *τῇ προωρισμένῃ* πρὸ αἰώνων εἶναι διὰ παντὸς εἰς δόξαν παράμονον ἄτρεπτον *ἡνωμένῃ* καὶ *ἐκλελεγμένῃ* ἐν πάθει ἀληθινῷ ἐν θελήματι τοῦ πατρὸς καὶ Ἰησοῦ Χριστοῦ τοῦ θεοῦ ἡμῶν τῇ ἐκκλησίᾳ τῇ ἀξιομακαρίστῳ τῇ οὔσῃ ἐν Ἐφέσῳ τῆς Ἀσίας πλεῖστα ἐν Ἰησοῦ Χριστῷ καὶ ἐν ἀμώμῳ χαρᾷ χαίρειν] *Ἀποδεξάμενος* ἐν θεῷ τὸ πολυαγάπητόν σου ὄνομα ὃ κέκτησθε φύσει δικαίᾳ κατὰ πίστιν καὶ ἀγάπην ἐν Χριστῷ Ἰησοῦ τῷ σωτῆρι ἡμῶν μιμηταὶ *ὄντες* θεοῦ *ἀναζωπυρήσαντες* ἐν αἵματι θεοῦ τὸ συγγενικὸν ἔργον τελείως ἀπηρτίσατε

[Ignatius, [also called] Theophorus, *being blessed* in the greatness and fullness of God the father, *being predestined* before the beginning of the ages to an enduring and immutable glory, *being united* and *being elected* through true suffering by the will of the Father, and Jesus Christ our God, to the Church which is at Ephesus, in Asia, deservedly most happy. Abundant happiness through Jesus Christ, and His undefiled grace.] *Receiving gladly*, much-beloved in God, news about you, regarding the nature of righteousness, according to the faith and love in Jesus Christ our Savior.

Being imitators of God, and *stirring up* yourselves by the blood of God, you have perfectly completed the work assigned to you.

The classification of the adverbial participle as cause (because), condition (if), concession, purpose (telic), result, and even the attendant circumstance (upgraded effect) are influences of the context from a translational perspective.[150] Clark rightly asserts, "no translation opens a transparent window onto the meaning of the original text. Translation must also be guided by the characteristics of the intended audience of the translation."[151]

In itself a participle is a +factive presupposition and must be primarily analyzed in contrast to +assertion or −assertion. If an author wants to grammaticalize any of these pragmatic effects, he would have available different parts of the grammar. By choosing a participle, however, these pragmatic effects can be seen (but it would be a tertiary effect), sometimes as a result of translation into another language.

Notes

1. Halliday, *On Language and Linguistics*, 2.
2. Sim, "Undeterminacy," 348.
3. Ibid.
4. M. A. K. Halliday, *English Language*, 55.
5. M. A. K. Halliday, "Notes on Transitivity," 38.
6. *TBF*, 41.
7. Butler, *Systemic*, 164.
8. *SRG*, 244.
9. Anders Cavallin, "Verb un Participium coniunctum," 280.
10. *SRG*, 245. For the same analysis in Classical Greek, see Lang, "Participial Motivation," 49.
11. Burton calls it the logical force of modal function. See *BMT*, 163.
12. Porter poses, "a distinction must be made between the participle as grammaticalizing an essential semantic feature and its pragmatic usage. The participle is a participle by form, with its concomitant semantic meaning." See *PVA*, 374.
13. *GGBB*, 642–43. *Italics his.*
14. *LDF*, 183.
15. Porter, *Verbal Aspect*, 375.
16. *LDF*, 183. Levinsohn's statement includes all the anarthrous adverbial participles that precede the main clause whether present or aorist. The Healeys says, "in narrative the circumstantial participial [nominative adverbial participial] clause usually appears initially in the sentence, or it is found within a cluster of syntactically subordinate items itself which presents the first main clause." Healey and Healey, "Circumstantial Participles," 179.
17. See Healey and Healey, "Greek Circumstantial Participles," 247; See also Greenlee, *A Concise Exegetical Grammar*, 66–67 for the same position. From a modal semantics perspective, the participle as a presupposition has by its semantic nature this secondary importance.
18. *PVA*, 184.
19. Porter, *Idioms*, 289.
20. It must be said from the outset that Buist Fanning does not state a particular linguistic theory that he adopted in his study of the Greek verbal system. It may be that he has surveyed several different approaches on verbal aspect and moved on to apply his particular analysis of the verb

in the New Testament. He does seem to see pairs of opposition and does not handle the verbs based on this binary opposition. Fanning, *Verbal Aspect*, 83–84.

21. Decker, *Temporal Deixis*, 26.

22. Porter, *Idioms*, 21. Cf. Fanning, *Verbal* 84–5. Cf. also Porter, *Verbal Aspect*, 88 where he defines aspect as "a synthetic semantic category (realized in the forms of verbs) used of meaningful oppositions in a network of tense systems to grammaticalize the author's reasoned subjective choice of conception of a process."

23. Naselli, Andrew David, "A Brief Introduction to Verbal Aspect in New Testament Greek," *Detroit Baptist Seminary Journal* 12 (2007): 23.

24. Porter, "Greek Grammar and Syntax," 89.

25. Decker, *Temporal Deixis*, 26.

26. Decker adds, "aspect expresses a view of the process grammatically, *Aktionsart* expresses it lexically and contextually. The web of semantic factors comprised by aspect, lexis, and *Aktionsart*, along with other grammatical and contextual factors … is referred to … as the verbal complex." It must be remembered that tense usage "is not dependent upon lexis, otherwise there is no accounting for the number of different tense forms in Greek that may be used with the same lexical item within the same temporal contexts." Ibid., 27. See *PVA*, 87. For Porter, lexis may provide a point at which *Aktionsart* can be joined with a theory of verbal aspect, but this is exactly what is pointed out by Decker's definition of verb complex.

27. *TBF*, 51.

28. Markedness is a linguistic issue by which in opposition to two or more members in the speech act, "it is felt to be more usual, more normal, less specific than the other." Bernard Comrie, *Aspect: An Introduction to the Study of Verbal Aspect and Related Problems*, CTL (Cambridge, MA: Cambridge University Press, 1976), 111. See also Stephanie L., *Sentence Conjunction in the Gospel of Matthew: Kai, De, Tote, Gar, Syn and Asyndeton in Narrative Discourse*, JSNTSup 216 (London: Sheffield Academic Press, 2002), 65.

29. *PVA*, 90.

30. Porter, *Idioms*, 188.

31. Decker, *Temporal Deixis*, 107.

32. Buist Fanning, "Greek Presents, Imperfects, and Aorists in the Synoptic Gospels: Their Contribution to Narrative Structuring," in *Discourse Studies & Biblical Interpretation: A Festschrift in Honor of Stephen H. Levinsohn*, edited by Steven E. Runge (Bellingham, WA: Logos Bible Software, 2011), 185.

33. See Campbell, *Non-Indicative Verbs*, 10–11.

34. See Fanning, "Greek Presents," 172–173.

35. *PVA*, 92–93.

36. Paul J. Hopper, "Aspect and Foregrounding in Discourse," in *Discourse and Syntax*, edited by Talmy Givón, Syntax and Semantics 12 (New York, NY: Academic Press, 1979), 213.

37. Campbell, *Verbal Aspect*, 14.

38. Fanning perceived this need of interaction of the aspect with several other features right after his dissertation. He states that the understanding of aspect in the NT requires the interpreter to see "aspect for what it really is, in and of itself, apart from these wider features (the "definition" or semantic level) and tracing its significant interactions with these other features in actual usage." Fanning, "Greek Presents," 186.

39. *GGBB*, 615. Wallace asserts that it was the adjectival nature of participle that broke down any remnants of verbal aspect. See also *ATR*, 1111.

40. Ibid., 615. Italics his.
41. *PVA*, 366.
42. See the following verses for more examples: Matthew 15:12; Mark 8:1, 10:1, 14:67; Luke 11:26, 14:32. An important observation that must be made here is that though the tense of the main verb may vary, the participle is always in the aorist nominative in the upgraded effect.
43. *GGBB*, 643.
44. Ibid., 527. Since the whole debate on the aspectual legitimacy of the "historical present" is dealt with extensively in Greek studies, especially recent literature on verbal aspect, it will not be considered in this paper. The most recent works on verbal aspect in the NT agree with idea of vividness or dramatic narration. C. M. J Sicking, and P. Stork, "The Grammar of the So-Called Historical Present in Ancient Greek," in *Grammar As Interpretation: Greek Literature in Its Linguistic Contexts,* Mnemosyne Bibliotheca Classica Batava 171 (Leiden: Brill, 1997), 131–168. See also *GGBB*, 526–32; Fanning, *Verbal Aspect*, 226–39; *PVA*, 189–98; Decker, *Temporal Deixis*, 40–1; 101–04.
45. Decker, *Temporal Deixis*, 41.
46. *GGBB*, 507–09.
47. *PVA*, 189.
48. Bernard Comrie, *Tense*, 85.
49. See Fanning's most recent essay on the historical present, Fanning, "Greek Presents," 157–190, especially, 182–185.
50. Porter, *Linguists as a Pedagogue*, 54.
51. *SRG*, 249.
52. Ibid.
53. There are two reasons for including the treatment of verbal aspect here: first, the study of verbal aspect has shown that in planes of discourse, the perfective aspect realized by the aorist tense-form has the background function; second, while proponents of verbal aspect theory relate this background function to the aorist, the proposal here is that while the verbal aspect is important, the primary clue for the background function is found in the opposition of the participle (modulation) to the mood and/or modality, along with several other features. For aspect theory see *PVA*, Decker, *Deixis*, Fanning, *Verbal Aspect*. For a further development of the background function that goes beyond aspect theory, see *TBF*, 63–64.
54. *PVA*, 104.
55. Ibid., 106. See McKay, *Syntax*, 46. See also Porter, *Idioms*, 188. Fanning has a different approach in applying SFL to the New Testament. He sees that in narrative the background function is not associated with aorist aspect, at least in the indicative verbs. According to him aorists are used to carry the main or foreground narration. See Fanning, *Verbal Aspect*, 74–75, 255–290. However, Martin-Asensio has posed a strong critique to Fanning's perspective: "Fanning's wholesale adoption of Wallace's scheme is ill-informed given that Fanning's subject is New Testament Greek. Wallace's argument is that '… part of the meaning of the perfective aspect, at least in narration, is to specify major, sequential, foregrounded events, while part of the meaning of the contrasting non-perfective aspects, particularly an imperfective, is to give supportive, background information' (Wallace, 'Figure and Ground', p. 209). But in the Mark passage we could also argue that the aorist is used to set the scene for the two dialogues between the demonized man and Jesus (5:7–10, 18–19) in both of which the present and imperfects dominate. Another climactic point in this passage is 5:15, again built upon the present tense: καὶ ἔρχονται πρὸς τὸν Ἰησοῦν καὶ θεωροῦσιν τὸν δαιμονιζόμενον καθήμενον ἱματισμένον καὶ σωφρονοῦντα, τὸν ἐσχηκότα

τὸν λεγιῶνα, καὶ ἐφοβήθησαν. *TBF*, 62 note 42. These events can hardly be said to be 'subsidiary'." One wonders, however, why such a hard critique comes without numbering one page of Fanning's book. See Fanning's suggestion of the three-part structure of aorist and imperfect in narrative in his "Greek Presents," 179.

56. *PVA*, 380.

57. Campbell, *Verbal Aspect*, 29–30.

58. Not that they adopt any idea of the participle having temporal reference. The term background seems to be related to discourse prominence. See *SRG*, 248.

59. *LDF*, 183. See also *SRG*, 249.

60. *LDF*, 183.

61. First, there are examples where the aorist participle precedes the main clause and the present participle follows it (see footnote below). Second, there are examples where both the aorist and present participle precede the main clause (cf. Luke 15:5, 9). 3) There are examples where the present participle precedes the main clause (Luke 9:5–6; Act 4:34). 4) There are examples where the aorist follows the main clause (Matthew 27:4; Acts 10:33). Whatever order occurs, the spotlighting function is present.

62. The aorist participle is in *italics*, the main verb in **boldface**, and the present participle is underlined. See Matt 8:25; 9:18; 14:26; 15:22, 23; 16: 13, 22; 18:26, 28–29; 19:22; 20:11–12; 21:20; 25:20; 26:8, 42; 27:3–4, 29,35; 28:13, 18–21; Mark 6:25; 14:60; Luke 1:63; 5:8, 12, 13; 7:18–19, 39; 8:24, 54; 24:23; Acts 3:26; 5:22–23; 12:7; 22:26.

63. Keaton, M. *The Lexham Propositional Outlines Glossary*. Bellingham, WA: Lexham Press, 2014.

64. *PVA*, 382.

65. *SRG*, 249.

66. Ibid., 252.

67. See Decker's display for Mark. He notes that in his displayed passages (Mark 2, 6, and 15) there are a great number of participles and 85 % of the aorist participles precede the main verb. See Decker, *Temporal Deixis*, 121.

68. See Mark 15:15,17 Ὁ δὲ Πιλᾶτος βουλόμενος τῷ ὄχλῳ τὸ ἱκανὸν ποιῆσαι ἀπέλυσεν αὐτοῖς τὸν Βαραββᾶν, καὶ παρέδωκεν τὸν Ἰησοῦν *φραγελλώσας* ἵνα σταυρωθῇ, καὶ ἐνδιδύσκουσιν αὐτὸν πορφύραν καὶ περιτιθέασιν αὐτῷ *πλέξαντες* ἀκάνθινον στέφανον·. See also Mark 15:30.

69. The aorist participle is in italics, the present participle underlined and the main verb in boldface.

70. See *PVA*, 383.

71. *LDF*, 183. *SRG*, 251.

72. The semantics of the Greek verb contains at least 14 systems within its network. The verbal forms are what give realization to the verbal network. Porter, "The Greek Verbal Network," 17.

73. Runge declares, "a choice to use a participle to grammaticalize an action represents the choice to use a verb form that is less specific than a finite verb, whether in paratactic or hypotactic relation." See *SRG*, 248.

74. Fanning, *Verbal Aspect*, 65. This opposition seems to involve the contrast between mood, modality, and modulation. If this idea does not transcend verbal aspect, coherence would be impossible in cases where the most marked tense (in the participle) occurs side by side with the less marked tense (in the indicative), placing the foreground information with the less marked (aorist) indicative. Information given by the modulation is lesser marked than the information given by the mood. See Act. 16:9: "Καὶ ὅραμα διὰ [τῆς] νυκτὸς τῷ Παύλῳ ὤφθη, ἀνὴρ Μακεδών τις **ἦν** *ἑστὼς* καὶ *παρακαλῶν* αὐτὸν καὶ underlined{λέγων}· διαβὰς εἰς Μακεδονίαν **βοήθησον** ἡμῖν." Even though the actions described by the participle are heavily marked (stative, present), the most heavily marked

action is in the aorist. The reason why this occurs is due the opposition between modulation (less heavily marked) and the modal (more marked compared to the semantic presupposition realized by the participles). See Porter's thesis that says that based on the concept of markedness the stative aspect is the most heavily marked formally (perfect tense-form) and forms an opposition with the perfective aspect which is the least marked. See *PVA*, 90.

75. Porter and O'Donnel say, "each grammatical category in a particular system is given meaning by its relationship to the other categories within the system." See Porter, "The Greek Verbal," 11.

76. Ibid.

77. Halliday, *On Grammar*, 189.

78. Teun A. Van Dijk, *Cognição, Discurso e Interação*, Coleção Caminhos da Linguística, Apresentação e Organização de Ingedora Villaça Kock (São Paulo: Editora Contexto, 2011), 48.

79. Robert W. Funk, *A Beginning-Intermediate Grammar of Hellenistic Greek*. 2nd ed. SBLSBS 2 (Missoula: Scholars, 1973), § 845.

80. *LDF*, 184.

81. Buijs, *Participle*, 32.

82. *SRG*, 250.

83. *SRG*, 245.

84. Not all the New Testament examples of the aorist adverbial participle that begins a sentence have been analyzed in this study. Nonetheless, this principle is valid with almost all that have the upgraded participial effect. This is common with adverbial constituents. See *LDF*, 14.

85. See *PVA*, 94.

86. This is basically aligned with *LDF*, 181.

87. The abstraction of meaning involved in the participle can also be seen by this clause chain function. In Greek this quality of continuity and discontinuity can be described by the Greek conjunctions καί and δέ. However, the upgraded effect is able to present this continuity without distributing equal weight for both the participle and the main verb. See *SRG*, 23.

88. C. M. J. Sicking, and Peter Stork, *Two Studies in the Semantics of the Verb in Classical Greek*, Mnemosyne, Bibliotheca Classica Batava, 160 (Leiden: E.J. Brill, 1996), 6.

89. Campbell, *Verbal Aspect*, 15.

90. It may be that this clause chain was so easily noted that Codex Bezae changed the read of an aorist participle within the upgraded context into two subjunctives coordinated by καί. Several features can be used to explain this effect. Close association (*association étroite*) with the main verb following the specific structure, is crucially, even primarily, affected by the verbal complex, that is, lexis + form + context = pragmatic (and/or discourse) function. Sicking, *Two Studies in the Semantics*, 6.

91. Sicking, *Two Studies in the Semantics*, 42.

92. This is basically aligned with Sicking and Stork, *Two Studies in the Semantics*, 17.

93. In this case the connection is made by the connective with the semantic continuity assignment καί. To use καί may give the impression that all coordinate verbal forms have the same semantic weight, especially if the main verb is connected by καί.

94. See *SRG*, 254.

95. Luke 8:44 *προσελθοῦσα* ὄπισθεν **ἥψατο** τοῦ κρασπέδου τοῦ ἱματίου αὐτοῦ καὶ παραχρῆμα ἔστη ἡ ῥύσις τοῦ αἵματος αὐτῆς. (She *came up* behind him [and] **touched** the fringe of his garment, and immediately her discharge of blood ceased).

96. *SRG*, 255. The participle should be viewed as in contrast to the assertion whether +assertion or −assertion. Therefore, as a presupposition the participles invite the readers' to "participate" in the event (ideationally) so that the main action can be in the spotlight.

97. In the NT the aorist tends to precede the main verb and the present to follow it. See *PVA*, 382.

98. Daniel Wallace points out that "the telic participle almost always *follows* the controlling verb [main verb]. Thus, the word order emulates what it depicts. Some participles, when following their controlling verb [main verb], virtually demand to be taken as telic (e.g., πειράζω). "Although presenting the information in this way, Wallace is very sensitive to the discussion between semantic and pragmatic when he says, "as we have seen, there are eight kinds of adverbial participles: temporal, manner, means, cause, condition, concession, purpose, and result. Yet, it should be stressed that the participle in itself means none of these ideas." See *GGBB*, 636, 639. This has been mentioned by Robertson when he says "these ideas are not in the participle but are merely suggested by the context. See *ATR*, 1124. The telic idea is a pragmatic event. The only point signaled by the semantic of the participle is that of a factive presupposition and as such its secondary importance concerning the main verb, which is an assertion.

99. Bekalu, "Presupposition, 152.

100. See *BDF* § 417.

101. NLT, NRS, NAS, NIV, NJB, NLT, NRS, RSV, NAB.

102. *GGBB*, 637. See O'Brien, *Ephesians*, 386.

103. The scope of this idea is from Wallace, Ibid., 638.

104. Sim, "Undeterminacy," 349.

105. Ibid., 348. Jannaris notes that the participle "did not appeal to the taste and needs of popular speech because of its ambiguity and inconvenient inflection. For apart from its vagueness in regard to person, it did not even specify its own nature and meaning, but subordinated it to the context." See Antonius N. Jannaris, *A Historical Greek Grammar Chiefly of the Attic Dialect* (London: Macmillan, 1897), 504.

106. Although Halliday is dealing with modality and modulation in English, his theory can be applied effectively to the Greek verbal system, though the differences should not be ignored. Thus, the dependence on systemic functional linguistics can be seen in this approach. See Halliday, *System and function*, 209. *Italics* added.

107. See *GGBB*, 485 for a description of the imperatival function.

108. Porter presents some examples of an aorist preceding the main verb and a present participle following it. See *PVA*, 382.

109. Steven Runge sees a similar event occurring in Matthew 28:17–20. *SRG*, 251–52.

110. *SRG*, 266.

111. See *LDF*, 184.

112. Bekalu, "Presupposition," 152.

113. Ibid., 5. The relation of the adverbial participle with emotion is suggested here in hope that the future researches can extend this discussion.

114. Some manuscripts have the imperative form. The participle ἐγερθείς is well attested ℵ C K L N W Δ Θ *f*[1.13] 33. 565. 579. 700. 892. 1424. *l* 844. *l* 2211 m q.

115. Few manuscript replaced the participle by the imperatival form (αρον ℵ D 1424).

116. Some mss bring the participles "being angry" οργισθεις D a ff² r¹. The emotional context still visible.

117. Classical scholars have already mentioned these aspects. See Bakker, *Grammar As Interpretation*, 1–16; Sicking, and Stork, *Semantics of the Verb*, 6, 42–43. Lang, *Herodotean Narrative*, 2, 13; Lang, "Participial Motivation," 48–65, especially 49.

118. Egbert J. Bakker, "Verbal Aspect and Mimetic Description in Thucydides," in *Grammar As Interpretation: Greek Literature in Its Linguistic Contexts*, edited by Egbert J. Bakker, Mnemosyne, Bibliotheca Classica Batava 171 (Leiden: Brill, 1997), 7. The whole relation is crucially, even primarily, affected by the verbal complex, that is, lexis + form + context = pragmatic (and/or discourse) function. The speaker subjectively determines the use of indicatives and participles related to certain types of context.

119. See other examples with other participial functions in emotional environment. Matthew 19:22, Luke 2:48, 7:38, 8:47; John 20:11; Acts 2:13, 5:41; Phil 3:18.

120. See Appendix.

121. Sicking, and Stork, *Semantics*, 17.

122. Ibid.

123. Leckie-Tarry, *Language and Context*, 6.

124. Reed, "Language of Change and the Changing of Language," 131.

125. Robertson deals with the relation of the participles with verbs of emotion, but considers only the difference between the supplementary and the adverbial participle without any further discussion. See *ATR*, 1121.

126. Lang. *Herodotean Narrative*, 2.

127. Lang, "Participial Motivation," 49.

128. Ibid.

129. The number can vary because of its subjective nature and the lack of parallel passage to compare.

130. See Appendix.

131. There are forty occurrences of κλαίω in the New Testament within an emotional environment. The participle is present in all the examples whether as the participle of κλαίω or as indicating some movement toward the main clause with κλαίω. See Matt. 2:18; 26:75; Mk. 5:38–39; 14:72; 16:10; Lk. 6:21, 25; 7:13, 32, 38; 8:52; 19:41; 22:62; 23:28; Jn. 11:31, 33; 16:20; 20:11, 13, 15; Acts 9:39; 21:13; Rom. 12:15; 1 Co. 7:30; Phil. 3:18; Jas. 4:9; 5:1; Rev. 5:4–5; 18:9, 11, 15, 19.

132. Thuc. 4.27.2. It is interesting to note words in the same context such as ἐφοβοῦντο, and ἔχοντάς τι ἰσχυρὸν contribute for the feeling communicated.

133. Soph. El. 1160. Another example is τι δ' εν δολω δει μαλλον η *πεισαντ' αγειν* (why must we use trickery rather than persuasion, to lead him?) See Moorhouse, *The Syntax of Sophocles*, 251.

134. Egbert J. Bakker, "Verbal Aspect," 7.

135. Ludwig Radermacher, *Neutestamentliche Grammatik: das Griechische des Neuen Testaments im Zusammenhang mit der Volkssprache* (Tübingen: Mohr, 1911), 209. According to him, the use of the participle is a matter of a personal style, especially after the verbs γινώσκω, εἶδαν, and ἐπίσταμαι.

136. George M. Bolling, "The Participle in Hesiod," *CUB* 3 no. 4 (1897): 426.

137. Lang, *Herodotean Narrative*, 13.

138. One alternative name for this participle is that of *style* according to Wallace. This type of participle "adds color" to the story. See *GGBB*, 627.

139. *ATR*, 1136 (Cf. 2 Cor. 3:8–10; 6:9 f.; 9:11 ff).

140. Wallace refers to this participle as "pleonastic". See *GGBB*, 650.

141. *SRG*, 154.

142. *SRG*, 145.

143. Ibid. For a detailed presentation on redundant quotative frames see *SRG*, 145–162. There is a considerable agreement that this use was a natural feature of the Greek language and it does not need to be understood as Hebraism.

144. Ibid., 152.

145. Other participles of sorrow-regret sub-domain are found in Matthew: 26:22; 27:3.

146. Levinsohn, *Discourse*, p. 86

147. Ibid., p. 97.

148. Sicking and Stork, *Two Studies in the Semantics*, 43.

149. In a private e-mail, Daniel Wallace observes, "Poetry often changes the forms and structure from prose, so it's not at all a reliable guide for later prose usage."

150. Stahl observes that all of these features are the result of the context: "erscheint es in verschiedenen logischen Beziehungen, die sonst durch Bestimmungssatze mit dem Verbum finitum ausgedruckt werden. Dabei ist also festzuhalten, dass die logische Besonderheit solcher Partizipialsatze nicht im Partizipium selbst liegt, sondern bei ihm nur durch den Zusammenhang angedeutet wird." Johann M. Stahl, *Kritisch-historische Syntax des griechischen Verbums der klassischen Zeit. Indogermaqnische Bibliothek*, 4 (Heidelberg: Winter, 1907), 681–682.

151. Greg Clark, "General Hermeneutics" in *The Face of New Testament Studies: A Survey of Recent Research*, edited by Scot McKnight and Grant R. Osborne (Grand Rapids, MI: Baker Academia/ Apollos, 2004), 106.

CHAPTER FIVE

Semantics of the Upgraded Participle

The specific semantics realized by the Greek participle with its functional roles, are generally applied to the upgraded participial effect. The association of this specific pragmatic effect to the anarthrous aorist nominative participle that precedes the main verb simultaneously establishes several functional roles. The embedded clause is so closely connected to the main clause that the readers see two different actions in *association étroite* and mentally the participle is upgraded into the same mood or modality of the main verb.

It is not as though "the participle ... takes on the force of a finite verb and ceases, in some sense, to behave like a participle."[1] Rather, the impression that the participle is upgraded into the same mood of the main verb is just a functional result of being a semantic presupposition. In other words, it is because a participle behaves as a participle that the reader has this impression. Participle is a formal designation and as such will never cease to be a participle. This textual component can never be changed, and it is not changed with the aorist participle implicatures.

We divided this chapter into three main sections. The first, under the head of upgraded participle in the New Testament, introduces the semantics of the participle in contrast to the semantics of mood. Two subdivisions are added to analyze the structure of the upgraded participial effect with its relation to grammar, and the structure of the upgraded participle and its relation to pragmatics. The second section presents the upgraded function in the LXX, which agrees with Classical usage. The third section argues that the upgraded function, which is a pragmatic effect, was present in the classical period of the Greek language; therefore, it is a natural function of the participle.

The Upgraded Participle in the New Testament

What is the semantic or pragmatic relationship of an anarthrous aorist (adverbial) participial clause that precedes the main clause? There is much more than merely conveying information of secondary importance compared to that of the main clause.[2] As Campbell states, "a semantic value may be expressed through several different pragmatic implicatures, none of which should be confused with the semantic value itself."[3] Since the upgraded participle is just a pragmatic effect of the aorist participle due to several factors, it is necessary to reiterate here that the only semantic to be noted regarding the participle is that of +factive presupposition.

The analysis of any adverbial participle deals with its internal logic relation in the embedded clause, which denotes something in the imagination, whose existence is only ideational. It is a stylistic feature of the author through which he invites the readers to agree with the truthfulness of the embedded clause for the sake of the argument at hand. Again, as Palmer clarifies, "it is not factuality, certainty or truth that is at issue here. What is at issue is that nothing is being asserted, that there is no information value, because both the speaker and hearer accept the proposition."[4]

The information value used as the established information is derived directly or indirectly from the preceding discourse content, or from the generally accessible knowledge of every person.[5] Non-established information is the ultimate goal of a discourse, thus, as Runge states, "the presupposed information provides the framework for processing and understanding the focal information."[6]

Understanding focal information is often related to understanding the information structure. Writers of break default expectation of the flow of information in some marked ways that signal or point to some prominent feature of the discourse. For instance, verbs in Greek quite often occur in the beginning of the clause,[7] and when this normally expected information flow and prominence are violated, then it is because the writer wants to make something stand out.

With the upgraded participle function, it is possible to observe one of these natural flows being broken as the participle of the embedded clause is set at the beginning of the complex clauses. Examples, Matthew 2:11 ... **πεσόντες** *προσεκύνησαν* ... (... **they fell down** [and] *worshiped* ...), Matthew 2:14 ... **ἐγερθεὶς** *παρέλαβεν* ... (**he rose** [and] *took*); John 12:32 ... **ἀπελθὼν** *ἐκρύβη* ... ([Jesus] **departed** [and] *hid* [himself]); Acts 5:6 ... **ἐξενέγκαντες** *ἔθαψαν* ... ([the young men] **carried** him **out** [and] *buried* him); 2 Tim 4: 11 ... **ἀναλαβὼν** *ἄγε* ... (**take** [Mark] [and] *bring* ....)

All the examples above have in common the fact that the embedded clause with an anarthrous aorist participle with the upgraded function is placed at the beginning of a clause or sentence. The participles are factive presuppositions and "placing presupposed information in a place of prominence has the effect of establishing an explicit frame of reference, providing the reader with the primary basis for connecting what follows with what precedes" (backward-forward function).[8] The readers must exercise their minds to be able to connect many parts of the narrative or discourse. Knowing what was going on from the previous context, the readers now focus on the verb of the primary clause. The verb of the embedded clause has the functional role of hierarchization. The aorist participle of the embedded clause serves as a background to the main clause and it sets the main clause in the spotlight.

The readers are able to relate the verb of the embedded clause to the verb of the primary clause. When the upgraded effect is involved, this relation is such that readers mentally see the two actions so closely associated that they intellectually upgrade the aorist participle to the mood of the main clause. Although the participle in this function seems to be finite, the semantic value of its action is completely out of the finiteness system. Actually, the lack of limitation of the verbal form takes the participle out of the attitude subsystem. The action of the primary clause is in the spotlight, while the participle in this relation plays a "second fiddle".

The lexeme of the participles is not a necessary part for the communication of the main event. It could be removed, and the sentence would still make sense. Generally, the upgraded effect presents a circumstance in the form of movement, though unspecified, and the meaning seems to trigger the readers to make a mental exercise by assuming that the two actions are so associated that they look like one.

Structure of the Upgraded Participle: Grammar

The upgraded participial function occurs with an anarthrous aorist participle of the embedded clause preceding the main clause. The main verb can vary, but it is usually another aorist tense-form, with any mood (indicative, imperative, subjunctive, or infinitive).[9] In dealing with the structure of the upgraded participial and its relation to grammar, Porter's hypothesis is adopted here, although with a specific application to the moods, that is, patterns of textual usage readily illustrate that certain textual conditions become associated with particular mood/modality/

modulation forms, so that the use of the mood/modality/modulation form in the textual environment readily implicates the associated conventionalized meaning.[10]

Halliday defines structure as "the ordered repletion of like events that make up the patterns."[11] It represents experiential meaning, which tends to follow these common elements: "it will be a configuration, or constellation, of discrete elements, each of which makes its own distinctive contribution to the whole."[12] He goes on to say, "what the textual component does is to express the particular semantic status of elements in the discourse by assigning them to the boundaries ... and so marks off units of the message as extending from one peak of prominence to the next."[13]

Difference in sequence produces difference in meaning and this meaning can vary in degrees of delicacy, as is true in almost every language.[14] Since structure is realized by making a systemic choice, grammar in this case shows how a given choice made by the writer is realized in structural items.[15]

The relationship between the anarthrous participle of the embedded clause and the main clause establishes a process of hierarchization of clausal relationships in which mood as an interpersonal metafunction and modulation (ideational metafunction) indicate a high degree of compression of meaning.[16] For instance, Mat 27:4 ἥμαρτον **παραδοὺς** αἷμα ἀθῷον (I have sinned betraying innocent blood) and 28:7 καὶ ταχὺ **πορευθεῖσαι** εἴπατε τοῖς μαθηταῖς αὐτοῦ (so **go** quickly [and] *tell* his disciples).[17]

The example of Matthew 28:7 finds a parallel in Mark 16:7. Mark opts to coordinate the two-movement having equal status with two finite verbs "*ὑπάγετε εἴπατε* τοῖς μαθηταῖς αὐτοῦ" ("but go, tell his disciples"). Two finite verbs do not mark hierarchization, so the readers can take both verbs as having the same importance. In the broad context we see that the command is to tell, *going* is the attendant circumstance to perform central direction (*εἴπατε* τοῖς μαθηταῖς αὐτοῦ).

The urgency of the command is described by Matthew by the choice of the participle ταχύ (quickly) having the focus on the main verb (*εἴπατε*). We know that originally the two sentences had an imperatival force, assuming that Matthew used Mark as one of his sources. The difference between Matthew and Mark is related to their particular choices. Matthew chose to utter this command preceded by an attendant circumstance in a clause chain. The readers will take the participle as a command, not because of the participle in itself, but because of the *association étroite*. The participle with a lexeme of movement indicate an urgent, mentally unspecified movement made by both the direct addressees of the passage and by extension, all the readers.

Both evangelists had different options to communicate this event, but Matthew's choice opens a slot to be filled and felt by the readers because participles present with vividness what could be a very boring or cold command. The use of the participle in this clause chain helps the readers to keep focus on the main command (tell), but the readers cannot escape the urgency presented to themselves because of the its drawing function.

It is important to mention here that the classification of the different types of participles (means, manner, condition, etc.) is applied to the analysis of the internal structure of the participial adverbial clauses. In the examples above Matthew 28:7 is not the only case of upgraded function. Both of them demand a mental exercise from the readers to handle the internal structural and its external relation to the main clause.

How meaning is compressed in the Matthew 27:4 can be seen by the relationship of the embedded clause with the main clause. The structure of this participle is different from that of the upgraded in Matthew 28:7. In the former, the participle designates a meaning (ideational) that is part of a clause, which describes one single, even if complex, event. The predicates in this clause are characterized by the obligatory sharing of arguments (I have sinned by betraying innocent blood!). The example in 28:7, on the other hand, seems to present two independent events in close association, making the readers to take them as one event.

The participle of the embedded clause is not independent at all. However, the *association étroite* of the embedded clause and the main clause acts in the readers' mind by making them to see an implicit coordination (ideationally) plus the necessity of seeing the participle in the same mood as the main clause. These mental features plus the close association and the prominence of the participle at the beginning of the clause all indicate a lot of simultaneous meaning compressed into two verbs without losing track on focus of the main command.

The participial clause involves the need to process dependency relationships having the flexibility to realize meanings at various points on the presuppositional scale.[18] Matthew 2:8 illustrates the occurrence of the upgraded participial effect with the imperative mood. "καὶ πέμψας αὐτοὺς εἰς Βηθλέεμ εἶπεν· πορευθέντες **ἐξετάσατε** ἀκριβῶς περὶ τοῦ παιδίου· ἐπὰν δὲ εὕρητε, ἀπαγγείλατέ μοι, ὅπως κἀγὼ ἐλθὼν προσκυνήσω αὐτῷ"[19] ("And sending them to Bethlehem, he said, 'Go [and] *search* diligently for the child, and when you have found, tell me, that I will come and worship him.'"). *Going* is clearly part of the way that the *searching* is to take place.

By failing to see that the participle πορευθέντες is a formal designation, which grammaticalizes presupposition realized by modulation, one fails to grasp the author's main command, *search* (ἐξετάσατε) diligently for the child. The participle πορευθέντες provides the frame work for processing and understanding the focal information of the main clause. The clause chain helps the readers to keep track of the main clause but inevitably they drawn inside of the event by the presupposition.

The focal information resides in searching (ἐξετάσατε), but both the speakers and the readers must agree for the sake of the command that πορευθέντες is a prerequisite to achieve the directive. Thus, the aorist imperative is so associated with the participial embedded clause that the readers get the impression that the aorist participle was upgraded into the same mood as the main clause.

Two imperatives connected with καί or separated by a comma would utter two equal commands with the same level of prominence. However, by rendering one of the verbs with an aorist participle with the upgraded effect, Matthew wants the readers to take the participle seriously, but without giving it the prominence that belongs to the main command. Thus, to translate it as *going* would be ambiguous, since none of the tertiary implicatures fit well in this context. The best option here is to upgrade the participle into the same mood of the main clause. This is confirmed by the parallel passages above when two finite forms are replaced by a participle preceding the main verb with the upgraded effect.

The upgraded participial effect occurs with the indicative mood in the NT. Mark 2:14 καὶ παράγων εἶδεν Λευὶν τὸν τοῦ Ἀλφαίου καθήμενον ἐπὶ τὸ τελώνιον καὶ λέγει αὐτῷ ἀκολούθει μοι καὶ *ἀναστὰς* **ἠκολούθησεν** αὐτῷ (And passing by, he saw Levi the son of Alphaeus sitting at the tax booth, and he said to him, "Follow me." And **he rose** [and] *followed* him.). Sometimes the command comes alone, but the evangelist opts to describe the result of the command with the indicative (+assertion) preceded by a participle. Matthew 9:9 has the same structure of Mark FINITE VERB + καί + PARTICIPLE + FINITE VERB. Luke (5:28) adds an extra participle (καταλιπὼν) but follows the same structure of the other evangelists.

Luke 4:20 "καὶ *πτύξας* τὸ βιβλίον *ἀποδοὺς* τῷ ὑπηρέτῃ **ἐκάθισεν** καὶ πάντων οἱ ὀφθαλμοὶ ἐν τῇ συναγωγῇ ἦσαν ἀτενίζοντες αὐτῷ" ("and he closed the book [and] gave it back to the attendant [and] he sat down. And the eyes of all in the synagogue were fixed on him").

The quotation in Luke 4:18–19 is framed by a chiasm formed by the verbs ἀνέστη (indicative), ἐπεδόθη (indicative), and ἀνοίξας (aorist participle). Thus, "stood up," "was handed," "unrolling"—vv 16–17).[20] In the second part of the chiasm Luke seems to invert, bringing this narrative set to a peak. Thus, πτύξας (aorist participle), ἀποδούς (aorist participle), and ἐκάθισεν (indicative). Therefore, "rolled up," "handed," "sat down"—v 20).[21]

The first of part of the chiasm moves the narrative strongly by two indicatives and slows it down by the aorist participle. Then the second part starts slowly with two aorist participles, and then it brings the narrative back to an assertion that will culminate in the most prominent point of the narrative, that is, ἤρξατο δὲ λέγειν πρὸς αὐτοὺς ὅτι σήμερον πεπλήρωται ἡ γραφὴ αὕτη ἐν τοῖς ὠσὶν ὑμῶν

(Luk 4:21). Although another adverbial function would fit here, the necessary continuity of text demands that one recognizes the upgraded participial effect.[22]

The upgraded participial effect occurs with the subjunctive. Hebrews 6:1 "Διὸ ἀφέντες τὸν τῆς ἀρχῆς τοῦ Χριστοῦ λόγον ἐπὶ τὴν τελειότητα **φερώμεθα**, μὴ πάλιν θεμέλιον καταβαλλόμενοι μετανοίας ἀπὸ νεκρῶν ἔργων καὶ πίστεως ἐπὶ θεόν." ("Therefore, *let us leave* the doctrine of the first principles of Christ [and] **go on** in the perfection, not laying again a foundation of repentance from dead works and of faith toward God"). Lane renders this participle as having the upgraded effect. He says that participle "gains an imperatival force from the hortatory subjunctive φερώμεθα, "let us be carried forward."[23]

The main action is related to the main clause, the participle here not only gives background to the main verb but also sets it under the spotlight. The Hebrews should move on in the perfection, which is the author's projection with no expectation of fulfillment.[24] The close connection of the aorist participle with the main verb makes the readers take the participle as upgraded into the subjunctive. The hortatory subjunctive, *to move on in the perfection*, is the most prominent part, but the attendant circumstance "*leaving*," an unspecified movement, must be taken as a true proposition to achieve the action of the main clause.

The upgraded participial effect occurs with the infinitive. Luke 14:18 "καὶ ἤρξαντο ἀπὸ μιᾶς πάντες παραιτεῖσθαι. ὁ πρῶτος εἶπεν αὐτῷ· ἀγρὸν ἠγόρασα καὶ ἔχω ἀνάγκην *ἐξελθὼν ἰδεῖν* αὐτόν· ἐρωτῶ σε, ἔχε με παρῃτημένον" ("And they all began unanimously to refuse. The first said to him, 'I have bought a field and I have a need **to go out** [and] *see* it; I ask you, have me excused").[25] Infinitive expresses an action without referring to person, tense, gender, or number. An infinitive almost always occurs in relation to another verb.

Both the participle and the infinitive demand from the readers some mental exercise to relate them to their respective connections. The participle is connected in such a way to the infinitive that it precedes that whoever sees it will upgrade the participle to the same modulation to which it is pointing. "To go" is related to "to see." It is a background for the action of the infinitive that follows. The aorist participle sets the infinitive in the spotlight. The excuse is that the person bought a field, so he must see it, but that requires motion, he must go.

The aorist participle and ἰδεῖν are so closely associated that the reader tends to upgrade the anarthrous aorist nominative participle mentally to the same modulation as what follows. Thus, the phenomenon can relate the ideational metafunction of the modal semantic of the participle to the interpersonal metafunction realized by mood and modals, and another modulation grammaticalized by the Greek infinitive.

These functional components realized by finite verbs (e.g., indicative, subjunctive, or imperative) or non-finite verbs (e.g., infinitives), allow the writer to centralize the main sentence (spotlight) by rendering the rest of the actions as participles.[26] This is true on both sides of the main clause. Participles that precede the main clause have a function distinct from those that follow the main clause. However, the upgraded effect not only has a specific structure but also it describes the aorist participle clearly as part of the way that the main action takes place.

Word Order with the Upgraded Participle

There is a common word order related to the upgraded function. As already affirmed, the upgraded function is an anarthrous aorist nominative participle that precedes the main clause. Is this word order determinative to this specific function of the participle or is it not worth considering? For Wallace, the word order of the aorist participle seems to have a negative function, that is, to limit other choices of the aorist that precedes the main clause.[27]

Porter, in discussing patterns of constituent order and clause structure in New Testament Greek, says, "the flexibility of Greek syntax, because of its inflected endings and its various ways of forming clauses, does not mean that the order of various elements makes no difference."[28] This is exactly what syntax does. It deals with analysis of meaningful order of various structural elements that are parts of units.[29]

Words, phrases, and sentences normally occupy an established position in the Greek clause. Obviously, one's explanation for this assumption will depend on one's methodology. Dover notes that there are ten different views for explaining word order in Greek, but four are predominant: lexical and semantic, syntactical, logical, and stylistic determinants. Dover works much more with statistical patterns in order to determine word order in Greek.[30]

Winer explains Greek word order as both nature and convention. He says, "the arrangement of the several words of a sentence is in general determined by the order in which the conceptions are formed."[31] Another methodological explanation is presented by BDF who see the word order as a result of style.[32] Davison sees word order from a typological perspective, that is, a theory of Word Order Universals.[33]

Among several different functions, word order is a signaling device of prominence. Reed has established the importance of word order when he says,

> various word order constructions are motivated by informational requirements of the discourse and they should not be understood simply as stylistic variants. Since word order in Greek is somewhat flexible, the use of prominence may help to explain

apparently random variations of word order, which many have dismissed as an insig-
nificant feature of an inflected language[34]

There are other focal pointers in Greek and style can be added in some cases.
The specific discussion in the present study is related to the anarthrous aorist
(adverbial) participial clause that precedes the main verb. There is a complexity of
meaning and the specific word order of the upgraded effect seems to have a purposeful choice related to the specific semantic of the participle with its resultant
functional roles.

We understand that "prominence is rarely signaled by one grammatical device,
but more commonly is the result of a combination of grammatical categories. The
analyst should not depend on the presence of one grammatical category to determine prominence, but an analysis of all signaling devices."[35] The flexibility of the
Greek participle makes it suitable for use in environments where other forms are
often found (e.g., verbs, adverbs, adjectives, and nouns).[36] Therefore, the participial
order occurs according to the slot that it will fill. If a participle fills the slot of verb
then the word order will follow the anticipated verb's position. Although a Greek
participle does not convey time, the temporal reference of the participle is established relative to its use in context.[37]

This is not to say that it is necessary to determine time with the participle in
every instance.[38] Depending on the context, time could be important, and if that
is the case, then syntax will have an important role. Otherwise, Campbell's general rule should be accepted, that is, "the ability of the aorist participle to express
contemporaneous temporal reference, and indeed even future temporal reference,
in relation to its principal verb, indicates the weakness of the relative temporal
reference model of the participle."[39]

Generally, we observe that verbal aspect seems to influence the participial
order. An author is more prone to choose an aorist participle to express a complete
action and position it before the main verb in order to describe a background
circumstance to the main clause. Although no precise rule can be pointed out for
the upgraded effect because of its ambiguity (there is more than one discrete interpretation),[40] a set of data based on Logos Bible syntactical research shows that the
aorist normally precedes the finite verb of the clause that is related to it.[41] A search
in Logos Bible results in 886 places where the aorist nominative participle precedes the main clause.

Acknowledging that there are no Bible-search tools that are completely free
from error, this study uses Logos searches in an attempt to set boundaries by clause.
The reason for setting this limitation and establishing this specific relation comes
from the assumption that all the adverbial participles in the New Testament are in
the nominative.[42]

The exception has been already established by Culy who states, "Adverbial participles will always be nominative, except in genitive absolute constructions or when they modify an infinitive."[43] If the adverbial participial clause is searched only in the Gospels of Mark and Luke, the result will be Mark 562 and Luke 1,068. However, by narrowing the search to include only the aorist participle nominative in an embedded clause placed at the beginning of the sentence, the Marcan occurrences decrease from 562 to 162.

Applying the same limited syntactical search to the entire New Testament yields only 1030 adverbial participial embedded clauses that precede the main clause. Of these, the Gospels break down as follows: Matthew 223, Mark 160, Luke 208, and John 52. Logos presents the following results, 886 (88.3 %) out of 1030 anarthrous aorist adverbial participles in the nominative that precede the main clause in the New Testament, and 127 (12.4 %) anarthrous present adverbial participles in the nominative that precede the main clause.[44]

The following chart presents the result for the upgrade participial effect. The statistics below follow Wallace's qualification that "If a participle makes good sense when treated as an adverbial participle, we should not seek to treat it as attendant circumstance."[45] Based on the structure information common to the upgraded function, our study takes the open text syntactical relation from established examples of the participle of the embedded clause with the upgraded function and sets it as the criterion to produce the following statistics. It must be said, however, that the key determining factor for identifying the upgraded function is the analysis of each context.[46]

Considering the fact that 88.3 % of the adverbial participles that precede the verb are aorist and 12.4 % are present participles,[47] nothing can be said regarding the structure of the upgraded effect, since these 88.3 % involve all kinds of contextual meaning. Of the 886 aorist participles in embedded clauses that precede the main clause, 25.6 % are found having the upgraded effect, but there is no way to assign a pattern of usage for the upgraded based on this.

In the above constructions, there is an embedded clause, that is, a shifting, a linguistic element embedded to a level of grammar lower than the typical level at which it functions. This type of secondary clause is realized by the adverbial participle. The upgraded function is realized by this aorist participle, which is placed at the beginning of the clause having two simultaneous functions. All the above participles are readers-oriented that draw them into the context opening a slot so that the readers can infer important information to give vividness to the communication of the action.

The participial embedded clause before (in this case placed at the beginning of) the main clause indicates a switch from the previous context. It cohesively

UPGRADED	MATTHEW	MARK	LUKE/ACTS=	MOOD/ MODAL
Indicative	39	28	39/49 = 88	155
Imperative	11	11	14/9 = 23	45
Subjunctive	5	7	6/2 = 8	20
Infinitive	1	1	2/3 = 5	7
TOTAL	56	47	61/63 = 124	227

Figure 5.1. The upgraded effect in the NT.

connects something already in the previous context that the readers are able to access mentally (factive presupposition), and at same time, it renews the information by connecting the same embedded clause (participle) to the main clause.

The participial embedded clause also indicates a prioritization of the action of the main clause by giving to it focus. The following examples with different moods illustrate the point. The first example is with the indicative, the second subjunctive, the third imperative, and finally infinitive:

Matthew 2:11 καὶ *ἐλθόντες* εἰς τὴν οἰκίαν **εἶδον** τὸ παιδίον μετὰ Μαρίας τῆς μητρὸς αὐτοῦ καὶ *πεσόντες* **προσεκύνησαν** αὐτῷ καὶ *ἀνοίξαντες* τοὺς θησαυροὺς αὐτῶν **προσήνεγκαν** αὐτῷ δῶρα χρυσὸν καὶ λίβανον καὶ σμύρναν (And *going* into the house they **saw** the child with Mary his mother, and *they fell down* [and] **worshiped** him. And *they opened* their treasures, [and] **they offered** him gifts, gold and frankincense and myrrh.)

Observe that there are three primary clauses related to three embedded clauses. Each embedded clause depends on a primary clause. They are 1) *ἐλθόντες* … **εἶδον**; 2) *πεσόντες* **προσεκύνησαν**; 3) *ἀνοίξαντες* … **προσήνεγκαν**. All of the embedded clauses are aorist adverbial participles that form a logical clause chain. The conjunction καί connects the main clauses, not the participial clauses. The embedded clause should not be seen as a disconnected entity type, but as clause association.

Each embedded clause is logically connected to the main clause and each complex clause (embedded and main clause) are connected by καί. As already stated, καί has two functions: linking items of equal status,[48] and marking the transition to or from background information.[49] Conjunctions such as καί, δέ and οὖν should not be counted when identifying the initial element. In other words, καί "does not mark a distinction of semantic continuity or discontinuity,"[50] the participle placed in the beginning of the complex relational clause does—backward-forward function.

Matthew provides for the reader an indication that there is a backward-forward function (point of departure involving renewals) by means of the upgraded participle πεσόντες. The first one, ἐλθόντες, signals to the readers the starting point for communication, thus the readers must think, who is coming? What is going on? ἐλθόντες, though it answers something, is still vague. Runge recognizes that "the focus of the clause may be more specifically defined as the difference between what is presupposed in a context and what is asserted."[51]

The main difference between the present study and Runge's statement is that this study sees the participle as a semantic presupposition. Of course, the complexity of the relation between the embedded clause and the main clause involves a high degree of compressed meaning, thus the reader must appeal to the previous context to better know what they already know. Matthew 2:7 introduces two participants, Herod and the Magi;

the participles stimulate the readers' mind to connect circumstance to participants. Thus, ἐλθόντες, a plural nominative participle, must be referring to the Magi.[52]

The readers are looking at the broad context in order to infer the necessary information for the understanding of what the author is assigning for them. Being able to perceive the participants, the readers can move on to the main clause to which their focus was directed. Thus, "εἶδον τὸ παιδίον μετὰ Μαρίας τῆς μητρὸς αὐτοῦ" ("they saw the child with Mary his mother"). After doing that, Matthew presents a sequence of two pairs of main clauses preceded by two pairs of embedded clauses. The point of departure and renewal connected by καί does a simultaneous function by pointing backward-forward, that is, πεσόντες **προσεκύνησαν** …. The readers were already called to participate in the construction of meaning with the first participle but now there is a clause chain that makes the readers to look backward and move forward to participate in the emotional atmosphere.

The following examples with the anarthrous aorist adverbial participle preceding the main clause with an imperative illustrate the statement above.

Acts 10:20, "ἀλλὰ ἀναστὰς **κατάβηθι** καὶ **πορεύου** σὺν αὐτοῖς μηδὲν διακρινόμενος ὅτι ἐγὼ ἀπέσταλκα αὐτούς" ("Get up [and] *go down* and *go* with them nothing doubting, for I have sent them").

Acts 10:17–23a shows the culmination of Peter's vision, and while he was recovering from the shock of the vision on the roof of the tanner's house, the Spirit told him the messengers from Cornelius arrive at Joppa. Thus, the Spirit urged him to go with them back to Cornelius Acts 10: 20.

There are two primary clauses in this passage, ἀλλὰ ἀναστὰς **κατάβηθι** and πορεύου σὺν αὐτοῖς μηδὲν διακρινόμενος. There is a secondary clause type introduced by ὅτι, i.e., ἐγὼ ἀπέσταλκα αὐτούς. The embedded clause is introduced by ἀναστάς and has the upgraded effect in this context. The function of the embedded clause placed in the beginning of the sentence indicates the double functions backward (Given) and forward (New).

ἀναστάς grammaticalizes several features, but it is still fluctuating in some points, thus who is receiving this direction, what is going on? The readers already know who is who and what is going on. Luke signals all this by giving a grammatical feature that not only sets the main verb in the spotlight, but also indicates that this information is related to the previous context.

This factive presupposition (reader's mental exercise realized by the adverbial participle), is so closely associated with the main verb that it causes the reader to mentally render the aorist participle as though it were upgraded to the same mood as that of the primary clause.[53]

The last illustration brings the infinitive. The reason for presenting two illustrations is to show that the upgraded effect seems to place the main clause in the spotlight with more emphasis than is the case with the other clauses.

Acts 6:2 *προσκαλεσάμενοι* δὲ οἱ δώδεκα τὸ πλῆθος τῶν μαθητῶν **εἶπαν** οὐκ ἀρεστόν ἐστιν ἡμᾶς *καταλείψαντας* τὸν λόγον τοῦ θεοῦ διακονεῖν τραπέζαις (and the twelve *summoned* the full number of the disciples and **said**, "It is not right *to give up preaching* the word of God to serve tables.

There are two primary clauses and two embedded clauses in these verses. The first primary clause is οἱ δώδεκα εἶπαν …, the second primary clause οὐκ ἀρεστόν ἐστιν ἡμᾶς. The first embedded clause προσκαλεσάμενοι indicates a starting point for the forward communication, at the same time it activates the readers' mind to relate the information about who is who and what is going on from the previous context so that New information can be placed in the spotlight.

In summary, if Porter's hypothesis that patterns of textual usage readily illustrate that certain textual conditions become associated with particular forms, it may be said that all upgraded effect clauses are placed at the beginning of the principal clause or sentence and have a dual function: point of departure (pointing backward) involving a renewal (pointing forward). The focus will be on the main action even if this action is another modulation.

This is what happens to the infinitive in close association to the aorist participle. The aorist participle is upgraded in the readers' mind to the other modulation, and both modulations draw the readers' attention to the previous co-text and context. However, the infinitive refers to situations in which the event denoted by it is necessarily unrealized or uncompleted at the time of the matrix event.[54]

The nuances of the upgraded participle should be considered case by case in context since it deals with implicature; nonetheless, grammarians present the following features:

Grammatical (Morphological, Structural)

- The upgraded participle is always anarthrous.[55]
- Like all adverbial participles, it is nominative.[56] When referring to more than one person, the plural is used, while the singular refers to one person.
- The tense of the participle in the upgraded effect is always aorist.
- The aorist adverbial participle with the upgraded effect is placed at the beginning of the clause or sentence, because of the backward-forward function of the embedded clause.[57]
- There are no fixed rules on the mood of the main verb. The majority of the main verbs with the upgraded participial effect are indicative, subjunctive, imperative, and infinitive.[58]
- Verbs of motion such as πορεύομαι, ἔρχομαι are preferred for the upgraded effect, but others occur as well (ἐγείρω, λαμβάνω).[59]

Contextual

- Greek participles are factive presupposition (semantic value), and one of its functional roles, which operates within the readers' mind, indicates that in the upgraded pragmatic effect the aorist participle functions as a prerequisite to main clause.[60] The semantic value of the participle (factive presupposition) enables the readers to relate the participle with several parts of the context.
- The upgraded pragmatic effect relates to the embedded clause, which is so closely associated with the primary clause (main clause) that in the readers' mind it is as though the participle were in the mood of the main verb.[61]
- The upgraded participle occurs in a context where a particular author wants to describe the event of the main verb, and the participle is seen as part of the way the main action takes place.
- The upgraded participle appears in a context where something of an ingressive idea is expressed.[62] To accomplish the action of the main verb, the aorist participle in the embedded clause seems to be a starting point for the communication. In the context, the participle initiates an unspecified movement toward the action of the main verb.
- The upgraded participle gives new information with more emphasis on the main verb in contrast to the other aorist adverbial participles.[63]
- In emotional environment the upgraded participle draws the readers to be involved. In context of emotion the upgraded participle seems to combine in some examples both emotion and motion ([e]motion).[64]

Structure of the Upgraded: Pragmatics

The essential semantic feature governs the range of pragmatic usage; thus the participle is always a participle by form with its own meaning, and as such it grammaticalizes an essential semantic feature.[65] It is being argued here that the Greek participle is a semantic presupposition that does not exhaust the information, but is open. Thus, it lacks certain information, which is then added by the relationship with the main verb, and which can be grasped by the readers in a logical way.

The very fact the participle stimulates the readers to look at the previous context and then points to the main verb shows that the participle is a presupposition. Factive verbs are called as such because they presuppose the factivity of their complements; and as presupposition, they constitute background in linguistic expressions.[66]

The general observations on both the modal semanticis and the functional roles of the anarthrous aorist nominative participle are being here applied to the upgraded effect, which is a result of the semantic of the context. The two features seen in the adverbial participles placed at the beginning of the clause or sentence are applied below to the upgraded effect, that is, prioritizing, background.

The majority of scholars see the upgraded participle as communicating an action that is coordinate with the finite verb of the main clause.[67] With respect to logical relation, it is presented merely as an accompaniment of the action of the verb. Wallace states, "the participle then, in effect, 'piggy-backs' on the mood of the main verb."[68] The conventional explanation for an upgraded participle is commonly illustrated in the following way.

Matt. 2:13   Ἀναχωρησάντων δὲ αὐτῶν ἰδοὺ ἄγγελος κυρίου φαίνεται κατ᾽ ὄναρ τῷ Ἰωσὴφ λέγων· *ἐγερθεὶς* **παράλαβε** τὸ παιδίον καὶ τὴν μητέρα αὐτοῦ καὶ φεῦγε εἰς Αἴγυπτον καὶ ἴσθι ἐκεῖ ἕως ἂν εἴπω σοι· μέλλει γὰρ Ἡρῴδης ζητεῖν τὸ παιδίον τοῦ ἀπολέσαι αὐτό.

            And having departed, behold, an angel of the Lord appeared to Joseph in a dream, saying, "*Get up* [and] **take** the Child and His mother, and flee to Egypt, and remain there until I tell you; for Herod is going to search for the Child to destroy Him."

In chapters one and three we already discussed some aspects of this passage. Here we present some complements about the upgraded effect. In this passage as the angel is speaking to Joseph, the participle ἐγερθείς relates to the imperative παράλαβε, creating a clause chain. The participle here is still grammatically subordinate to the main clause in the imperative (παράλαβε), and from a trans-lational perspective does not fall into any of the adverbial categories.[69] Of course, if a nominative anarthrous participle is related to the main verb, the syntactical relation is adverbial.

Dana-Mantey admit that here the English participle fails to extend its use in order to render the entire force of the Greek participle.[70] For lack of other options, the participle in this function is translated as a finite verb connected to the main verb by the word *and* or a simple *comma*.[71]

In the translation, the participle ἐγερθείς piggy-backs on the mood of the main verb and is perceived as an imperative "get up". It may immediately be noted that there are three imperatives in the verse: παράλαβε which is perfective (aorist),[72] φεῦγε and ἴσθι which are imperfective (present).[73]

The conventional explanation for the upgraded participle is that it derives its "mood" semantically from that of the main verb παράλαβε,[74] and as such is very similar to the independent use of the participle, where a participle functions like a finite verb. Therefore, the participle here is a kind of a prerequisite before the main verb. "Get up" (ἐγερθείς) is not the main event; otherwise two imperatives would be used.[75]

The participle is not used as a finite verb since it is outside the attitude system, but in this context, it gives this impression because this is a part of the functional role of semantic presupposition. In the end, it is because of a lack of a better term in English that this participial effect is translated like an imperative.[76] Campbell states, "the participle, therefore, takes on the force of a finite verb and ceases, in some sense, to behave like a participle."[77] A participle, however, being a semantic presupposition, never ceases being a presupposition in contrast to ±assertion. The effect is ideational that causes the readers to make a mental exercise of an unspec-ified movement giving color to the event described.

Matt. 2:14   ὁ δὲ *ἐγερθεὶς* **παρέλαβεν** τὸ παιδίον καὶ τὴν μητέρα αὐτοῦ νυκτὸς καὶ ἀνεχώρησεν εἰς Αἴγυπτον.

And he *got up* [and] **took** the child and his mother by night and departed to Egypt.

Matthew 2:14 entails the same feature but now the same participle (ἐγερθείς) is related not to an imperative, but to an indicative (παρέλαβεν). Rather than translate it as "Get up" (2:13), here the participle is upgraded to the same notion described by the indicative mood. While related to the imperative, the impression that one gets from this participle is that Joseph was commanded not only to take his child and wife and flee, but to do so immediately.

Here with the indicative, the circumstance described by the aorist participle receives the pragmatic effect though now it is in the same mood as the interpersonal component realized by the indicative and becomes "he [Joseph] got up and took ... by night." The occurrence of νυκτός (genitive—time during the night) not only cuts off the possibility of translating ἐγερθείς as a temporal adverb like "*after you have risen*," but it also shows the urgency of this command. He obeyed immediately as the imperative requires, "he took" his child and wife.[78] In other words, ἐγερθείς is upgraded to the same mood as the main verb, that is, an indicative.

Recognizing that the upgraded participle is one of those Greek idioms that has no exact parallel in English, scholars tend to render it as two finite verbs coordinated by the English conjunction *and* or sometimes a comma to avoid repeating *and*. Burton, who calls the upgraded participle attendant circumstance, states that the upgraded participle function is "often equivalent to a coordinate verb with καί. Though grammatically not an independent element of the sentence, the participle in such cases becomes in thought assertive, hortatory, optative, imperative, etc., according to the function of the principal verb."[79] Since choice determines meaning, had an author wanted to coordinate two verbs with καί he would have produced a different relation than if he had used an adverbial participle.

The opposite of the Burton assertion is true. Because an author does not want to coordinate two actions, he chooses sometimes to set the embedded clause in a clause chain with the main clause and the formal way to do it is by the use of the Greek participle. Different effects can happen by different structure and relation of the embedded clause with the main clause.

At the level of the semantic category realized by the form, it is impossible to find principled grounds for distinguishing among means, manner, cause, result, and even the upgraded participle. The particular choice of the participle occurs in relation to the indicative, imperative, subjunctive, optative, and infinitive. The choice to use a participle to grammaticalize an action may be defined in terms of what is not chosen, in contrast to what is chosen.

Runge rightly observes, "The verbal participle does not explicitly specify the grammatical categories assigned to it, and this fact is widely acknowledged."[80] Therefore, since form and function are integral parts in semantic analysis, it can be said that the semantics realized by the Greek participle is that of presupposition, and its function "concerns knowledge which a speaker/writer does not assert but presumes as part of the background of a sentence, knowledge presumed to be already known to the hearer/reader."[81]

Knowing that form and function are integral to semantics does not mean that they are the same. Thus, as Comrie states, "The separation of meaning from implicature thus enables us, first to give a more accurate characterization of the meaning of a linguistic form, and second given to a theory of implicatures, to account for the implicatures that are assigned to linguistic forms in the absence of any cancellation of those implicatures."[82] The choice of the participial form blocks the +finiteness system which in turn blocks the attitude system. Here is a place to understand the participle on its own ground for the sake of the readers.

A participle is always a participle by form, so caution is recommended every time the upgraded function occurs. Although the majority of versions translate this participle as two coordinate verbs, scholars should be aware that statements such as the upgraded construction that says, "two verbs connected by καί would serve equally well, since the participle of attendant circumstance [upgraded participle] does not specify the relationship between the action of the main verb and the attendant circumstance."[83] Rather, the choice of the participle breaks the idea of coordination and sets a clause chain where the participle is so connected to the main verb that they look like one.

We have seen in the parallel examples that some evangelists of the synoptical Gospels chose to communicate the very same event using two finite verbs while others take one of the finite verbs and transforms it into a -finite in order to draw the readers to be part of a meaningful construction. As a matter of fact, the participle is grammatically dependent and thus not coordinate. Therefore, "to overlook this point is to miss the distinction between using a participle rather than a finite verb form that is truly coordinate."[84]

The coordinate idea is always available, and it is possible as we have seen in passages where Mark, for example, uses two finite forms connected by καί while another Gospel writer replaces one of the finite verbs (usually a verb of movement) and sets it in the upgraded structure to form a clause chain. The coordinate idea comes from translation and there are times when it is inappropriate to use it to express meaning.[85] The importance of the upgraded participial effect then appears as the participle is translated into English, and that is a different matter. This is not to say, however, that there is no exegetical significance in Greek to this function of the participle.

In Matthew 2:13, the participle is a presupposition which is listener/reader oriented and therefore it invokes the articulation of the text in the way that the readers will immerse themselves as part of the event itself since they are constructing meaning. The text of Matt 2:13 says ἰδοὺ ἄγγελος κυρίου φαίνεται κατ' ὄναρ τῷ Ἰωσὴφ λέγων· ἐγερθεὶς **παράλαβε** τὸ παιδίον καὶ τὴν μητέρα αὐτοῦ καὶ **φεῦγε** εἰς Αἴγυπτον.

The first participle λέγων is a shift[86] in the narrative that functions to capture the reader's attention for the discourse that follows.[87] Its function is to introduce a dramatic pause just before a (or the) significant point of the speech.[88] The atmosphere is surrounded by fear and the participle adds flavor to the narrative like a 'color commentator'.[89] The participle λέγων introduces a pause in the narrative and has the effect of attracting more of the reader's attention to the speech or segment of speech that follows.[90]

The other participle ἐγερθείς draws him or her into the event as though the same urgency being described invites the reader to perceive himself/herself as being part of the dynamic of the narrative by connecting the participle to the main verb as though the participle and the main verb form one action. What is explicit seems to be obvious and easy for the readers to follow. What is ideational (presupposition) demands more attention from the readers and therefore highlights points of focus demanding more mental effort from the readers.

Schlatter has stated, "wenn zwei Handlungen zu einem Vorgang verbunden sind, wird für die vorbereitende Handlung das Partizip des Aorists vor den Aorist des Hauptverbums gestellt."[91] Thus, the upgraded function indicates an action that is so connected with the action of the main verb that the two are seen as one process/action.

This connection of the participle with the main verb shows the versatility of a presupposition, which resides exactly in its capacity to work within readers at two levels: first, by reading a participle the reader perceives that "a greater emphasis is placed on the action of the main verb than on the participle."[92] Second, the connection of the participle ἐγερθείς with παράλαβε in this construction presuppositionally upgrades the participle to the mood of παράλαβε.

The writer, by choosing a presupposition is not only doing something herself/himself, but also demanding something of the listener.[93] Hence, the upgraded function gives its importance to the flow of the narrative. In both cases, ἐγερθείς precedes the main verb. If the main verb is παράλαβε (imperative), ἐγερθείς has the effect of being taken as imperative.[94] Joseph grasped the direction in which the participle was upgraded, since he immediately got up and obeyed the Angel's command according to verse 14. In this passage, then, ἐγερθείς is not only listener/reader oriented but it also communicates listener/reader *reaction*.

In summary, the abstraction of meaning can be seen in the use of the upgraded participle. the upgraded participle refers to an action that is so connected with the action of the main verb that the two are seen as one process/action. Although connected, the participle and the main clause do not describe the same perspective on the action. However, they are so related that the participle shows the hierarchization by setting the main verb in the spotlight and "piggy backing" the mood of the main clause. Therefore, ἐγερθείς is not equally important to παραλαμβάνω, but it is not unimportant, allowing the reader to ignore the urgency of the situation at hand.

Functions of the Upgraded Participle

Prioritizing Function

Greek participles are *modulations*, and the information given by a modulation is less heavily marked than that given by a *mood/modality*. Their relationship represents a process of hierarchization. Thus, the anarthrous aorist participle is a modulation that has a meaningful distinction first of all in contrast to the attitude system, mood (+assertion) and modal (-assertion).

In discourse, everything is important, but not important for the same reason. The role of the participle is to mark what is of primary importance, as though the participle is the spotlight illuminating the main verb. Therefore, the first function of the upgraded participle is that of prioritizing the action of the main clause.

By choosing a participle over an indicative, an original writer made a decision of emphasis and meaning.[95] From the -finiteness system an author has the option of choosing a factive presupposition, which lacks limitation on the form of the verb that blocks the person of the verb opening a slot for the readers to fill.

One of the functions of a presupposition is that of prioritizing the main action. Runge states, "speakers tend to start with what is already established or knowable in the context and then add new or 'nonestablished' information to it."[96] Focal point is added by 'nonestablished' elements, and non-focal information is established.

Palmer sees communication with irrealis (non-assertion) as being without information value since both speaker and hearer accept the proposition.[97] For example, Matthew 28:19 "*πορευθέντες* οὖν **μαθητεύσατε** πάντα τὰ ἔθνη, βαπτίζοντες αὐτοὺς εἰς τὸ ὄνομα τοῦ πατρὸς καὶ τοῦ υἱοῦ καὶ τοῦ ἁγίου πνεύματος" ("*Go*, then, [and] **disciple** all the nations, baptizing them in the name of the Father and the Son and the Holy Spirit").[98] πορευθέντες is not the focal information of the sentence, but the speaker stimulates the readers to presuppose with him that "going" is indispensable for a correct understanding of the command. The command is "*make disciples*," but both the speaker and the readers must see the participle and the main verb as one process/action.

The main verb is an aorist imperative μαθητεύσατε (*make disciple*) which is then complemented by three anarthrous participles—one that precedes (aorist πορευθέντες [going]) and two that follow (present βαπτίζοντες[99] [baptizing] and διδάσκοντες [teaching]). Although there are three participles in the passage above, the focus of the discussion below is on πορευθέντες because it is an upgraded participial clause.

Based on the examples of passages that occur in the synoptical Gospels, we have places where one or two of the evangelists use two finite verbs while others take one of the finite verbs and changes it into an aorist participle preceding the main clause. We have seen two imperatives in one of the evangelists while other grammaticalizes one of the verbs with an aorist participle preceding the main clause. It is a matter of choice, but choosing a participle is different from a choice of a finite verb.

There are examples where the evangelists record the same event with virtually the same verbal lexemes but different choices from the verbal network. Mark 2:9 has a sequence of finite forms.

Mark 2:9–11	ἔγειρε καὶ ἆρον … καὶ περιπάτει; … ἔγειρε ἆρον … καὶ ὕπαγε
Matthew 9:5–6	ἔγειρε καὶ περιπάτει; … *ἐγερθεὶς* **ἆρον** … καὶ ὕπαγε
Luke 5:23–24	ἔγειρε καὶ περιπάτει; … ἔγειρε καὶ *ἄρας* … **πορεύου**

Every author grammaticalizes the same event with different choices. Matthew takes originally Mark's two present imperatives (ἔγειρε, ἆρον) and changes the imperative ἔγειρε into an aorist participle ἐγερθείς preceding an aorist imperative resulting in the upgraded effect. It is not a participle functioning as an imperative, rather it is a participle functioning according to its own nature.

Back to the analysis of πορευθέντες in Matthew 28:19, there are two extreme views regarding this participle: first, there is a tendency to render πορευθέντες as an imperative so that the great commission is not seen as a great suggestion.[100] Second, there are others that deemphasize πορευθέντες to the point of omitting it in translation. Paul Gaechter purposes this omission when he says that "'Geht' hat also keinen eigenen Akzent und ist darum nicht wörtlich zu übersetzen."[101] Both extremes should be avoided.

As Rogers says, "the participle is not to be weakened to a secondary option which is not as important."[102] The fact is, however, that it should not be seen as equally important, since not every action is equally important, and that is one of the most important functions of the aorist participle in this verse. The upgraded participial effect prioritizes the central action described by the main verb.[103] The imperative flavor rather than being something in the written text it has an imperative flavor in the reader's mind as a result of the *association étroite* of the participle. Two events become one jointed event in the upgraded relation. This is what Matthew is doing, he is assigning something to his reader both at the semantic level and at the structure level.[104]

The participle is less specific at rendering any coordination since it does not gramaticalize direction (imperative), but only presupposition. Therefore, by choosing πορευθέντες, Matthew describes some condensing action, at the same time that he is prioritizing the action of the main clause, μαθητεύσατε but surrounded by a color and vivid attendant circumstance.

Rogers again perceives that "the major emphasis of the commission lies in the aorist imperative ("make disciples") which is complemented by an aorist participle ("go") which is also part of the command."[105] This feature is noted by Wallace who says, "the relative semantic weight in such constructions is that *a greater emphasis is placed on the action of the main verb than on the participle.*"[106]

Language is an exchange of meaning, and Matthew is imposing his specific point of view on the text in order to highlight various levels of meaning.[107] Finite verbs are more central than non-finite verbs (participle and infinitive). He knows that not every action is equally important, and he is marking this by using the aorist participle.[108] This is a rhetorical strategy. The imperative (μαθητεύσατε) is the most prominent part of this relation and the participle (πορευθέντες) points to it. The main command is directly addressed to the disciples, but the readers cannot escape the command since the aorist participle drew them into the attendant circumstance with the upgraded effect.

There is another syntactical structure with the upgraded effect in this passage. When the aorist anarthrous participle preceding the main clause is used, it serves to prepare the readers for what comes; the upgraded participial function is upgraded to the mood of the main clause only ideationally. Formally, a participle can never be an imperative (+direction), and since the semantics of the participle realized by its form grammaticalizes presupposition in contrast to +finite system, two features should be highlighted.

First, Matthew does not reduce the participle πορευθέντες to a mere non-imperative sense in this passage.[109] Rather the upgraded construction indicates that πορευθέντες is an integral part of the main verb as though the participle were describing attitude. This a mental exercise in written form making an unspecified movement toward the realization of the action of the main clause.

Second, Matthew does not use πορευθέντες as an imperative. Had Matthew used two imperatives he would have introduced ambiguity about which of the two imperatives was more important to him. In the upgraded construction the participle is so related to the main verb that it sounds like an imperative, but that happens without ambiguity. The main verb is the priority in the speech act, while the participle plays a "'second fiddle' to the main action."[110]

Background Function

The upgraded participle is like any participle. Semantically, a participle is a +factive presupposition. Hierarchization is a functional role of being a presupposition. Hierarchization has two resulting functions: prioritizing, which was just treated, and background function. After discussing the prioritizing function in Matthew 28:19 with the upgraded participle, the background function will now be considered.

Background provides the context within which the main events (foreground) take place. It is background primarily because *it does not advance the narrative or argument.* When a term is combined with others, there is a logical opposition[111] between the central meaning of one term and the central meaning of the other term.[112] The central meaning of πορευθέντες grammaticalized by form is that of presupposition while the central meaning of μαθητεύσατε is that of direction or command. The action of the participle is backgrounded with respect to the main action (μαθητεύσατε). πορευθέντες has a supportive role and thereby keeps the reader's attention focused on the μαθητεύσατε.[113]

In terms of background, there are two things in the upgraded function: 1) πορευθέντες serves as a background action to the main verb, 2) it also sets the main verb in the spotlight. The use of the participle ensures that the main action, μαθητεύσατε, is obviously marked as the most important in the sentence.

Three participles are connected with the main clause in this passage. The aorist participle (πορευθέντες) serves as the background while the present participles (βαπτίζοντες, διδάσκοντες) develop the idea commanded by the main verb. It is like a puzzle: the aorist participles are the background, the main verb is the central part of the image, and the present participles are the pieces that implement the landscape.

By starting this sentence with πορευθέντες (an anarthrous participle), Matthew does not assign any discontinuity. He assigns continuity that indicates to the readers the necessary connection between the previous narrative with what is ahead.[114] In other words, he has given lots of new information in the previous context and by using participles, Matthew wants to prepare the readers for more new information.

With this upgraded function, Matthew assigns something to the readers in order to specify the most prominent part, μαθητεύσατε πάντα τὰ ἔθνη.[115]

A logical 'clause chain' (πορευθέντες) is thus formed, that logically connects two sentences by assigning continuity between them "ἐδόθη μοι πᾶσα ἐξουσία ἐν οὐρανῷ καὶ ἐπὶ [τῆς] γῆς" ("All authority in heaven and on earth has been given to me") and "μαθητεύσατε πάντα τὰ ἔθνη" ("make disciples of all nations"). The aorist participle is dependent on μαθητεύσατε and the continuation has the forward pointer as focal. The verbal complex formed by the participle (πορευθέντες) of the embedded clause and the finite verb of the main (μαθητεύσατε) should not be taken as two distinct commands that are equal to each other. But neither should it be treated as though Jesus is giving a suggestion "as you go," or the like.[116]

Upgraded Participle and Verbs of Motion

The background and prioritizing functions are extended into a clause chain by which the speaker/writer expects to draw the readers into the environment of the narrative.[117] The participle occurs in different types of context, not necessarily an emotional one, but as has been argued, when it commonly occurs in context of emotion the readers are drawn into it. Since the function of the participle is related to main clause, the participle with verbs of movement are common in order to express an unspecified movement toward the main action.

The same features are commonly observed with the upgraded participial effect: a preference for verbs of movement (motion) and, though there is a high degree of subjectivity, a tendency to occur in an environment with some sort of feelings when the author wants to get the readers involved in it. For instance, there are twenty-one occurrences of the motion verb πορεύομαι in the aorist participle.[118] Twelve are anarthrous aorist (adverbial) participles that precede an imperative and are upgraded to the same mood.[119] The very use of the participial form of πορεύομαι connected to a different mood shows that any attempt to see it idiomatically fails.

Another verb of motion that occurs with the participial upgraded function is ἀνίστημι. Of the approximately one hundred eight occurrences, sixty fit in the upgraded function. It is possible that the conventionalized usage somehow influenced it to such an extent that this participial usage became idiomatically fixed.[120] Even in classical Greek, Thucydides used the anarthrous aorist (adverbial) participial clause ἀναστήσας with the upgraded function (… καὶ κατὰ τάχος ἀναστήσας ἦγε τὸν στρατόν … - … and quickly he *rose up* and **led** his army …).[121]

The choice from the verbal system in regard to these two verbs does not occur at the cost of any semantic value of both participle and mood/modal. The participle in these two verbs grammaticalizes +factive presupposition that automatically block the attitude system. The main point is asserted while the presupposition brings readers to participate on the construal of meaning. (See Figure 5.2 below)

What is true for the participle generally is true for the upgraded function specifically, the extension into a clause chain[122] and the preference for contexts involving [e]motion when an author wants to get the readers involved with it.

| Matt 9:13 | *πορευθέντες* δὲ **μάθετε** τί ἐστιν· ἔλεος θέλω καὶ οὐ θυσίαν· οὐ γὰρ ἦλθον καλέσαι δικαίους ἀλλὰ ἁμαρτωλούς. |
| | But *Go* [and] **learn** what is, 'I desire mercy, and not sacrifice.' For I did not come to call the righteous, but sinners. |

The narrative of verses 11–13 contains several different actions. The Pharisees saw Jesus and questioned why he was eating with sinners. Jesus replied to them by saying that those who are healthy do not need a doctor but the sick ones.

In the first part of verse 13 the use of the anarthrous aorist (adverbial) participial clause backgrounds the action of *learning*, indicating that the prominent part of the contrast (presupposition vs. -assertion) is in the main action (μάθετε). The main clause is set in the spotlight of the participle, which also adds the background idea. While the focus is on "learning," there are two simultaneous features in the context - one indicated by the lexis (motion) and the other defined by the co-text (emotion).[123]

Matthew communicates two connected actions. The use of the participle as a factive presupposition with its functional role serves as the background and prioritizes the action of "learning." He invites the readers to feel the environment of [e]motion assigned by ἔλεος θέλω καὶ οὐ θυσίαν (I desire mercy, and not sacrifice). It is as though Jesus is saying to the reader as well "*Go* and **learn**" what I expect from you.

The reader will perceive that there is a slight departure from the shared information of the preceding verses involving a renewal in verse 13 where the focal information can be found. By rendering "go" as a participle in this association Jesus is doing more than simply suggesting (as you are going), but he is not saying "go" as an imperative. Rather, the participle as a presupposition, is able to be upgraded in the reader's mind to the mood of the main. The anarthrous aorist (adverbial) participial clause in this function is relegated into a supportive role and thereby sets the focus on the reader's perspective of the main action of the direction.

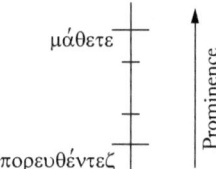

Figure 5.2. Prominence: spotlighting main verb. Developed from Jeffrey T Reed, *A Discourse Analysis of Philippians*, 108.

| Matt 11:4 | καὶ ἀποκριθεὶς ὁ Ἰησοῦς εἶπεν αὐτοῖς· *πορευθέντες* **ἀπαγγείλατε** Ἰωάννῃ ἃ ἀκούετε καὶ βλέπετε· |
| | And Jesus answering them said, *Go* [and] **report** to John what you hear and see. |

This verse is introduced by a "quotative frame" (ἀποκριθεὶς ... εἶπεν) which signals a transition from narrative proper to a speech or dialogue embedded within the narrative.[124] The narrative switches into a dialog because John the Baptist sent his disciples to know if Jesus was the one who he was expecting. The focal part is ἀπαγγείλατε (report). The participle πορευθέντες (going) is a clause chain with the main clause. This chain sets the main verb in the spotlight and serves as background for the main action.

The semantic domain of motion occurs in a context where unbelief seems to hit John the Baptist, who then sent messengers to Jesus with his question. His answer draws the readers' attention to one segment of the discourse by slowing down the narrative at the same time that a renewal occurs. The environment involves a sort of [e]motion since the emotive tone is felt in the following verses (20-25) describing the unrepentant city. Again the participle (πορευθέντες) and the main verb (ἀπαγγείλατε) are so closely related that the participle seems to adopt the same mood of the main verb.

| Luke 17:19 | καὶ εἶπεν αὐτῷ· *ἀναστὰς* **πορεύου**· ἡ πίστις σου σέσωκέν σε. |
| | Then he said to him, *Get up* [and] **go**; your faith has saved you. |

Luke 17:11-19 shows a natural feature of the upgraded participle, namely [e]motion. The emotional atmosphere is highlighted in 17:11 with Jesus' final journey to Jerusalem (see 9:51-53; 10:38; 13:22, 33; 14:25; 17:11; 18:35; 19:1, 11, 28, 41).[125] There two stages in this narrative: 1) the miracle itself (17:11-14), and 2) the Samaritan's disposition to come back to thank and praise Jesus

(17:15-19).[126] Verse 14 has two anarthrous aorist participles that precede their main clauses (ἰδών … εἶπεν and πορευθέντες … ἐπιδείξατε).

Both participles spotlight the main verb and serve as the background and prioritization of the main verb. However, only πορευθέντες is so connected to the main verb that the reader gets the idea that the participle works as an imperative. Both verbs in this passage have the reader as its goal. While the imperative gives direction to the original addressee, the participle invites the reader to feel as though the command is for him or her.

There is another clause chain in verse 15 that also involves two participles. These two participles have a spotlighting function for the main verb. An anarthrous aorist participle (ἰδών) precedes the main verb (ὑπέστρεψεν) and an anarthrous present participle (δοξάζων) that follows it.[127] The present participle describes some aspect of the event of the main verb, as though it is an addition to the main clause.[128] The environment of gratitude highlights the [e]motion involved in the context.[129] The participles invoke *perception*, and the man has correctly connected Jesus with God's work. His actions simply reveal the depth of his perception. Therefore, the participle demands something from the readers.[130]

In verse 18, Jesus asked "οὐχ εὑρέθησαν ὑποστρέψαντες δοῦναι δόξαν τῷ θεῷ εἰ μὴ ὁ ἀλλογενὴς οὗτος" ("Has no one been found returning to give glory to God except this foreigner?").[131] There are three verbal forms (εὑρέθησαν ὑποστρέψαντες δοῦναι) connected in this passage.[132] While some scholars see an emotive edge in the choice of this NT *hapax legomenon* (ἀλλογενής),[133] it is possible that the emotive tone has to do with the combination of several features in the context, and this is the type of context that the participle is used to draw the readers into the environment of the event.

Verse 19 culminates this narrative. Jesus says to the leper, "Ἀναστὰς πορεύου·" ("*get up* and **go**"). The participle is what gives color to the narrative and, at the same time, points to the main verb. The participle ἀναστάς is related to a present indicative creating some sort of suspense related to a future event.[134] There is such a close relationship between ἀναστάς and the present imperative that the reader gets the impression that there is only one action being described. The participle sets the background for the present imperative. These accumulated features together point to the climax of the narrative, that is, "ἡ πίστις σου σέσωκέν σε" ("your faith has saved you").[135]

In summary, the analysis of the upgraded function of the participle is primarily a pragmatic one. This particular function follows the normal semantics of all adverbial participles, and the only semantics of +factive presupposition. The abstraction of meaning of the participle shows that the functional role of being a presupposition results in hierarchization, which has background and prioritizing functions. These two functions extend to be a clause chain by which the speaker/ writer captures the reader's attention.

The Upgraded Participle in the LXX

Because of the presence of the upgraded function in the LXX,[136] some scholars have seen this function as a Hebraism.[137] However, the number of the so-called "Hebraisms"[138] has been reduced since the discovery of the papyri. After Moulton's research in the papyri anything which has ever been termed a "Hebraism" at once arouses his suspicion.[139]

The purpose of this section is to investigate the presence of the upgraded function of the participle in the Greek translation of the Hebrew Bible. The viewpoint defended here is that the upgraded function of the participle is a natural feature of Greek language and should not be considered as Hebraism since, as will be seen in the next part, this function was already present in the Classical period.

Williams observes,

> A little less than one-half of the participles in the Septuagint translate participles in the Hebrew, that is, over half of the participles in the Septuagint translate something else (infinitive absolute, infinitive construct, or a finite verb ....The Hebrews knew not the adverbial use of the participle until they learned it from Greek-speaking peoples. The forty-one cases of the adverbial, and the four cases of the complementary, participles in the Septuagint show how the translators were influenced by Hellenism (as to grammatical constructions at least).[140]

The use of this function of the participle is quite old. More than that, idioms of a language by nature are set patterns of accepted usage, and this function, though not so frequent, was present in the use of the participle.[141] Of course, even if two bodies of material are contemporary, a cause and effect relationship has not been established.[142] In other words, the upgraded function occurs in the LXX, but it is also part of the Classical period. Curiously, the translational technique of the LXX calls attention to this. When Hebrew reads two imperatives, the translators of the LXX would sometimes render the first imperative as an anarthrous aorist participle preceding the other verb having the upgraded participial effect.[143] Something common in the synoptical Gospels.

Our research does not deal with translational techniques of the LXX,[144] which is beyond the scope of this study. However, it must be admitted that the translation of the Hebrew Bible into Greek represents, at least with the upgraded function, more than a mechanical reproduction of a Hebrew *vorlage* into Greek.

Upgraded Function with Verbs of Motion in the LXX

Gen. 27:9	καὶ *πορευθεὶς* εἰς τὰ πρόβατα **λαβέ** μοι ἐκεῖθεν δύο ἐρίφους ἀπαλοὺς καὶ καλούς, καὶ ποιήσω αὐτοὺς ἐδέσματα τῷ πατρί σου, ὡς φιλεῖ.
	And *Go* to the flock [and] **take** for me two young goats, tender and good, and I will make them meats for your father, as he loves.
	לֶךְ־נָא אֶל־הַצֹּאן וְקַח־לִי מִשָּׁם שְׁנֵי גְּדָיֵי עִזִּים טֹבִים וְאֶעֱשֶׂה אֹתָם מַטְעַמִּים לְאָבִיךָ כַּאֲשֶׁר אָהֵב׃

Assuming that the translators of the LXX found the two imperatives as the Massoretic Text presents them, this translation is valuable for supplying social and historical information. The two Hebrew imperatives לֶךְ (verb qal imperative masculine singular) and קַח (verb qal imperative masculine singular) were translated by an anarthrous aorist participial clause (πορευθείς [לֶךְ]) and a finite aorist imperative (λαβέ [קַח]). The translators of the LXX in Genesis assumed that these two Hebrew imperatives were so connected that the first could fit well as a Greek participle and the second as a normal imperative.

The problem here could be like what Sirach asserted in his prologue 1:22–26, "22 αὐτὰ ἐν ἑαυτοῖς Εβραϊστὶ λεγόμενα καὶ ὅταν μεταχθῇ εἰς ἑτέραν γλῶσσαν 23 οὐ μόνον δὲ ταῦτα24 ἀλλὰ καὶ αὐτὸς ὁ νόμος καὶ αἱ προφητεῖαι25 καὶ τὰ λοιπὰ τῶν βιβλίων26 οὐ μικρὰν ἔχει τὴν διαφορὰν ἐν ἑαυτοῖς λεγόμενα" (The same things uttered in Hebrew, and when translated into another tongue, and not only these things, but even the law itself, and the prophets, and the rest of the books, have no small difference) (Sirach Prolog 1:22–26). Another explanation could be a matter of choice, namely the translators chose to render one of the verbs as a participle so that the second verb could be in the spotlight.

Waltke and O'Connor agree with this when they say, "the choice of a word may express one type of meaning, its morphology another, and its position in sequence another; and any element is likely to have more than one structural role, like a chord in a polyphonic structure which participates simultaneously in a number of melodic lines."[145] The choice to use a participle to grammaticalize the first imperatival form of the Hebrew represents, at least in this case, the choice of using a form that is less specific, less determined so that the reader could participate in the meaning uttered.[146]

In Genesis 27:9 the translators had the choice of translating as two Greek imperatives, but they did not. They chose to render one of the Hebrew imperatives as a +factive presupposition and the other as an imperative. The choice of a presupposition brings a resultant functional role of hierarchization, which in turn, has a double function of background and prioritizing function. The basis for the choice seems to be the translators' interpretation.

In Hebrew, on the other hand, a "clausal *waw* is a simple conjunction, that is, it places propositions or clauses one after another, without indicating the hierarchical relation between them."[147] The translators of Genesis in this passage decided to render it with two nuances. 1) They rendered it as though the two verbs could be taken as describing one only action. The Hebrew language tends to use the conjunctive *waw* "to join two clauses which describe interrelated or overlapping situations not otherwise logically related."[148] 2) The best option to keep, at some level an imperatival flavor with the two verbs, is to render one of the Hebrew imperatives as a participle and preserve the other as an imperative. This secondary function is called the upgraded participle. The focal point is λαβέ [קַח], but this does not mean that the participle is just a suggestion. πορευθείς is so closely connected to the imperative that from the reader's perspective, it should be seen with this imperatival flavor.

Gen. 27:13   εἶπεν δὲ αὐτῷ ἡ μήτηρ ἐπ' ἐμὲ ἡ κατάρα σου τέκνον μόνον ὑπάκουσον τῆς φωνῆς μου καὶ *πορευθείς* **ἔνεγκέ** μοι

[His] mother, however, said to him: "Let your curse be on me, my son; only obey my voice, and *go* [and] **bring** them to me."

וַתֹּאמֶר לוֹ אִמּוֹ עָלַי קִלְלָתְךָ בְּנִי אַךְ שְׁמַע בְּקֹלִי וְלֵךְ קַח־לִי׃

In Genesis 27:9 the *waw* precedes only the second imperative while in 27:13 the *waw* precedes the first imperative. וְלֵךְ קַח **and go, bring** are both imperative, however, the Septuagint text of MS B has an aorist participle followed by an imperative, both in the aorist. To take the Greek participle as any other adverbial function but upgraded would suggest that Rachel is giving Jacob an option. In Hebrew it is transparent that Rachel is commanding Jacob not only to bring a goat, but also to go. However, it is not different with this function of the participle. Two imperatives coordinated by a conjunctive *waw* present both commands with the same weight. The upgraded function has a pragmatic effect on the participle causing the participle to get this imperatival flavor with a specific result: the readers, by looking at this construction, understand promptly that the main action is *bring them to me*."[149]

It is interesting to note that Genesis 27:13 is connected to 27:14 where there is a change of mood from imperative into three qal *waw* conjunctive imperfects.

Gen. 27:14   *πορευθεὶς δὲ* **ἔλαβεν** *καὶ ἤνεγκεν τῇ μητρί καὶ ἐποίησεν ἡ μήτηρ αὐτοῦ*
ἐδέσματα καθὰ ἐφίλει ὁ πατὴρ αὐτοῦ.

So he *went* [and] **took** them and *brought* them to his mother, and his
mother made the meats such as his father loved.

וַיֵּלֶךְ וַיִּקַּח וַיָּבֵא לְאִמּוֹ וַתַּעַשׂ אִמּוֹ מַטְעַמִּים כַּאֲשֶׁר אָהֵב אָבִיו׃

In this construction when the participle was related to an imperative, the
reader was invited to taste its imperatival flavor but not make it prominent, and
when the Hebrew switched into other form, the participle linked to it did the
same thing with the new form. Therefore, in this case the conclusion is that the
upgraded function is valid with these two sets of reference.[150]

Deut. 11:28   *καὶ τὰς κατάρας ἐὰν μὴ ἀκούσητε τὰς ἐντολὰς κυρίου τοῦ θεοῦ ὑμῶν*
ὅσας ἐγὼ ἐντέλλομαι ὑμῖν σήμερον καὶ πλανηθῆτε ἀπὸ τῆς ὁδοῦ ἧς
ἐνετειλάμην ὑμῖν **πορευθέντες** *λατρεύειν θεοῖς ἑτέροις οὓς οὐκ οἴδατε*

and the curse, if you do not hear the commandments of your Lord God,
as many as I command you today, and turn aside from the way that I am
commanding you, *to go* to worship other gods, which you do not know.

וְהַקְּלָלָה אִם־לֹא תִשְׁמְעוּ אֶל־מִצְוֹת יְהוָה אֱלֹהֵיכֶם וְסַרְתֶּם מִן־הַדֶּרֶךְ אֲשֶׁר אָנֹכִי מְצַוֶּה אֶתְכֶם
הַיּוֹם לָלֶכֶת אַחֲרֵי אֱלֹהִים אֲחֵרִים אֲשֶׁר לֹא־יְדַעְתֶּם׃ ס

In Deut. 11:28 the upgraded participle precedes an infinitive *πορευθέντες*
λατρεύειν. There is an unusual feature in this passage. The LXX adds an extra verb
(*λατρεύειν*) that is not in the Hebrew text. This extra verb is an infinitive, which is
a –factive presupposition. "To go after other gods" is "to worship other gods."

By seeing a presupposition (*πορευθέντες*) the readers were able to understand
that "going" to other gods is "worshiping" them, however, the translators here preferred to translate הלך (verb qal infinitive construct) as an aorist participle and add
an extra verb that develops this idea. Both infinitives and participles are semantic
presuppositions, and as such, they do not exhaust the information, namely it lacks
certain information that is added by the relationship with the main clause, which
can be caught by the reader in a logical way.[151]

In Hebrew, the infinitive construct expresses an action without referring to
person, gender, number, or tense. For this reason, this infinitive may not be used
independently as the main verb of a clause, and almost always occurs in relation to
another verb or to an independent verbless clause). Since there is no finite form in
this construction, it is possible to say that when the participle is closely connected
with the infinitive in Greek, the focal point is on the participle. The infinitive
adds more information, that is, it develops the action (+ the logical actor) of the

participle.[152] Van der Merwe rightly states that "semantically speaking the infinitive has no function in itself. The functions of an infinitive refer either to the syntactic function that it fulfils in a clause or to the semantic relationship between itself and the finite verb."[153]

The choices were available and the LXX translators of the Pentateuch chose to replace an infinitive construct in Hebrew with an aorist participle plus an extra verb in the infinitive. Of course, "every language community has its own conventions that determine the form that their texts should take in order to be understood as coherent texts. This includes conventions regarding the manner in which semantic links are made between the relevant people and things in a text."[154]

Semantics of the Anarthrous Aorist Participial Clause Preceding the Main Action in the LXX

The goal here is to demonstrate that the inclusion of the semantics of the participle with its functional results is the key to explain the upgraded participle in the New Testament. The semantics of the participle is +factive presupposition. In a factive presupposition, the "fact" is a representation at the semantic level and on it the truth lies in the meaning shared by the reader.

The best explanation for the upgraded participial effect is found in the reader's way of seeing the process uttered by the participle. A participle is a participle by form and as such it grammaticalizes a presupposition. The upgraded participial effect is so called because it is found where an anarthrous aorist participle in the nominative case precedes the main verb and is closely connected with main clause (mostly with an aorist imperative, indicative, subjunctive, and even an infinitive) and has its modal semantic ideationally upgraded into the mood of the main action in the form of mental exercise.[155]

This anarthrous aorist participle works at the semantic level having the ideational metafunction so connected to the interpersonal metafunction that the reader has the impression that both the ideational and the interpersonal metafunctions grammaticalize the speaker's attitude.

The upgraded function is a sort of implicature resulting from several features in the context. The essential semantic value of the participle is presupposition which primarily has a hierarchization functional role, which in turn, has two other functions: background and prioritizing functions. The analysis of this kind of structure in the LXX has shown that the participle works as a clause chain, which typically resembles the conjunctive *waw*. However, no fixed rule was observed that could explain the relation of the *waw* with this effect, since sometimes there are two verbs with only the first verb having a *waw* conjunctive, sometimes the second has it, and other times there is no *waw*.

In practical terms, the translators of the LXX needed to determine where Greek words fit on the continuum in order to render the Greek accurately. They seem to follow precisely the semantics of the participle, but their decision regarding which verb will function in this or that way seems to be arbitrary. However, almost every time they chose an anarthrous participle with a specific structure, the aorist participle connects itself with the main verb and at the same, sets the main verb in the spotlight. While these two functional roles normally seem to be related to the upgraded participial effect, no pattern of usage that indicates emotion was perceived, although it was not absent in some contexts. The general observation is that the use of the participles draws the readers into the environment of the event. It is possible to say that every time that the upgraded participial effect occurs, and the context of the situation indicates emotion, the participles become a very suitable tool because they are readers-oriented.[156]

The Upgraded Participle in Classical Greek

The upgraded participial effect is a natural feature of the Greek language and not a Hebraism as some scholars used to think. This section is not designed to evaluate all the data available but to synthesize and affirm that the functional role of the anarthrous aorist (adverbial) participle that precedes the main verb (mostly the imperative) was used in Classical Greek with the pragmatic effect as observed in both LXX and New Testament.

The common structure of the upgraded function observed in both LXX and NT involves an anarthrous aorist (adverbial) participle that precedes the main verb. This aorist participle is so closely related to the main verb that the readers tend to see the participle as being upgraded into the mood of the verb to which it is related. There are two types of context in some of the Classical Greek writings where the upgraded function is found: poetry and prose.

The upgraded participial effect has already been discussed by scholars of Classical Greek. Moorhouse, for example, sees the adverbial participle as circumstantial in general and has a twofold division of the "circumstantial participle", that is, (a) the conjunctive use of the participle, which consists "of a verb co-ordinate with the existing principal verb of its clause"[157] and (b) the autonomous use of the participle in which the verb is not to be assimilated. He adds,

> it is important to note that in the conjunctive use (upgraded participial effect) the modal force of the principal verb, not only in the indicative but in the other moods

also, is shared by the participle: hence, if the participle were 'upgraded', it would take the same mood (indic., imper., subj., opt., infin.) as the former principal verb with which it had now become co-ordinate.[158]

This coordination does not occur at the textual level, but at the semantic level. The participle formally and semantically is outside of the attitude system, which is grammaticalized by the moods.[159] However, the relation of the participle to the main verb should be seen synoptically, in close union (*association étroite*). In this upgraded participial effect, the construction serves to stress the indissoluble nature of the union of these two verbs.[160]

The set of data below is brief and seeks to show that this specific function was part of Classical Greek period. In Homer as well as in Aeschylus, the anarthrous aorist (adverbial) participle is upgraded to the same mood as that of the main verb. However, in terms of structure, the aorist participle follows the main verb. Poetry often changes the forms and structure of regular prose, so it is not at all a reliable guide for later prose usage. Euripides, in the drama of Orestes, however, has one use of the aorist participle that precedes the main verb and has the upgraded function.

Iliad 16.521 (7th Century B.C)	ἔγχος δ᾽ οὐ δύναμαι σχεῖν ἔμπεδον, οὐδὲ *μάχεσθαι ἐλθὼν* **δυσμενέεσσιν**
	and I choose not to have my lance firmly, neither *to go* [and] **fight** with the foolish-men
Iliad 16. 668 (7th Century B.C)	φίλε Φοῖβε, κελαινεφὲς αἷμα **κάθηρον** *ἐλθὼν* ἐκ βελέων Σαρπηδόνα
	Dear Phoebus, *go* [and] **cleanse** from Sarpedon the dark blood.
Eur. Orest. 884–85 (480–406 B.C)	ἐπεὶ δὲ πλήρης ἐγένετ᾽ Ἀργείων ὄχλος, κῆρυξ *ἀναστὰς* **εἶπε**: Τίς χρῄζει λέγειν, πότερον Ὀρέστην κατθανεῖν ἢ μὴ χρεών, μητροκτονοῦντα
	But when the crowd of the city of Argos got together, a herald *got up* [and] **said**: "Who desires to say whether Orestes should be slain or not for the murder of his mother?"[a]
Aeschylus Supp. 928. (525–456 BC)	κηρῦξ
	λέγοιμ᾽ ἂν *ἐλθὼν* παισὶν αἰγύπτου τάδε
	Herald
	May I go [and] *tell* Aegyptus' sons about this.

[a] The Greek edition of these two instances is from Homer. Homeri Opera in five volumes (Oxford, UK: Oxford University Press), 1920.

The Greek of Aristophanes could well serve the purpose here, but we are presenting some examples in order to show that the upgraded construction in the classical period follow the typical structure. For instance, Aristophanes, Clouds 634 "Σω. ἀνύσας τι **κατάθου** καὶ πρόσεχε τὸν νοῦν" ("Soc. Hurry up, lay down and pay attention"). His structure is quite similar to some of the examples we find in the Gospels, PARTICIPLES [aorist] + FINITE VERB [imperative] + καί FINITE VERB [imperative].

In line 838 we have another example of the upgrade participle, "ἀλλ᾽ ὡς τάχιστ᾽ ἐλθὼν ὑπὲρ ἐμοῦ **μάνθανε**." ("but go as quickly as possible [and] **learn** instead of me"). The unspecified movement is typically part of the upgraded with this lexeme. The mental exercise in written form makes the readers to see the relation of the attendant circumstance in a clause chain with the main clause. Two events are in close association that readers ideationally see one main event, that is, "learn".

We observe that for some unknown reason, sometimes the order of the constituent changes but the upgraded effect probably still occurs. Whether coming before or after the main verb this functional role of the participle is valid. ἐλθὼν sets the main verb (λέγοιμ᾽) in the spotlight prioritizing the action of the main clause. Even coming after the main verb, the aorist participle serves as background to the action of the main clause. The ingressive context set up the background ("go") so the focal point could be expressed.

The poetic examples above show that even preceding the main verb when the participle occurs in an [e]motional context, the readers are drawn into the emotional context. The upgraded effect not only catches the readers' attention, but also makes them upgrade the participle ideationally into the mood of the main verb. This agrees with what Lightfoot suggests, "the use of a participle construction indicates that the author of the sentence presupposes and wishes the hearer to think that he presupposes that the complement reflects a real, actual, existing state of affairs."[161] Lightfoot's observation can be applied to the upgraded effect as a real grammatical presupposition.

The examples below were taken from Greek prose, which uniformly follows the pattern of usage that was observed in the NT and LXX, that is, the anarthrous aorist (adverbial) participle precedes the main verb.

Xen Ana 1. 6. 10	μετὰ ταῦτα, κύρου κελεύοντος ἄπαντες καὶ οἱ συγγενεῖς ἀναστάντες **ἔλαβον** τὸν Ὀρόντην τῆς ζώνης ἐπὶ θανάτῳ …
	After these things, Cyrus ordered [it], all even the siblings [of Orontes] *got up* [and] *took* Orontes with a strap until death …[a]

Xen Ana 1. 1. 7   ὁ δὲ κῦρος *ὑπολαβὼν* τοὺς φεύγοντας *συλλέξας* στράτευμα **ἐπολιόρκει** μίλητον καὶ κατὰ γῆν καὶ κατὰ θάλατταν καὶ ἐπειρᾶτο κατάγειν τοὺς ἐκπεπτωκότας.[b]

But Cyrus *received* the banished ones, *collected* them an army [and] **laid siege** to Miletus by land and sea, and endeavored to restore the exiles.[c]

---

[a] Xenophon, *The Anabasis of Xenophon: with an interlinear translation, for the use of schools and private learners on the Hamiltonian system* (Philadelphia, PA: David McKay, 1887), 64. The Greek text is from Thomas Clark's edition, the translation it is mine.

[b] The Greek text is from William W. Goodwin and John Williams White, *The First Four Books of Xenophon's Anabasis*, Revised Edition (Boston, MA: Published By Ginn and Co, 1896), the translation it is my own.

[c] See Sophocles, Antigone 1107 (496–406 B. V); Further instances in the Classical Period are Phe. Cor. 21; Thuc. 4.93, 112; Od. 6.7; Xen. An. 3.2.34; Xen. Cyr. 5.2.14; Ar. Nub 181.

The structure in the examples above show no difference with the structure we find in the Koiné Greek, PARTICIPLE + FINITE VERB. It is a matter of choice, but the choice to set the participle preceding the main verb communicate an action with color and vividness that attracts the readers to participle in the construction of meaning.

The context speaks of Tissaphernes who brought an accusation of murder against Cyrus to king Artaxerxes. Cyrus escaped because of his mother's intercession and started to gather an army, so that he might take the king by surprise. Cyrus was sending message to the cities in order to get people on his side but Tissaphernes discovered that Miletus had been in favor of the idea, and to stop the uprising he killed some and banished others. Thus, Xenophon makes a contrast between Tissaphernes and Cyrus at this point by saying that the former banished them, but the latter received them and made them part of his army (Xen Ana 1. 1. 7).

There are two aorist participles before the main verb, and at least one must be seen by the readers as upgraded into the same mood of the main verb. The reader is invited to make a logical coordination (not grammatical one) as though the participle presents an assertion (role of the indicative mood). By using a participle, an author is not concerned with statements of fact, but with presupposition. It is possible to see these aorist participles as temporal, *"when he received them ..."* or *"after received them ...."* However, the upgraded effect seems to fit better in this context.

First, it is a contrastive clause, *"But Cyrus received them ... and laid siege ...."* Second, Xenophon makes the contrast, saying that Tissaphernes banished them but Cyrus welcomed them, and that is the translation of H. G. Dakyns.[162] Third, the emphasis is that Cyrus gathered them into an army, but "receive" is a prerequisite to "collect," and "collect" is a prerequisite to "lay siege". Fourth, the structure fits the upgraded pragmatic effect.

Oguse deals with the modal relations of the participles in ancient Greek. He observes some similarities and differences between the pre-classical and classical period. He says, "les écrivains de l'époque hellénistique aient présenté un tableau différent. En fait, une enquête qui avait porté non sur ces auteurs, mais sur des inscriptions de leur temps, avait confirmé ce qui était évident a priori."[163]

Oguse deals with two examples from Xenophon, that is, Xen Ana 3. 1.46 "καὶ νῦν, ἔφη, μὴ μέλλωμεν, ὦ ἄνδρες, ἀλλ᾽ ἀπελθόντες ἤδη **αἱρεῖσθε** οἱ δεόμενοι ἄρχοντας ...." ("And now that he has gone, let us not delay, oh gentlemen, but *go* immediately [and] **take** your officers).[164] The other case is Xen. Cyrop. 5.4.22 "ἀπελθόντες ... ἕλεσθε". He thinks that the author would have rendered the same meaning if he had chosen two imperatives. He says that to characterize the upgraded participle [étroitement associé] "à son verbe principal on peut noter que dans l'ensemble des exemples qui seront cités à propos de cet emploi un renversement des rapports de dèpendance laisse le sens, sinon intact, du moins relativement peu altéré".[165]

Oguse sees the use of either two imperatives or the upgraded function as having the same importance. The semantic unity of the presupposition has been identified as the key to understand the participle. The author had a choice of having two finite forms, but by choosing a participle, he sets the main verb in the spotlight, the participle serving as a background for it.

He goes on to say,

> Il va de soi que pareilles façons de s'exprimer ne sauraient convenir dans le premier membre de la phrase à cet endroit, l'auteur aurait pu faire usage d'un imperátif, et écrire ἀπέλθετε καὶ ἕλεσθε, coordonnant les indications relatives aux deux actions voulues. On a, en effet, nettement l'impression qu'il s'agit d'ordres auxquels il faut accorder la même importance, l'exécution du premier étant une condition nécessaire de celle du second.[166]

Oguse does not explain why that is the case, even though he mentions that the action of the participle is a necessary condition for performing the action of the main verb.[167] The confusion arises when analysis seems to fail to realize that the participle remains a participle. Oguse argues that these two commands have equal importance. If that is true, it must be asked why a given author chooses to render one of these verbs as an aorist participle and the other as an imperative.

The choice of the participle in this effect makes the information of the participle to be of secondary importance to that conveyed by the main clause.[168] This is *contra* Oguse who thinks that the meaning of the participle in this context is just as important as the meaning of the main verbal.[169] He presents the following examples.

Xen. *An.* 3.2.39a	νῦν τοίνυν, ἔφη, *ἀπιόντας* ποιεῖν δεῖ τὰ δεδογμένα.[a]
	Therefore, now, he says, it is necessary *to depart* [and] to do the things expected.
Xen. *An.* 3.3.1a	Τούτων λεχθέντων ἀνέστησαν καὶ *ἀπελθόντες* **κατέκαιον** τὰς ἁμάξας καὶ τὰς σκηνάς.
	After saying this they rose, and *they went* [and] **burned** the wagons and tents.[b]
Xen. *An.* 2.2.4	ὧδε οὖν χρὴ ποιεῖν *ἀπιόντας* δειπνεῖν, ὅτι τις ἔχει
	See, then, what is necessary to do: *to leave* [and] to dine on whatever one has.[c]
Dem. 18.118b	*λαβὼν* **ἀνάγνωθι** τὸ ψήφισμ᾿ ὅλον τὸ γραφέν μοι
	take [and] **read**, please, the entire decree written to me[d]

---

[a] Although ἀπιόντας seems to be an aorist form, it is a participle pl pres active masculine accusative, probably from Doric.

[b] The first participle λεχθέντων is adverbial. The context of this passage is in proximity with that of the previous passage and shows that these two participles are clearly an effect of the upgraded function.

[c] Xen. *An.* 2.2.5 mentions that the generals and captains who heard this statement went away and did as such "ἀπῆλθον καὶ ἐποίουν. " However, the result is uttered with a explicit coordination. Further examples are found in Xen. Ana 1.2.17; 3.2.39; 3.3.1.

[d] See Dem. 19.276, 57.31. In Dem 20.27 two imperatives are used connected with καί in an analogous passage. Therefore, the choice was available, but the author chooses the form according to what meaning he wants to render.

The best explanation to the upgraded participial effect has to do with Greek modal semantics, in which the essential semantics of the participle is factive presupposition. The finite idea that the participle gets in this context is because in the factive presupposition, the "fact" is a representation at the semantic level and on it the truth lies in the meaning shared by the reader. The validity of this function is present not only in the Greek New Testament, but also in both the LXX and Classical Greek.

Notes

1. Campbell, *Verbal Aspect and the Non-Indicative*, 19.

2. *Contra LDF*, 186.
3. Campbell, *Verbal Aspect and the Non-Indicative*, 18.
4. Palmer, *Mood*, 4.
5. *SRG*, 188.
6. Ibid., 189.
7. Stephen H. Levinsohn, *Self-Instruction Material on Narrative Discourse Analysis* (Dallas, TX: SIL International, 2007), §§4A.2.2, 4B.2.2; Porter, *Idioms*, 293.
8. *SRG*, 194.
9. There is no case with the optative mood in the NT.
10. Adapted from *PVA*, 104.
11. Halliday, *On Grammar*, 18.
12. Ibid., 203. For a discussion, see Butler, *Systemic*, 86–88.
13. Halliday, *On Grammar*, 208.
14. Halliday, *Halliday: System and Function in Language*, Selected Papers, edited by Cunther Kress (Oxford, UK: Oxford University Press, 1976), 85.
15. Halliday, "*On Language and Linguistics*," 183.
16. *SRG*, 244, points out that "not every action is equally important, and participles provide the grammatical means of explicitly marking this."
17. Observe that the order of the participle (preceding or following) does not change the focus from the main clause. Only the second is in the upgraded effect.
18. For the non-finite structural relations see Leckie-Tarry, *Language and Context*, 128–129.
19. It may be that ἐλθὼν **προσκυνήσω** is also an upgraded participial effect with the future tense. Whether the Greek future is a tense, or a mood has not been established. Whatever conclusion one comes to, the occurrence of the upgraded participial effect with the future could be one indication of the modal side of future tense.
20. ἀναπτύξας verb participle aorist active nominative masculine singular from ἀναπτύσσω. The progressive idea of the narrative seems to take the reader from one verb to other and finally to the motivational part (the Greek participle) followed by the periphrastic perfect use of the participle. It is possible that this participle has the upgraded function, although a temporal translation such as *when* or *after* is also possible.
21. John Nolland, *Luke 1:1–9:20*, WBC (Dallas, TX: Word, Incorporated, 2002), 191.
22. Almost all the English versions translated these two aorist participles as upgraded.
23. William Lane, *Hebrews 1–8*, WBC (Dallas, TX: Word, Incorporated, 1998), 131.
24. This type of subjunctive is known as volitive. Of course, volitive is just a pragmatic usage of the subjunctive. See *PVA*, 171.
25. The history of the transmission of this passage shows that the upgraded participial effect is related. There are MSS that have two infinitives coordinated by καί. It may be that some amanuenses noticed the close relation between the anarthrous aorist participle and the infinitive and, thinking it was a wrong reading, corrected it to be two infinitives connected by καί. The Byzantine textual tradition has ἐξελθεῖν supported by the Byzantine text A E G H K M N P S U W Y D L P W 1 2 13 28 69 118 124 157 209 346 565 700 788 1071 1346 1424 1582 2358 1 13 MT TR a b c e f ff2 q. The reading that explains the origin of the other and has support of the papyrus and support of both western mss and Alexandrian mss is ἐξελθών î75 a B D L Q Y.
26. *SRG*, 244.
27. *GGBB*, 623.
28. Porter, *Idioms*, 289.

29. Ibid., 288.
30. K. J. Dover, *Greek Word Order* (Cambridge, MA: University Press, 1960), 12–24, 25–31, 32–34, 66–68.
31. Winer, *Grammar*, 684.
32. BDF, § 472.
33. M. E. Davison, "NT Greek Word Order," *Literary and Linguist Computing 4 no. 1 (1989)*:19–28.
34. Jeffrey T. Reed, "Identifying Theme," 87–88.
35. Ibid., 83
36. It does not mean that the participle becomes any of these, but that the participle may function similarly to a verb, adverb, adjective, or noun.
37. Porter, *Idiom*, 187.
38. The evidence is compelling that the anarthrous aorist participle that precedes the main verb which is other aorist tense-form both form a contemporaneous temporal reference. In this sense, the circumstance described by the participle is clearly part of the way that the action of the main clause takes place.
39. Campbell, *Verbal Aspect and Non-Indicative*, 15.
40. *PVA*, 442.
41. There may be some ambiguity, but there is a high agreement among scholars that the aorist participle tends to precede the main clause while the present participle follows the main clause. See *PVA*, 380. The above statistic seems to avoid some ambiguities as pointed out by Lars Hartman. See *Id.*, "Testimonium Linguae: Participial Constructions in the Synoptic Gospels: A linguistic examination of Luke 21:13," *Coniectanea Neotestamentica* 19 (Lund: Gleerup, 1963), 5–56. Porter presents similar statistics, although he deals only with examples where both a present and an aorist participle modifies the same main verb. He states that of approximately 85 instances in the NT with the above relation, in approximately 75 of the instances, the aorist precedes the main verb and the present follows it. See *PVA*, 383.
42. Scholars are not unanimous on this matter.
43. Culy, "Adverbial Participles," 441.
44. There is a lack of 17 adverbial participles that Logos does not include in this research. The reason for such lack is unknown.
45. *GGBB*, 640
46. The reason to limit the set of data above is that the majority of the upgraded function occurs in the Gospels and Acts.
47. We already mentioned that there are 127 present adverbial participles in embedded clauses that precede the main verb. Ignoring the redundant quotative frame, the number decreases to 66 out of 127. Those are embedded clauses in the present tense that precede the main clause. With few exceptions, it can be said that the present adverbial participial clause has the function of point of departure involving renewal.
48. See *LDF*, 71.
49. *SDG*, 17.
50. Ibid., 16.
51. *SRG*, 189.
52. Again, "if the subject of the participle is also the subject of the main clause, a nominative form is typically used. See *SRG*, 199.
53. This very same impression seems to have affected the understanding of the copyist of codex D, since he must have fixed the "apparent" imperative of the *vorlage* he was using. He probably

imagined that the *vorlage* was mistaken by having an aorist participle where an imperative seems to be the best choice. This is a typical characteristic of the upgraded particle preceding an imperatival main clause.

54. Susanne Wurmbrand, *Infinitives: Restructuring and Clause Structure*, Studies in Generative Grammar 55 (Berlin: Mouton de Gruyter, 2003), 62

55. Culy, "Adverbial Participles," 441–453. *GGBB*, 617.

56. Culy rightly declares, "Adverbial participles will always be nominative, except in genitive absolute constructions or when they modify an infinitive." See Culy, "Adverbial Participles," 441.

57. See *GGBB*, 642.

58. Ibid., 642. See *GCG*, 58.

59. Fanning, *Verbal Aspect*, 341–342. BDAG include ἐγείρω at least in the imperative as some sort of verbs of motion. ἐγείρω appear "in a command to evoke movement from a fixed position ἔγειρε, ἐγείρου *get up! come!* impv. BDAG, 272.

60. McKay rightly affirms that "context is always important in deciding the precise significance of a particular form. Words lose much of their meaning when they are isolated, and syntax involves the interplay of combinations of possible meaning. Cf. McKay, "Syntax in Exegesis," *TynBul* 23 (1972):56.

61. According to Wallace, the participle "piggy-backs" on the mood of the main verb. See *GGBB*, 640.

62. Ingressive action: Ingressive action may be represented by a point. It is the point of entrance into a state or the initial point of an action. The inception of the state or action precedes the action of the principal verb, but the ingressive state or action itself may continue simultaneously with that of the principal verb. Henry Barton Robinson, *Syntax of the Participle in the Apostolic Fathers in the Editio Minor of Gebhardt-Harnack-Zahn* (Chicago, IL: University of Chicago Press, 1913), 19. See *PVA*, 184. Porter proposes to abandon this label because of confusion over the difference between a sentence and the meaning of the individual verb form. See also Charles R. Smith, "Errant Aorist Interpreters" *GTJ* 2 no 2 (1981):221. It is possible to affirm that the ingressive idea is the meaning of a given aorist participle based on the entire proposition in context, not any individual semantic value of its component parts. Cf., *PVA*, 184.

63. *GCG*, 58.

64. This specific feature is in contrast to verbs of motion that idiomatically appear in the present form in specific commands. Normally πορεύου, πορεύεσθε prefers the imperative present (twenty-three times in the NT) over the aorist (four times). See Fanning, *Verbal Aspect*, 341–348. The upgraded function contrasts with these idioms since it prefers the aorist participle that is anarthrous and precedes the main verb, which in almost all the occurrences is aorist as well.

65. *PVA*, 104, 374.

66. Hardy, *Narrating Knowledge*, 48–51.

67. *GGBB*, 640; *GCG*, 58; Young, *Intermediate NT Greek*, 158; *DMG*, 228. Campbell, *Verbal Aspect and Non-Indicative*, 19. William Sanford LaSor, Peter Hintzoglou, and Eric N. Jacobsen, *Handbook of New Testament Greek: An Inductive Approach Based on the Greek Text of Acts* (Grand Rapids, MI: Eerdmans, 1985), §. 14.416. *BMT*, 174.

68. *GGBB*, 641 has a long discussion on the passage about to be treated here.

69. Young, *Intermediate New Testament Greek*, 158. Some scholars have confused the above declaration and have asserted that each category that does not fit in their own adverbial system should be treated as an attendant circumstance participle. See Hewett, *New Testament Greek*, 197. Hewett calls 'attendant activity' what virtually is the attendant circumstance participle; however, his example in Act 13:11 fits better as a redundant participle. The attendant circumstance

participle has its own structure in semantics and occurs frequently in both the LXX and the NT as will be seen.

70. *DMG*, 228.

71. *GGBB*, 640. ESV uses a comma to separate the participle and the imperative.

72. Porter comments that the aorist imperative is the less heavily marked form and normally used when a command is uttered, treating it as a complete process. The present imperative is the more heavily marked imperative and is used when the speaker wishes in some way to specify this command, treating it as in progress, or to deny this process as being in progress. Cf. *PVA*, 351.

73. The different verbal aspects remain the same and are not affected at all.

74. *GGBB*, 640; *GCG*, 58; *BMT*, 174.

75. *GGBB*, 643.

76. *DMG*, 229.

77. Campbell, *Verbal Aspect and Non-Indicative*, 19.

78. The majority of the versions in English, Portuguese, Spanish, and German translate it as a coordinate clause. Some versions use a comma to separate the participle from the finite verb [to avoid repeating the word "and"].

79. *BMT*, 174.

80. *SRG*, 248.

81. G. Hudson, *Essential Introductory Linguistics* (Ann Arbor, MI: Blackwell Publishers Inc. 2000), 322. See Kempson. *Presupposition*, 50. See also R. Garner, "Presupposition in Philosophy and Linguistics," in *Studies in Linguistic Semantics*, edited by Charles J. Fillmore and D. Terence Langendoen (New York, NY: Holt, Rinehart and Winston, 1971), 23–42.

82. Comrie, *Tense*, 25.

83. Funk, *Grammar of Hellenistic* § 846.8.

84. *SRG*, 249, note 20.

85. Lyons, *Structural Semantics*, 97–99; Gleason, Jr. "Some Contributions," *HQ* 4 (1963): 54–55; Henry A. Gleason, *An Introduction to Descriptive Linguistics* (London: Holt, Rinehart & Winston, 1978), 77; Greg Clark, "General Hermeneutics" in *The Face of New Testament Studies: A Survey of Recent Research*, edited by Scot McKnight and Grant R. Osborne (Grand Rapids, MI: Baker Academia/Apollos, 2004), 106; *SRG*, 249, note 20.

86. *GGBB*, 642.

87. *SRG*, 145.

88. *SRG*, 151.

89. *GGBB*, 628.

90. Greenlee uses different terminology regarding the attendant circumstance participle. For him the attendant circumstance participle follows the leading verb in word order and normally it is a present tense-form. The upgraded participial function fits better in his coordinate circumstance. See *GCG*, 57–58.

91. Adolf Schlatter, "*Der Evangelist Matthäus: Seine Sprache, sein Ziel, seine Sebständigkeit*" (Stuttgart: Calwer Verlag, 1836), 23.

92. *GGBB*, 643–644. Greenlee recognizes this very same aspect when he points out that although the participle and the main verb are connected, they do not describe an action with equal importance. See *GCG*, 58.

93. Halliday, *Introduction to Functional Grammar*, 68.

94. By using the subcategorization upgraded it does not mean that it is part of the semantic meaning of the participle, rather it is part of the semantics of the context. Even though Wallace, for

example, divides the participle into several of these subcategorizations. After dealing with all of them, he comments with a caveat: "Yet, it should be stressed that the participle in itself means none of these ideas." *GGBB*, 638.

95. See *SRG*, 248.

96. *SRG*, 187.

97. Palmer, *Mood*, 4.

98. οὖν is missing from ℵ A 0148^vid f^13 etc. bo^pt. νυν ('now') in D it. The first part of Matt 28:19 has a firm textual tradition. Codex Bezae D05 illustrated the upgraded participle with its hindrance. D05 reads πορεύεσθαι (verb infinitive present middle from πορεύομαι) which could be only a misspelling of the imperative form πορεύεσθε. Tischendorf understood it as an imperative transcripted wrongly. See Constantinus von Tischendorf; Gregory, Caspar René (Hrsg.); Abbot, Ezra (Hrsg.): *Novum Testamentum Graece* (Lipsiae: Giesecke & Devrient, 186), 9–94, Mt 28:19. Origen wrote two finite verbs without any coordinate conjunction, he reads πορεύεσθε μαθητεύσατε.

99. B and D read an aorist participle βαπτίσαντες, but evidence confirms the present tense-form for this text. Cf. Karl Barth, "An Exegetical Study of Matthew 28:16–20," in *The Theology of the Christian Mission*, edited by Gerald H. Anderson (New York, 1961), 67.

100. Cleon Rogers, Jr. "The Great Commission," 258. Wallace says, "to turn πορευθέντες into an adverbial participle is to turn the Great Commission into the Great Suggestion!" See *GGBB*, 645. Although Wallace states this, it must be said that the upgraded participle is an adverbial participle since it is related to the main clause. It is only from translation that πορευθέντες sounds independent from the main clause. Thus, as Wallace has said that to translate πορευθέντες into an adverbial clause in English is to turn the Great Commission into the Great Suggestion!

101. Paul Gaechter, *Das Matthäus-Evangelium* (München: Wien, 1963), 965.

102. Roger, "The Great Commission," 262.

103. *SRG*, 244.

104. See Van Dijk. *Cognição*, 48.

105. Roger, "The Great Commission," 262.

106. *GGBB*, 642–643.

107. *TBF*, 51.

108. See *SRG*, 244.

109. Roger, "The Great Commission," 266.

110. *SRG*, 250.

111. Fanning, *Verbal Aspect*, 65; *PVA*, 90.

112. Porter, "The Greek Verbal," 11.

113. See *SRG*, 251.

114. This is basically aligned with *LDF*, 181.

115. Teun A. Van Dijk, *Cognição, Discurso e Interação*, 48.

116. *Contra* Robert D. Culver, "What Is the Church's Commission? Some Exegetical Issues in Matthew 28:16–20," *BSac* 125 no. 499 (1968):244. Zuck follows the same idea when he says, "the other verbal forms ("go," "baptizing," and "teaching") are all present participles. "Go ye therefore" should be rendered, "Therefore as ye are going." Roy B. Zuck, "Greek Words for Teach," *BSac* 130 no. 519 (1973):163. Of course, the first participle πορευθέντες is not present, but only "baptizing" and "teaching."

117. Bekalu, "Presupposition," 152.

118. Only the adverbial use of the participle is included here. See Matt. 2:8; 9:13; 11:4; 17:27; 18:12; 21:6?; 22:15 25:16; 26:14; (can be rendered as temporal, but it is ambiguous); 27:66 (adjectival participial clause); 28:19; Mk. 16:15; Lk. 7:22; 9:12, 13, (verse 52 adjectival, see NVI); 13:32; 14:10; 15:15; 17:14; 22:8; 1 Pe. 3:19 (maybe temporal); 3:22 (maybe adjectival).

119. Matt 2:8; 9:13; 11:4; 17:27; 28:7; 28:19; Mark 16:15; Luke 7:22; 13:32; 14:10; 17:14; 22:8.

120. With indicative (Matt 9:9; 26:62; Mark 1:35; 2:14; 7:24; 10:1; 14:57, 60; 16:9; Luke 1:39; 4:29, 38, 39; 5:25, 28; 6:8; 11:8; 15:18, 20; 17:19; 22:45, 23:1; 24:12, 33; Acts 1:15; 3:26; 5:6; 5:17, 34; 8:27; 9:11, 18, 39; 10:20, 23; 11:28; 13:16, 33; 14:20; 15:7; 22:10; 23:9); with imperative (Matt 2:8; 9:13; 11:4; 17:27; 28:7,19; Mark 16:15); Luke 7:22; 13:32; 14:10; 17:14; 22:8); with subjunctive Luke 22:46.

121. Thuc. 4.93.

122. Bekalu, "Presupposition," 152.

123. Louw and Nida say, "Of all the semantic domains, *Attitudes and Emotions* (25) is most likely to consist of numerous idiomatic and figurative expressions. The reason for this is that attitudes and emotions are essentially subjective events and states, and there is a marked tendency in languages to describe such subjective experiences in terms of figurative expressions or idioms". See domain 25.

124. *SRG*, 145.

125. Darrel L. Bock, *Luke 9:51–24:53*, ECNT (Grand Rapids, MI: Baker Academic, 1996), 1397.

126. Ibid.

127. εὐχαριστῶν add the emotional tone that antecedes verse 19. ("adds" is the correct verb 3ʳᵈ person.

128. *LDF*, 186. The nominative case to both participles (a clause chain) indicates that the subject of the participle is the same subject of the main clause. See *SRG*, 250.

129. εὐχαριστῶν (17:16) and δοξάζων (Luk 17:15) contribute to the emotional environment.

130. Bock, *Luke*, 1403.

131. Condex D presents couple of variations in this passage. It reads ἐξ αὐτῶν οὐδεὶς εὑρέθη ὑποστρέφων δώσει δόξαν. It changes the aorist participle into a present participle.

132. δοῦναι is dependent on ὑποστρέψαντες, both of them are a factive presupposition. The infinitive form emphasizes the verbal action itself while the nominative participle tracks the participant of the process. Marshall comments that "the use of εὑρίσκω with the participle is unusual". He sees this verb as the Greek equivalent to the Hebrew niphal of *māṣāʾ*, 'to be found, appear, prove, be shown (to be)'." I. Howard Marshall, *The Gospel of Luke: A Commentary on the Greek Text*, NIGTC (Exeter: Paternoster Press, 1978), 652.

133. Ibid., 1404. Marshall comments that "ἀλλογενής, 'foreign', is used of non-Jews in the LXX and on the well-known 'keep out' signs on the inner barrier in the temple. The non-Jew with no religious privileges has shown a better understanding of the situation than the Jews." See Marshall, *Luke*, 652.

134. Here we have the infrequent structure of an anarthrous aorist participle preceding a present imperative with the upgraded function. See *GGBB*, 644.

135. According to verbal aspect theory as pointed out by Porter, the perfect tense-form is the most heavily marked aspect that in planes of discourse marks frontground information. Thus, the main point of the narrative is the assertion that the leper's faith has saved him. Bock points out that "it is here that the Samaritan reflects a surprise. Such reaction often comes from a person that we might not expect to respond sensitively. Here a foreigner is the model. Bock, *Luke*, 1406.

136. LXX (Septuagint) is a collective term referring to the translations of the books of the Hebrew Bible.

137. Rogers, "The Great Commission," 58–61; C. K. Barrett, "The Imperatival Participle," *ExpTim* 59 (1947–48): 165–166; C. F. D. Moule, *An Idiom Book of New Testament Greek* (Cambridge, MA: Cambridge University Press, 1959), 179–180.

138. As Payne says "the term is usually applied to linguistic elements (whether words, expressions, idioms, syntax, grammar or style) which are alien to Greek and which owe their origin to either Aramaic or Hebrew." D. F. Payne, "Semitisms in the Books of Acts," in *Apostolic History and the Gospel: Essays Presented to F. F. Bruce*, edited by W. Ward Gasque and Ralph P. Martin (Exeter: The Paternoster Press, 1970), 135–136.

139. Henry St. John Thackeray, A *Grammar of the Old Testament in Greek: According to the Septuagint* (Cambridge, MA: University Press, 1909), 26.

140. Charles Bray Williams, *The Participle in the Book of Acts* (Chicago, IL: The University of Chicago Press, 1909), 8.

141. *PVA*, 376.

142. Ibid., 374.

143. There is no uniformity of usage of this function in the LXX.

144. For detailed study see John H. Sailhamer, *The Translational Technique of the Greek Septuagint for the Hebrew Verbs and Participles in Psalms 3–41*, SBG 2 (New York, NY: Peter Lang, 1991).

145. Bruce K. Waltke, and M. O'CONNOR, *An Introduction to Biblical Hebrew Syntax* (Winona Lake: Eisenbrauns, 1990), 42.

146. *SRG*, 248.

147. Waltke, *Hebrew Syntax*, 649.

148. Ibid., 653.

149. Van der Merwe notes that the stem דלה often expresses a figurative movement. See Christo H. J. van der Merwe, Jackie A. Naudé, and Jan H. Kroeze, *A Biblical Hebrew Reference Grammar*, Biblical Languages: Hebrew 3 (Sheffield: Sheffield Academic Press, 1999), 164.

150. Other examples in Genesis with the participle of πορεύομαι include: Passages with πορεύομαι singular Gen. 27:9, 13–14; Gen. 37:14; Gen. 45:28; 37:14; πορεύομαι with plural Gen. 22:8–9 "... πορευθέντες [וַיֵּלְכוּ] δὲ ἀμφότεροι ἄμα ... ἦλθον [וַיָּבֹאוּ] ἐπὶ τὸν τόπον ὃν εἶπεν αὐτῷ ὁ θεός ..." (They both *went* together ... [and] arrived at the place which God had told him ..."); Gen. 43:2 "... πορευθέντες [שֻׁבוּ] **πρίασθε** [שִׁבְרוּ] ... ("*Go* ... [and] buy ..."). There is no *waw* conjunctive in this example, which means that the translator of the LXX was not limited to the presence of *waw*. Two imperatives in the Hebrew Pentateuch connected logically led the LXX's interpreter to render the first one as an anarthrous aorist participle while the second imperative kept the same mood. The varying positions of the *waw* conjunctive, with the first verb or the second, and sometimes not even present, indicates that the choice for transforming one of the verbs into a aorist participle with the upgraded function seems to be subjective, that is, it is how the translators saw it in the context. Here it a place where one can see grammar as interpretation. See also Exod. 5:18; 2 Ki. 5:10, 12.

151. Hardy, *Narrating Knowledge*, 48–51.

152. Van der Merwe, *Biblical Hebrew*, 153.

153. Ibid., 154.

154. Ibid., 65. See Exod. 12:32; Deut. 29:25; Jos. 2:1; 23:16 (**πορευθέντες** λατρεύσητε [aorist participle preceding a subjunctive]); 2 Ki. (LXX 4 Kings) 2:16; 1 Ma. 7:7; 9:59. Examples with ἀναστας: Gen. 13:17; 19:15; 22:3; 23:7; 24:10, 54; 27:19; 28:2; 31:17; 32:23; 35:1; 44:4; Exod.

2:17; 24:13; Num. 24:25; Josh 1:2; 7:13; 8:1; Judg. 7:9; 8:20; 9:32; 2 Sam. 15:9; 19:8; 2 Kgs. 1:3; 1 Esd. 4:47; 8:91 f; 9:1, 7; Tob. 8:10; 9:5; 10:10; Ps. 101:14; Job 1:20; Dan. 4:18; Bel. 1:37; 1:39. Examples with ἀναλαβόντες: Gen. 45:19; 46:6; Exod. 12:32; Deut. 1:41; 1 Esd. 1:32, 51; Jdt. 7:5; 14:3; 2 Macc. 10:27; Job 21:12; Jer. 4:6; Dan. 3:51(BGT: This database is from the LXT databases in Bible Works 9).

155. There is no example of this function with an optative.

156. For more information about the translation technique of the LXX see Dirk Büchner, "Translation Technique in the Septuagint Leviticus," in *Diglossia and Other Topics in New Testament Linguistics, JSNTSup* 193 (Sheffield: Sheffield Academic Press, 2000), 92–106.

157. Moorhouse, *The Syntax of Sophocles*, 250.

158. Ibid.

159. *PVA*, 375.

160. Moorhouse, *Syntax of Sophocles*, 255.

161. Lightfoot, *Natural Logic*, 41–42.

162. Xenophon, *The anabasis of Cyrus*. Trans. H. G. Dakyns. Smyth under the head, any attendant circumstance, confirms this participle as a participle of attendant circumstance since he translates: "*he collected them an army and laid siege to Miletus.*" Cf. Herbert Weir Smyth, *A Greek Grammar for Schools and Colleges* (New York, NY: American Book Co, 1916), 315.

163. Oguse, *le Participe Circonstanciel*, 64.

164. verb 2ⁿᵈ pl pres imperat mp attic epic.

165. Oguse, *le Participe Circonstanciel*, 65.

166. Ibid.

167. Ibid., 65.

168. See *LDF*, 186.

169. Oguse, *le Participe Circonstanciel*, 65. In his own words, "les Grecs ont euxmêmes coordonné, à l'occasion, lá où ils auraient pu employer un verbe principal et un participe circonstanciel dont le contenu aurait été de la même importance que celui du verbe dominant."

CHAPTER SIX

Examination of New Testament Examples of the Upgraded Participle

This chapter is a collection of data that shows the relation of the upgraded effect with different mood/modalities in the NT. First, the upgraded participial effect with the indicative will be analyzed understanding that this pragmatic effect is often ambiguous because there are multiple instances where more than one option is available. Second, the occurrences with the subjunctive. Third, it will be shown that every time an anarthrous aorist (adverbial) participle precedes an aorist imperative in the main clause the participle is upgraded to the same mood in the reader's perspective. Finally, a few examples with the infinitive.[1]

We have been arguing that the inclusion of the semantics of the participle with its functional results is the key to explaining the Greek participles, and the upgraded participial effect is a good case study in the New Testament. The only semantics of the participle is that of +factive presupposition. The analysis of any adverbial participle is the analysis of the internal logical relation of the participle in the embedded clause, which denotes something that is imagined, whereby the author wants the readers to presuppose the truthfulness of the proposition uttered by the participle for the sake of the argument. That is why it is not factuality, certainty or truth that is at issue. In a factive presupposition, the "fact" is a representation at the semantic level and on it the truth lies in the meaning shared by the reader. That is why both the speaker and hearer accept the validity of the proposition at hand.

Further, semantic presupposition represents a stage of hierarchization, an abstraction of meaning whose specific functional roles have two further functions: background and prioritizing. The participle, a clause chain, connects itself with the main verb while setting the main verb in the spotlight. These characteristics signal the degree of importance of that clause chain in relation to the main action. The context oftentimes involves [e]motion and that is a good opportunity to draw the readers in to it.

The specific semantics realized by the Greek participles with its functional roles are generally applied to the upgraded participial effect. The association of this specific pragmatic effect to the anarthrous aorist participle that precedes the main verb simultaneously establishes several functional roles. It sets the main verb in the spotlight, it "serves as the background to" the main clause, it prioritizes the action of main clause, and it serves as a logical clause chain that is so closely connected to the main verb that the participle is upgraded into the same mood or modality of the main verb.

The close relation of the two functional components (ideational and interpersonal) realized by modulation and mood should be taken as stressing the indissoluble nature of this union. However, though the participle is upgraded and in close relation to the main verb, the two are not identical, the participle is on the side of the ideational metafunction, while mood (± assertion) is on the side of the interpersonal metafunction.

Valid Examples with the Indicative Mood

The explanation for this contextual phenomenon has its origin in the semantics of the participle. Language is a semiotic system with specific functions. There are three metafunctions in language: ideational, interpersonal, and textual. The first two are more germane to the present discussion. The upgraded participial effect occurs as a result of several features within the context. Ideational metafunction with its functional role, namely, modulation is realized in Greek by the participle and infinitive. Interpersonal metafunction with its functional role, namely, mood and modal/modality are realized in Greek by indicatives and non-indicatives.

The contextual relation of these two metafunctions with their functional roles modulation and mood/modal is the origin of this pragmatic effect called upgrading. They are so closely connected that the fluctuating part of the clause (a participial form), which is outside of the attitude system realized by the moods that belong to the interpersonal metafunction, acts as though it is on the inside.

The relation that occurs within a specific context gives the impression that the participial modulation is "upgraded" (cognitively) to the same mood of the main clause, no matter if the mood is imperative, indicative, subjunctive, optative, or infinitive.[2]

The functional roles realized by finite verbs (e.g., indicative, subjunctive, or imperative) and non-finite verbs (e.g., participles), allow the writer to centralize the main sentence (spotlight) by using the participle to point to the prominent verb.[3] There is a necessary distinction to be made that involves these functional components. While the interpersonal meaning relates to language as a social action, the ideational meanings relates to language as reflection.[4] The participle under analysis here belongs to the ideational meanings, thus it relates to language as reflection. In other words, the participle is a semantic presupposition. The relation of the participle to the different mood or modals "gives structure to experience and helps to determine our way of looking at things, so that it requires some intellectual effort to see them in any other way than that which our language suggests to us."[5]

Matthew

2:11 καὶ ἐλθόντες εἰς τὴν οἰκίαν εἶδον τὸ παιδίον μετὰ Μαρίας τῆς μητρὸς αὐτοῦ καὶ πεσόντες **προσεκύνησαν** αὐτῷ καὶ ἀνοίξαντες τοὺς θησαυροὺς αὐτῶν προσήνεγκαν αὐτῷ δῶρα χρυσὸν καὶ λίβανον καὶ σμύρναν (And going into the house they saw the child with Mary his mother, and *they fell down* [and] **worshiped** him. And opening their treasures, they offered him gifts, gold and frankincense and myrrh.)

While the first relation of the aorist participle to the indicative verb is unanimously accepted,[6] the second pair of verbs is rendered differently by various English versions. Some English versions translated the second pair using the upgraded effect, thus, they opened … [and] they offered.[7] Both Hagner and Morris translated the two pairs of verbs as having the upgraded participial effect.[8] The two pairs of verbs above are coordinated by καί, and this coordination indicates to the reader the close association to the connected clause.[9]

The relation of these two clauses connected by the coordinating conjunction indicates that there is continuity within the event narrated. This continuity is not a function of καί since it "does not mark a distinction of semantic continuity or discontinuity."[10] There are two functions of καί in the narrative: first, it links items of equal status, thus, the author judged that events described have equal status;[11] second, καί marks the transition to or from background information.[12]

Matthew seems to assign continuity based on the aorist participle, which is a clause chain that precedes each of the two main verbs. Thus, πεσόντες

προσεκύνησαν (*they fell down* [and] **worshiped**) and ἀνοίξαντες ... **προσήνεγκαν**
(*they opened* ... [and] **they offered**) could be translated with a temporal idea, especially the second pair, but the upgraded participial implicature seems to be the
better option for the first occurrence, and a possible, but probably the second
occurrence indicates to different movement in different logical chronology.

There are several reasons to believe that the first clause chain has the upgraded
effect: first, the temporal idea would give new information in contrast to the other
adverbial participle that qualify the action of the main verb;[13] second, the context
presents an ingressive idea, a typical function of the upgraded effect;[14] third, this
context presents the participle as something of a prerequisite to the main clause.[15]
Therefore, the first pair is doubtless the upgraded participial effect, while the second pair of verbs might not be.

> 2:14 ὁ δὲ *ἐγερθεὶς* **παρέλαβεν** τὸ παιδίον καὶ τὴν μητέρα αὐτοῦ νυκτὸς καὶ ἀνεχώρησεν
> εἰς Αἴγυπτον (And *he rose* [and] **took** the child and his mother by night and departed
> to Egypt).

> 2:16 τότε Ἡρῴδης ἰδὼν ὅτι ἐνεπαίχθη ὑπὸ τῶν μάγων ἐθυμώθη λίαν καὶ *ἀποστείλας*
> **ἀνεῖλεν** πάντας τοὺς παῖδας τοὺς ἐν Βηθλέεμ ... (Then Herod, seeing that he had been
> tricked by the magi, became furious, and *he sent* [and] **killed** all the male children in
> Bethlehem ...)

In this case, the syntax of the aorist participle presents some oddities, since there
is no explicit object. However, when the verb "send" is used with other verbs "it
often means simply that the action in question has been performed by someone
else, like ... *he had (them) killed*."[16] The act of killing was performed by someone
else, but Herod was responsible for it.[17] The relation of this aorist participle to the
main verb ἀνεῖλεν has the upgraded effect. Levinsohn has observed that τότε is a
marker of continuity,[18] and if continuity is assigned, the upgraded implicature is
more probable.[19]

> 2:23 καὶ *ἐλθὼν* **κατῴκησεν** εἰς πόλιν λεγομένην Ναζαρέτ ὅπως πληρωθῇ τὸ ῥηθὲν
> διὰ τῶν προφητῶν ὅτι Ναζωραῖος κληθήσεται (And *he went* [and] **lived** in a city
> called Nazareth, so to fullfil that what was spoken by the prophets, that he would be
> called a Nazarene).

> 4:13 καὶ καταλιπὼν τὴν Ναζαρὰ *ἐλθὼν* **κατῴκησεν** εἰς Καφαρναοὺμ τὴν
> παραθαλασσίαν ἐν ὁρίοις Ζαβουλὼν καὶ Νεφθαλίμ (And leaving Nazareth *he went*
> [and] **lived** in Capernaum by the sea, in the territory of Zebulun and Naphtali).

> 4:20 οἱ δὲ εὐθέως *ἀφέντες* τὰ δίκτυα **ἠκολούθησαν** αὐτῷ (Immediately they *left* their
> nets [and] **followed** him).

4:22 οἱ δὲ εὐθέως ἀφέντες τὸ πλοῖον καὶ τὸν πατέρα αὐτῶν **ἠκολούθησαν** αὐτῷ (Immediately they *left* the boat and their father [and] **followed** him).

8:2 καὶ ἰδοὺ λεπρὸς προσελθὼν **προσεκύνει** αὐτῷ λέγων κύριε ἐὰν θέλῃς δύνασαί με καθαρίσαι (And behold, a leper *came* [and] **worshiped** him, saying, "Lord, if you will, you can make me clean").

The parallel passages in Mark (1:40–42) and Luke (5:12–13) include participles with differences that deserve more attention. Mark for example has the following structure, "… παρακαλῶν αὐτὸν [καὶ γονυπετῶν] καὶ λέγων"" (PARTICIPLE + καί PARTICIPLE + καί + PARTICIPLE). Mark's structure has the main clause first (καὶ ἔρχεται πρὸς αὐτὸν λεπρὸς …) the two present participles develop the action of the main clause culminating in a dramatic pause with λέγων (saying).

Luke's structure fits in the upgraded participle (ἰδὼν δὲ τὸν Ἰησοῦν, πεσὼν ἐπὶ πρόσωπον ἐδεήθη …) The first participle is clearly marking a temporal feature ("when he saw Jesus"), then an ingressive dialog starts, but before that there is the following upgraded structure PARTICIPLE [aorist] + FINITE VERB [aorist]. The aorist participle fits better in the upgraded than the other adverbial logical relation and the scribe of Codex Bezae has a finite verb (ἔπεσε – aorist indicative) instead of the participle.

Matthew presents the best structure for the typical upgraded participle. The aorist participle is placed right before the main clause. None of the temporal ideas would fit in the translation, therefore, the upgraded effect is a matter of choice according to the observation of the other evangelists. Both Matthew and Luke chose to communicate the attendant circumstance in a clause chain result in the upgraded effect.

8:7 καὶ λέγει αὐτῷ ἐγὼ ἐλθὼν **θεραπεύσω** αὐτόν (And he said to him, "*I will come* [and] **heal** him").

8:25 καὶ προσελθόντες **ἤγειραν** αὐτὸν λέγοντες κύριε σῶσον ἀπολλύμεθα (And *they went* [and] **woke** him, saying, "Save us, Lord; we are perishing").

8:26 καὶ λέγει αὐτοῖς τί δειλοί ἐστε ὀλιγόπιστοι τότε ἐγερθεὶς **ἐπετίμησεν** τοῖς ἀνέμοις καὶ τῇ θαλάσσῃ καὶ ἐγένετο γαλήνη μεγάλη (And he said to them, "Why are you afraid, O you of little faith?" Then **he rose** [and] *rebuked* the winds and the sea, and there was a great calm.)

9:7 καὶ ἐγερθεὶς **ἀπῆλθεν** εἰς τὸν οἶκον αὐτοῦ (And *he rose* [and] **went** home.)

This is another passage that records the healing and forgiveness of a paralytic and found parallel in the other Synoptic Gospels. Mark's structure is FINITE VERB [aorist] καί + PARTICIPLE [aorist] + FINITE VERB [aorist]. He coordinates two main clauses and adds between these two one participial embedded clauses.

Mark 2:12	"καὶ ἠγέρθη καὶ εὐθὺς *ἄρας* τὸν κράβαττον **ἐξῆλθεν** ..."
	"and he rose and immediately *took* his bed [and] **went out** ..."

The finite verb in Mark (ἠγέρθη) becomes a participle in Matthew 9:7 (ἐγερθείς). The typical upgraded structure is that of Matthew, but Mark also presents a clause chain between the aorist participle (ἄρας) with the main verb (ἐξῆλθεν). Luke uses two embedded clauses (ἀναστὰς ... ἄρας) preceding the main clause (ἀπῆλθεν) establishing a clause chain with the upgraded effect. Although the parallel examples are minimal they highlight one feature, the choice of Matthew to present an attendant circumstance for the main action realized by the participle, indicates that the mental coordination between the participle and the main verb has a real coordination by two finite verbs in Mark.

The upgraded participle acts like a topic shift by which the readers get them awake by the participle but change from the activity of the attendant circumstance into that of the main clause. In other words, the participle points out a new direction for the action of the spotlight.

9:9 ... καὶ λέγει αὐτῷ ἀκολούθει μοι καὶ *ἀναστὰς* **ἠκολούθησεν** αὐτῷ (and he said to him, "Follow me." And *he rose* [and] **followed** him.)

9:18 ταῦτα αὐτοῦ λαλοῦντος αὐτοῖς ἰδοὺ ἄρχων εἷς *ἐλθὼν* **προσεκύνει** ... (saying these things to them, behold, a ruler *came* in [and] **knelt** before him ...).

Matthew's upgraded structure (*ἐλθὼν* **προσεκύνει** – he came [and] knelt) is described by Luke with a finite verb ("ἦλθεν ἀνὴρ ..." – "a man came ..."). While Matthew use a finite verb for the reverent action ("προσεκύνει ..." – "he knelt), Luke takes the same lexeme and writes it in a participle ("πεσών"). Mark uses a present finite verb ("ἔρχεται") and the present verbal form ("πίπτει"). The main difference between two finite verbs and one participle preceding a finite verb is that the action of the participle sets the main verb in the spotlight indicating a topic shift from the attendant circumstance to the main clause.

9:25 ὅτε δὲ ἐξεβλήθη ὁ ὄχλος *εἰσελθὼν* **ἐκράτησεν** τῆς χειρὸς αὐτῆς καὶ ἠγέρθη τὸ κοράσιον (But when the crowd had been put outside, *he went in* [and] **took** her by the hand, and the girl arose).

Both Luke and Matthew trimmed the remainder of the story of the raising of the daughter of the synagogue's ruler. Mark (5:39) presents the following structure, καί + PARTICIPLE [aorist] + FINITE VERB [present] ("καὶ εἰσελθὼν λέγει αὐτοῖς" – "and when he had entered, he said to them"). Mark's structure looks like the upgraded structure, except that he uses a present finite verb for the main clause. The participle is still a factive presupposition, but the mental exercise is marking a logical time frame about when Jesus said to them, the answer is when he entered.

Matthew presents the upgraded typical structure and the temporal idea of the participle does not fit in this sentence. The time frame is related to the passive finite clause that says, "ὅτε δὲ ἐξεβλήθη ὁ ὄχλος" ("when the crowd had been put outside"). The position of the aorist participle immediately preceding the main verb is a backward-forward pointer. There is a clear transition from the main clause related to the crowd into the main clause that describes the action of Jesus taking the girl by the hand. The upgraded participle here also indicates as normally indicated a transition from the participial circumstance into the main action. The relation between the participle is so close of the main verb that the readers see mentally a coordination between the two clauses.

9:31 οἱ δὲ *ἐξελθόντες* **διεφήμισαν** αὐτὸν ἐν ὅλῃ τῇ γῇ ἐκείνῃ (But they *went out* [and] **spread** his fame through all that district).[20]

12:45 … καὶ *εἰσελθόντα* **κατοικεῖ** ἐκεῖ καὶ γίνεται τὰ ἔσχατα τοῦ ἀνθρώπου ἐκείνου χείρονα τῶν πρώτων … (… and they *enter* and **dwell** there, and the last state of that person is worse than the first …).

13:36 τότε *ἀφεὶς* τοὺς ὄχλους **ἦλθεν** εἰς τὴν οἰκίαν … (Then *he left* the crowds [and] **went** into the house).

13:46 *εὑρὼν* δὲ ἕνα πολύτιμον μαργαρίτην *ἀπελθὼν* **πέπρακεν** πάντα ὅσα εἶχεν καὶ ἠγόρασεν αὐτόν (and when he found one pearl of great value, *he went* [and] **sold** all that he had and bought it.)

14:12 καὶ *προσελθόντες* οἱ μαθηταὶ αὐτοῦ **ἦραν** τὸ πτῶμα καὶ ἔθαψαν αὐτόν καὶ *ἐλθόντες* ἀπήγγειλαν τῷ Ἰησοῦ (And his disciples *came* [and] **took** the body and buried it, and *they went* [and] **told** Jesus.)

14:31 εὐθέως δὲ ὁ Ἰησοῦς *ἐκτείνας* τὴν χεῖρα **ἐπελάβετο** αὐτοῦ καὶ λέγει αὐτῷ ὀλιγόπιστε εἰς τί ἐδίστασας (Jesus immediately *reached out* his hand [and] **took hold of** him, and said to him, "O you of little faith, why did you doubt?").

15:22 καὶ ἰδοὺ γυνὴ Χαναναία ἀπὸ τῶν ὁρίων ἐκείνων *ἐξελθοῦσα* **ἔκραζεν**[21] λέγουσα ἐλέησόν με κύριε υἱὸς Δαυίδ ἡ θυγάτηρ μου κακῶς δαιμονίζεται (And behold, a

Canaanite woman from that region *came out* [and] **was crying**, "Have mercy on me, O Lord, Son of David; my daughter is severely oppressed by a demon").

15:25 ἡ δὲ *ἐλθοῦσα* **προσεκύνει** αὐτῷ λέγουσα κύριε βοήθει μοι (and she *came* [and] **worshiped** him, saying, "Lord, help me").

15:29 καὶ μεταβὰς ἐκεῖθεν ὁ Ἰησοῦς ἦλθεν παρὰ τὴν θάλασσαν τῆς Γαλιλαίας καὶ *ἀναβὰς* εἰς τὸ ὄρος **ἐκάθητο** ἐκεῖ (Jesus going on from there, walked beside the Sea of Galilee. And *he went up* on the mountain [and] **sat down** there).

20:6 περὶ δὲ τὴν ἑνδεκάτην *ἐξελθὼν* **εὗρεν** ἄλλους ἑστῶτας καὶ λέγει αὐτοῖς τί ὧδε ἑστήκατε ὅλην τὴν ἡμέραν ἀργοί (And about the eleventh hour *he went out* [and] **found** others standing. And he said to them, 'Why do you stand here idle all day?')

21:29 ὁ δὲ ἀποκριθεὶς εἶπεν οὐ θέλω ὕστερον δὲ *μεταμεληθεὶς* **ἀπῆλθεν** (And answering, he answered, 'I do not want' but afterward *he repented* [and] **went**).

22:7 ὁ δὲ βασιλεὺς ὠργίσθη καὶ *πέμψας* τὰ στρατεύματα αὐτοῦ **ἀπώλεσεν** τοὺς φονεῖς ἐκείνους καὶ τὴν πόλιν αὐτῶν ἐνέπρησεν (The king was furious, and *he sent* his troops [and] **destroyed** those murderers and burned their city).

22:15 Τότε *πορευθέντες* οἱ Φαρισαῖοι συμβούλιον **ἔλαβον** ὅπως αὐτὸν ἐν λόγῳ. (Then the Pharisees *went* [and] **plotted** how to entangle him in his words).

22:22 καὶ *ἀκούσαντες* ἐθαύμασαν καὶ *ἀφέντες* αὐτὸν **ἀπῆλθαν** (When they heard it, they marveled. And *they left* him [and] **went** *away* …).

26:14–15 τότε *πορευθεὶς* εἷς τῶν δώδεκα ὁ λεγόμενος Ἰούδας ἰσκαριώτης πρὸς τοὺς ἀρχιερεῖς **εἶπεν** τί θέλετέ μοι δοῦναι κἀγὼ ὑμῖν παραδώσω αὐτόν οἱ δὲ ἔστησαν αὐτῷ τριάκοντα ἀργύρια (Then one of the twelve, whose name was Judas Iscariot, *went* to the chief priests [and] **said**, "What will you give me if I deliver him over to you?" And they paid him thirty pieces of silver)

Matthew's structure is quite complicated because there is one embedded clause within the embedded clause. The parallel passage of both Mark and Luke present some different structure. Mark (14:10) records Judas' plan to betray Jesus with a finite verb only (ἀπῆλθεν – he went). He uses an aorist indicative while Luke (22:4) records it with the upgraded effect (καὶ ἀπελθὼν συνελάλησεν … – he went way [and] talked …). The presence of τότε (Matthew 26:14) indicates continuity of time and points out to the next development in the storyline as we have mentioned above.[22]

The relation between the embedded clause and the main clause was seen as coordinate in some Greek manuscripts with καί followed by a finite verb (aorist).[23]

Different authors have different options to portray the event, Mark chose a finite verb while Luke and Mathew decided to present the same event with more color and vividness by choosing a participle in a clause chain with the main clause.

26:42 πάλιν ἐκ δευτέρου ἀπελθὼν **προσηύξατο** λέγων· πάτερ μου, εἰ οὐ δύναται τοῦτο παρελθεῖν ἐὰν μὴ αὐτὸ πίω, γενηθήτω τὸ θέλημά σου. (Again, for the second time, *he went away* [and] **prayed** saying, "My Father, if this cannot pass unless I drink it, your will be done.")

26:50 ὁ δὲ Ἰησοῦς εἶπεν αὐτῷ ἑταῖρε ἐφ᾽ ὃ πάρει τότε *προσελθόντες* **ἐπέβαλον** τὰς χεῖρας ἐπὶ τὸν Ἰησοῦν καὶ ἐκράτησαν αὐτόν (Jesus said to him, "Friend, do what you came to do." Then *they came up* [and] **laid** hands on Jesus and seized him).

26:51 καὶ ἰδοὺ εἷς τῶν μετὰ Ἰησοῦ *ἐκτείνας* τὴν χεῖρα **ἀπέσπασεν** τὴν μάχαιραν αὐτοῦ καὶ *πατάξας* τὸν δοῦλον τοῦ ἀρχιερέως ἀφεῖλεν αὐτοῦ τὸ ὠτίον (And behold, one of those who were with Jesus *stretched out* his hand [and] **drew** his sword and *struck* the servant of the high priest [and] **cut off** his ear).

26:56 τοῦτο δὲ ὅλον γέγονεν ἵνα πληρωθῶσιν αἱ γραφαὶ τῶν προφητῶν τότε οἱ μαθηταὶ πάντες *ἀφέντες* αὐτὸν **ἔφυγον** (But all this has taken place that the Scriptures of the prophets might be fulfilled." Then all the disciples *left* him [and] **fled**).

26:75 καὶ ἐμνήσθη ὁ Πέτρος τοῦ ῥήματος Ἰησοῦ εἰρηκότος ὅτι πρὶν ἀλέκτορα φωνῆσαι τρὶς ἀπαρνήσῃ με καὶ *ἐξελθὼν* ἔξω **ἔκλαυσεν** πικρῶς (And Peter remembered the saying of Jesus, "Before the rooster crows, you will deny me three times." And *he went out* [and] **wept** bitterly).

27:30 καὶ *ἐμπτύσαντες* εἰς αὐτὸν **ἔλαβον** τὸν κάλαμον καὶ ἔτυπτον εἰς τὴν κεφαλὴν αὐτοῦ (And *they spit* on him [and] **took** the reed and **struck** him on the head).

28:9 καὶ ἰδοὺ Ἰησοῦς ὑπήντησεν αὐταῖς λέγων χαίρετε αἱ δὲ *προσελθοῦσαι* **ἐκράτησαν** αὐτοῦ τοὺς πόδας καὶ **προσεκύνησαν** αὐτῷ (And behold, Jesus met them saying, "Greetings!" And *they came up* [and] **took hold of** his feet and **worshiped** him).

28:11 πορευομένων δὲ αὐτῶν ἰδού τινες τῆς κουστωδίας *ἐλθόντες* εἰς τὴν πόλιν **ἀπήγγειλαν** τοῖς ἀρχιερεῦσιν ἅπαντα τὰ γενόμενα (And going, behold, some of the guard *went* into the city [and] **told** the chief priests all the state of affair).

28:13 λέγοντες εἴπατε ὅτι οἱ μαθηταὶ αὐτοῦ νυκτὸς *ἐλθόντες* **ἔκλεψαν** αὐτὸν ἡμῶν κοιμωμένων (saying, "Tell that 'his disciples *came* by night [and] **stole** him while we were asleep.')

Mark

1:18 καὶ εὐθὺς *ἀφέντες* τὰ δίκτυα **ἠκολούθησαν** αὐτῷ (And immediately *they left* their nets [and] **followed** him).

1:20 καὶ εὐθὺς ἐκάλεσεν αὐτούς καὶ *ἀφέντες* τὸν πατέρα αὐτῶν Ζεβεδαῖον ἐν τῷ πλοίῳ μετὰ τῶν μισθωτῶν **ἀπῆλθον** ὀπίσω αὐτοῦ (And immediately he called them, and *they left* their father Zebedee in the boat with the hired servants [and] **followed** him).

1:35 καὶ πρωὶ ἔννυχα λίαν *ἀναστὰς* **ἐξῆλθεν** καὶ **ἀπῆλθεν** εἰς ἔρημον τόπον κἀκεῖ προσηύχετο (And *he got up* early in the morning, while it was still dark, [and] **went out** and **departed** to a desolate place, and there he prayed).

2:14 ... καὶ λέγει αὐτῷ ἀκολούθει μοι καὶ *ἀναστὰς* **ἠκολούθησεν** αὐτῷ (... and he said to him, "Follow me." And *he rose* [and] **followed** *him*)

4:39 καὶ *διεγερθεὶς* **ἐπετίμησεν** τῷ ἀνέμῳ καὶ εἶπεν τῇ θαλάσσῃ σιώπα πεφίμωσο καὶ ἐκόπασεν ὁ ἄνεμος καὶ ἐγένετο γαλήνη μεγάλη (And *he got up* [and] **rebuked** the wind and said to the sea, "Quiet! Be still!" And the wind died down, and there was a great calm).

5:27 ἀκούσασα περὶ τοῦ Ἰησοῦ *ἐλθοῦσα* ἐν τῷ ὄχλῳ ὄπισθεν **ἥψατο** τοῦ ἱματίου αὐτοῦ (having heard the things concerning Jesus, *she came* in the crowd behind, [and] **touched** his garment).

5:30 καὶ εὐθὺς ὁ Ἰησοῦς ἐπιγνοὺς ἐν ἑαυτῷ τὴν ἐξ αὐτοῦ δύναμιν ἐξελθοῦσαν *ἐπιστραφεὶς* ἐν τῷ ὄχλῳ **ἔλεγεν** τίς μου ἥψατο τῶν ἱματίων (And Jesus, immediately perceiving in himself that power went out from him, *turned* to the crowd [and] **was saying**, "Who touched my garments?")

6:12 καὶ *ἐξελθόντες* **ἐκήρυξαν** ἵνα μετανοῶσιν (So *they went out* [and] **proclaimed** that they should repent).

6:27 καὶ εὐθὺς ἀποστείλας ὁ βασιλεὺς σπεκουλάτορα ἐπέταξεν ἐνέγκαι τὴν κεφαλὴν αὐτοῦ καὶ *ἀπελθὼν* **ἀπεκεφάλισεν** αὐτὸν ἐν τῇ φυλακῇ (And immediately the king sent an executioner with orders to bring his [John's] head. And *he went* [and] **beheaded** him in the prison).

7:8 *ἀφέντες* τὴν ἐντολὴν τοῦ θεοῦ **κρατεῖτε** τὴν παράδοσιν τῶν ἀνθρώπων (*you leave* the commandment of God [and] **hold** to the tradition of men).

7:24 ἐκεῖθεν δὲ *ἀναστὰς* **ἀπῆλθεν** εἰς τὰ ὅρια τύρου καὶ εἰσελθὼν εἰς οἰκίαν οὐδένα ἤθελεν γνῶναι καὶ οὐκ ἠδυνήθη λαθεῖν (And from there *he arose* [and] **departed** to the region of Tyre. And entering a house he did not want anyone to know, but he could not be hidden).

7:25 ἀλλ᾽ εὐθὺς ἀκούσασα γυνὴ περὶ αὐτοῦ ἧς εἶχεν τὸ θυγάτριον αὐτῆς πνεῦμα ἀκάθαρτον *ἐλθοῦσα* **προσέπεσεν** πρὸς τοὺς πόδας αὐτοῦ (But immediately hearing of him, a woman whose little daughter had an unclean spirit *came* [and] **fell down** at his feet).

7:30 καὶ ἀπελθοῦσα εἰς τὸν οἶκον αὐτῆς **εὗρεν** τὸ παιδίον βεβλημένον ἐπὶ τὴν κλίνην καὶ τὸ δαιμόνιον ἐξεληλυθός (And *she went* home [and] **found** the child lying in bed and the demon gone).

7:33 καὶ ἀπολαβόμενος αὐτὸν ἀπὸ τοῦ ὄχλου κατ᾽ ἰδίαν **ἔβαλεν** τοὺς δακτύλους αὐτοῦ εἰς τὰ ὦτα αὐτοῦ καὶ πτύσας ἥψατο τῆς γλώσσης αὐτοῦ (And *he took* him aside from the crowd privately [and] *he put* his fingers into his ears, and spitting touched his tongue).

8:10 καὶ εὐθὺς ἐμβὰς εἰς τὸ πλοῖον μετὰ τῶν μαθητῶν αὐτοῦ **ἦλθεν** εἰς τὰ μέρη Δαλμανουθά (And immediately *he got* into the boat with his disciples [and] **went** to the district of Dalmanutha).

8:13 καὶ ἀφεὶς αὐτοὺς πάλιν ἐμβὰς **ἀπῆλθεν** εἰς τὸ πέραν (And leaving them, *he* again *embarked* [and] **departed** to the other side).

9:20 καὶ ἤνεγκαν αὐτὸν πρὸς αὐτόν καὶ ἰδὼν αὐτὸν τὸ πνεῦμα εὐθὺς συνεσπάραξεν αὐτόν καὶ πεσὼν ἐπὶ τῆς γῆς **ἐκυλίετο** ἀφρίζων (And they brought the boy to him. And when the spirit saw him, immediately it convulsed the boy, and *he fell* on the ground [and] **rolled** about, foaming).

10:1 καὶ ἐκεῖθεν ἀναστὰς ἔρχεται εἰς τὰ ὅρια τῆς Ἰουδαίας καὶ πέραν τοῦ Ἰορδάνου καὶ συμπορεύονται πάλιν ὄχλοι πρὸς αὐτόν καὶ ὡς εἰώθει πάλιν ἐδίδασκεν αὐτούς (And he **got up** there [and] *went* to the region of Judea and beyond the Jordan, and crowds gathered to him again. And again, as was his custom, he taught them).

10:50 ὁ δὲ ἀποβαλὼν τὸ ἱμάτιον αὐτοῦ ἀναπηδήσας **ἦλθεν** πρὸς τὸν Ἰησοῦν (And throwing off his cloak, *he sprang up* [and] *came* to Jesus).

14:3 καὶ ὄντος αὐτοῦ ἐν βηθανίᾳ ἐν τῇ οἰκίᾳ Σίμωνος τοῦ λεπροῦ κατακειμένου αὐτοῦ ἦλθεν γυνὴ ἔχουσα ἀλάβαστρον μύρου νάρδου πιστικῆς πολυτελοῦς *συντρίψασα* τὴν ἀλάβαστρον **κατέχεεν** αὐτοῦ τῆς κεφαλῆς (And while he was at Bethany in the house of Simon the leper, as he was reclining, a woman came having an alabaster flask of ointment of pure nard, very costly, *she broke* the flask [and] **poured** it over his head).

14:39 καὶ πάλιν ἀπελθὼν **προσηύξατο** τὸν αὐτὸν λόγον εἰπών (And again *he went away* [and] **prayed**, saying the same words).

14:45 καὶ ἐλθὼν εὐθὺς προσελθὼν αὐτῷ **λέγει** ῥαββί καὶ κατεφίλησεν αὐτόν (And coming, *he went up* to him at once [and] **said**, "Rabbi!" And he kissed him).[24]

14:50 καὶ ἀφέντες αὐτὸν **ἔφυγον** πάντες (And they all *left* him [and] **fled**).

14:57 καί τινες ἀναστάντες **ἐψευδομαρτύρουν** κατ᾽ αὐτοῦ λέγοντες (And some *got up* [and] **bore false witness** against him, saying).

14:63 ὁ δὲ ἀρχιερεὺς *διαρρήξας* τοὺς χιτῶνας αὐτοῦ **λέγει** τί ἔτι χρείαν ἔχομεν μαρτύρων (And the high priest **tore** his garments [and] *said*, "What further witnesses do we need?").[25]

Mark's structure in this passage is set by the aorist participle preceding what seems to be a historical present. PARTICIPLES [aorist] + FINITE VERB [present]. Luke presents only a summary of the larger discourse of Jesus before the high priest. Matthew uses the same lexeme of Mark but with different choices from the verbal network system, FINITE VERB [aorist] + PARTICIPLE [present].

Matthew uses a finite verb followed by the present participle (λέγων) giving a dramatic pause, while Mark choses the upgraded effect. It is possible that Matthew wants to emphasize the forbidden act of tearing the high priest garment. Mark wants to take his readers to what is being said.

14:67 καὶ ἰδοῦσα τὸν Πέτρον θερμαινόμενον *ἐμβλέψασα* αὐτῷ **λέγει** καὶ σὺ μετὰ τοῦ Ναζαρηνοῦ ἦσθα τοῦ Ἰησοῦ (and seeing Peter warming himself, *she looked at* him [and] **said**, "You also were with the Nazarene, Jesus").

14:72 καὶ εὐθὺς ἐκ δευτέρου ἀλέκτωρ ἐφώνησεν καὶ ἀνεμνήσθη ὁ Πέτρος τὸ ῥῆμα ὡς εἶπεν αὐτῷ ὁ Ἰησοῦς ὅτι πρὶν ἀλέκτορα φωνῆσαι δὶς τρίς με ἀπαρνήσῃ καὶ *ἐπιβαλὼν* **ἔκλαιεν** (And immediately the rooster crowed a second time and Peter remembered the word Jesus had said to him, "Before the rooster crows twice, you will deny me three times" and *he broke down* [and] **wept**).[26]

16:8 καὶ *ἐξελθοῦσαι* **ἔφυγον** ἀπὸ τοῦ μνημείου … (And they *went out* [and] **fled** from the tomb …).

16:20 ἐκεῖνοι δὲ *ἐξελθόντες* **ἐκήρυξαν** πανταχοῦ τοῦ κυρίου συνεργοῦντος καὶ τὸν λόγον βεβαιοῦντος διὰ τῶν ἐπακολουθούντων σημείων (And they *went out* [and] **preached** everywhere, the Lord working with them, and confirming the word by the signs that followed).

Luke

1:28 καὶ *εἰσελθὼν* πρὸς αὐτὴν **εἶπεν** χαῖρε κεχαριτωμένη ὁ κύριος μετὰ σοῦ (And *he came* to her [and] **said**, "Greetings, O favored one, the Lord is with you!")

4:20 καὶ πτύξας τὸ βιβλίον *ἀποδοὺς* τῷ ὑπηρέτῃ **ἐκάθισεν** καὶ πάντων οἱ ὀφθαλμοὶ ἐν τῇ συναγωγῇ ἦσαν ἀτενίζοντες αὐτῷ (And *he rolled up* the book [and] *gave* it back to the attendant and **sat down**. And the eyes of all in the synagogue were fixed on him).

4:29 καὶ **ἀναστάντες** *ἐξέβαλον* αὐτὸν ἔξω τῆς πόλεως καὶ ἤγαγον αὐτὸν ἕως ὀφρύος τοῦ ὄρους ἐφ᾽ οὗ ἡ πόλις ᾠκοδόμητο αὐτῶν ὥστε κατακρημνίσαι αὐτόν (And **they rose up** [and] *drove* him out of the city and brought him to the brow of the hill on which their city was built, so that they could throw him down the cliff).

4:38 *ἀναστὰς* δὲ ἀπὸ τῆς συναγωγῆς **εἰσῆλθεν** εἰς τὴν οἰκίαν Σίμωνος πενθερὰ δὲ τοῦ Σίμωνος ἦν συνεχομένη πυρετῷ μεγάλῳ καὶ ἠρώτησαν αὐτὸν περὶ αὐτῆς (And *he got up* from the synagogue [and] **entered** Simon's house and Simon's mother-in-law was sick with a high fever, and they requested him on her behalf).

4:39 καὶ *ἐπιστὰς* ἐπάνω αὐτῆς **ἐπετίμησεν** τῷ πυρετῷ καὶ ἀφῆκεν αὐτήν παραχρῆμα δὲ *ἀναστᾶσα* **διηκόνει** αὐτοῖς (And *he bent over* her [and] **rebuked** the fever, and it left her, and immediately she *got up* [and] **was serving** them).

5:11 καὶ καταγαγόντες τὰ πλοῖα ἐπὶ τὴν γῆν *ἀφέντες* πάντα **ἠκολούθησαν** αὐτῷ (And bringing the boats to land, *they left* everything [and] **followed** him).

5:12 καὶ ἐγένετο ἐν τῷ εἶναι αὐτὸν ἐν μιᾷ τῶν πόλεων καὶ ἰδοὺ ἀνὴρ πλήρης λέπρας ἰδὼν δὲ τὸν Ἰησοῦν *πεσὼν* ἐπὶ πρόσωπον **ἐδεήθη** αὐτοῦ λέγων κύριε ἐὰν θέλῃς δύνασαί με καθαρίσαι (While he was in one of the cities, and behold a man full of leprosy and seeing Jesus, *he fell on* his face [and] **begged** him saying "Lord, if you will, you can make me clean.")

5:25 καὶ παραχρῆμα *ἀναστὰς* ἐνώπιον αὐτῶν *ἄρας* ἐφ᾽ ὃ κατέκειτο **ἀπῆλθεν** εἰς τὸν οἶκον αὐτοῦ δοξάζων τὸν θεόν (And immediately *he got up* before them [and] *picked up* what he had been lying on [and] **went** home, glorifying God).

5:28 καὶ καταλιπὼν πάντα *ἀναστὰς* **ἠκολούθει** αὐτῷ (And leaving everything, *he got up* [and] **followed** him).

6:8 αὐτὸς δὲ ᾔδει τοὺς διαλογισμοὺς αὐτῶν εἶπεν δὲ τῷ ἀνδρὶ τῷ ξηρὰν ἔχοντι τὴν χεῖρα ἔγειρε καὶ στῆθι εἰς τὸ μέσον καὶ *ἀναστὰς* **ἔστη** (but he knew their thoughts, and he said to the man with the withered hand, "rise and stand forth in the midst" and *he rose* [and] **stood**).

7:14 καὶ *προσελθὼν* **ἥψατο** τῆς σοροῦ οἱ δὲ βαστάζοντες ἔστησαν καὶ εἶπεν νεανίσκε σοὶ λέγω ἐγέρθητι (and *he came up* [and] **touched** the bier, and the bearers stood still, and he said, "boy I say to you, get up.")

8:24 *προσελθόντες* δὲ **διήγειραν** αὐτὸν λέγοντες ἐπιστάτα ἐπιστάτα ἀπολλύμεθα ὁ δὲ *διεγερθεὶς* **ἐπετίμησεν** τῷ ἀνέμῳ καὶ τῷ κλύδωνι τοῦ ὕδατος καὶ ἐπαύσαντο καὶ ἐγένετο γαλήνη (and *they went* [and] **woke** him, saying, "master, master, we are perishing!" and *he awoke* [and] **rebuked** the wind and the raging waves, and they ceased, and there was a calm).

8:37 καὶ ἠρώτησεν αὐτὸν ἅπαν τὸ πλῆθος τῆς περιχώρου τῶν γερασηνῶν ἀπελθεῖν ἀπ' αὐτῶν ὅτι φόβῳ μεγάλῳ συνείχοντο αὐτὸς δὲ *ἐμβὰς* εἰς πλοῖον **ὑπέστρεψεν** (and all the multitude of the surrounding country of the Gerasenes asked him to depart from them, for they were seized with great fear. So, *he embarked* [and] **returned**).

8:41 καὶ ἰδοὺ ἦλθεν ἀνὴρ ᾧ ὄνομα Ἰάϊρος καὶ οὗτος ἄρχων τῆς συναγωγῆς ὑπῆρχεν καὶ *πεσὼν* παρὰ τοὺς πόδας τοῦ Ἰησοῦ **παρεκάλει** αὐτὸν εἰσελθεῖν εἰς τὸν οἶκον αὐτοῦ (and behold, there came a man named Jairus, and he was a ruler of the synagogue: and *he fell down* at Jesus' feet, [and] **implored** him to come to his house).

8:44 *προσελθοῦσα* ὄπισθεν **ἥψατο** τοῦ κρασπέδου τοῦ ἱματίου αὐτοῦ καὶ παραχρῆμα ἔστη ἡ ῥύσις τοῦ αἵματος αὐτῆς (*she came up* behind [and] **touched** the fringe of his garment, and immediately her hemorrhage ceased).

9:28 ἐγένετο δὲ μετὰ τοὺς λόγους τούτους ὡσεὶ ἡμέραι ὀκτὼ καὶ *παραλαβὼν* Πέτρον καὶ Ἰωάννην καὶ Ἰάκωβον **ἀνέβη** εἰς τὸ ὄρος προσεύξασθαι (and it came to pass about eight days after these words and *he took* Peter and John and James, [and] **went up** into a mountain to pray).

9:47 ὁ δὲ Ἰησοῦς εἰδὼς τὸν διαλογισμὸν τῆς καρδίας αὐτῶν *ἐπιλαβόμενος* παιδίον **ἔστησεν** αὐτὸ παρ' ἑαυτῷ (but Jesus, knowing the thoughts of their hearts, *took* a child [and] **put** him by his side).

10:34 καὶ *προσελθὼν* **κατέδησεν** τὰ τραύματα αὐτοῦ ἐπιχέων ἔλαιον καὶ οἶνον *ἐπιβιβάσας* δὲ αὐτὸν ἐπὶ τὸ ἴδιον κτῆνος **ἤγαγεν** αὐτὸν εἰς πανδοχεῖον καὶ ἐπεμελήθη αὐτοῦ (*he went* [and] **bound up** his wounds, pouring on oil and wine and *set* him on his own animal [and] **brought** him to an inn and took care of him).

10:35 καὶ ἐπὶ τὴν αὔριον *ἐκβαλὼν* **ἔδωκεν** δύο δηνάρια τῷ πανδοχεῖ καὶ εἶπεν ἐπιμελήθητι αὐτοῦ καὶ ὅ τι ἂν προσδαπανήσῃς ἐγὼ ἐν τῷ ἐπανέρχεσθαί με ἀποδώσω σοι (and the next day *he took out* two denarii [and] **gave** them to the innkeeper, and said, 'take care of him, and whatever more you spend, I will repay you when I come back').

11:8 λέγω ὑμῖν εἰ καὶ οὐ δώσει αὐτῷ *ἀναστὰς* διὰ τὸ εἶναι φίλον αὐτοῦ διά γε τὴν ἀναίδειαν αὐτοῦ *ἐγερθεὶς* **δώσει** αὐτῷ ὅσων χρήζει (I say to you, though he will not give anything when he gets up because he is his friend, yet because of his impudence *he will rise* [and] **give** him whatever he needs).

11:26 τότε πορεύεται καὶ παραλαμβάνει ἕτερα πνεύματα πονηρότερα ἑαυτοῦ ἑπτά καὶ *εἰσελθόντα* **κατοικεῖ** ἐκεῖ καὶ γίνεται τὰ ἔσχατα τοῦ ἀνθρώπου ἐκείνου χείρονα τῶν πρώτων (Then it goes and brings seven other spirits more evil than itself, and *they enter* and **dwell** there and the last state of that man is worse than the first").

13:15 ἀπεκρίθη δὲ αὐτῷ ὁ κύριος καὶ εἶπεν ὑποκριταί ἕκαστος ὑμῶν τῷ σαββάτῳ οὐ λύει τὸν βοῦν αὐτοῦ ἢ τὸν ὄνον ἀπὸ τῆς φάτνης καὶ *ἀπαγαγὼν* **ποτίζει** (and the Lord answered him and said hypocrites! Does not each of you on the Sabbath untie his ox or his donkey from the manger and *lead it away* [and] **give** water to it?)

14:4 οἱ δὲ ἡσύχασαν καὶ *ἐπιλαβόμενος* **ἰάσατο** αὐτὸν καὶ ἀπέλυσεν (but they remained silent and *he took him* [and] **healed** him and sent him away).

14:25 συνεπορεύοντο δὲ αὐτῷ ὄχλοι πολλοί καὶ *στραφεὶς* **εἶπεν** πρὸς αὐτούς (and great crowds accompanied him, and *he turned* [and] **said** to them).

14:28 τίς γὰρ ἐξ ὑμῶν θέλων πύργον οἰκοδομῆσαι οὐχὶ πρῶτον *καθίσας* **ψηφίζει** τὴν δαπάνην εἰ ἔχει εἰς ἀπαρτισμόν (for which of you, desiring to build a tower, does not first *sit down* [and] **count** the cost, whether he has enough to complete it?)

14:32 εἰ δὲ μή γε ἔτι αὐτοῦ πόρρω ὄντος πρεσβείαν *ἀποστείλας* **ἐρωτᾷ** τὰ πρὸς εἰρήνην (And if not, while the other is yet a great way off, *he sends* a delegation [and] **asks** for terms of peace).

15:15 καὶ *πορευθεὶς* **ἐκολλήθη** ἑνὶ τῶν πολιτῶν τῆς χώρας ἐκείνης καὶ ἔπεμψεν αὐτὸν εἰς τοὺς ἀγροὺς αὐτοῦ βόσκειν χοίρους (So *he went* [and] **hired** himself out to one of the citizens of that country and he sent him into his fields to feed pigs).

15:18 *ἀναστὰς* **πορεύσομαι** πρὸς τὸν πατέρα μου καὶ ἐρῶ αὐτῷ πάτερ ἥμαρτον εἰς τὸν οὐρανὸν καὶ ἐνώπιόν σου (*I will get up* [and] **go** to my father, and I will say to him, "father, I have sinned against heaven and before you).

15:20 καὶ *ἀναστὰς* **ἦλθεν** πρὸς τὸν πατέρα ἑαυτοῦ ἔτι δὲ αὐτοῦ μακρὰν ἀπέχοντος εἶδεν αὐτὸν ὁ πατὴρ αὐτοῦ καὶ ἐσπλαγχνίσθη καὶ *δραμὼν* **ἐπέπεσεν** ἐπὶ τὸν τράχηλον αὐτοῦ καὶ κατεφίλησεν αὐτόν (and *he got up* [and] **came** to his father, and while he was still a long way off, his father saw him and felt compassion, and *ran* [and] **embraced** him and kissed him).

15:26 καὶ *προσκαλεσάμενος* ἕνα τῶν παίδων **ἐπυνθάνετο** τί ἂν εἴη ταῦτα (And *he called* one of the servants [and] **asked** what these things meant).

15:28 ὠργίσθη δὲ καὶ οὐκ ἤθελεν εἰσελθεῖν ὁ δὲ πατὴρ αὐτοῦ *ἐξελθὼν* **παρεκάλει** αὐτόν (but he was angry and did want to enter, but his father *came out* [and] **pleaded** him).

18:22 εἶπεν δὲ ὁ Πέτρος ἰδοὺ ἡμεῖς *ἀφέντες* τὰ ἴδια **ἠκολουθήσαμέν** σοι (and Peter said, "behold, *we have left* our homes [and] **followed** you").

19:4 καὶ *προδραμὼν* εἰς τὸ ἔμπροσθεν **ἀνέβη** ἐπὶ συκομορέαν ἵνα ἴδῃ αὐτόν ὅτι ἐκείνης ἤμελλεν διέρχεσθαι (So *he ran* on ahead [and] **climbed up** into a sycamore tree to see him, for he was about to pass that way).

19:6 καὶ *σπεύσας* **κατέβη** καὶ ὑπεδέξατο αὐτὸν χαίρων (So *he hurried* [and] **came down** and received him joyfully).

20:29 ἑπτὰ οὖν ἀδελφοὶ ἦσαν καὶ ὁ πρῶτος *λαβὼν* γυναῖκα **ἀπέθανεν** ἄτεκνος (for there were seven brothers and the first *took* a wife, [and] **died** without children).

22:4 καὶ *ἀπελθὼν* **συνελάλησεν** τοῖς ἀρχιερεῦσιν καὶ στρατηγοῖς τὸ πῶς αὐτοῖς παραδῷ αὐτόν (*He went away* [and] **discussed** with the chief priests and officers how he might betray him to them).

22:62 καὶ *ἐξελθὼν* ἔξω **ἔκλαυσεν** πικρῶς (And *he went* out [and] **wept** bitterly)

23:1 Καὶ *ἀναστὰν* ἅπαν τὸ πλῆθος αὐτῶν **ἤγαγον** αὐτὸν ἐπὶ τὸν Πιλᾶτον (and the whole assembly of them **rose up** [and] *brought* him to Pilate).

24:12 ὁ ἰδοὺ Πέτρος *ἀναστὰς* **ἔδραμεν** ἐπὶ τὸ μνημεῖον καὶ παρακύψας βλέπει τὰ ὀθόνια μόνα καὶ ἀπῆλθεν πρὸς ἑαυτὸν θαυμάζων τὸ γεγονός (Behold Peter **got up** [and] *ran* to the tomb and stooping he saw the linen cloths by themselves; and he departed marveling at what had happened).

John

12:36 ὡς τὸ φῶς ἔχετε πιστεύετε εἰς τὸ φῶς ἵνα υἱοὶ φωτὸς γένησθε ταῦτα ἐλάλησεν Ἰησοῦς καὶ *ἀπελθὼν* **ἐκρύβη** ἀπ᾽ αὐτῶν (while you have the light, believe in the light, that you may become sons of light." Jesus said these things and *departed* [and] **hid** himself from them).

This is the only occurrence of the upgraded participial effect with the indicative in the Gospel of John. The logical sequence in the narrative makes more sense if one renders the anarthrous aorist participle as being upgraded into the mood of the main clause.[27]

Acts

3:7 καὶ πιάσας αὐτὸν τῆς δεξιᾶς χειρὸς **ἤγειρεν** αὐτόν παραχρῆμα δὲ ἐστερεώθησαν αἱ βάσεις αὐτοῦ καὶ τὰ σφυδρά (and *he took* him by the right hand [and] **raised** him *up*, and immediately his feet and ankles were made strong).

5:6 ἀναστάντες δὲ οἱ νεώτεροι **συνέστειλαν** αὐτὸν καὶ ἐξενέγκαντες **ἔθαψαν** (the young men **rose** [and] *wrapped* him up and *carried* him *out* [and] **buried** him).

5:10 ἔπεσεν δὲ παραχρῆμα πρὸς τοὺς πόδας αὐτοῦ καὶ ἐξέψυξεν εἰσελθόντες δὲ οἱ νεανίσκοι εὗρον αὐτὴν νεκράν καὶ *ἐξενέγκαντες* **ἔθαψαν** πρὸς τὸν ἄνδρα αὐτῆς (immediately she fell down at his feet and breathed her last and the young men coming in found her dead, and *they carried* her *out* [and] **buried** her beside her husband).[28]

7:4 τότε *ἐξελθὼν* ἐκ γῆς Χαλδαίων **κατῴκησεν** ἐν Χαρράν κἀκεῖθεν μετὰ τὸ ἀποθανεῖν τὸν πατέρα αὐτοῦ μετῴκισεν αὐτὸν εἰς τὴν γῆν ταύτην εἰς ἣν ὑμεῖς νῦν κατοικεῖτε (then *he went out* from the land of the Chaldeans [and] **lived** in Haran and after his father died, God removed him from there into this land in which you are now living).

8:5 Φίλιππος δὲ *κατελθὼν* εἰς τὴν πόλιν τῆς Σαμαρείας **ἐκήρυσσεν** αὐτοῖς τὸν Χριστόν (Philip *went down* to the city of Samaria [and] **proclaimed** to them the Christ).

8:27 καὶ *ἀναστὰς* **ἐπορεύθη** καὶ ἰδοὺ ἀνὴρ Αἰθίοψ εὐνοῦχος δυνάστης Κανδάκης βασιλίσσης Αἰθιόπων ὃς ἦν ἐπὶ πάσης τῆς γάζης αὐτῆς ὃς ἐληλύθει προσκυνήσων εἰς Ἰερουσαλήμ (and *he got up* [and] **went** and behold a man, an Ethiopian, eunuch, a court official of Candace, queen of the Ethiopians, who was in charge of all her treasure, who had come to Jerusalem to worship).

9:1–2 ὁ δὲ Σαῦλος ἔτι ἐμπνέων ἀπειλῆς καὶ φόνου εἰς τοὺς μαθητὰς τοῦ κυρίου *προσελθὼν* τῷ ἀρχιερεῖ **ἠτήσατο** παρ᾽ αὐτοῦ ἐπιστολὰς … (but Saul, still breathing threats and murder against the disciples of the Lord, *went* to the high priest [and] **asked** him for letters …).

9:18 καὶ εὐθέως ἀπέπεσαν αὐτοῦ ἀπὸ τῶν ὀφθαλμῶν ὡς λεπίδες ἀνέβλεψέν τε καὶ *ἀναστὰς* **ἐβαπτίσθη** (and immediately something like scales fell from his eyes, and he regained his sight and he rose [and] **was baptized**).

9:27 Βαρναβᾶς δὲ *ἐπιλαβόμενος* αὐτὸν **ἤγαγεν** πρὸς τοὺς ἀποστόλους καὶ **διηγήσατο** αὐτοῖς πῶς ἐν τῇ ὁδῷ εἶδεν τὸν κύριον καὶ ὅτι ἐλάλησεν αὐτῷ καὶ πῶς ἐν Δαμασκῷ ἐπαρρησιάσατο ἐν τῷ ὀνόματι τοῦ Ἰησοῦ (but Barnabas *took* him [and] **brought** him to the apostles and **declared** to them how on the road he saw the Lord and that he spoke to him, and how at Damascus was bold in the name of Jesus).

9:40 ἐκβαλὼν δὲ ἔξω πάντας ὁ Πέτρος καὶ *θεὶς* τὰ γόνατα **προσηύξατο** καὶ ἐπιστρέψας πρὸς τὸ σῶμα εἶπεν Ταβιθά ἀνάστηθι ἡ δὲ ἤνοιξεν τοὺς ὀφθαλμοὺς αὐτῆς καὶ ἰδοῦσα τὸν Πέτρον ἀνεκάθισεν (but Peter put them all outside, and *knelt down* [and] **prayed**; and turning to the body he said, "Tabitha, arise." And she opened her eyes and seeing Peter she sat up).

10:23 εἰσκαλεσάμενος οὖν αὐτοὺς ἐξένισεν τῇ δὲ ἐπαύριον *ἀναστὰς* **ἐξῆλθεν** σὺν αὐτοῖς καί τινες τῶν ἀδελφῶν τῶν ἀπὸ Ἰόππης συνῆλθον αὐτῷ (for he invited them in to be guests and the next day *he got up* [and] **went out** with them, and some of the brothers from Joppa went with him).

10:25 ὡς δὲ ἐγένετο τοῦ εἰσελθεῖν τὸν Πέτρον συναντήσας αὐτῷ ὁ Κορνήλιος *πεσὼν* ἐπὶ τοὺς πόδας **προσεκύνησεν** (and as Peter was coming in, Cornelius met him, and *fell down* at his feet, [and] **worshipped**).

12:9 καὶ *ἐξελθὼν* **ἠκολούθει** καὶ οὐκ ᾔδει ὅτι ἀληθές ἐστιν τὸ γινόμενον διὰ τοῦ ἀγγέλου ἐδόκει δὲ ὅραμα βλέπειν (and *he went out* [and] **followed** him and he did not know that what was being done by the angel was true, but thought he was seeing a vision).

12:19 Ἡρῴδης δὲ ἐπιζητήσας αὐτὸν καὶ μὴ εὑρὼν ἀνακρίνας τοὺς φύλακας ἐκέλευσεν ἀπαχθῆναι καὶ *κατελθὼν* ἀπὸ τῆς Ἰουδαίας εἰς Καισάρειαν **διέτριβεν** (and Herod searching for him and not finding, he examined the sentries and ordered that they should be killed, and *he went down* from Judea to Caesarea [and] **spent** time there).

13:13 ἀναχθέντες δὲ ἀπὸ τῆς Πάφου οἱ περὶ Παῦλον ἦλθον εἰς Πέργην τῆς Παμφυλίας Ἰωάννης δὲ *ἀποχωρήσας* ἀπ᾽ αὐτῶν **ὑπέστρεψεν** εἰς Ἰεροσόλυμα (and Paul and his fellows set sail from Paphos and came to Perga in Pamphylia and John *left* them [and] **returned** to Jerusalem)

13:29 ὡς δὲ ἐτέλεσαν πάντα τὰ περὶ αὐτοῦ γεγραμμένα *καθελόντες* ἀπὸ τοῦ ξύλου **ἔθηκαν** εἰς μνημεῖον (and when they had carried out all that was written of him, *they took* him down from the tree [and] **laid** him in a tomb).[29]

14:14–15 ἀκούσαντες δὲ οἱ ἀπόστολοι Βαρναβᾶς καὶ Παῦλος *διαρρήξαντες* τὰ ἱμάτια αὐτῶν **ἐξεπήδησαν** εἰς τὸν ὄχλον ... (but the apostles Barnabas and Paul hearing [this], *they tore* their garments [and] *rushed out* into the crowd ...)

14:20 κυκλωσάντων δὲ τῶν μαθητῶν αὐτὸν *ἀναστὰς* **εἰσῆλθεν** εἰς τὴν πόλιν καὶ τῇ ἐπαύριον ἐξῆλθεν σὺν τῷ Βαρναβᾷ εἰς Δέρβην (but the disciples gathering about him, *he got up* [and] *entered* the city, and on the next day he went on with Barnabas to Derbe).

15:7 Πολλῆς δὲ ζητήσεως γενομένης *ἀναστὰς* Πέτρος **εἶπεν** πρὸς αὐτούς· ἄνδρες ἀδελφοί, ὑμεῖς ἐπίστασθε ὅτι ἀφ' ἡμερῶν ἀρχαίων ἐν ὑμῖν ἐξελέξατο ὁ θεὸς διὰ τοῦ στόματός μου ἀκοῦσαι τὰ ἔθνη τὸν λόγον τοῦ εὐαγγελίου καὶ πιστεῦσαι (and after there had been much debate, Peter *stood up* [and] **said** to them, "men, brothers, you know that in the early days God chose among you, that by my mouth the Gentiles should hear the word of the gospel and believe).

16:18 τοῦτο δὲ ἐποίει ἐπὶ πολλὰς ἡμέρας. *διαπονηθεὶς* δὲ Παῦλος καὶ *ἐπιστρέψας* τῷ πνεύματι **εἶπεν**· παραγγέλλω σοι ἐν ὀνόματι Ἰησοῦ Χριστοῦ ἐξελθεῖν ἀπ' αὐτῆς· καὶ ἐξῆλθεν αὐτῇ τῇ ὥρᾳ (and this she kept doing for many days and Paul, *became annoyed* and *turned* [and] **said** to the spirit, "I command you in the name of Jesus Christ to come out of her" and it came out that very hour).[30]

16:22 καὶ συνεπέστη ὁ ὄχλος κατ' αὐτῶν καὶ οἱ στρατηγοὶ *περιρήξαντες* αὐτῶν τὰ ἱμάτια **ἐκέλευον** ῥαβδίζειν (the crowd joined against them, and the magistrates **tore** the garments **off** them [and] *commanded* to beat them with rods).

16:27 ἔξυπνος δὲ *γενόμενος* ὁ δεσμοφύλαξ καὶ *ἰδὼν* ἀνεῳγμένας τὰς θύρας τῆς φυλακῆς *σπασάμενος* τὴν μάχαιραν **ἤμελλεν** ἑαυτὸν ἀναιρεῖν νομίζων ἐκπεφευγέναι τοὺς δεσμίους (And the jailor, being roused out of sleep and seeing the prison doors open, *he drew* his sword [and] **was about** to kill himself, supposing that the prisoners had escaped).

16:33 καὶ *παραλαβὼν* αὐτοὺς ἐν ἐκείνῃ τῇ ὥρᾳ τῆς νυκτὸς **ἔλουσεν** ἀπὸ τῶν πληγῶν καὶ ἐβαπτίσθη αὐτὸς καὶ οἱ αὐτοῦ πάντες παραχρῆμα (and *he took* them in that hour of the night [and] **washed** their wounds; and he was baptized and immediately all with him).

16:39 καὶ *ἐλθόντες* **παρεκάλεσαν** αὐτούς καὶ *ἐξαγαγόντες* ἠρώτων ἀπελθεῖν ἀπὸ τῆς πόλεως (and **they came** [and] *apologized* to them and *they took* them *out* [and] **asked** them to leave the city).

17:19 *ἐπιλαβόμενοί* τε αὐτοῦ ἐπὶ τὸν Ἄρειον πάγον **ἤγαγον** λέγοντες· δυνάμεθα γνῶναι τίς ἡ καινὴ αὕτη ἡ ὑπὸ σοῦ λαλουμένη διδαχή (and *they took* him [and] **brought** him to the Areopagus, saying, "may we know what this new teaching is that you are speaking?).

17:34 τινὲς δὲ ἄνδρες *κολληθέντες* αὐτῷ **ἐπίστευσαν** ἐν οἷς καὶ Διονύσιος ὁ Ἀρεοπαγί της καὶ γυνὴ ὀνόματι Δάμαρις καὶ ἕτεροι σὺν αὐτοῖς (but some men *joined* him [and] **believed**, among whom also were Dionysius the Areopagite and a woman named Damaris and others with them).

18:1 μετὰ ταῦτα *χωρισθεὶς* ἐκ τῶν Ἀθηνῶν **ἦλθεν** εἰς Κόρινθον (After this *Paul left* Athens [and] **went** to Corinth).

18:6 ἀντιτασσομένων δὲ αὐτῶν καὶ βλασφημούντων *ἐκτιναξάμενος* τὰ ἱμάτια **εἶπεν** πρὸς αὐτούς τὸ αἷμα ὑμῶν ἐπὶ τὴν κεφαλὴν ὑμῶν καθαρὸς ἐγώ ἀπὸ τοῦ νῦν εἰς τὰ ἔθνη πορεύσομαι (and [they] resisting and blaspheming, *he shook out* his garments [and] **said** to them, "your blood be on your own heads! I am innocent. From now on I will go to the Gentiles").[31]

18:7 καὶ *μεταβὰς* ἐκεῖθεν **εἰσῆλθεν** εἰς οἰκίαν τινὸς ὀνόματι Τιτίου Ἰούστου σεβομένου τὸν θεόν οὗ ἡ οἰκία ἦν συνομοροῦσα τῇ συναγωγῇ (and *he left* there [and] **went** to the house of a man named Titius Justus, a worshiper of God. His house was next door to the synagogue).

18:17 *ἐπιλαβόμενοι* δὲ πάντες Σωσθένην τὸν ἀρχισυνάγωγον **ἔτυπτον** ἔμπροσθεν τοῦ βήματος καὶ οὐδὲν τούτων τῷ Γαλλίωνι ἔμελεν (and *they all seized* Sosthenes, the ruler of the synagogue, [and] **beat** him in front of the tribunal and Gallio paid no attention to any of this).

18:22 καὶ κατελθὼν εἰς Καισάρειαν *ἀναβὰς* καὶ *ἀσπασάμενος* τὴν ἐκκλησίαν **κατέβη** εἰς Ἀντιόχειαν (and landing at Caesarea, *he went up* and *greeted* the church, [and] **went down** to Antioch)

19:8 *εἰσελθὼν* δὲ εἰς τὴν συναγωγὴν **ἐπαρρησιάζετο** ἐπὶ μῆνας τρεῖς διαλεγόμενος καὶ πείθων τὰ περὶ τῆς βασιλείας τοῦ θεοῦ (and *he entered* the synagogue [and] **spoke** boldly for three months reasoning and persuading them about the kingdom of God).

19:9 ὡς δέ τινες ἐσκληρύνοντο καὶ ἠπείθουν κακολογοῦντες τὴν ὁδὸν ἐνώπιον τοῦ πλήθους *ἀποστὰς* ἀπ' αὐτῶν **ἀφώρισεν** τοὺς μαθητὰς καθ' ἡμέραν διαλεγόμενος ἐν τῇ σχολῇ Τυράννου (but when some became stubborn and continued in unbelief, speaking evil of the way before the congregation, *he withdrew* from them [and] **took** the disciples with him, reasoning daily in the school of Tyrannus).

19:19 ἱκανοὶ δὲ τῶν τὰ περίεργα πραξάντων *συνενέγκαντες* τὰς βίβλους **κατέκαιον** ἐνώπιον πάντων καὶ συνεψήφισαν τὰς τιμὰς αὐτῶν καὶ εὗρον ἀργυρίου μυριάδας πέντε (and a number of those who had practiced magic arts *brought* the books [and] **burned** before all and they counted the value of them and found it came to fifty thousand pieces of silver).

20:5 οὗτοι δὲ *προελθόντες* **ἔμενον** ἡμᾶς ἐν Τρῳάδι (these *went on* ahead [and] **were waiting** for us at Troas).

20:10 *καταβὰς* δὲ ὁ Παῦλος **ἐπέπεσεν** αὐτῷ καὶ συμπεριλαβὼν εἶπεν μὴ θορυβεῖσθε ἡ γὰρ ψυχὴ αὐτοῦ ἐν αὐτῷ ἐστιν (but Paul *went down* [and] **bent over** him, and taking him in his arms, said, "Do not be alarmed, for his life is in him").

20:14 ὡς δὲ συνέβαλλεν ἡμῖν εἰς τὴν Ἄσσον *ἀναλαβόντες* αὐτὸν **ἤλθομεν** εἰς Μιτυλήνην (and when he met us at Assos, *we took* him on board [and] **went** to Mitylene)

20:17 ἀπὸ δὲ τῆς Μιλήτου *πέμψας* εἰς Ἔφεσον **μετεκαλέσατο** τοὺς πρεσβυτέρους τῆς ἐκκλησίας (and from Miletus **he sent** to Ephesus [and] *called* the elders of the church).

20:36 καὶ ταῦτα εἰπὼν *θεὶς* τὰ γόνατα αὐτοῦ σὺν πᾶσιν αὐτοῖς **προσηύξατο** (And when he had said these things, *he knelt down* [and] **prayed** with them all).

20:37 ἱκανὸς δὲ κλαυθμὸς ἐγένετο πάντων καὶ *ἐπιπεσόντες* ἐπὶ τὸν τράχηλον τοῦ Παύλου **κατεφίλουν** αὐτόν (and there was much weeping on the part of all and *they embraced* Paul [and] **kissed** him).

21:8 τῇ δὲ ἐπαύριον ἐξελθόντες ἤλθομεν εἰς Καισάρειαν καὶ *εἰσελθόντες* εἰς τὸν οἶκον Φιλίππου τοῦ εὐαγγελιστοῦ ὄντος ἐκ τῶν ἑπτὰ **ἐμείναμεν** παρ᾽ αὐτῷ (On the next day we departed and came to Caesarea, and *we entered* the house of Philip the evangelist, who was one of the seven, [and] **stayed** with him).

21:15 μετὰ δὲ τὰς ἡμέρας ταύτας *ἐπισκευασάμενοι* **ἀνεβαίνομεν** εἰς Ἱεροσόλυμα (After these days *we made preparations* [and] **went up** to Jerusalem)

22:6 ἀκούσας δὲ ὁ ἑκατοντάρχης *προσελθὼν* τῷ χιλιάρχῳ **ἀπήγγειλεν** λέγων τί μέλλεις ποιεῖν ὁ γὰρ ἄνθρωπος οὗτος Ῥωμαῖός ἐστιν (and hearing the centurion, *he went* to the tribune [and] **said** to him, "What are you about to do? For this man is a Roman citizen").

22:30 τῇ δὲ ἐπαύριον βουλόμενος γνῶναι τὸ ἀσφαλὲς τὸ τί κατηγορεῖται ὑπὸ τῶν Ἰουδαίων ἔλυσεν αὐτόν καὶ ἐκέλευσεν συνελθεῖν τοὺς ἀρχιερεῖς καὶ πᾶν τὸ συνέδριον καὶ *καταγαγὼν* τὸν Παῦλον **ἔστησεν** εἰς αὐτούς (but on the next day, desiring to know the real reason why he was being accused by the Jews, he unbound him and commanded the chief priests and all the council to meet, and *he brought* Paul *down* [and] **set** him before them).

23:16 ἀκούσας δὲ ὁ υἱὸς τῆς ἀδελφῆς Παύλου τὴν ἐνέδραν *παραγενόμενος* καὶ *εἰσελθὼν* εἰς τὴν παρεμβολὴν **ἀπήγγειλεν** τῷ Παύλῳ (and the son of Paul's sister heard of their ambush, and he went and *entered* the barracks [and] **told** Paul)

23:18 ὁ μὲν οὖν *παραλαβὼν* αὐτὸν **ἤγαγεν** πρὸς τὸν χιλίαρχον καὶ φησίν ὁ δέσμιος Παῦλος *προσκαλεσάμενός* με **ἠρώτησεν** τοῦτον τὸν νεανίσκον ἀγαγεῖν πρὸς σέ ἔχοντά τι λαλῆσαί σοι (therefore *he took* him [and] **brought** him to the tribune and said, "Paul the prisoner *called* me [and] **asked** me to bring this young man to you, as he has something to say to you").

23:31 οἱ μὲν οὖν στρατιῶται κατὰ τὸ διατεταγμένον αὐτοῖς *ἀναλαβόντες* τὸν Παῦλον **ἤγαγον** διὰ νυκτὸς εἰς τὴν Ἀντιπατρίδα (therefore the soldiers, according to their instructions, *took* Paul [and] **brought** him by night to Antipatris)

25:6 διατρίψας δὲ ἐν αὐτοῖς ἡμέρας οὐ πλείους ὀκτὼ ἢ δέκα *καταβὰς* εἰς Καισάρειαν τῇ ἐπαύριον *καθίσας* ἐπὶ τοῦ βήματος *ἐκέλευσεν* τὸν Παῦλον ἀχθῆναι (and staying among them not more than eight or ten days, *he went down* to Caesarean and the next day he *took* his seat on the tribunal [and] **ordered** Paul to be brought).

27:35 εἴπας δὲ ταῦτα καὶ λαβὼν ἄρτον εὐχαρίστησεν τῷ θεῷ ἐνώπιον πάντων καὶ *κλάσας* **ἤρξατο** ἐσθίειν (and when he had said these things, he took bread, and giving thanks to God in the presence of all *he broke* it [and] **began** to eat)

2 Corinthians 2:13

οὐκ ἔσχηκα ἄνεσιν τῷ πνεύματί μου τῷ μὴ εὑρεῖν με Τίτον τὸν ἀδελφόν μου ἀλλὰ *ἀποταξάμενος* αὐτοῖς **ἐξῆλθον** εἰς Μακεδονίαν (my spirit was not at rest because I did not find my brother Titus, So *I took leave* of them [and] **went on** to Macedonia)

Valid Examples with the Subjunctive Mood

As already stated, the subjunctive and the imperative are both modals or modality. Both move in the realm of *volition and* are thus deontic. The subjunctive grammaticalizes +projection = +volition, +visualization according to a modal semantic theory. The relation of the participle to the subjunctive fulfills a rhetorically supportive role. Like the participle, the subjunctive occurs within direct, indirect, or authorial discourse within narrative.[32] The insistence of some on seeing the subjunctive as indicating nothing but future fails to appreciate the semantic richness of this modal.[33]

Although the subjunctive is not an assertion, it is still part of the attitude system, and therefore, its modality or modal is used to realize the interpersonal metafunction. The difference between a participle and a subjunctive occurs not only at the semantic level, but also in the functional roles realized by modulation and by mood. The interpersonal meaning (subjunctive) is related to language as a social action, that is, the subjunctive is related to the will of the speaker. Of course, this will is projected, and "when no claim is made about the state of the world, but some non-existent state is hypothesized or projected, whatever its relationship to the actual world,"[34] the subjunctive will be the mood used.

While interpersonal meaning to which the subjunctive belongs relates language social action, the ideational meanings to which the participle belongs are related to language as reflection.[35] Therefore, the modal semantics of the subjunctive grammaticalizes "projection with no expectation of fulfillment,"[36] and the modal semantics of the participle grammaticalizes presupposition, that is, reflection. When the upgraded participial effect occurs with subjunctive, it is necessary to say that the participle always will be a participle, however, the upgraded effect occurs because of several features within the context that give the impression to the readers as they are drawn into the environment of the event at hand.

Matthew

4:9 καὶ εἶπεν αὐτῷ ταῦτά σοι πάντα δώσω, ἐὰν *πεσὼν* **προσκυνήσῃς** μοι (and he said to him, "All these I will give you, if *you fall down* [and] **worship** me")

13:28 ὁ δὲ ἔφη αὐτοῖς ἐχθρὸς ἄνθρωπος τοῦτο ἐποίησεν. οἱ δὲ δοῦλοι λέγουσιν αὐτῷ θέλεις οὖν *ἀπελθόντες* **συλλέξωμεν** αὐτά (and he said to them, 'an enemy has done this.' but the servants said to him, 'then do you want us *to go* [and] **gather** them?').[37]

14:15 Ὀψίας δὲ γενομένης προσῆλθον αὐτῷ οἱ μαθηταὶ λέγοντες ἔρημός ἐστιν ὁ τόπος καὶ ἡ ὥρα ἤδη παρῆλθεν ἀπόλυσον τοὺς ὄχλους, ἵνα *ἀπελθόντες* εἰς τὰς κώμας **ἀγοράσωσιν** ἑαυτοῖς βρώματα (and when it was evening, the disciples came to him saying, "this is a desert place, and the hour is already over; dismissed the crowds so that *they go into* the villages [and] **buy** food for themselves")

26:36 Τότε ἔρχεται μετ' αὐτῶν ὁ Ἰησοῦς εἰς χωρίον λεγόμενον Γεθσημανὶ καὶ λέγει τοῖς μαθηταῖς καθίσατε αὐτοῦ ἕως [οὗ] *ἀπελθὼν* ἐκεῖ **προσεύξωμαι** (then Jesus went with them to a place called Gethsemane, and he said to his disciples, "sit here, while *I go* over there [and] **pray**.").

27:64 κέλευσον οὖν ἀσφαλισθῆναι τὸν τάφον ἕως τῆς τρίτης ἡμέρας, μήποτε *ἐλθόντες* οἱ μαθηταὶ αὐτοῦ **κλέψωσιν** αὐτὸν καὶ εἴπωσιν τῷ λαῷ ἠγέρθη ἀπὸ τῶν νεκρῶν, καὶ ἔσται ἡ ἐσχάτη πλάνη χείρων τῆς πρώτης (therefore order the tomb to be made secure until the third day, lest his disciples *go* [and] **steal** him away and say to the people, 'he was risen from the dead,' and the last fraud will be worse than the first.")

Mark

5:23 καὶ παρακαλεῖ αὐτὸν πολλὰ λέγων ὅτι τὸ θυγάτριόν μου ἐσχάτως ἔχει, ἵνα *ἐλθὼν* **ἐπιθῇς** τὰς χεῖρας αὐτῇ ἵνα σωθῇ καὶ ζήσῃ (and implored him many times saying, "my daughter is at the last. *Come* [and] **lay** your hands on her, so that she may be saved and live.")

6:36 ἀπόλυσον αὐτούς, ἵνα *ἀπελθόντες* εἰς τοὺς κύκλῳ ἀγροὺς καὶ κώμας **ἀγοράσωσιν** ἑαυτοῖς τί φάγωσιν. (dismiss them *to go* into the surrounding countryside and villages [and] **buy** themselves something to eat").

6:37 ὁ δὲ ἀποκριθεὶς εἶπεν αὐτοῖς δότε αὐτοῖς ὑμεῖς φαγεῖν. καὶ λέγουσιν αὐτῷ *ἀπελθόντες* **ἀγοράσωμεν** δηναρίων διακοσίων ἄρτους καὶ δώσομεν αὐτοῖς φαγεῖν; (but [he] answering said to them, "give them something to eat." And they said to him, "*shall we go* [and] **buy** two hundred denarii worth of bread and give it to them to eat?").

13:36 μὴ *ἐλθὼν* ἐξαίφνης **εὕρῃ** ὑμᾶς καθεύδοντας. (lest he *come* suddenly [and] **find** you asleep).

14:1 ᾿Ην δὲ τὸ πάσχα καὶ τὰ ἄζυμα μετὰ δύο ἡμέρας. καὶ ἐζήτουν οἱ ἀρχιερεῖς καὶ οἱ γραμματεῖς πῶς αὐτὸν ἐν δόλῳ *κρατήσαντες* **ἀποκτείνωσιν** (and it was now two days before the Passover and the Feast of Unleavened Bread. And the chief priests and the scribes were seeking how *to arrest* him by stealth [and] **kill** him).

14:12 Καὶ τῇ πρώτῃ ἡμέρᾳ τῶν ἀζύμων, ὅτε τὸ πάσχα ἔθυον, λέγουσιν αὐτῷ οἱ μαθηταὶ αὐτοῦ ποῦ θέλεις *ἀπελθόντες* **ἑτοιμάσωμεν** ἵνα φάγῃς τὸ πάσχα; (and on the first day of unleavened bread, when they sacrificed the Passover lamb, his disciples said to him, "where will you have us **go** [and] *prepare* for you to eat the Passover?").

16:1 Καὶ διαγενομένου τοῦ σαββάτου Μαρία ἡ Μαγδαληνὴ καὶ Μαρία ἡ [τοῦ] Ἰακώβου καὶ Σαλώμη ἠγόρασαν ἀρώματα ἵνα *ἐλθοῦσαι* **ἀλείψωσιν** αὐτόν. (and the Sabbath was past, Mary Magdalene, Mary the mother of James, and Salome bought spices, so that *they might go* [and] **anoint** him.

Luke

7:3 ἀκούσας δὲ περὶ τοῦ Ἰησοῦ ἀπέστειλεν πρὸς αὐτὸν πρεσβυτέρους τῶν Ἰουδαίων ἐρωτῶν αὐτὸν ὅπως *ἐλθὼν* **διασώσῃ** τὸν δοῦλον αὐτοῦ. (hearing the centurion about Jesus, he sent to him elders of the Jews, asking him *to come* [and] **heal** his servant.

8:12 οἱ δὲ παρὰ τὴν ὁδόν εἰσιν οἱ ἀκούσαντες, εἶτα ἔρχεται ὁ διάβολος καὶ αἴρει τὸν λόγον ἀπὸ τῆς καρδίας αὐτῶν, ἵνα μὴ *πιστεύσαντες* **σωθῶσιν**. (the ones along the path are those who have heard; then the devil comes and takes away the word from their hearts, so that *they may* not *believe* [and] **be saved**.

9:12 Ἡ δὲ ἡμέρα ἤρξατο κλίνειν προσελθόντες δὲ οἱ δώδεκα εἶπαν αὐτῷ ἀπόλυσον τὸν ὄχλον, ἵνα *πορευθέντες* εἰς τὰς κύκλῳ κώμας καὶ ἀγροὺς **καταλύσωσιν** καὶ εὕρωσιν ἐπισιτισμόν, ὅτι ὧδε ἐν ἐρήμῳ τόπῳ ἐσμέν (and the day began to wear away, and the twelve came and said to him, "dismiss the crowd so that *they may go* into the surrounding villages and countryside [and] **find** lodging and get provisions, for we are here in a desolate place").

9:13 εἶπεν δὲ πρὸς αὐτούς δότε αὐτοῖς ὑμεῖς φαγεῖν. οἱ δὲ εἶπαν οὐκ εἰσὶν ἡμῖν πλεῖον ἢ ἄρτοι πέντε καὶ ἰχθύες δύο, εἰ μήτι *πορευθέντες* ἡμεῖς **ἀγοράσωμεν** εἰς πάντα τὸν λαὸν τοῦτον βρώματα (but he said to them, "give them something to eat." They said, "we have no more than five loaves and two fish—unless we are **to go** [and] *buy* food for all these people").

15:23 καὶ φέρετε τὸν μόσχον τὸν σιτευτόν, θύσατε, καὶ *φαγόντες* **εὐφρανθῶμεν** (and bring the fattened calf and kill it, and *let us eat* [and] **celebrate**).

John

12:24 ἀμὴν λέγω ὑμῖν, ἐὰν μὴ ὁ κόκκος τοῦ σίτου *πεσὼν* εἰς τὴν γῆν **ἀποθάνῃ**, αὐτὸς μόνος μένει ἐὰν δὲ ἀποθάνῃ, πολὺν καρπὸν φέρει (truly, truly, I say to you, unless a grain of wheat *falls* into the earth [and] **dies**, it remains alone; but if it dies, it bears much fruit.

Acts

15:36 Μετὰ δέ τινας ἡμέρας εἶπεν πρὸς Βαρναβᾶν Παῦλος *ἐπιστρέψαντες* δὴ **ἐπισκεψώμεθα** τοὺς ἀδελφοὺς κατὰ πόλιν πᾶσαν ἐν αἷς κατηγγείλαμεν τὸν λόγον τοῦ κυρίου πῶς ἔχουσιν (and after some days Paul said to Barnabas, "*Let us return* [and] **visit** the brothers in every city where we proclaimed the word of the Lord, and see how they are").

23:24 κτήνη τε παραστῆσαι ἵνα *ἐπιβιβάσαντες* τὸν Παῦλον **διασώσωσι** πρὸς Φήλικα τὸν ἡγεμόνα (also to provide mounts *to put* Paul *on* [and] **bring him safely** to Felix the governor).

27:42 Τῶν δὲ στρατιωτῶν βουλὴ ἐγένετο ἵνα τοὺς δεσμώτας ἀποκτείνωσιν, μή τις *ἐκκολυμβήσας* **διαφύγῃ** (The soldiers' plan was to kill the prisoners, lest any *should swim away* [and] **escape**).

Romans

15:32 ἵνα ἐν χαρᾷ **ἐλθὼν** πρὸς ὑμᾶς διὰ θελήματος θεοῦ *συναναπαύσωμαι* ὑμῖν (so that by God's will *I may come* to you with joy [and] **be refreshed** in your company).

1 Corinthians

6:15 οὐκ οἴδατε ὅτι τὰ σώματα ὑμῶν μέλη Χριστοῦ ἐστιν; ἄρας οὖν τὰ μέλη τοῦ Χριστοῦ **ποιήσω** πόρνης μέλη; μὴ γένοιτο (do you not know that your bodies are members of Christ? *Shall I then take* the members of Christ [and] **make** them members of a prostitute? Never!).

Hebrews

6:1 Διὸ ἀφέντες τὸν τῆς ἀρχῆς τοῦ Χριστοῦ λόγον ἐπὶ τὴν τελειότητα **φερώμεθα**, μὴ πάλιν θεμέλιον καταβαλλόμενοι μετανοίας ἀπὸ νεκρῶν ἔργων καὶ πίστεως ἐπὶ θεόν (therefore *let us leave* the elementary doctrine of Christ [and] **go on** to maturity, not laying again a foundation of repentance from dead works and of faith toward God).

1 Peter

2:24 ὃς τὰς ἁμαρτίας ἡμῶν αὐτὸς ἀνήνεγκεν ἐν τῷ σώματι αὐτοῦ ἐπὶ τὸ ξύλον, ἵνα ταῖς ἁμαρτίαις *ἀπογενόμενοι* τῇ δικαιοσύνῃ **ζήσωμεν**, οὗ τῷ μώλωπι ἰάθητε (He himself bore our sins in his body on the tree, that *we might die to sin* [and] **live** to righteousness. By his wounds you have been healed).

2 Peter

3:17 Ὑμεῖς οὖν, ἀγαπητοί, προγινώσκοντες φυλάσσεσθε, ἵνα μὴ τῇ τῶν ἀθέσμων πλάνῃ *συναπαχθέντες* **ἐκπέσητε** τοῦ ἰδίου στηριγμοῦ (You therefore, beloved, knowing this beforehand, take care that *you are not carried away* with the error of lawless people [and] **lose** your own stability).[38]

Valid Examples with the Imperative Mood

Modal semantics of the Greek imperative sees its essential semantic value as a strong direction—direction as attitude. As already stated, the imperative has been treated here as part of the attitude system, but it has not been considered as a pure mood that grammaticalizes assertion, rather, it is modal or modality. As Porter states, "the command attitudinally grammaticalizes the speaker's desire to give direction to a process."[39]

The imperative and the subjunctive are modals or modality. Both move in the realm of *volition* and are thus deontic. However, while the subjunctive grammaticalizes +projection = +volition, +visualization[40], the imperative grammaticalizes +direction = volition, which involves the imposition of one's will upon another.[41] The attitudinal system that includes the Greek modals (imperative, subjunctive, and optative) makes no assertions in contrast to the indicative mood. Further, they describe some deontic attitude hypothesized or projected to a non-existent state, and they have in common the fact that they grammaticalize the volition of the speaker.[42] This attitudinal system, whether +assertion or −assertion, belongs to the interpersonal metafunction realized by the mood and modals, and stands in contrast to the ideational metafunction realized by modulation.

In the New Testament there are eleven uses of the upgraded participial effect with verbs of motion πορεύομαι in close connection with the aorist imperative.

Matthew

2: 8 καὶ πέμψας αὐτοὺς εἰς Βηθλέεμ εἶπεν· *πορευθέντες* **ἐξετάσατε** ἀκριβῶς περὶ τοῦ παιδίου· ἐπὰν δὲ εὕρητε, ἀπαγγείλατέ μοι, ὅπως κἀγὼ ἐλθὼν προσκυνήσω αὐτῷ (And sending them to Bethlehem, he said, *Go* [and] **search** diligently for the child, and when you have found him, bring me word, that I too may come and worship him).

There is a clear outline of this narrative (1) the arrival and message of the magi (vv 1–2); (2) the troubled reaction of Herod (vv 3–8); and (3) the completion of the journey of the magi in the worship of the child (vv 9–12).[43] Matthew brings the narrative to a climax through three aorist indicative verbs (προσεκύνησαν, "they worshiped"; προσήνεγκαν, "they offered" [gifts]; ἀνεχώρησαν, "they departed"). The drama of the passage can be felt by the use of the aorist participles where each main verb is colored by an accompanying adverbial participle (πεσόντες, "having fallen to the ground"; ἀνοίξαντες, "having opened"; χρηματισθέντες, "having been warned").

The discourse function of the anarthrous aorist nominative participle that precedes the main verb is a result of its modal semantics. Semantic presupposition has its functional role of hierarchization. The reader is capable of identifying each point of prominence at the same time that he or she is drawn into the drama of the narrative. Thus, this abstraction of meaning, namely, hierarchization, provides the background for the foreground events. The foreground events are described by the indicative verbs προσεκύνησαν, "they worshiped"; προσήνεγκαν, "they offered" [gifts]; ἀνεχώρησαν, "they departed", while the background is set by the aorist participle πεσόντες, "having fallen to the ground"; ἀνοίξαντες, "having opened"; χρηματισθέντες, "having been warned".

What is true of every anarthrous (adverbial) aorist participle that precedes the main verb is true of the upgraded participial effect with one further point. *πορευθέντες* **ἐξετάσατε** seems to invite the reader to be part of the environment of the narrative. The participle can fluctuate to invite the reader to share information with the narrator. *Go* [and] **search** are so closely connected that these two verbs become virtually a single unit from the readers' perspective.

The participle is upgraded into the imperative mood ideationally. There is no other way to render the participle here. It is not that the participle became an imperative grammatically, it is still a participle that is taking the readers to get so involved with this semantic ideational unity that readers in thought at the semantic level image this participle as having the modal force of an imperative.

2:13 Ἀναχωρησάντων δὲ αὐτῶν ἰδοὺ ἄγγελος κυρίου φαίνεται κατ᾽ ὄναρ τῷ Ἰωσὴφ λέγων· *ἐγερθεὶς* **παράλαβε** τὸ παιδίον καὶ τὴν μητέρα αὐτοῦ καὶ *φεῦγε* εἰς Αἴγυπτον καὶ ἴσθι ἐκεῖ ἕως ἂν εἴπω σοι· μέλλει γὰρ Ἡρῴδης ζητεῖν τὸ παιδίον τοῦ ἀπολέσαι αὐτό (Departing, behold, an angel of the Lord appeared to Joseph in a dream saying, "**Rise**, *take* the child and his mother, [and] *flee* to Egypt, and remain there until I tell you, for Herod is about to search for the child, to destroy him.")

2:20 λέγων· *ἐγερθεὶς* **παράλαβε** τὸ παιδίον καὶ τὴν μητέρα αὐτοῦ καὶ *πορεύου* εἰς γῆν Ἰσραήλ· τεθνήκασιν γὰρ οἱ ζητοῦντες τὴν ψυχὴν τοῦ παιδίου (saying, "*Rise* [and] **take** the child and his mother and *go* to the land of Israel, for those who sought the child's life are dead.")

5: 14 καὶ αὐτὸς παρήγγειλεν αὐτῷ μηδενὶ εἰπεῖν, ἀλλὰ *ἀπελθὼν* **δεῖξον** σεαυτὸν τῷ ἱερεῖ καὶ προσένεγκε περὶ τοῦ καθαρισμοῦ σου καθὼς προσέταξεν Μωϋσῆς, εἰς μαρτύριον αὐτοῖς (And he charged him to tell no one, but "*go* and **show** yourself to the priest, and make an offering for your cleansing, as Moses commanded, for a proof to them."

5: 24 ἄφες ἐκεῖ τὸ δῶρόν σου ἔμπροσθεν τοῦ θυσιαστηρίου καὶ ὕπαγε πρῶτον διαλλάγηθι τῷ ἀδελφῷ σου, καὶ τότε *ἐλθὼν* **πρόσφερε** τὸ δῶρόν σου (leave your gift there before the altar and go. First be reconciled to your brother, and then *come* and **offer** your gift).

9: 6 ἵνα δὲ εἰδῆτε ὅτι ἐξουσίαν ἔχει ὁ υἱὸς τοῦ ἀνθρώπου ἐπὶ τῆς γῆς ἀφιέναι ἁμαρτίας τότε λέγει τῷ παραλυτικῷ· *ἐγερθεὶς* **ἆρόν** σου τὴν κλίνην καὶ ὕπαγε εἰς τὸν οἶκόν σου.[44] (But that you may know that the Son of Man has authority on earth to forgive sins"—he then says to the paralytic—"*Rise*, **pick up** your bed and go home").

9: 13 *πορευθέντες* δὲ **μάθετε** τί ἐστιν· ἔλεος θέλω καὶ οὐ θυσίαν· οὐ γὰρ ἦλθον καλέσαι δικαίους ἀλλὰ ἁμαρτωλούς (*Go* [and] **learn** what this means, 'I desire mercy, and not sacrifice.' For I came not to call the righteous, but sinners").

9: 18 Ταῦτα αὐτοῦ λαλοῦντος αὐτοῖς, ἰδοὺ ἄρχων εἷς *ἐλθὼν* **προσεκύνει** αὐτῷ λέγων ὅτι ἡ θυγάτηρ μου ἄρτι ἐτελεύτησεν· ἀλλὰ *ἐλθὼν* **ἐπίθες** τὴν χεῖρά σου ἐπ᾽ αὐτήν, καὶ ζήσεται (saying these things to them, behold, a ruler *came in* [and] **worshiped** him, saying, "My daughter has just died, but *come* [and] **lay** your hand on her, and she will live.").

11: 4 καὶ ἀποκριθεὶς ὁ Ἰησοῦς εἶπεν αὐτοῖς· *πορευθέντες* **ἀπαγγείλατε** Ἰωάννῃ ἃ ἀκούετε καὶ βλέπετε (And answering, Jesus said to them, "*Go* [and] **announce** to John things that you hear and see).

17: 27 ἵνα δὲ μὴ σκανδαλίσωμεν αὐτούς, *πορευθεὶς* εἰς θάλασσαν **βάλε** ἄγκιστρον καὶ τὸν ἀναβάντα πρῶτον ἰχθὺν ἆρον, καὶ ἀνοίξας τὸ στόμα αὐτοῦ εὑρήσεις στατῆρα· ἐκεῖνον *λαβὼν* **δὸς** αὐτοῖς ἀντὶ ἐμοῦ καὶ σοῦ (So not to cause offense to them, *go* to the sea [and] **cast** a hook and take the first fish you that comes up, and openning its mouth you will find a shekel. *Take* that [and] **give** it to them for me and for yourself").

28: 7 καὶ ταχὺ *πορευθεῖσαι* **εἴπατε** τοῖς μαθηταῖς αὐτοῦ ὅτι ἠγέρθη ἀπὸ τῶν νεκρῶν, καὶ ἰδοὺ προάγει ὑμᾶς εἰς τὴν Γαλιλαίαν, ἐκεῖ αὐτὸν ὄψεσθε· ἰδοὺ εἶπον ὑμῖν (so *go* quickly [and] **tell** his disciples that he was risen from the dead, and behold, he is going before you to Galilee; behold you will see him. See, I have told you").

28:19 *πορευθέντες* οὖν **μαθητεύσατε** πάντα τὰ ἔθνη, βαπτίζοντες αὐτοὺς εἰς τὸ ὄνομα τοῦ πατρὸς καὶ τοῦ υἱοῦ καὶ τοῦ ἁγίου πνεύματος (*Go* therefore [and] **make disciples** of all nations, baptizing them in the name of the Father and of the Son and of the Holy Spirit).

Mark

16: 15 καὶ εἶπεν αὐτοῖς· *πορευθέντες* εἰς τὸν κόσμον ἅπαντα **κηρύξατε** τὸ εὐαγγέλιον πάσῃ τῇ κτίσει (and he said to them, "*Go* into all the world [and] **proclaim** the gospel to the whole creation).

Luke

5:24 ἵνα δὲ εἰδῆτε ὅτι ὁ υἱὸς τοῦ ἀνθρώπου ἐξουσίαν ἔχει ἐπὶ τῆς γῆς ἀφιέναι ἁμαρτίας - εἶπεν τῷ παραλελυμένῳ· σοὶ λέγω, *ἔγειρε* καὶ *ἄρας* τὸ κλινίδιόν σου **πορεύου** εἰς τὸν οἶκόν σου (but that you may know that the Son of Man has authority on earth to forgive sins"—he said to the paralytic—I say to you, *rise* and *pick up* your bed [and] **go** to your home").[45]

7:22 καὶ ἀποκριθεὶς εἶπεν αὐτοῖς· *πορευθέντες* **ἀπαγγείλατε** Ἰωάννῃ ἃ εἴδετε καὶ ἠκούσατε ... (and answering he said to them, "*Go* [and] **tell** John what you have seen and heard).

9:60 εἶπεν δὲ αὐτῷ· ἄφες τοὺς νεκροὺς θάψαι τοὺς ἑαυτῶν νεκρούς, σὺ δὲ ἀπελθὼν **διάγγελλε** τὴν βασιλείαν τοῦ θεοῦ (And he said to him, "Leave the dead to bury their own dead. But you, *go* [and] **proclaim** the kingdom of God.").

10: 10 εἰς ἣν δ᾽ ἂν πόλιν εἰσέλθητε καὶ μὴ δέχωνται ὑμᾶς, *ἐξελθόντες* εἰς τὰς πλατείας αὐτῆς **εἴπατε** (But whenever you enter a city and they do not receive you, *go* into its streets [and] **say**).

13: 32 καὶ εἶπεν αὐτοῖς· *πορευθέντες* **εἴπατε** τῇ ἀλώπεκι ταύτῃ· ἰδοὺ ἐκβάλλω δαιμόνια καὶ ἰάσεις ἀποτελῶ σήμερον καὶ αὔριον καὶ τῇ τρίτῃ τελειοῦμαι (And he said to them, "*Go* [and] **say** to that fox, 'Behold, I cast out demons and perform healings today and tomorrow, and the third day I will finish).

16:6 ὁ δὲ εἶπεν· ἑκατὸν βάτους ἐλαίου. ὁ δὲ εἶπεν αὐτῷ· δέξαι σου τὰ γράμματα καὶ *καθίσας* ταχέως **γράψον** πεντήκοντα. (and he said, a hundred measures of oil. And he said to him, take your bill, and *sit down* quickly [and] **write fifty**).

17: 7 Τίς δὲ ἐξ ὑμῶν δοῦλον ἔχων ἀροτριῶντα ἢ ποιμαίνοντα, ὃς εἰσελθόντι ἐκ τοῦ ἀγροῦ ἐρεῖ αὐτῷ· εὐθέως *παρελθὼν* **ἀνάπεσε** (Who among you having a servant who came in from plowing or tending sheep, will say '*Come* here immediately [and] **recline** at table'?).

17: 14 καὶ ἰδὼν εἶπεν αὐτοῖς· *πορευθέντες* **ἐπιδείξατε** ἑαυτοὺς τοῖς ἱερεῦσιν. καὶ ἐγένετο ἐν τῷ ὑπάγειν αὐτοὺς ἐκαθαρίσθησαν (and seeing them he said to them, "*Go* [and] **show** yourselves to the priests." And as they went they were cleansed).

17: 19 καὶ εἶπεν αὐτῷ· *ἀναστὰς* **πορεύου**· ἡ πίστις σου σέσωκέν σε (Then he said to him, *Get up* [and] **go**; your faith has saved you.)

19:5 καὶ ὡς ἦλθεν ἐπὶ τὸν τόπον, ἀναβλέψας ὁ Ἰησοῦς εἶπεν πρὸς αὐτόν· Ζακχαῖε, *σπεύσας* **κατάβηθι**, σήμερον γὰρ ἐν τῷ οἴκῳ σου δεῖ με μεῖναι. (And when Jesus came to the place, looking up he said to him, "Zacchaeus, *hurry* [and] **come down**, for today I must stay at your house").

22:8 καὶ ἀπέστειλεν Πέτρον καὶ Ἰωάννην εἰπών· *πορευθέντες* **ἑτοιμάσατε** ἡμῖν τὸ πάσχα ἵνα φάγωμεν[46] (and Jesus sent Peter and John, saying, "*Go* [and] **prepare** the Passover for us, that we may eat it.").

22:46 καὶ εἶπεν αὐτοῖς τί καθεύδετε; *ἀναστάντες* **προσεύχεσθε**, ἵνα μὴ εἰσέλθητε εἰς πειρασμόν (and he said to them, "Why are you sleeping? *Rise* [and] **pray** lest you may enter into temptation.").

Acts

9:11 ὁ δὲ κύριος πρὸς αὐτόν· *ἀναστὰς πορεύθητι* ἐπὶ τὴν ῥύμην τὴν καλουμένην Εὐθεῖαν καὶ ζήτησον ἐν οἰκίᾳ Ἰούδα Σαῦλον ὀνόματι Ταρσέα· ἰδοὺ γὰρ προσεύχεται (And the Lord [said] to him, "*Rise* [and] go to the street called Straight, and look for at the house of Judas a man of named Saul of Tarsus, for behold, he is praying).
10:13 καὶ ἐγένετο φωνὴ πρὸς αὐτόν· *ἀναστάς*, Πέτρε, **θῦσον** καὶ **φάγε** (And there came a voice to him: "*Rise*, Peter; **kill** and **eat**").

The use of the aorist participial effect of ἀνίστημι with the imperative seems to be the favorite of Luke. It may be Luke's attempt of reproduce the original set as found in the LXX. Every time when there is a reminiscence of the Old narrative, Luke seems to try to reproduce not only the vocabulary, but also the LXX structure. This same situation is quoted *ipsis litteris* in Acts 11:7. The anarthrous aorist participial effect serves as a background of the main action, and it prioritizes the two main verbs θῦσον καὶ φάγε.

The use of the participle ἀναστάς enables the author to express details "without bestowing upon them a prominence that would distort the perspective, the finite verb giving the outline of the action while the participle supplies the coloring."[47] Because θῦσον καὶ φάγε are imperatives and the aorist participle forms a united action, it is upgraded in the readers' perspective into the same modal semantic, namely, imperative.

10:20 ἀλλὰ *ἀναστὰς* **κατάβηθι** καὶ **πορεύου** σὺν αὐτοῖς μηδὲν διακρινόμενος ὅτι ἐγὼ ἀπέσταλκα αὐτούς (*Get up* [and] **go down** and **go** with them nothing doubting, for I have sent them).

The relation of the anarthrous aorist participle ἀναστάς with the two imperatives **κατάβηθι** καὶ **πορεύου** has the upgraded implicature. The copyist of codex D decided to render the idea of *get up* as an imperatival verb ἀναστά, with a grammatical oddity since he did not use the conjunction καί to coordinate the two verbs. There are two coordinate imperatival verbs that the participle precedes with the upgraded participial effect. As already mentioned, the continuity between backward information with forward information is being called in this study point of departure involving renewal.

The adverbial participle is this logical clause chain that assigns this point of departure involving renewal. The present participle follows the two imperatives as it develops the speech already announced by the modal. The culmination of the narrative is a huge encouragement, that is, ἐγὼ ἀπέσταλκα αὐτούς.[48]

16:9 Καὶ ὅραμα διὰ [τῆς] νυκτὸς τῷ Παύλῳ ὤφθη, ἀνὴρ Μακεδών τις ἦν ἑστὼς καὶ παρακαλῶν αὐτὸν καὶ λέγων· διαβὰς εἰς Μακεδονίαν **βοήθησον** ἡμῖν (And a vision appeared to Paul in the night: a man of Macedonia was standing and urging him and saying, "*Come over* to Macedonia [and] **help** us).

16:15 ὡς δὲ ἐβαπτίσθη καὶ ὁ οἶκος αὐτῆς, παρεκάλεσεν λέγουσα· εἰ κεκρίκατέ με πιστὴν τῷ κυρίῳ εἶναι, εἰσελθόντες εἰς τὸν οἶκόν μου **μένετε**· καὶ παρεβιάσατο ἡμᾶς (When she was baptized and her household, she urged saying "If you have judged me to be faithful to the Lord, *come in* my house [and] **stay.**" And she prevailed upon us).

16:36 ἀπήγγειλεν δὲ ὁ δεσμοφύλαξ τοὺς λόγους [τούτους] πρὸς τὸν Παῦλον ὅτι ἀπέσταλκαν οἱ στρατηγοὶ ἵνα ἀπολυθῆτε· νῦν οὖν ἐξελθόντες **πορεύεσθε** ἐν εἰρήνῃ (And the jailer announces these words to Paul: "The magistrates have sent to let you go. Therefore, *come out* now [and] **go** in peace").

16:37 ὁ δὲ Παῦλος ἔφη πρὸς αὐτούς· δείραντες ἡμᾶς δημοσίᾳ ἀκατακρίτους, ἀνθρώπους Ῥωμαίους ὑπάρχοντας, ἔβαλαν εἰς φυλακήν, καὶ νῦν λάθρᾳ ἡμᾶς ἐκβάλλουσιν; οὐ γάρ, ἀλλὰ ἐλθόντες αὐτοὶ ἡμᾶς ἐξαγαγέτωσαν (but Paul said to them, "beating us publicly, uncondemned, men being Roman, They put us in a prison and now do they now throw us out secretly? No! *Let* them *come* themselves [and] **lead** us **out**").

21:24 τούτους παραλαβὼν **ἁγνίσθητι** σὺν αὐτοῖς καὶ δαπάνησον ἐπ᾽ αὐτοῖς ἵνα ξυρήσονται τὴν κεφαλήν, καὶ γνώσονται πάντες ὅτι ὧν κατήχηνται περὶ σοῦ οὐδέν ἐστιν ἀλλὰ στοιχεῖς καὶ αὐτὸς φυλάσσων τὸν νόμον (*take* these men [and] **purify** yourself along with them and pay their expenses, so that they may shave the head. And everyone will know that there is nothing in what they have been told about you, but that you also walk keeping of the law.

22:13 ἐλθὼν πρός με καὶ ἐπιστὰς **εἶπέν** μοι· Σαοὺλ ἀδελφέ, ἀνάβλεψον. κἀγὼ αὐτῇ τῇ ὥρᾳ ἀνέβλεψα εἰς αὐτόν (He *came* to me, and *stood* next to me [and*] **said** to me, 'Brother Saul, receive your sight.' And at that very hour I received my sight and saw him).

2 Timothy

2 Tim 4:11 Λουκᾶς ἐστιν μόνος μετ᾽ ἐμοῦ. Μᾶρκον ἀναλαβὼν **ἄγε** μετὰ σεαυτοῦ, ἔστιν γάρ μοι εὔχρηστος εἰς διακονίαν (Luke alone is with me. **Take** Mark [and] *bring* him with you, for he is helpful to me for ministry).

James

1:21 διὸ *ἀποθέμενοι* πᾶσαν ῥυπαρίαν καὶ περισσείαν κακίας ἐν πραΰτητι **δέξασθε** τὸν ἔμφυτον λόγον τὸν δυνάμενον σῶσαι τὰς ψυχὰς ὑμῶν (therefore *put away* all filthiness and overflowing of wickedness [and] **receive** with meekness the implanted word, which is able to save your souls).

It is possible that the NASB renders the participle with a subordinate idea without deciding any contextual implicature, thus "therefore putting aside all filthiness and *all* that remains of wickedness, in humility receive the word implanted, which is able to save your souls." However, the upgraded participial implicature is the best option to the anarthrous aorist participle in this passage. Moo sees as an upgraded implicature when he states, "Greek participles in these situations often become virtually equivalent to the imperative verbs they depend on."[49] So does Martin in his translation "get rid of all [moral] filth …."[50]

As already stated, the anarthrous aorist adverbial participle placed in the beginning of a clause or sentence has two functions: to indicate point of departure, thus who is doing that action since the participle does grammaticalize that? 1:19 says "ἀδελφοί μου ἀγαπητοί)", and in verse 21, the main verb grammaticalizes the subject of verse 19, that is, δέξασθε ("receive"). The function then is backward-forward. The focus is in the main verb, but the author appeals to their readers' mind (factive presupposition) that the participle already indicates to them that they need to interact with the context.

Valid Examples with the Infinitive Modulation

The infinitive (modulation) deserves an analysis of its own. However, since there are only few examples of the participle having the upgraded implicature, the discussion is brief. Both the participle and the infinitive are modulation, not literally mood.[51] Therefore, they both are outside of the attitude system. They belong to the ideational meanings, which relates language as reflection.[52] Robertson says,

The infinitive never developed personal endings and remained undefined, unlimited. The infinitive and the participle are thus both infinitives in this sense, that they are the unlimited verb so far as personal endings are concerned. They are both participles in that they participate in both noun and verb. The terms have no inherent distinction, but serve merely as a convenience. In the nature of the case neither can have a subject in any literal sense.[53]

Although neither infinitives nor participles grammaticalize attitudes within modal semantics, they have a distinct semantic that distinguishes them when they are involved within the same syntactical configuration.[54] Lightfoot tries to establish a difference, but his explanation seems to hit only the participial side, and he also assumes something untenable, that is, that the indicative is the mood for factual proposition. He says, "Use of a participle construction indicates that the author of the sentence presupposes and wishes the hearer to think that he presupposes that the complement reflects a real, actual, existing state of affairs."[55]

The distinction between these two modulations cannot be suitably defined here, but suffice it to say, the use of the participle "presupposes that the speaker is committed to the truth of the proposition, and not with statements of fact, but with presupposition."[56] When verbs of perception have the infinitive as a complement, there is an indirect perception involved, but when the complement is a participle a direct perception is being uttered. When the aorist occurs with the infinitive, it denotes a situation necessarily unrealized or incomplete,[57] while the participle presupposes the truthfulness of the proposition so that the argument of the main clause can make sense.

Matthew

5:13 Ὑμεῖς ἐστε τὸ ἅλας τῆς γῆς· ἐὰν δὲ τὸ ἅλας μωρανθῇ, ἐν τίνι ἁλισθήσεται; εἰς οὐδὲν ἰσχύει ἔτι εἰ μὴ *βληθὲν* ἔξω **καταπατεῖσθαι** ὑπὸ τῶν ἀνθρώπων ("you are the salt of the earth, but if salt has lost its taste, how shall its saltiness be restored? It is no longer good for anything but *to be thrown out* [and] **to trample** under people's feet).

Mark

1:7 Καὶ ἐκήρυσσεν λέγων ἔρχεται ὁ ἰσχυρότερός μου ὀπίσω μου, οὗ οὐκ εἰμὶ ἱκανὸς *κύψας* **λῦσαι** τὸν ἱμάντα τῶν ὑποδημάτων αὐτοῦ (and he preached, saying, "after me comes he who is mightier than I, the strap of whose sandals I am not worthy *to bend down* [and] **untie**).

Luke

11:7 κἀκεῖνος ἔσωθεν ἀποκριθεὶς εἴπῃ μή μοι κόπους πάρεχε ἤδη ἡ θύρα κέκλεισται καὶ τὰ παιδία μου μετ᾽ ἐμοῦ εἰς τὴν κοίτην εἰσίν οὐ δύναμαι *ἀναστὰς* **δοῦναί** σοι (and he answering from within, will say, 'do not bother me; the door is already shut, and my children are with me in bed. I cannot *get up* [and] **give** you anything'?).

14:18 καὶ ἤρξαντο ἀπὸ μιᾶς πάντες παραιτεῖσθαι. ὁ πρῶτος εἶπεν αὐτῷ· ἀγρὸν ἠγόρασα καὶ ἔχω ἀνάγκην *ἐξελθὼν* **ἰδεῖν** αὐτόν ἐρωτῶ σε, ἔχε με παρῃτημένον (but they all began to make excuses. The first said to him, 'I have bought a field, and I must *go out* [and] **see** it. Please have me excused').

Acts

6:2 προσκαλεσάμενοι δὲ οἱ δώδεκα τὸ πλῆθος τῶν μαθητῶν εἶπαν οὐκ ἀρεστόν ἐστιν ἡμᾶς *καταλείψαντας* τὸν λόγον τοῦ θεοῦ **διακονεῖν** τραπέζαις (and the twelve summoned the full number of the disciples and said, "It is not right *to give up* preaching the word of God [and] **serve** tables).

19:21 Ὡς δὲ ἐπληρώθη ταῦτα, ἔθετο ὁ Παῦλος ἐν τῷ πνεύματι *διελθὼν* τὴν Μακεδονίαν καὶ Ἀχαΐαν **πορεύεσθαι** εἰς Ἱεροσόλυμα εἰπὼν ὅτι μετὰ τὸ γενέσθαι με ἐκεῖ δεῖ με καὶ Ῥώμην ἰδεῖν (now after these events Paul resolved in the Spirit *to pass through* Macedonia and Achaia [and] **go** to Jerusalem, saying, "After I have been there, I must also see Rome").

25:9 Ὁ Φῆστος δὲ θέλων τοῖς Ἰουδαίοις χάριν καταθέσθαι ἀποκριθεὶς τῷ Παύλῳ εἶπεν θέλεις εἰς Ἱεροσόλυμα *ἀναβὰς* ἐκεῖ περὶ τούτων **κριθῆναι** ἐπ᾽ ἐμοῦ (but Festus, wishing to do the Jews a favor, answered to Paul, "do you want *to go up* to Jerusalem [and] *there be tried* on these charges before me?

Notes

1. The collected data is from Logos Bible software.
2. Moorhouse, *The Syntaxe of Sophocles*, 250.
3. *SRG*, 244.
4. Halliday, *Functional Grammar*, 26–27.
5. Halliday, *On Grammar*, 175.
6. ASV, ESV, KJG, NAS, NET, NIV, NLT, and NAB.
7. NET, NIV, NLT, and NAB. ASV, ESV, and NAS translated with a gerund, thus "opening …". KJG renders it with as temporal, thus "when …."
8. Hagner, *Matthew 1–13*, 23. See Leon Morris, *The Gospel According to Matthew*, PNTC (Grand Rapids, MI: W.B. Eerdmans, 1992), 33.
9. *SRG*, 16.
10. Ibid., 16.
11. See *LDF*, 71.
12. *SRG*, 17.
13. *GCG*, 58.
14. See Chapter 5.
15. See notes on Chapter 5

16. Morris, *Matthew*, 45. BDAG ἀποστέλλω 2 ⓑ says that "when used w. other verbs, ἀ. often functions like our verbal auxiliary 'have' and means simply that the action in question has been performed by someone else (Gen 31:4; 41:8, 14; Ex 9:27; 2 Km 11:5 al.; X., Cyr. 3, 1, 6; Plut., Mor. 11c μεταπέμψας ἀνεῖλε τ. Θεόκριτον) ἀποστείλας ἀνεῖλεν *he had (them) killed* Mt 2:16. ἀ. ἐκράτησεν τ. Ἰωάννην *he had John arrested* Mk 6:17. ἀ. μετεκαλέσατο *he had (him) summoned* Ac 7:14. ἐσήμανεν ἀ. διὰ τ. ἀγγέλου αὐτοῦ *he had it made known by his angel* Rv 1:1. Sim. ἀπέστειλαν αἱ ἀδελφαὶ πρὸς αὐτὸν λέγουσαι *the sisters had word brought to him* J 11:3. ἀ. ἐν ἀφέσει *set free* Lk 4:18b (Is 58:6). BDAG, 121.

17. Ibid.

18. *LDF*, 95–96.

19. Hagner, *Matthew 1–13*, 32. See also Morris, *Matthew*, 44

20. It is difficult without a parallel passage to help us to establish the type of relationship with the participle such as this. The classification of the upgraded function is ambiguous in this passage. Usually in construction such as this the upgraded effect comes with a particle indicating an urgency (εὐθέως) or immediate at beginning of the action. It is possible that this participle could easily describe a sequence of a logical temporal frame (after leaving …), and therefore is not in the upgraded effect.

21. There is an aorist in some mss instead of an imperfect see. εκραξεν ℵ* Z 0281 *f*[13] 579. 1241. Mark 7:25 has a different lexeme for the main verb, but it is an aorist indicative.

22. Levinsohn, *Discourse*, p. 97.

23. και ειπεν αυτοις D latt (sa[ms] bo).

24. The upgraded effect with historic present.

25. Upgraded effect with historic present

26. Some manuscript has (he began to cry) ηρξατο κλαιειν D Θ 565 latt sa[mss], presenting an ingressive idea, something that occurs with the upgrade effect itself. Two other mss keep Mark's aorist participle but change the main verb from an imperfect to an aorist indicative (ℵ* C).

27. The major commentaries on the Gospel of John render this passage as having the upgraded effect. See George R. Beasley-Murray, *John*, WBC 36 (Dallas: Word, Incorporated, 2002), 204. D. A. Carson, *The Gospel According to John*, PNTC (Grand Rapids, MI: Inter-Varsity Press, 1991), 446.

28. Codex Bezae and all Syriac version and Peshitta have a finite verb preceded by a participle (συστειλαντες εξηνεγκαν και). Instead of the participle ἐξενέγκαντες, the copyist of D writes the finite form ἐξήνεγκαν. The upgraded effect typically causes this type of reading, specially that the participle is in clause chain with the main clause which presents the coordinate idea in the readers mind.

29. The ideational function of the participle with the upgraded effect cause a mental coordination because of the close association of the participle with the main verb. It is possible that the copyist of Codex Bezae felt the mental coordination and decided to write the relation between the participle and the main verb with καί.

30. The different word order does not change the upgraded effect in this passage. See επιστρεψας δε ο Παυλος τω πνευματι και διαπονηθεις 𝔓[127vid] D.

31. δέ indicates that the subject of the absolute genitive is "they".

32. Campbell, *Verbal Aspect*, 50.

33. See José Antonio Septién, *El Griego Bíblico al Alcance de Todos: Un Estudio Programado del Griego del Nuevo Testamento* (Barcelona: Editorial Clie, 2007), 907.

34. *PVA*, 168, 173.

35. Halliday, *Functional Grammar*, 26–27.
36. *PVA*, 170.
37. There are three Byzantine MSS that read an indicative rather than the subjunctive of συλλέγω.
38. NAB and ESV render this participial as upgraded. So does Bauckman. See Richard J. Bauckham, *2 Peter, Jude*, WBC 50 (Dallas, TX: Word, Incorporated, 1998), 336.
39. *PVA*, 335
40. Ibid.
41. *GGBB*, 485. See *DMG*, 174.
42. *PVA*, 168, 322. Wallace seems to position the subjunctive and optative on the side of the indicative in the sense that they address congnition, that is, an appeal to the mind, and the imperative is set apart since it addresses to the volition. However, this dichotomy (volition and mind) is hard to maintain. See *GGBB*, 446.
43. Donald A. Hagner, *Matthew 1–13*, WBC 35a (Dallas, TX: Word, Incorporated, 1998), 24.
44. Only Matthew has any examples of the aorist participial effect with the ἐγείρω.
45. The upgraded participial implicature might be the cause to the copist of א D 157 1424 to change the participial upgraded effect into the finite imperatival form ἀρόν.
46. LXX examples with this same verb include Gen 12:9; 27:9, 13 f; 37:14; 45:28; 2 Kgs 5:10, 12; Tob 1:19; 1 Macc 7:7; Dan (Th) 6:20.
47. George M. Bolling, "The Participle in Hesiod," *CUB* 3, no 4 (1897): 422–423. In Acts 12:7 καὶ ἰδοὺ ἄγγελος κυρίου ἐπέστη καὶ φῶς ἔλαμψεν ἐν τῷ οἰκήματι· πατάξας δὲ τὴν πλευρὰν τοῦ Πέτρου ἤγειρεν αὐτὸν λέγων· ἀνάστα ἐν τάχει. καὶ ἐξέπεσαν αὐτοῦ αἱ ἁλύσεις ἐκ τῶν χειρῶν.) Luke uses the imperatival form ἀνάστα alone.
48. Peter's struggle against eating shows his fear of disobeying God. Therefore, the [e]motional environment is still favored by the participle to draw the readers into the context. Further examples with ἀνίστημι include 22:10 εἶπον δέ· τί ποιήσω, κύριε; ὁ δὲ κύριος εἶπεν πρός με· ἀναστὰς πορεύου εἰς Δαμασκὸν κἀκεῖ σοι λαληθήσεται περὶ πάντων ὧν τέτακταί σοι ποιῆσαι. 22:16 καὶ νῦν τί μέλλεις; ἀναστὰς βάπτισαι καὶ ἀπόλουσαι τὰς ἁμαρτίας σου ἐπικαλεσάμενος τὸ ὄνομα αὐτοῦ. Examples of the participle of ἀνίστημι with the participial upgraded effect in the LXX include Gen 13:17; 19:15; 22:3; 23:7; 24:10, 54; 25:34 (?); 27:19; 28:2; 31:17; 32:1(?), 23; 35:1; 44:4; Exod 2:17; 24:13; Num 22:20 (?); 24:25; Deut 17:8 (?); 31:16 (?); Josh 1:2; 7:13; 8:1; Jda. 8:20; Judg 7:9; 8:20; 9:32; 2 Sam 15:9; 19:8; 2 Kgs 1:3; 1 Esd 4:47; 8:91 f; 9:1, 7; Tob 8:10; 10:10; Tbs. 8:10; 9:5; 10:10; Ps 101:14; Job 1:20; Dan 4:18; Bel 1:37; Bet. 1:39.
49. Douglas J. Moo, *The Letter of James*, PNTC (Grand Rapids, MI: Eerdmans, 2000), 86.
50. Ralph P. Martin, *James*, WBC, 48 (Dallas, TX: Word, Incorporated, 1998), 48.
51. Septién sees it that way when he states, "… el Infinitivo no es un modo aunque se le clasifica a menudo de esa manera. El modo es la manera como se realiza o relaciona un acción verbal de acuerdo con la actitud del sujeto que la ejecuta." Septién, *El Griego Bíblico*, 274.
52. Halliday, *Functional Grammar*, 26–27.
53. *ATR*, 370.
54. See *PVA*, 391.
55. Lightfoot, *Natural Logic*, 41–42. See also Bakker, "Verbal Aspect," 7.
56. Palmer, *Mood*, 18, see also 140–141.
57. Wurmbrand, *Infinitives*, 62.

CHAPTER SEVEN

Conclusion

This study has attempted to develop the use of the participle in general and the upgraded effect in particular. Our study involves two features: first, it involves the general modal semantics of the participle; second, it includes the analysis of emotional context and the use of participles as a fascinating tool to draw the readers into it. Thus, the thesis of this study is that the participle is a factive presupposition by which the author invites the readers to participate in the construal of meaning and upgraded participial effect as a result of a very complex construction involving structure, lexis, and the choices available in the verbal network.

Semantic presupposition is a mental exercise demanded by a written verbal form (participle and/or infinitive) from the readers/hearers in order to construct the intended wide meaning. Typically, in a factive presupposition the "fact" resides at the semantic level, and the truth then lies in the meaning shared by the reader.

The upgraded effect has a specific structure throughout all the observed data, that is, PARTICIPLE [aorist nominative] + FINITE VERB [any tense/any mood]. There are other pragmatic effects realized by this specific structure, specifically the logical temporal relation of antecedent or subsequent time occurs. Generally, the upgraded effect loves the imperative, likes the indicative, tolerates the other moods. We have not found any upgraded effect that the participle is not an aorist preceding the main verb typically an aorist, but not always.

The comparison between the synoptic Gospels revealed that some parallel passages have TWO FINITE VERBS coordinated by καί in one or two of the evangelists while another switches one of the aorist forms to an aorist nominative participle removing the conjunction καί leaving out only the mental coordination because of the participial function, that is, ideational that puts the participle in a clause chain with the main verb. All the Gospel writers have different choices available and there is clear indication about what makes them choose the participles besides the semantic function of the participle of drawing the readers into the construal of meaning.

The choice of the participle is more sophisticated because two actions are set as one, where the first (participial clause) is taken as a written mental exercise of an unspecified movement toward the main action. The relation of the two is so connected that the readers will read/hear the attendant circumstance of the main clause in the same mood. The participle sets the main verb in the spotlight so that the readers can use their creative mind to fill some information purposefully blocked by the author.

The upgraded effect works both at the semantic level as a factive presupposition and at the pragmatic level as result of the functional roles of the modal semantic of the aorist participle. This adverbial bifunctional role (backward-forward) ⟷ occurs with every aorist adverbial participle that initiates the clause association, but the upgraded effect seems to be stronger than the clause association since the readers mentally upgrade the participle of the embedded clause to the mood of the primary clause.

This study has sought to demonstrate that a semantic presupposition represents a stage of hierarchization. This linguistic feature is an abstraction of meaning whose specific functional roles have two further functions: background and prioritizing. The background and prioritizing functions presumably demonstrate that the Greek participle is a logical clause chain.

The assumption that motivated this work is that a general understanding of the semantics of the participle will help to avoid any confusion between a participle (modulation), and the other Greek moods. To do so, a specific method was adopted related to a theory of language, which in itself defines the method to be used. Systemic functional linguistics is a system-structure theory, which views language as a network of interrelated sets of options.

This study attempts to apply descriptive methods as opposed to prescriptive methods, hence the use of systemic functional linguistics as the adopted theory. It is descriptive linguistics, which defines language in terms of its use, as opposed to prescriptive linguistics, which attempts to define what a language should be like. The choice to use a functional linguistics theory is due to its functional paradigm, which indicates that there is a difference in meaning when an author chooses to utter something with a participle, even if it is related to the main verb in such a way that the participle seems to have upgraded its modulation.

For instance, to say that the use of the upgraded effect represents the same meaning as though the author had chosen two imperatives coordinated by καί fails to see the essential difference between a mood and its semantics on the one hand, and a modulation with its essential semantic value on the other.

The point here is that the choice that the language user makes not only highlights the meaning of that choice but also eliminates the meanings of the other options. Thus, the choice of a participle is made at the cost of the attitude system, since the participle is formally and semantically outside the attitude system. This assertion moves beyond the normal conception of the systemic functional linguistics network, since it contrasts the finiteness system (±finite system), and not merely the −finite subsystem (±factive presupposition).

This study seeks to distinguish semantics and pragmatics. The assumption is that if the supposed meaning of a grammatical feature can be canceled in a specific use, this meaning is not part of the semantics of the form itself, but of its context. Recognizing the upgraded effect as a contextual meaning, this study includes the study of register, which is the study of the context. Register indicates the most common context where a speaker/writer uses a grammatical form.

In general, the richness of the participle serves as an excellent tool when a context of the situation presents emotion because the author has a choice of inviting the readers to participate of the event at hand. The goal of the participle is to draw the readers into the environment of the narrative. Thus, the relation of the aorist participle to the main verb is what gives structure to the readers' experience and helps to determine how they should be looking at things. The participle requires intellectual effort from the readers to appreciate what the language is suggesting to them. This interaction between a modulation (participle) and the mood and modals is possible because of the close association of the two functional components of language, that is, interpersonal and ideational metafunction.

This study has demonstrated the necessary distinction between these functional components. The interpersonal meaning relates to language as a social action, while the ideational meanings relates to language as reflection. The failure to balance the relation of these two metafunctions and what they realize has been the cause of confusion and has underestimated the value of participles in general and upgraded participial function in particular.

The upgraded choice is a natural feature of the Greek language since the Classical period and occurs throughout the Greek period. Our conclusion is that the upgraded effect is one option among others that an author has available on the verbal network system. Knowing the choice implies meaning to a participle to block the attitude system because of the lack of limitation on the verbal form. The lack of limitation opens a slot for the readers to fill with significant mental information. All the participles are factive presupposition, and this book is concerned with the anarthrous aorist nominative participles that precedes the main verb. Sometimes this structure has a temporal logical relation but most of the examples of this structure fit the upgraded.

Multiple language theories are helpful with their different methodology to the study of particular features in language, but any approach to the field of language should consider including a balanced perspective of language as taught by Halliday. It is possible that some have taken his conclusions farther than he would appreciate, but this does not mean that his theory of language should be rejected. Rather, the analysis of the functional components (ideational, interpersonal, and textual) must be part of any attempt to understand how meaning is exchanged.

Appendix

Sample of Emotional Description in Matthew and Acts with the Upgraded Participle

Matthew	Emotion	Maybe	No-Emotion
2: 8	x		
2:11	x		
2:13	x		
2:14	x		
2:16	x		
2:20	x		
2:23			x
4:9	x		
4:13			x
4:20		x	
4:22		x	
5:13			x
5:14		x	
5: 24	x		
8:2	x		
8:7	x		
8:25	x		
8:26	x		

continued

Matthew	Emotion	Maybe	No-Emotion
9:6	x		
9:7	x		
9:9		x	
9:13	x		
9:18	x		
9:25	x		
9:31	x		
11: 4		x	
12:45	x		
13:28	x		
13:36			x
13:46	x		
14:12		x	
14:31	x		
15:22	x		
15:25	x		
15:29			x
17: 27	x		
20:6		x	
21:29	x		
22:7	x		
22:15	x		
22:22	x		
26:14–15	x		
26:42	x		
26:50	x		
26:51	x		
26:56	x		
26:75	x		
27:30	x		
28:7	x		
28:9	x		
28:11			x
28:13	x		
28:19	x		

Acts	Emotion	Maybe	No-Emotion
3:7	x		
5:6	x		
5:10	x		

Acts	Emotion	Maybe	No-Emotion
6:2		x	
7:4		x	
8:5		x	
8:27			x
9:1–2	x		
9:11			x
9:18	x		
9:27		x	
9:40	x		
10:13	x		
10:20	x		
10:23			x
10:25	x		
12:9		x	
12:19	x		
13:13	x		
13:29	x		
14:14–15	x		
14:20	x		
15:7		x	
15:36		x	
16:9	x		
16:15	x		
16:18	x		
16:22	x		
16:27	x		
16:33	x		
16:36	x		
16:37	x		
16:39	x		
17:19		x	
17:34	x		
18:1			x
18:6	x		
18:7	x		
18:17	x		
18:22			x
19:8		x	

continued

Acts	Emotion	Maybe	No-Emotion
19:9	x		
19:21	x		
20:5			x
20:10	x		
20:17			x
20:37	x		
21:8			x
21:15		x	
21: 24		x	
22:6		x	
22:13	x		
22:30		x	
23:16	x		
23:18		x	
23:24		x	
23:31			x
25:6			x
25:9		x	
27:35	x		

Bibliography

Books

Adrados, Francisco Rodríguez. *Lingüística Estructural.* Madrid: Gredos, 1974.

Anderson, Gerald H. *The Theology of the Christian Mission.* Nashville, TN: Abingdon, 1961.

Arnold, C. E., *Ephesians: Power and Magic: The Concept of Power in Ephesians in Light of Its Historical Setting.* Cambridge, MA: Cambridge University Press, 1989.

Bakker, Egbert J. *Grammar as Interpretation: Greek Literature in Its Linguistic Contexts.* Mnemosyne, Bibliotheca Classica Batava 171. Leiden: Brill, 1997.

Ball, Francis Kingsley. *The Elements of Greek: A First Book with Grammar, Exercises, and Vocabularies.* New York, NY: Macmillan, 1913.

Battistella, Edwin L. *Markedness: The Evaluative Superstructure of Language.* Albany, NY: State University of New York Press, 1990.

Bauckham, Richard J. *2 Peter, Jude,* Word Biblical Commentary, vol. 50. Dallas, TX: Word, Incorporated, 1998.

Bauer, Walter, William F. Arndt, F. Wilbur Gingrich, and Frederick W. Danker. *A Greek-English Lexicon of the New Testament and Other Early Christian Literature.* 2nd ed. Chicago, IL: University of Chicago, 1979.

Bauer, Walter, Frederick W. Danker, William F. Arndt, and F. Wilbur Gingrich. *A Greek-English Lexicon of the New Testament and Other Early Christian Literature.* 3rd ed. Chicago, IL: University of Chicago, 2000.

Beasley-Murray, George R. *John*. Word Biblical Commentary, edited by David A. Hubbard and Glenn W. Barker, vol. 36. Waco, TX: Word, 1987.

Bechara, Evanildo. *Moderna Gramática Portguesa*. 17th ed. Rio de Janeiro: Nova Fronteira, Lucerna, 2009.

Benson, James D. and William S. Greaves. *Systemic Perspectives on Discourse*. Norwood, NJ: Ablex Pub. Corp, 1985.

Berch, E. A. *Einige Bemerkungen über die modale und temporale Bedeutung des griechischen Participis*. Kiel: Kiel Universität, 1869.

Bernard Comrie. *Tense*. Cambridge Textbooks in Linguistics. Cambridge, MA: Cambridge University Press, 1985.

Bierwisch, Manfred, and Karl Erich Heidolph. *Progress in Linguistics: A Collection of Papers*. Berlin: Mouton, 1970.

Binnick, Robert I. *Time and the Verb: A Guide to Tense and Aspect*. New York, NY: Oxford University Press, 1991.

Black, David Alan. *Linguistics for Students of New Testament Greek: A Survey of Basic Concepts and Applications*. Grand Rapids, MI: Baker Book House, 1988.

Blass, Friedrich. *Grammar of New Testament Greek*, translated and rvised by Henry St. John Thackeray, 2nd ed. London: Macmillan Company, 1905.

Blass, F., and A. Debrunner. *A Greek Grammar of the New Testament and Other Early Christian Literature*. Translated and revised by Robert W. Funk. Chicago, IL: University of Chicago Press, 1961.

Bock, Darrell L. *Luke*. Baker Exegetical Commentary on the New Testament 3. 2 vols. Grand Rapids, MI: Baker Academic, 1996.

Brooks, James A., and Carlton L. Winbery. *Syntax of New Testament Greek*. Washington, DC: University Press of America, 1988.

Brugmann, Karl, and Berthold Delbrück. *Grundriss der Vergleichenden Grammatik der Indogermanischen Sprachen. Kurzgefasste Darstellung der Geschichte des Altindischen, Altiranischen (avestischen u. altpersischen) Altarmenischen, Altgriechischen, Albanesischen, Lateinischen, Oskischumbrischen, Altirischen, Gotischen, Althochdeutschen, Litauischen und Altkirchenslavischen*. Strassburg: K. J. Trübner, 1897.

Buijs, Michel. *Ancient Greek Narrative Discourse: The Distribution of Subclauses and Participial Clauses in Xenophon's Hellenica and Anabasis*. Mnemosyne, 260. Leiden/Londo: Brill, 2005.

Burton, Ernest De Witt. *Syntax of the Moods and Tenses in New Testament Greek*. 3rd ed. Edinburg: T&T Clark, 1898.

Butler, Christopher S. *Systemic Linguistics: Theory and Applications*. London: Batsford, 1985.

Buttmann, Alexander. *A Grammar of the New Testament Greek*. Andover, MA: Warren F. Draper Publisher, 1878.

Campbell, Constantine R. *Verbal Aspect and Non-Indicative Verbs: Further Soundings in the Greek of the New Testament*. Studies of Biblical Greek 15. New York, NY: Peter Lang, 2008.

Carson, D. A. *Exegetical Fallacies*. Grand Rapids, MI: Baker, 2003.

Carson, D. A. *The Gospel According to John*, The Pillar New Testament Commentary. Grand Rapids, MI: Inter-Varsity Press, 1991.

Chierchia, Gennaro, and Sally McConnell-Ginet. *Meaning and Grammar: An Introduction to Semantics*. Cambridge, MA: MIT Press, 2000.

Christie, Frances. *Classroom Discourse Analysis: A Functional Perspective*. London: Continuum, 2005.

Connor, W. Robert. *Thucydides*. Princeton, NJ: Princeton University Press, 1984.

Cooper, Guy L., and K. W. Krüger. *Attic Greek Prose Syntax*. Ann Arbor, MI: University of Michigan Press, 1998.

Crespo, Emilio, Jesús de la Villa, and A. R. Revuelta. *Word Classes and Related Topics in Ancient Greek: Proceedings of the Conference on 'Greek Syntax and Word Classes' Held in Madrid on 18–21 June 2003*. Louvain-la-Neuve: Peeters, 2006.

Croy, N. Clayton. *A Primer of Biblical Greek*. Grand Rapids, MI: Eerdmans, 2007.

Dana, H. E., and Julius R. Mantey. *A Manual Grammar of the Greek New Testament*. New York, NY: Macmillan, 1957.

Decker, Rodney J. *Temporal Deixis of the Greek Verb in the Gospel of Mark with Reference to Verbal Aspect*. Studies in Biblical Greek 10. New York, NY: Peter Lang, 2001.

Delville, Jean-Pierre. *L'Europe de L'exégèse au XVIe Siècle: Interprétations de La Parabole des Ouvriers à La Vigne, Matthieu 20:1–16*. Leuven: University Press, 2004, xxix.

Dik, Simon. *The Theory of Functional Grammar: Part 1: The Structure of the Clause*. Dordrecht: Foris, 1989.

Dooley, Robert A., and Stephen H. Levinsohn, *Analyzing Discourse: A Manual of Basic Concepts*. Dallas, TX: SIL International, 2001.

Dover, K. J. *Greek Word Order*. Cambridge, MA: Cambridge University Press, 1960.

Duhoux, Yves. *Le Verbe Grec Ancien: Éléments de Morphologie et de Syntaxe Historiques*. Louvain-la-Neuve: Peeters, 2000.

Eriksson, Karl. *Das Präsens Historicum in der Nachklassischen Griechischen Historiographie*. Lund: Gleerupska Universitetsbokhandeln, 1943.

Fanning, Buist M. *Verbal Aspect in New Testament Greek*. Oxford Theological Monographs. Oxford, UK: Clarendon Press, 1990.

Fantin, Joseph D. *The Greek Imperative Mood in the New Testament: A Cognitive and Communicative Approach*. Studies in Biblical Greek 12. New York, NY: Peter Lang, 2010).

Farrar, F. W. *A Brief Greek Syntax and Hints on Greek Accidence: With Some Reference to Comparative Philology, and with Illustrations from Various Modern Languages*. London: Longmans, Green, and Co, 1905.

Fawcett, Robin P. *A Theory of Syntax for Systemic Functional Linguistics*. Current Issues in Linguistic Theory 4. Amsterdam: Benjamins, 2000.

Fillmore, Charles J., and D. Terence Langendoen. *Studies in Linguistic Semantics*. New York, NY: Holt, Rinehart and Winston, 1971.

Firbas, Jan. *Functional Sentence Perspective in Written and Spoken Communication*. Cambridge, MA: Cambridge University Press, 1992.

Firth, J. R. "Selected papers of J. R. Firth, 1952–1959", edited by F. R. Palmer. London: Longmans, 1968.

Firth, J. R. *Speech*. London: Benn's Sixpenny Library, 1930.

Gaechter, Paul. *Das Matthäus-Evangelium*. München: Wien, 1963.

Gildersleeve, Basil L. *Stahl's Syntax of the Greek Verb*. Analecta Gorgiana 393. Piscataway, NJ: Gorgias Press, 2009.

Gildersleeve, Basil L. *Syntax of Classical Greek: From Homer to Demosthenes*. Ann Arbor, MI: University Microfilms International, 1980.

Givón, Talmy. *Syntax 1*. Amsterdam: Benjamins, 2001.

Givón, Talmy. *Syntax and Semantics*. Discourse and Syntax 12. New York, NY: Academic Press, 1979.

Givón, Talmy. *Syntax: A Functional Typological Introduction*, 1. New York, NY: John Benjamins, 1984.

Gleason, Henry A. *An Introduction to Descriptive Linguistics*. London: Holt, Rinehart & Winston, 1978.

Gonda, J. *The Character of the Indo-European Moods with Special Regard to Greek and Sanskrit*. Wiesbaden: O. Harrassowitz, 1956.

Goodwin, William Watson. *Syntax of the Moods and Tenses of the Greek Verb*. Boston, MA: Ginn and Co, 1897.

Greenlee, J. Harold. *A Concise Exegetical Grammar of New Testament Greek*. Grand Rapids, MI: W.B. Eerdmans, 1986.

Hagner, Donald A. *Matthew*. Word Biblical Commentary, 2 vols. Dallas, TX: Word, Incorporated, 1998.

Halliday, M. A. K, and Jonathan J. Webster. *The Essential Halliday*. London: Continuum, 2009.

Halliday, M. A. K. *Introduction to Functional Grammar*. 2nd ed. London: Edward Arnold, 1994.

Halliday, M. A. K. *Language as Social Semiotic: The Social Interpretation of Language and Meaning*. London: Edward Arnold, 1978.

Halliday, M. A. K. *Computational and Quantitative Studies*. The Collected Works of M. A. K. Halliday, edited by Jonathan J. Webster, vol. 6. London: Continuum, 2005.

Halliday, M. A. K. *Explorations in the Functions of Language*. London: Edward Arnold, 1976.

Halliday, M. A. K. *Halliday: System and Function in Language. Selected papers*, edited by Gunther Kress. London: Oxford University Press, 1978.

Halliday, M. A. K. *Learning How to Mean—Explorations in the Development of Language*. London: Edward Arnold, 1975.

Halliday, M. A. K. *On Language and Linguistics*. The Collected Works of M. A. K. Halliday, edited by Jonathan J. Webster, vol. 3. London: Continuum, 2003.

Halliday, M. A. K. *Studies in Chinese Language*. The Collected Works of M. A. K. Halliday, edited by Jonathan J. Webster, vol. 8. London: Continuum, 2006.

Halliday, M. A. K. *Studies in English Language*. The Collected Works of M. A. K. Halliday, edited by Jonathan J. Webster, vol. 7. London: Continuum, 2005.

Halliday, M. A. K. *On Grammar.* The Collected Works of M. A. K. Halliday, edited by Jonathan J. Webster, vol. 1. London: Continuum, 2002.

Hardy, Donald E. *Narrating Knowledge in Flannery O'Connor's Fiction.* Columbia, SC: University of South Carolina Press, 2002.

Hartman, Lars. *Testimonium Linguae: Participal Constructions in the Synoptic Gospels: A Linguistic Examination of Luke 21:13.* Coniectanea Neotestamentica 19. Lund: Gleerup, 1963.

Heiser, Michael S. *Glossary of Morpho-Syntactic Database Terminology.* Bellingham, WA: Logos Bible Software, 2005.

Hengeveld, Kees. *Non-Verbal Predication Theory, Typology, Diachrony.* Berlin: Mouton de Gruyter, 1992.

Hewett, James Allen, C. Michael Robbins, and Steven R. Johnson. *New Testament Greek: A Beginning and Intermediate Grammar.* Peabody, MA: Hendrickson, 2009.

Holton, David, Peter Mackridge, and Irene Philippaki-Warburton. *Greek: A Comprehensive Grammar of the Modern Language.* London: Routledge, 1997.

House, Juliane. *Translation Quality Assessment: A Model Revisited,* Tübingen Beiträgen zur Linguistik 410. Tübingen: Narr, 1997.

Hudson, G. *Essential Introductory Linguistics.* Oxford, UK: Blackwell Publishers, 2000.

Jannaris, Antonius N. *An Historical Greek Grammar, Chiefly of the Attic Dialect as Written and Spoken from Classical Antiquity Down to the Present Time, Founded Upon the Ancient Texts, Inscriptions, Papyri and Present Popular Greek.* London: Macmillan Co, 1897.

Jaszczolt, Katarzyna. *Semantics, Pragmatics and Beyond: Meaning in Language and Discourse.* Harlow: Longman, 2002.

Jones, Frank Pierce. *The Ab Urbe Condita Construction in Greek: A Study in the Classification of the Participle.* New York, NY: Kraus, 1973.

Karleen, Paul Stuart. *The Syntax of the Participle in the Greek New Testament.* Ann Arbor, MI: A Bell & Howell Company, 1994.

Kavčič, Jerneja. *The Syntax of the Infinitive and the Participle in Early Byzantine Greek: An Interpretation in Terms of Naturalness Theory.* Ljubljana, Slovenia: Znanstvenoraziskovalni inštitut, Filozofske fakultete, 2005.

Keaton, Mark. *The Lexham Propositional Outlines Glossary.* Bellingham, WA: Lexham Press, 2014.

Kempchinsky, Paula Marie, and Roumyana Slabakova. *Aspectual Inquiries.* Studies in Natural Language and Linguistic Theory 62. Dordrecht: Springer, 2005.

Kempson, Ruth M. *Presupposition and the Delimitation of Semantics.* Cambridge Studies in Linguistics 15. Cambridge, MA: Cambridge University Press, 1975.

Knight. George W. Knight. *The Pastoral Epistles: A Commentary on the Greek Text.* New International Greek Testament Commentary. Grand Rapids, MI: William B. Eerdmans, 1992.

Kortmann, Bernd. *Adverbial Subordination: A Typology and History of Adverbial Subordinators Based on European Language.* Berlin: Mouton de Gruyter, 1997.

Krüger, Karl Wilhelm. *Griechische Sprachlehre für Schulen Th. 1, H. 1, Ueber die Gewöhnliche, Vorzugsweise die Attische Prosa. Formlehre.* Berlin: Krüger, 1846.

Kühner, Raphael. *Ausführliche Grammatik der griechischen Sprache: Wissenschaftlich und mit Rücksicht auf den Schulgebrauch.* Hannover: Hahnsche Hofbuchhandlung, 1834.

Lambrecht, Knud. *Information Structure and Sentence Form: Topic, Focus, and the Mental Representations of Discourse Referents.* Cambridge, MA: Cambridge University Press, 1994.

Lane, William L. *Hebrews.* Word Biblical Commentary, 2 vols. Dallas, TX: Word, Incorporated, 1998.

Lang, Mabel L. *Herodotean Narrative and Discourse.* Cambridge, MA: Harvard University Press, 1984.

Leckie-Tarry, Helen. *Language and Context: A Functional Linguistic Theory of Register,* edited by David Birch. London: Pinter, 1995.

Levinsohn, Stephen H. *Discourse Features of New Testament Greek: A Coursebook on the Information Structure of New Testament Greek.* 2nd ed. Dallas, TX: International Academic Bookstore, 2000.

Levinson, Stephen C. *Pragmatics.* Cambridge, MA: Cambridge University Press, 2000.

Lightfoot, David. *Natural Logic and the Greek Moods: The Nature of the Subjunctive and Optative in Classical Greek.* Janua Linguarum: Series Practica 230. Berlin: Mouton, 1975.

Lopes, Jose Manuel. *Foregrounded Description in Prose Fiction: Five Cross-Literary Studies.* Toronto: University of Toronto Press, 1995.

Louw, Johannes P. and Eugene A. Nida, eds. *Greek-English Lexicon of the New Testament Based on Semantic Domains.* 2nd ed. 2 vols. New York, NY: United Bible Societies, 1989.

Lundholt, Marianne Wolff. *The Linguistic Manifestation of Literary Communication in Narrative Fiction.* Ph.D. diss., University of Southern Denmark, 2004.

Lyons, John. *Language and Linguistics: An Introduction.* Cambridge, MA: Cambridge University Press, 2002.

Lyons, John. *New Horizons in Linguistics.* Harmondsworth: Penguin, 1970.

Lyons, John. *Structural Semantics: An Analysis of Part of the Vocabulary of Plato.* Oxford, UK: Basil Blackwell, 1963.

Mackridge, Peter. *The Medieval Greek Infinitive in the Light of Modern Dialectical Evidence.* Venice: n.p., 1996.

Mandēlaras, Vasileios G. *The Verb in the Greek Non-Literary Papyri.* Athens: Hellenic Ministry of Culture and Sciences, 1973.

Marshall, I Howard. *The Gospel of Luke: A Commentary on the Greek Text.* New International Greek Testament Commentary. Exeter: Paternoster Press, 1978.

Martín-Asensio, Gustavo. *Transitivity-Based Foregrounding in the Acts of the Apostles: A Functional-Grammatical Approach to the Lukan Perspective.* Journal for the Study of the New Testament Supplement Series 202. Sheffield: Sheffield Academic Press, 2000.

Martin, Ralph P. *James,* Word Biblical Commentary, vol. 48. Dallas, TX: Word, Incorporated, 1998.

Mathesius, Vilém, and Josef Vachek. *A Functional Analysis of Present Day English on a General Linguistic Basis,* edited by Janua Linguarum. Series Practica 208. Berlin: Mouton, 1975.

McKay, K. L. *Greek Grammar for Students: A Concise Grammar of Classical Attic with Special Reference to Aspect in the Verb.* Canberra: Department of Classics, Australian National University, 1974.

McKay, K. L. A New Syntax of the Verb in New Testament Greek: An Aspectual Approach. Studies in Biblical Greek 5. New York, NY: Peter Lang, 1994.

Moo, Douglas J. *The Letter of James.* Pillar New Testament Commentary. Grand Rapids, MI: Eerdmans Publishing Company, 2000.

Moorhouse, A. C. *The Syntax of Sophocles.* Mnemosyne Bibliotheca Classica Batava, Supplementum 75. Leiden: Brill, 1982.

Morris, Leon. *The Gospel According to Matthew.* The Pillar New Testament Commentary. Grand Rapids, MI: W.B. Eerdmans, 1992.

Moule, C. F. D. *An Idiom-Book of New Testament Greek*, 2nd ed. Cambridge, MA: Cambridge University Press, 1963.

Moulton, James Hope. *A Grammar of New Testament Greek. Volume I, Prolegomena.* Edinburgh: T. & T. Clark, 1998.

Neves, Maria Helena de Moura. *Gramática dos Usos do Português.* São Paulo: UNESP, Ed. Universidade Estadual Paulista, 2000).

Nolland, John. *Luke.* Word Biblical Commentary, 3 vols. Dallas, TX: Word, Incorporated, 2002.

Nunn, H. P. V. *A Short Syntax of New Testament Greek.* Cambridge, MA: Cambridge University Press, 1920.

Nunn, H. P. V. *The Elements of New Testament Greek.* Cambridge, MA: Cambridge University Press, 1923.

Oguse, André. *Recherches sur le Participe Circonstanciel en Grec Ancien.* Wetteren, Belgique: Des Press de L'Imprimerie Cultura, 1962.

Oh, Choon-Kyu, and David A. Dinneen. *Syntax and Semantics.* New York, NY: Academic Press, 1979.

Palmer, Frank Robert. *Mood and Modality*, 2nd ed. Cambridge Textbooks in Linguistics. Cambridge, MA: Cambridge University Press, 2006.

Palmer, Micheal W. Levels of Constituent Structure in New Testament Greek. Studies in Biblical Greek 4. New York, NY: Peter Lang, 1995.

Palmer, Richard E. *Hermeneutics; Interpretation Theory in Schleiermacher, Dilthey, Heidegger, and Gadamer.* Northwestern University Studies in Phenomenology & Existential Philosophy. Evanston: Northwestern University Press, 1969.

Paul, Hermann. *Principien der Sprachgeschichte.* Halle: Max Niemeyer, 1880.

Porter, Stanley E. *Verbal Aspect in the Greek of the New Testament, with Reference to Tense and Mood.* Studies in Biblical Greek 1. New York, NY: Peter Lang, 1993.

Porter, Stanley E. *Idioms of the Greek New Testament.* 2nd ed. Biblical Language 2. Sheffield: Sheffield Academic Press, 1999.

Porter, Stanley E. "Prominence: An Overview". In *The Linguist as Pedagogue: Trends in the Teaching and Linguistic Analysis of the Greek New Testament*, edited by Stanley E. Porter and Matthew Brook O'Donnell. Sheffield: Sheffield Phoenix Press, 2009.

Poythress, Vern S. Science and Hermeneutics: Implications of Scientific Method for Biblical Interpretation. Foundations of Contemporary Interpretation, vol. 6. Grand Rapids, MI: Zondervan, 1988.

Quintero, María Jesús Pérez. *Adverbial Subordination in English: A Functional Approach.* Language and Computers Series 41. Amsterdam: Rodopi, 2002.

Reed, Jeffrey T. *A Discourse Analysis of Philippians: Method and Rhetoric in the Debate over Literary Integrity.* Journal for the Study of the New Testament Supplement 136. Sheffield: Sheffield Academic Press, 1997.

Rijksbaron, Albert. *The Syntax and Semantics of the Verb in Classical Greek: An Introduction.* Chicago, IL: University of Chicago Press, 2006.

Robertson, A. T. *A Grammar of the Greek New Testament in the Light of Historical Research.* Nashville, TN: Broadman Press, 1934.

Runge, Steve. *Discourse Grammar of the Greek New Testament: A Practical Introduction for Teaching and Exegesis.* Peabody, MA: Hendrickson Publishers, 2010.

Sailhamer, John H. *The Translational Technique of the Greek Septuagint for the Hebrew Verbs and Participles in Psalms 3–41.* Studies in Biblical Greek 2. New York, NY: Peter Lang, 1991.

Saussure, Ferdinand de. *Course in Linguistics,* edited by C. Bally and A. Sechehaye, translated by W. Baskin. New York, NY: The Philosophical Library, 1959.

Schiffrin, Deborah Tannen, and Heidi Ehernberger Hamilton. *The Handbook of Discourse Analysis.* Malden, MA.: Blackwell Publishers, 2007.

Schiffrin, Deborah. *Approaches to Discourse.* Blackwell Textbooks in Linguistics 8. Oxford, UK: B. Blackwell, 1994.

Schlatter, Adolf von. *Der Evangelist Matthäus: seine Sprache, seine Ziel, seine Selbstständigkeit: ein Kommentar zum ersten Evangelium.* Stuttgart: Calwer Verlag, 1929.

Schnackenburg, R. *Ephesians: A Commentary.* Edinburgh: T & T Clark, 1991.

Schneider, Christoph. *Information und Absicht bei Thukydides: Untersuchung z. Motivation d. Handelns.* Hypomnemata, Untersuchungen zur Antike und zu ihrem Nachleben 41. Göttingen: Vandenhoeck und Ruprecht, 1974.

Schroeder, Leopold von. *Ueber die formelle Unterscheidung der Redetheile im Griechischen und Lateinischen, mit besonderer Berücksichtigung der Nominalcomposita.* Leipzig: K.F. Köhler, 1874.

Schwyzer, Eduard, and Albert Debrunner. *Griechische Grammatik, Auf der Grundlage von Karl Brugmanns. Griechischer Grammatik. Syntax und syntaktische Stilistik 2.* Münich: C. H. Beck 1959.

Septién, José Antonio. *El Griego Bíblico al Alcance de Todos: Un Estudio Programado del Griego del Nuevo Testamento.* Barcelona: Editorial Clie, 2007.

Sicking, C. M. J, and P. Stork. *Two Studies in the Semantics of the Verb in Classical Greek.* Mnemosyne Bibliotheca Classica Batava160. Leiden: E.J. Brill, 1996.

Silva, Moisés. *Biblical Words and Their Meaning: An Introduction to Lexical Semantics.* Revised and Expanded Edition. Grand Rapids, MI: Zondervan Publishing House, 1994.

Silva, Moisés. *God, Language and Scripture: Reading the Bible in the Light of General Linguistics.* Foundations of Contemporary Interpretation, vol. 4. Grand Rapids, MI: Zondervan, 1990.

Smyth, Herbert Weir. *Greek Grammar.* Oxford, UK: Benediction Classics, 2010.

Sophocles, and Jebb, Richard Claverhouse. *Sophocles: The Plays and Fragments.* Cambridge, MA: University Press, 1892.

Stahl, Johann M. *Kritisch-Historische Syntax des Griechischen Verbums der Klassischen Zeit.* Indogermaqnische Bibliothek 4. Heidelberg: Carl Winter's Universitätsbuchhandlung, 1907.

Steinberg, Danny D. and Leon A. Jakobovits. *Semantics: An Interdisciplinary Reader in Philosophy Linguistics and Psychology.* Cambridge, MA: Cambridge University Press, 1978.

Stork, Peter. *The Aspectual Usage of the Dynamic Infinitive in Herodotus.* Groningen: Bouma's Boekhuis, 1982.

Strawson, P. F. *Introduction to Logical Theory.* Abingdon, Oxon: Routledge, 2011.

Strawson, P. F. *Logic-Linguistic Papers.* London: Harvard University Press, 1962.

Selwyn, Edward Gordon. *The First Epistle of St. Peter: The Greek Text.* London: Macmillan, 1947.

Sweet, Henry. *A New English Grammar: Logical and Historical.* Oxford, UK: Clarendon Press, 1898.

Szabó, Zoltán Gendler. *Semantics vs. Pragmatics.* Oxford, UK: Clarendon Press, 2005.

Thackeray, Henry St. John. *A Grammar of the Old Testament in Greek: According to the Septuagint.* Cambridge, MA: University Press, 1909.

Thomson, George. *The Greek Language.* Cambridge, MA: W. Heffer & Sons, 1960.

Vachek, Josef, Josef Dubský, and Libuše Dušková. *Dictionary of the Prague School of Linguistics.* Amsterdam: Benjamins, 2003.

Van Dijk, Teun A. *Discourse and Context: A Sociocognitive Approach.* Cambridge, MA: Cambridge University Press, 2010.

Van Dijk, Teun A. *Cognição, Discurso e Interação,* Coleção Caminhos da Linguística, Apresentação e Organização de Ingedora Villaça Kock. São Paulo: Editora Contexto, 2011.

Van Dijk, Teun A. *Text and Context: Explorations in the Semantics and Pragmatics of Discourse.* London: Longman, 1977.

Van der Merwe, Christo H. J., Jackie A. Naudé, and Jan H. Kroeze. *A Biblical Hebrew Reference Grammar.* Biblical Languages: Hebrew 3. Sheffield: Sheffield Academic Press, 1999.

Voelz, James W. *Fundamental Greek Grammar.* 2nd ed. St. Louis, MI: Concordia, 1993.

Wallace, Daniel B. *Greek Grammar Beyond the Basics: An Exegetical Syntax of the New Testament.* Grand Rapids, MI: Zondervan, 1996.

Waltke, Bruce K. and M. O'CONNOR. *An Introduction to Biblical Hebrew Syntax.* Winona Lake, IN: Eisenbrauns, 1990.

Werner, Abraham, and Vladimir P. Nedjalkov. *Tense-Aspect, Transitivity and Causativity: Essays in Honour of Vladimir Nedjalkov.* Studies in Language Companion Series 50. Amsterdam: Benjamins, 1999.

Wilder, Amos N. *Early Christian Rhetoric: The Language of the Gospel.* Peabody, MA: Hendrickson Publishers, 1999.

Williams, Charles Bray. *The Participle in the Book of Acts*. Chicago, IL: The University of Chicago Press, 1909.

Winer, Georg Benedikt. *A Treatise on the Grammar of New Testament Greek: Regarded As a Sure Basis for New Testament Exegesis*. Edinburgh: Clark, 1882.

Wurmbrand, Susanne. *Infinitives: Restructuring and Clause Structure*. Studies in Generative Grammar 55. Berlin: Mouton de Gruyter, 2001.

Young, Richard A. *Intermediate New Testament Greek: A Linguistic and Exegetical Approach*. Nashville, TN: Broadman & Holman, 1994.

Zerwick, Maximilian. *Biblical Greek: Illustrated by Examples*. Translated by Joseph Smith. Scripta Pontificii Instituti Biblici 114. Rome: Pontificii Instituti Biblici, 1963.

Articles and Essays in Edited Collections

Barth, Karl. "An Exegetical Study of Matthew 28:16-20." In *The Theology of the Christian Mission*, edited by Gerald H. Anderson, 55–71. Nashville, TN: Abingdon, 1961.

Bosque, Ignacio. "Sobre el Aspecto en los Adjectivos y en los Participios." In *Tiempo y Aspecto en Español*, edited by Ignacio Bosque, 177–214. Madrid: Cátedra, 1990.

Büchner, Dirk. "Translation Technique in the Septuagint Leviticus." In *Diglossia and Other Topics in New Testament Linguistics*, edited by Stanley D. Porter, 92–106. Journal for the Study of New Testament Supplement Series 193. Sheffield: Sheffield Academic Press, 2000.

Chomsky, A. N. "Deep Structure, Surface Structure and Semantic Interpretation." In *Semantics*, edited by Danny D. Steinberg and Leon A. Jakobovits, 62–119. Cambridge: University Press, 1974.

Clark, Greg. "General Hermeneutics." In *The Face of New Testament Studies: A Survey of Recent Research*, edited by Scot McKnight and Grant R. Osborne, 104–117. Grand Rapids, MI: Baker Academia/Apollos, 2004.

Fanning, Buist M. "Greek Presents, Imperfects, and Aorists in the Synoptic Gospels: Their Contribution to Narrative Structuring." In *Discourse Studies & Biblical Interpretation: A Festschrift in Honor of Stephen H. Levinsohn*, edited by Steven E. Runge, 157–190. Bellingham, WA: Logos Software, 2011.

Fawcett, Robin P. "What Makes a 'Good' System Network Good?: Four Pairs of Concepts for Such Evaluations." In *Systemic Functional Approach to Discourse: Selected Papers from the 12th International Systemic Workshop*, edited by James D. Benson and William S. Greaves, 1–28. Advances in Discourse Processes 26. Norwood, NJ: Ablex Publishing Corporation, 1988.

Fillmore, C. J. "Types of lexical information." In *Studies in Syntax and Semantics*, edited by Ferenc Kiefer, 109–37. Dordrecht: D. Reidel, 1969.

Firth, J. R. "Selected papers of J. R. Firth, 1952–1959," edited by F. R. Palmer. London: Longmans, 1968.

Frisk, H. "Participium und Verbum Finitum im Spätgriechischen." In *Kleine Schriften zur Indogermanistik und zur Griechischen Wortkunde.* Studia Graeca et Latina Gothoburgensia, 431–342. Gotheburg: Acta Universitatis Gothoburgensis, 1966.

Fleischmann, Suzanne, and Linda R. Waugh. "Introduction." In *Discourse-Pragmatics and the Verb: The Evidence from Romance*, edited by Suzanne Fleischmann and Linda, R., 1–6. London: Routledge, 1991.

Fox, Barbara. "The Discourse Function of the Participle in Ancient Greek." In *Discourse Perspectives on Syntax*, edited by Flora Klein-Andreu, 23–41. New York, NY: Academic Press, 1983.

Garner, R. "'Presupposition' in Philosophy and Linguistic." In *Studies in Linguistic Semantics*, edited by C. J. Fillmore and D. T. Langendoen, 23–42. New York, NY: Holt, Rinehart and Winston, 1971.

Garner, R.. "Language as System and Language as Instance: The Corpus as a Theoretical Construct." In *Directions in Corpus Linguistics: Proceedings of Nobel Symposium*, edited by Jan Svartvik, 61–77. Berlin/New York, NY: Mouton de Gruyter, 1991.

Garner, R. "Lexis as a Linguistic Level." In *In Memory of J.R. Firth*, edited by C. E. Bazell et al, 150–161. London: Longman, 1996.

Garner, R. "Modes of Meaning and Modes of Expression: Types of Grammatical Structure, and their Determination by Different Semantic Functions." In *Function and Context in Linguistic Analysis: essays offered to William Haas*, edited by D.J Allerton, Edward Carney, and David Holdcroft, 57–79. London: Cambridge University Press.

Halle, Otto Michel. "μεταμέλομαι." In *Theological Dictionary of the New Testament*, vol 4, edited by Gerhard Kittel, translated by Geoffrey W. Bromiley, 626–629. Grand Rapids, MI: Eerdmans, 1964.

Hayase, Naoko. "The Cognitive Motivation for the use of Dangling Participles in English," In *Motivation in Grammar and the Lexicon*, edited by Klaus-Uwe Panther and Günter Radden, 89–106. Amsterdam: John Benjamins, 2011.

Hengeveld, Kees. "Adverbial Clauses in the Languages of Europe." In *Adverbial Constructions in the Languages of Europe*, edited by Johan van der Auwera 335–419. Berlin: Mouton de Gruyter, 1998.

Hopper, Paul J. "Aspect Between Discourse and Grammar: An Introductory Essay for the Volume." In *Tense-Aspect: Between Semantics & Pragmatics*, edited by Paul J. Hopper, 3–17. Amsterdam: John Benjamins, 1982.

Hopper, Paul J. "Aspect and Foregrounding in Discourse." In *Discourse and Syntax*, edited by Talmy Givón, Syntax and Semantics 12, 213–241. New York, NY: Academic Press, 1979.

Keenan, E. L. "Two Kinds of Presuppositon in Natural Language." In *Studies in Linguistic Semantics*, edited by Fillmore, C. J. and D. T. Langendoen, 45–54. New York, NY: Holt, Rinehart & Winston, 1971.

Kempson, Ruth M., and E. J. Lemmon. "Sentences, Statements, and Propositions." In *British Analytical Philosophy*, edited by Bernard Arthur, Owen Williams, and Alan Montefiore, 87–107. New York, NY: Humanities Press, 1966.

Kiparsky, P. and Kiparsky, C. "Facts." In *Progress in Linguistic: A Collection of Papers*, edited by Manfred Bierwish and Karl Erich Heidolph, 143–173. The Hague: Mouton, 1970.

Lunn, Patricia. "The Evaluative Function of the Spanish Subjunctive." In *Modality and Grammar in Discourse*, edited by Joan Bybee and Suzanne Fleischman, 419–449. Typological Studies in Language 32. Amsterdam: John Benjamins, 1995.

Matthiessen, Christian. "Representational Issues in Systemic Functional Grammar." In *Systemic Functional Approach to Discourse: Selected Papers from the 12th International Systemic Workshop*, edited by James D. Benson and William S. Greaves, 136–75. Advances in Discourse Processes 26. Norwood, NJ: Ablex Publishing Corporation, 1988.

O'Donnell, Matthew B. "Designing and Compiling a Register-Balanced Corpus of Hellenistic Greek for the Purpose of Linguistic Description and Investigation." In *Diglossia and Other Topics in New Testament Linguistics*, edited by Stanley D. Porter, 121–153. Journal for the Study of New Testament Supplement Series 193. Sheffield: Sheffield Academic Press, 2000.

Panther, Klaus-Uwe and Günter Radden, "Introduction: Reflections on motivation revisited," In *Motivation in Grammar and the Lexicon*, edited by Klaus-Uwe Panther and Günter Radden. Amsterdam: John Benjamins, 2011.

Payne, D. F. "Semitisms in the Books of Acts." In *Apostolic History and the Gospel: Essays Presented to F. F. Bruce*, edited by W. Ward Gasque and Ralph P. Martin, 134–150. Exeter: The Paternoster Press, 1970.

Porter, Stanley E. "Ancient Rhetorical Analysis and Discourse Analysis of the Pauline Corpus." In *The Rhetorical Analysis of Scripture: Essays from the 1995 London Conference*, edited by Stanley E. Porter and Thomas H. Olbricht, 49–274. Journal for the Study of the New Testament Supplement Series 146. Sheffield: Sheffield Academic Press, 1997.

Porter, Stanley E. "Greek Grammar and Syntax." In *The Face of New Testament Studies: A Survey of Recent Research*, edited by Scot McKnight and Grant R. Osborne, 76–103. Grand Rapids, MI: Baker Academic, 2004.

Porter, Stanley E. "Is Critical Discourse Analysis Critical? An Evaluation Using Philemon as a Test Case." In *Discourse Analysis and the New Testament: Approaches and Results*, edited by Stanley E. Porter and Jeffrey T. Reed, 47–70. Journal for the Study of New Testament Supplement Series 170. Sheffield: Sheffield Academic Press, 1999.

Porter, Stanley E. "Verbal Aspect and Discourse Function in Mark 16:1–8: Three Significant Instances." In *Studies in the Greek Bible: Essays in Honor of Francis T. Gignac, S.J.*, edited by Jeremy Corley and Vicent Skemp, 123–137. The Catholic Biblical Quarterly Monograph Series 44. Washington, DC: The Catholic Biblical Association of America, 2008.

Reed, Jeffrey T. "Identifying Theme in the New Testament: Insights from Discourse Analysis." In *Discourse Analysis and Other Topics in Biblical Greek*, edited by Stanley E. Porter and D. A. Carson, 75–101. Journal for the Study of the New Testament Supplement Series 113. Sheffield: Sheffield Academic Press, 1995.

Reed, Jeffrey T. "Language of Change and the Changing of Language: A Sociolinguistic Approach to Pauline Discourse." In *Diglossia and Other Topics in New Testament Linguistics*, edited by Stanley D. Porter, 121–153. Journal for the Study of New Testament Supplement Series 193. Sheffield: Sheffield Academic Press, 2000.

Salmon, Nathan. "Two Conceptions of Semantics." In *Semantics vs. Pragmatics*, edited by Zoltán Gendler Szabó, 317–328. Oxford, UK: Clarendon Press, 2005.

Schmidt, Daryl D. "The Study of Hellenistic Greek Grammar in the Light of Contemporary Linguistics." In *Perspectives on the New Testament: Essays in Honor of Frank Stagg*, edited by Charles H. Talbert, 27–38. Macon, GA.: Mercer University Press, 1985.

Sicking, C. M. J, and P. Stork. "The Grammar of the So-Called Historical Present in Ancient Greek." In *Grammar As Interpretation: Greek Literature in Its Linguistic Contexts*, edited by J. Egbert, 131–168. Mnemosyne, Bibliotheca Classica Batava 171. Leiden: Brill, 1997.

Sim, Margaret G. "Particles and Participles: A Helpful Partnership." In *Discourse Studies & Biblical Interpretation: A Festschrift in Honor of Stephen H. Levinsohn*, edited by Steven E. Runge, 225–243. Bellingham, WA: Logos Bible Software, 2011.

Stalnaker, Robert. "Pragmatic Presuppositions." In *Semantics and Philosophy*, edited by Milton K. Munitz and Peter K. Unger, 197–214. New York, NY: University Press, 1974.

Thiselton, A. C. "Semantics and New Testament Interpretation." In *New Testament Interpretation: Essays on Principles and Methods*, edited by I. Howard Marshall, 75–104. Grand Rapids, MI: Eerdmans Publishing Company, 1977.

Williams, M. P. "Functional Sentence Perspective in the Context of Systemic Functional Grammar." In *Pragmatics, Discourse and Text: Some Systemically-Inspired Approaches*, edited by E. M. Steiner and R. Veltman, 76–89. London: Pinter Publishers, 1988.

Wilson, Dan. "Relevance and Relevance Theory." In *MIT Encyclopedia of the Cognitive Sciences*, edited by R. Wilson and F. Keil, 719–720. Cambridge, MA: MIT Press, 1999.

Journal Articles

Armstrong, Paul B. "The Conflict of Interpretations and the Limits of Pluralism." *Modern Language Association* 98 (1983): 341–352.

Auld, A. Graeme, and Patrice Rolin. "Le Texte Hébreu et le Texte Grec de Josué: Une Comparaison à partir du Chapitre 5," *Foi et vie* 97, no. 4 (1998): 67–78.

Barrett, C. K. "The Imperatival Participle," *Expository Time* 59 (1947–48): 165–166.

Bolling, George M. "The Participle in Hesiod." *The Catholic University Bulletin* 3 (1897): 421–471.

Boyer, James L. "The Classification of Participles: A Statistical Study." *Grace Theological Journal* 5 (1984): 163–179.

Buttler, Christopher C. "Focusing on Focus: A Comparison of Functional Grammar, Role and Reference Grammar and Systemic Functional Grammar," *Language Sciences*, 27 (2005): 585–618.

Cavallin, A. "Zum Verhältnis Zwischen Regierendem Verb und Participium Conjunctum." *Eranos: Acta Philological Suecana* 44 (1946): 280–85.

Culver, Robert D. "What Is the Church's Commission?: Some Exegetical Issues in Matthew 28:16–20," *Bibliotheca Sacra* 125 (1968): 239–253.

Culy, Martin. "The Clue is in the Case: Distinguishing Adjectival and Adverbial." *Perspective in Religious Studies*, 30 (2003): 441–453.

Earl, Richard. "The Polemical Character of the Joseph Episode in Acts 7." *Journal of Biblical Literature* 98 (1979): 258–262.

Emden, Cecil S. "St Mark's Use of the Imperfect Tense." *Expository Times* 65 (1954): 146–149.

Fawcett, Robin P. "Some Proposal for Systemic Syntax." Part 1. *Midlands Association for Linguistic Study Journal* 1 (1974):1–15.

Freeman, Hal. "The Great Commission and the New Testament: An Exegesis of Matthew 28:16–20." *Southern Baptist Journal of Theology* 1, no. 4 (1997):14–23.

Gleason, H. A., Jr. "Some Contributions of Linguistics to Biblical Studies." *Hartford Quarterly* 4 (1963): 44–58.

Greenlee, J. Harold. "New Testament Circumstantial Participles." *Journal of Translation* 1 (2005): 57–59.

Halliday, M. A. K. "Notes on Transitivity and Theme in English. Part 1". *Journal of Linguistics* 3 (1967): 37–82.

Halliday, M. A. K. "Notes on Transitivity and Theme in English." Part 2. *Journal of Linguistics* 3 (1967): 199–244.

Halliday, M. A. K. "Options and Functions in the English Clause." *Brno Studies in English* 8 (1969): 81–88.

Healey, Phyllis M., and Alan Healey. "Greek circumstantial Participles: Tracking Participants with Participles in the Greek New Testament." *Journal of Translation and Text-Linguistics* 4 (1990): 173–259.

Hoopert, Daniel A. "Verb ranking in Koine Imperativals." *Journal of Translation* 3 (2007): 1–8.

Lang, Mabel L. "Participial Motivation in Thucydides." *Mnemosyne* 48 (1995): 48–65.

McHale, Brian. "Free Indirect Discourse: A Survey of Recent Accounts." *A Journal for Descriptive Poetics and Theory of Literature* 3 (1978): 249–87.

McKay, K. L. "Time and Aspect in New Testament Greek." *Novum Testamentum* 34 (1992): 209–228.

McKay, K. L. "Aspect in Imperatival Constructions in New Testament Greek". *Novum Testamentum* 27 (1985): 201–206.

McKay, K. L. "Syntax in Exegesis". *Tyndale Bulletin* 23 (1972): 39–57.

Meecham, H.G. "The Use of the Participle for the Imperative in the New Testament." *Expository Times* 58 (1947): 207–208.

Mesfin Awoke Bekalu. "Presupposition in News Discourse." *Discourse & Society SAGE Publication*, 17 (2006): 147–172.

Naselli, Andrew David. "A Brief Introduction to Verbal Aspect in New Testament Greek." *Detroit Baptist Seminary Journal* 12 (2007): 17–28.

Nida, Eugene A. "Implications of Contemporary Linguistics for Biblical Scholarship." *Journal of Biblical Literature* 91 (1972): 73–89.

Ouellet, Jacques. "Semantique Grammaticale du Verbe. I. *Langues et Linguistique*, 13 (1987): 183–230.

O'Rourke, John J. "The Historical Present in the Gospel of John." *Journal of Biblical Literature* 93 (1974): 585–90.

Porter, Stanley E. and Matthew B. O'Donnel. "The Greek Verbal Network Viewed from a Probabilistic Standpoint: An exercise in Hallidayan Linguistics." *Filologia Neotestamentaria* 14 (2001): 3–41.

Rogers, Cleon, Jr. "The Great Commission." *Bibliotheca Sacra* 130 (1973): 258–267.

Sim, Margaret. "Undeterminacy in Greek Participles," *The Bible Translator* 55 (2004): 348–359.

Van Valin, Robert D., Jr "Toward Understanding Grammar: Forma, Function, Evolution," *Lingua* 54 (1981): 47–87.

Voelz, James W. "Grammarian's Corner: Greek Participles, Part VII," *Concordia Journal* 34 (2008): 217–219.

———. "Grammarian's Corner: Participles, Part V," *Concordia Journal* 33 (2007): 299–301.

———. "Grammarian's Corner: Participles, Part VI," *Concordia Journal* 33 (2007): 379–380.

———. "Grammarian's Corner: Word Order, Part II, Adjectives." *Concordia Journal* 32 (2006): 79–80.

———. "Grammarian's Corner: Participles, Part II," *Concordia Journal* 32 (2006): 312–314.

———. "Grammarian's Corner: Participles, Part IV," *Concordia Journal* 33 (2007): 61–62.

———. "Grammarian's Corner: Word Order, Part III, Participles," *Concordia Journal* 32 (2006): 211–213.

———. "Grammarian's Corner: Word Order." *Concordia Journal* 31 (2005): 425–427

Whitelaw, R. and Frank Carter. "On Some Uses of the Aorist Participle." *The Classical Review* 5 (1891): 248–253.

Williams, Travis. "The Imperatival Participles in the New Testament." In http://bible.org/article/imperatival-participle-new-testament. (Accessed, June 20, 2010).

Zuck, Roy B. "Greek Words for Teach.," *Bibliotheca Sacra* 130 (1973): 158–168.

Zwicky, Arnold M. "On Markedness in Morphology," *Die Sprache* 24 no 2 (1978):129–143.

Unpublished and Informally Published Material

Edwards, Grant. "The Validity of Oblique Adverbial Participles in the Greek of the New Testament." Paper presented at the Regional Conference of the Evangelical Theological Society Southwest, New Orleans Baptist Seminary, March 11, 2005.

———. "The Validity of Oblique Adverbial Participles in the Greek of the New Testament." Th.M. thesis, Dallas Theological Seminary, 2007.

Rinker, Jonathan A. "The Genitive Absolute Participle in the Synoptic Gospels." Unpublished PhD paper, Baptist Bible Seminary, Clarks Summit, PA, 2009.

Reference Index

Subject Index

A

adverbial participle 4, 5, 19, 20, 21, 22, 25, 29, 31, 34, 35, 50, 52, 53, 54, 58, 59, 60, 62, 67, 72, 74, 75, 76, 77, 81, 82, 89, 90, 97, 110, 111, 112, 113, 115, 117, 119, 120, 121, 122, 123, 134, 137, 138, 146, 147, 158, 161, 163, 165, 166, 167, 168, 169, 170, 171, 172, 173, 180, 181, 183, 184, 186, 189, 190, 191, 203, 206, 207, 229, 233, 235

Anarthrous participle 1, 2, 3, 4, 32, 34, 52, 55, 62, 81, 112, 117, 118, 120, 121, 123, 134, 157, 158, 163, 164, 165, 166, 168, 170, 171, 172, 176, 177, 178, 179, 180, 181, 183, 184, 185, 188, 189, 190, 191, 204, 218, 229, 233, 235, 244

assertion 5, 6, 7, 8, 13, 14, 15, 24, 26, 29, 30, 31, 33, 34, 41, 44, 46, 47, 51, 56, 59, 67, 69, 70, 71, 76, 77, 78, 81, 93, 94, 96, 97, 99, 100, 101, 102, 103, 107, 111, 115, 116, 120, 122, 125, 126, 127, 135, 139, 148, 153, 162, 172, 173, 176, 181, 192, 204, 224, 228, 229, 243

attendant circumstance 19, 20, 21, 22, 34, 37, 38, 97, 111, 116, 147, 160, 162, 163, 166, 173, 174, 178, 191, 197, 198, 202, 207, 208, 215, 242

B

background 28, 29, 33, 34, 45, 44, 48, 58, 63, 64, 67, 70, 71, 72, 73, 74, 76, 79, 81, 94, 110, 111, 112, 113, 114, 115, 117, 118, 119, 120, 121, 123, 125, 127, 128, 129, 130, 136, 141, 144, 159, 163, 165, 167, 171, 173, 179, 180, 181, 183, 186, 188, 191, 193, 204, 205, 229, 233, 242

backward-forward 28, 81, 131, 142, 159, 168, 169, 170, 209, 233, 235, 242

bifunctional role 242

C

Clause-level analysis 1, 2, 3, 5, 6, 8, 9, 10, 11, 12, 13, 14, 15, 16, 17, 18, 19, 20, 21, 22, 23,

Name Index